PRAISE FOR

Named the Book of the Year for 2006 by *Books & Culture*

'Larsen's argument seems to me both convincing and important.'
Hugh McLeod, *Church History*

'A book which is so well written that it is very hard to put down.'
Journal of Theological Studies

'This is a really valuable corrective to the fashion for literary scepticism.'
The Tablet

'Tim Larsen has a keen eye for a good topic, and in *Crisis of Doubt* he has found his best yet.'
Journal of Ecclesiastical History

'Larsen's overall conclusion seems judicious and on the mark.'
Journal of the American Academy of Religion

'Around the case studies Larsen develops a wider argument that merits serious consideration by all historians of Victorian religion and culture.'
American Historical Review

Crisis of Doubt

Honest Faith in Nineteenth-Century England

TIMOTHY LARSEN

OXFORD
UNIVERSITY PRESS

OXFORD

UNIVERSITY PRESS

Great Clarendon Street, Oxford OX2 6DP

Oxford University Press is a department of the University of Oxford.
It furthers the University's objective of excellence in research, scholarship,
and education by publishing worldwide in

Oxford New York

Auckland Cape Town Dar es Salaam Hong Kong Karachi
Kuala Lumpur Madrid Melbourne Mexico City Nairobi
New Delhi Shanghai Taipei Toronto

With offices in

Argentina Austria Brazil Chile Czech Republic France Greece
Guatemala Hungary Italy Japan Poland Portugal Singapore
South Korea Switzerland Thailand Turkey Ukraine Vietnam

Oxford is a registered trade mark of Oxford University Press
in the UK and in certain other countries

Published in the United States
by Oxford University Press Inc., New York

© Timothy Larsen 2006

The moral rights of the author have been asserted
Database right Oxford University Press (maker)

First published 2006
First Published in Paperback 2008

British Library Cataloguing in Publication Data

Data available

Library of Congress Cataloging in Publication Data
Larsen, Timothy, 1967–Crisis of doubt : honest
faith in nineteenth century England / Timothy Larsen.

Includes bibliographical references and index.
ISBN-13: 978–0–19–928787–1 (alk. paper)
ISBN-10: 0–19–928787–2 (alk. paper)
1. England—Church history—19th century.   2. Skepticism—England—History—19th
century.   3. Secularism—England—History—19th century.   4. Belief and doubt.
5. Dissenters, Religious—England—History—19th century.   I. Title.
BR759. L25 2006
274.2′081–dc22   2006021997
Typeset by SPI Publisher Services, Pondicherry, India
Printed in Great Britain
on acid-free paper by
Biddles Ltd., King's Lynn, Norfolk

ISBN 978–0–19–928787–1 (Hbk.)
978–0–19–954403–5 (Pbk.)

1 3 5 7 9 10 8 6 4 2

For David Bebbington

Preface

This is a study of leading, popular, religious sceptics in nineteenth-century England who returned to the Christian faith. Although this story has not hitherto interested scholars, a remarkably high percentage of Secularist leaders did reconvert. There was a substantial crisis of doubt in the Victorian Secularist movement. A far greater percentage of Secularist leaders became Christians than Christian ministers became sceptics. These erstwhile freethinking leaders went on to become articulate defenders of the intellectual coherence of Christian thought—lecturing, writing, and debating in defence of their new-found convictions. This study explores the contours of the thought of these reconverts in every phase of their varied lives, from the Christianity of their youth, through their reasons for moving into scepticism and their articulation of sceptical ideas, to their reasons for ultimately rejecting freethought and reaffirming faith. *Crisis of Doubt* is partially intended as corrective to the dominance of the theme of the loss of faith or crisis of faith in the existing literature. So much attention has been paid to the lives and thought of figures who lost their faith that the intellectual cogency of Christianity for many Victorians has been obscured, sometimes even the very religiosity of the Victorians has been buried under a preoccupation with expressions of doubt. In some instances, the theme of 'honest doubt' has been so presented as to leave the impression that Victorians who were keeping up with their reading and had the wit to understand it would have inevitably lost their faith if they had the courage to face the truth. Alongside 'honest doubt', however, there was 'honest faith': Victorians who had fully imbibed, and indeed widely disseminated, all the latest ideas from German biblical criticism to Darwinism yet who ultimately came to the conviction that faith was more intellectually compelling than doubt. This book tells that story, the story of a Victorian crisis of doubt.

I have chipped away at this project since 1997, living in three different countries during that period. In the course of all that time and change, I have been helped by innumerable people. I have not kept track well of my debts, but I do want to acknowledge some of them here. Additional ones are also mentioned in the footnotes, and I want to also express my general thanks to all those who helped me but whom I have neglected to mention by name. First of all, I wish to express my tremendous gratitude to Nancy Falciani, Document Delivery Coordinator at the Wheaton College Library. Nancy has gone the extra mile more times than I would care to count to procure copies of extremely rare sources for me, and has put up with endless blizzards of electronic requests as I again and again decided that I needed everything ever written by or about some now-obscure Victorian. For the purpose of aiding my work, I cannot think of a more fortuitous position for my only sibling, Dr David K. Larsen, to hold than Head of Access Services at the University of Chicago Library, and I cannot imagine anyone who would be more patient and generous with a kid brother pestering them for help than David unfailingly is. Other particularly helpful librarians or archivists have been Jeffrey Abbott, Bishopsgate Reference Library; David Wykes, Dr Williams's Library; Sandy Finlayson and Diane Fisher, the Westminster Theological Seminary Library; Sue Mills, Regent's Park College, Oxford; Margaret Thompson, Westminster College, Cambridge; and Gillian Lonergan, The Co-operative College, Manchester. Fellow scholars who have graciously responded to my requests for information include Alan Ruston, Clyde Binfield, Marty Wauck, Ted Royle, James Moore, and Adrian Desmond.

It should also be acknowledged that an earlier sketch of part of the argument presented in this volume was published as 'The Regaining of Faith: Reconversions Among Popular Radicals in Mid-Victorian England', *Church History*, 70: 3 (Sept. 2001), 527–43. Also, aspects of the lives and thought of Joseph Barker and Thomas Cooper were treated in my book, *Contested Christianity: The Political and Social Contexts of Victorian Theology* (Waco, Tex.: Baylor University Press, 2004). Occasionally, I have found that this material still expressed what I wanted to say better than any new language I could devise. (On the other hand, both of those sources also advance arguments that I have not rehearsed here, but that I still believe make a contribution to these discussions.) I am grateful for the help of the various research assistants that I have had, including Derek Keefe, Sarah Jay,

Anna Thompson, Christa Countryman, and Ryan Peterson. My colleagues have been wonderful supporters of my work. Stephen Spencer and Daniel Treier read much more of my writings in draft than any colleague ought to expect from another, and Dan has been a particularly helpful sounding-board on this project. To move to more private debts, Jane ('the real doctor in our family') has not only allowed me to prioritize my work by doing so much else so willingly and well, but it has also been a great motivator that she consistently declared that this sounded like an interesting idea for a book (for a change?). I found occasion to mention our two daughters on a previous acknowledgments page and the oldest one rightly feels that I need to put her brother's name in print. I happen to be writing this on Theo's seventh birthday, and shall leave the office at noon so that I can join him at his Enchanted Castle party. Theo, I am very proud of you. Mark Smith graciously read a draft of the whole manuscript and offered astute comments on it, but his advice was not always taken, and the text has been tinkered with since he saw it last, so anything unfortunate in this book must be the responsibility of the author alone. Finally, I wish to offer a word about the dedication. I have never heard anyone speak of their doctoral supervisor in a way that made me jealous, and I would not trade my time with David Bebbington for the mentoring of any other scholar. Moreover, David has, year after year, continued to support my work in ways well beyond anything that a former research student could expect. This book is dedicated to him with profound thankfulness.

Contents

1

Crisis of Faith

> PROFESSOR CRABBIN: They want you to talk on the crisis of faith.
>
> HOLLY MARTINS: What's that?
>
> PROFESSOR CRABBIN: Oh, I thought you'd know—you're a writer.
>
> (Graham Greene, *The Third Man*, 1949)

The nineteenth-century crisis of faith is a motif that has become vastly overblown. Nevertheless, there really was a nineteenth-century crisis (or crises) of faith. This pattern of the loss of faith is a fascinating one, well worth thinking, reading, and teaching about. A focus on it, however, has repeatedly led to the loss of a sense of proportion. When the Victorian landscape is painted, doubt is frequently exaggerated and faith dwarfed. Too often, the crisis of faith is presented as the most important thing to be said about religion and the Victorians, or even the only thing to be said. What was in fact a telling counterpoint in any age in which religiosity in general and Christianity in particular were dominant and pervasive in so many ways, has often become the main story. If you asked any Victorian scholar whether or not the Victorian age was a religious one, you would be immediately told that it was very religious indeed. Warming to the theme, they might even go on to refer to it as 'the evangelical century', or 'the golden age of church attendance', or with some other such label. Yet, somehow all of that religion too often does not find a place in what is written in Victorian studies textbooks, or works of reference, or taught in courses. In such places, although there are laudable exceptions, one not infrequently learns simply that Victorians lost their faith. In terms of historians, this scholarly tendency is perhaps at its worst when it comes to intellectual history. There might have been hordes of earnest Christians running around trying to keep people from enjoying themselves, but thinking Victorians, at any rate, generally abandoned orthodox faith—or so the impression is left. The strength of the narrative of the Victorian crisis of faith has had the effect of excluding from view much of the religious life and history of the period.

It will be useful to illustrate this. There are three areas in which this tendency needs to be explored: (1) in intellectual history; (2) in general historical accounts of the period; and (3) in literary studies. First, in intellectual history, a recent example is the *Encyclopedia of Nineteenth-Century Thought*.[1] It is to hand because the editor kindly invited me to write the general entry on religion—an invitation I was honoured to receive and accept. My point is not at all that this reference work has undertaken its task poorly. It has done its work well, but within the limitations of the standard, prevailing assumption about the place of religion in nineteenth-century intellectual history. For the article on religion, I was given the title, 'Religion, Secularization, and the Crisis of Faith'. Such a title implies that the only thing that needs to be said about religion in regards to nineteenth-century thought was that it experienced a crisis and went into decline. There are entries with titles such as 'Main Currents in Scientific Thought' and 'Main Currents in Philosophy', but there is no 'Main Currents in Religious Thought' or 'Main Currents in Theology'. The tacit message is that religion and thought do not go together in the nineteenth century. The choices regarding biographical entries are also instructive. In addition to an array of seminal, leading doubters such as D. F. Strauss and Ludwig Feuerbach, there are also entries on more minor figures representing a range of views such as Charles Bradlaugh, Henry Buckle, George Combe, Frederic Harrison, W. E. H. Lecky, and Robert Owen. Nevertheless, orthodox Christian thought is so under-represented that there is not even an entry on John Henry Newman! Whether judged by the influence of his thought on his own times or on our own, the conclusion is inescapable that Newman must be regarded as an important thinker. Not only are a wide selection of Newman's books still in print with

---

[1] Gregory Claeys (ed.), *Encyclopedia of Nineteenth-Century Thought* (London: Routledge, 2005).

a variety of publishers, but they are often read by people who anticipate that his ideas still might have intrinsic merit—that they might help them think more clearly and profoundly about issues that concern them presently. Colleges, centres of research, and other scholarly endeavours are still being named after Newman. These are things that cannot be said of, for example, Frederic Harrison, whose thought, by way of contrast, was less significant both in his own day and in ours. One could then go on to other orthodox Christian thinkers missing from this volume, such as Thomas Chalmers (both Chalmers and Newman do not even show up in the index, revealing that they are not even referred to in passing in other articles). It is indicative of a strong and deeply ingrained tendency in Victorian studies to separate religion from any positive connection with thought, that a very fine scholar doing good editing work for an excellent academic publisher produced a work of reference shaped in this way. By a relentless focus on the stories of Victorians who experienced a loss of faith, these figures have often come to be viewed as merely famous examples of a rite of passage generally experienced by Victorians. Sally Mitchell, in *Daily Life in Victorian England* (1996), confidently informs her readers: 'Most thoughtful Victorians who lived through the middle years of the century experienced a crisis of faith.'[2] When religion and the life of the mind are spoken of together in Victorian studies the discussion is almost inevitably about doubt.

Second, there are the general books on the Victorian period. It is hard to know where to begin or where to end illustrating this tendency. Donald Read's *England: 1868–1914* (1979) can serve as an example.[3] Read's book contains three chronologically constructed sections: 1868–80, 1880–1900, and 1901–14. In each section, the chapters are given a simple theme such as 'Town Life' or 'Foreign Policy'. These themes generally reappear in each section. Each theme is followed by a primary source quotation that serves as a subtitle for the chapter. For example, 'Economic Life: *"The full morning of our national prosperity"* ' or 'Domestic Policy: *"My mission is to pacify*

---

[2] Sally Mitchell, *Daily Life in Victorian England* (Westport, Conn.: Greenwood Press, 1996), 246.
[3] Donald Read, *England 1868–1914* (London: Longman, 1979).

Ireland" '. Here are the subtitles for the three religion chapters (one
in each chronological section): '*Very hard to come at the actual belief of
any man*'; '*Post-Christian days*'; and '*A non-dogmatic affirmation of
general kindliness*'. The use of such subtitles serves to present Christianity as already a vague and instinctive thing in the mid-Victorian
period and something vanished altogether as far as the general
culture is concerned by the late Victorian period. Another example
is Thomas Heyck's *The Peoples of the British Isles: A New History*
(1992). Volume two covers the period from 1688 to 1870.[4] After
1815, the only mention of religion in a chapter or section title is one
section in the chapter 'Mid-Victorian Society and Culture, 1850–
1870'. The title of that section is 'Natural Science and the Decline of
Religion'. Having dispensed with religion by 1870, Volume 3, of
course, has no mention of religion in any chapter or section title.
The index has three pages listed under 'religion' in that volume. The
first one is to a section on 'Aestheticism', in which this trend is
partially explained by arguing that art filled the vacuum left by the
absence of religion. The second leads to a reference to Protestant–
Catholic tensions in Scotland. The final page-number sends one to a
discussion of secularization in a section on 'Popular Culture'.[5] Is
religion really irrelevant to the general history of Britain by 1870?
Likewise, *A History of England* (1991) by Clayton Roberts and David
Roberts begins the chapter entitled 'Victorianism' with a section on
'The Conquests of Science'.[6] This is then followed by one on 'Religion
and Doubt', ending on the later note as the last word on the matter.
Any reference to religion in the pages thereafter is found in the index
under the subheading 'decline of'. Indeed, the surest and quickest
way to find the discussion of religion in a general study of the
Victorian period is to look up 'Darwin, Charles' in the index. In
short, a skewed picture of religion in the Victorian period has often
been presented. *The Encyclopedia of the Victorian World: A Reader's
Companion to the People, Places, Events, and Everyday Life of the*

---

[4] Thomas William Heyck, *The People of the British Isles: A New History*. Volume 2:
From 1686 to 1870 (Belmont, Calif.: Wadsworth, 1992).

[5] Id., *The People of the British Isles: A New History*. Volume 3: *From 1870 to the
Present* (Belmont, Calif.: Wadsworth, 1992), 45, 57, 196.

[6] Clayton Roberts and David Roberts, *A History of England*: Volume II: *1688 to the
Present* (Englewood Cliffs, NJ: Prentice-Hall, 1991).

Victorian Era (1996) has entries on Madame Blavatsky, Charles Bradlaugh, Annie Besant, A. H. Clough, J. W. Colenso, J. A. Froude, and Sir John Robert Seeley, but none on Charles Spurgeon; entries on Babism, Bahaism, Spiritualism, the Theosophical Society, Transcendentalism, and Zionism, but none on Baptists, Congregationalists, Dissenters (or Nonconformists or Free Churches), Evangelicalism, or Methodism (if it be thought that these are too commonly known to necessitate an entry, there are entries on flowers, soccer, tennis, toilets, valentine cards, and much more).[7] It is hard to imagine a direct immersion in the primary sources of 'everyday life' in the Victorian era producing such a result: it betrays the cumulative effect of long-standing preoccupations by researchers, writers, and teachers gradually being transmuted from themes that scholars find telling and interesting into a misconception about the tone of the Victorian experience as a whole.

Third, a major contributor to this distortion is the field of English or literary studies. The theme of a crisis of faith can loom as large in their own field as people in that discipline wish it to or decide that it should: no corrective is being offered here to another discipline. What is being observed, however, is that a distinction needs to be clearly made between a theme in literature or English studies and a judgement regarding what a historical period itself was actually like. And the crisis of faith does loom very large indeed in English studies. For example, one can find posted on the web a syllabus for the course 'ENG 210: English Literature Since 1798', being offered at the University of Illinois—Urbana Champaign. In this lower level, general survey course, the entire Victorian period is covered in a unit entitled 'The Victorian Crisis of Faith'.[8] Presumably just about everything said about the Victorians in such a course would be in service of the theme of religious doubt. Books on the Victorians that are written in order to serve the needs of the field of literary studies tend to explain the Oxford Movement, evangelicalism, and Christianity generally as a way of setting a context for the loss of faith. Philip Davis's *The*

---

[7] Melinda Corey and George Ochoa, *The Encyclopedia of the Victorian World: A Reader's Companion to the People, Places, Events, and Everyday Life of the Victorian Era* (New York: Henry Holt and Co., 1996).

[8] www.english.uiuc.edu/facpages/Wood/syllabus.htm accessed on 27 May 2005.

Victorians, Volume 8 of the Oxford English Literary History, covering the period 1830–80 (2002), has a chapter on religion which is divided into two sections.[9] The first, entitled '1830–1850: Evangelicalism, the Broad Church, and Tractarianism', is significantly shorter than the second. This latter section, entitled 'The Mid-Victorian Change', is an exploration of religious doubt. It does not seem unfair to say that the first section serves primarily to set up the second, which is perceived as the real theme that needs to be grasped. In a like manner, Richard Altick's *Victorian People and Ideas: A Companion for the Modern Reader of Victorian Literature* (1973) has one chapter on religion, and it is entitled 'Religious Movements and Crises'.[10] Once again, it is apparent that the religious movements are explained in order to locate the crises. As students of nineteenth-century history often look to interdisciplinary forums that are dominated by scholars from the field of English studies (such as the journal *Victorian Studies*), it would take great vigilance to keep this sizeable literary theme from blurring into a misperception of the Victorians themselves.

Turning to scholarship that takes the Victorian crisis of faith as its main theme, it is fitting to start with Basil Willey. Not insignificantly, Willey was a professor of English literature rather than history. His 1950 book *Nineteenth Century Studies: Coleridge to Matthew Arnold* already had doubt as a strong theme. While there were chapters on Thomas Arnold and John Henry Newman, the heart of the book deals with figures who were not orthodox Christians: chapters on Thomas Carlyle, J. S. Mill, Auguste Comte, and George Eliot (thereby bringing in Charles Hennell, D. F. Strauss, and Ludwig Feuerbach, who are also named in that chapter's title). This would all be fine, were it not for the fact that already here in this first volume Willey begins to imagine and teach that these doubters typified the Victorian period. He says of George Eliot, for example:

In the present book, which attempts to follow some of the main currents of thought and belief in nineteenth century England, George Eliot must needs occupy a central place. Probably no English writer of the time, and certainly

---

[9] Philip Davis, *The Victorians*, The Oxford English Literary History: Volume 8: *1830–1880* (Oxford: Oxford University Press, 2002).

[10] Richard D. Altick, *Victorian People and Ideas: A Companion for the Modern Reader of Victorian Literature* (New York: W. W. Norton, 1973).

no novelist, more fully epitomizes the century; her development is a paradigm, her intellectual biography a graph, of its most decided trend. Starting from evangelical Christianity, the curve passes through doubt to a reinterpreted Christ and a religion of humanity: beginning with God, it ends with Duty.[11]

It is not enough to say that Eliot's story illuminates much about her times. A move from evangelicalism to doubt must be projected from her onto everything—it must be the story of 'the century'. Moreover, Willey's main contribution was yet to come. *Nineteenth-Century Studies* was followed by *More Nineteenth Century Studies: A Group of Honest Doubters* (1956). The first chapter is on F. W. Newman, and in the very first paragraph readers are told that they can take his story as that of a typical Victorian life: 'The spiritual history of Francis was in no way exceptional, as John [Henry Newman]'s was; what happened to him happened to so many in the nineteenth century that his life-story may be said to conform to the standard pattern.'[12] Not even 'a' standard pattern—*the* standard pattern. Thinking Victorians who never lost their faith were the odd ones, the exceptions. Or so Willey implies.

Willey set the template of a volume with chapter-length case studies giving intellectual biographies. It was followed by A. O. J. Cockshut in his *The Unbelievers: English Agnostic Thought, 1840–1890* (1964).[13] Cockshut revisited some of Willey's favourites such as George Eliot, Matthew Arnold, and J. S. Mill, and added others such as A. H. Clough, T. H. Huxley, and Samuel Butler. Thus the story has been set. When Joss Marsh thought of doing a doctoral thesis in this terrain she was discouraged: 'Chadwick, Cockshut, and Willey had settled the matter of the Victorian loss of faith, advisers said.'[14] The reference to Chadwick leads to another theme: the way that church historians have also fuelled this perception. Their interest in it is

---

[11] Basil Willey, *Nineteenth Century Studies: Coleridge to Matthew Arnold* (London: Chatto & Windus, 1950), 204–5.

[12] Id., *More Nineteenth Century Studies: A Group of Honest Doubters* (London: Chatto & Windus, 1956), 12.

[13] A. O. J. Cockshut, *The Unbelievers: English Agnostic Thought, 1840–1890* (London: Collins, 1964).

[14] Joss Marsh, *Word Crimes: Blasphemy, Culture, and Literature in Nineteenth-Century England* (Chicago: University of Chicago Press, 1998), 5.

hardly surprising. It is not unlike the tremendous interest that the Victorians themselves had in the theme: those most interested in faith are often the ones who are most preoccupied with doubt. As far back as 1970, Anthony Symondson recognized that this theme was so powerful it could be harnessed to market a book on church history. He therefore took a volume with essays on subjects as diverse as the missionary movement, the Oxford Movement, and the Prayer Book, and subsumed them under the alluring title, *The Victorian Crisis of Faith*.[15] The eminent Anglican church historian Owen Chadwick contributed *The Secularization of the European Mind in the Nineteenth Century* (1975).[16] Chadwick offered stimulating discussions of some real and important currents of thought. Unfortunately, for those trying to get a quick handle on a subject they do not know much about, Chadwick's title tended to add to a growing assumption that thinking people generally gave up on religion in the Victorian era. Another edited collection appeared in 1990: Richard J. Helmstadter and Bernard Lightman (eds.), *Victorian Faith in Crisis: Essays on Continuity and Change in Nineteenth-Century Religious Belief*.[17] It is a splendid book, written by careful scholars. Many of the essays seek to problematize or nuance the notion and contours of the Victorian crisis of faith (once again, it is not the aim of this study to halt crisis-of-faith studies—only to put them back into perspective). In 1996 Hugh McLeod observed that the multi-volume work from the Open University, *Religion in Victorian Britain*, mainly edited by Gerald Parsons, which had become the standard textbook in print on religion and the Victorians, reflected this imbalance: 'Meanwhile the Victorian "crisis of faith" continued to be a subject of absorbing interest, and, if anything, claimed a disproportionately large share of the space in the Parsons collection.'[18] The Willey template was again followed in a book by A. N. Wilson published

---

[15] Anthony Symondson (ed.), *The Victorian Crisis of Faith* (London: SPCK, 1970).

[16] Owen Chadwick, *The Secularization of the European Mind in the Nineteenth Century* (Cambridge: Cambridge University Press, 1975).

[17] Richard J. Helmstadter and Bernard Lightman (eds.), *Victorian Faith in Crisis: Essays on Continuity and Change in Nineteenth-Century Religious Belief* (London: Macmillan, 1990).

[18] Hugh McLeod, *Religion and Society in England, 1850–1914* (New York: St Martin's, 1996), 259.

in 1999. Rather brazenly left without a subtitle to add a descriptive tone, limit the context, or acknowledge chronological, geographical, or other boundaries, it was simply the story of *God's Funeral*.[19] Wilson can describe the theme of his book in an equally unqualified way as 'the demise of faith among the Victorians'.[20] Wilson's book also had chapters with individual intellectual biographies of Victorians, including Carlyle, Spencer, Eliot, and Swinburne. There also have been literary studies on this theme such as Robert Wolff's *Gains and Losses: Novels of Faith and Doubt in Victorian England* (1977), Elisabeth Jay's *Faith and Doubt in Victorian Britain* (1986), and R. L. Brett's *Faith and Doubt: Religion and Secularization in Literature from Wordsworth to Larkin* (1997).[21]

In fairness, it should be pointed out that, of course, not all studies of the Victorians do a disservice to religion. Social historians generally understand well the important place of religion in nineteenth-century Britain. As to general studies, just to name two, Edward Royle's *Modern Britain: A Social History, 1750–1997* (1997) and K. Theodore Hoppen's *The Mid-Victorian Generation, 1846–1886* (1998) are both books that give whole chapters to religion and take seriously its place in the lives of many Britons.[22] Others can be seen bravely trying to show a bit of resistance to the kind of tidal trends discussed here. Adam Roberts's *Victorian Culture and Society: The Essential Glossary* (2003) endearingly has an entry on 'religious certitude' as well as one on 'religious doubt'.[23] Granted, the 'certitude' article is quite short and the 'doubt' one quite long, and one might suspect that the former was thrown in as an afterthought. Still, if so, it was the right afterthought, and it shows that the editor

[19] A. N. Wilson, *God's Funeral* (New York: W. W. Norton, 1999).

[20] Ibid. 155.

[21] Robert Lee Wolff, *Gains and Losses: Novels of Faith and Doubt in Victorian England* (London: J. Murray, 1977); Elisabeth Jay, *Faith and Doubt in Victorian Britain* (London: Macmillan, 1986); R. L. Brett, *Faith and Doubt: Religion and Secularization in Literature from Wordsworth to Larkin* (Macon, Ga.: Mercer University Press, 1997).

[22] Edward Royle, *Modern Britain: A Social History, 1750–1997* (London: Arnold, 1997); K. Theodore Hoppen, *The Mid-Victorian Generation, 1846–1886* (Oxford: Clarendon Press, 1998).

[23] Adam C. Roberts, *Victorian Culture and Society: The Essential Glossary* (London: Arnold, 2003), 187–91.

realized that readers might otherwise be misled. Even some of the examples offered above sometimes began their discussions by emphasizing the strength of religion in the Victorian period before homing in on doubt as the *telos* of the piece. The discussion of 'Religion and Doubt' in Roberts and Roberts, for example, begins: 'When Queen Victoria died in 1901 the majority of her subjects were religious—many intensely so.'[24] Scholarship can be found that has not been completely overbalanced by the crisis-of-faith narrative.

This book is not a study of the Victorian crisis of faith, but rather of a crisis of doubt. Still, as it seeks to be a corrective, it is worth offering a few observations on the Victorian crisis of faith itself. Although this is not always noted, the Victorian crisis of faith was actually a by-product of the religiosity of the Victorians and, in particular, the influence of evangelicalism. The Victorians themselves frequently discussed and wrote about the crisis of faith. Many of them did this because they prized faith so much and therefore feared and cared about its loss. Their discussions and reading should not be seen as a measure of the extent of the crisis, but rather as a measure of the extent of their concern. This distinction must be maintained. Taking concern about doubt as a measure of its reality is like taking Victorian anti-Catholic rhetoric as a measure of how close England came to 'papal domination' in the nineteenth century. To make another point of comparison, Boyd Hilton, in his masterly study *The Age of Atonement: The Influence of Evangelicalism on Social and Economic Thought, 1795–1865* (1988), observes that narratives of financial ruin loomed large in the Victorian imagination and therefore were the theme of many novels.[25] It would be a mistake to move from this preoccupation to the assumption that the Victorian period was one in which the economy was shrinking and most people were experiencing dramatic decreases in their incomes and standards of living. People talk about what they fear, and they fear not only what is probable but also what would possibly strike at what they value most—even if that possibility is not the most likely outcome. Therefore, it is fitting that the crisis of faith is so entwined with literary

[24] Roberts and Roberts, *A History of England*, ii. 636.
[25] Boyd Hilton, *The Age of Atonement: The Influence of Evangelicalism on Social and Economic Thought, 1795–1865* (Oxford: Clarendon Press, 1988), 139–40.

studies, because that was how it was in the Victorian period. Mary Augusta Ward's crisis-of-faith novel, *Robert Elsmere* (1888), was the 'best-seller of the decade'.[26] In other words, many more Victorians were reading about, talking about, and perhaps worrying about the crisis of faith than were actually experiencing it themselves—let alone experiencing a loss of faith. Even for the Victorians themselves, the crisis of faith was more a literary than a historical theme. In a religious age, doubt loomed large as the bugbear of faith.

More specifically, the Victorian crisis of faith was in part a by-product of evangelicalism. Evangelicalism is a form of Protestantism that emphasizes personal religious experience: a conversion experience and a life of intimacy with God through prayer, Bible reading, worship, divine guidance, and the presence of the Holy Spirit. David Bebbington has said of evangelicalism: 'In the mid-nineteenth century it set the tone of British society.'[27] Many of the classic crisis-of-faith figures such as George Eliot and Leslie Stephen came out of evangelical commitments or contexts. James R. Moore has observed: 'Most of those who called themselves "agnostics" had an evangelical background.'[28] Frank Turner has offered an astute exploration of the way that evangelical expectations shaped the stories of those who lost their faith, such as how their notion of a deconversion was modelled on the evangelical idea of conversion.[29] My purpose here is to augment Turner's analysis with an additional line of argument: that the notion of honesty that created the Victorian category of 'honest doubt'—a major prompt for the crisis—was informed by evangelicalism. 'Honest doubt', a phrase from Tennyson's *In Memoriam*, has been latched onto as a way of expressing that the crisis-of-faith figures no longer found faith intellectually credible; they chose to be honest about that and face the consequences rather than to continue to give lip-service to religion. On one level, what had changed from the eighteenth century was not so much that some people now doubted, as that more of those who did now insisted on being honest and open about it. That leading eighteenth-century

---

[26] Helmstadter and Lightman, *Victorian Faith in Crisis*, 285.
[27] D. W. Bebbington, *Evangelicalism in Modern Britain: A History from the 1730s to the 1980s* (1989; London: Routledge, 1993), p. ix.
[28] Helmstadter and Lightman, *Victorian Faith in Crisis*, 173.
[29] Ibid. 9–38.

sceptic David Hume agreed with his sceptical friend, James Edmonstoune, that another freethinker in their circle should still pursue a career in the church:

It is putting too great a respect on the vulgar, and on their superstitions, to pique oneself on sincerity with regard to them. Did ever one make it a point of honour to speak truth to children or madmen? If the thing were worthy being treated gravely, I should tell him, that the Pythian oracle, with the approbation of Xenophon, advised everyone to worship the gods . . . I wish it were still in my power to be a hypocrite in this particular. The common duties of society usually require it; and the ecclesiastical profession only adds a little more to an innocent dissimulation, or rather stimulation, without which it is impossible to pass through the world. Am I a liar, because I order my servant to say, I am not at home, when I do not desire to see company?[30]

Here we have a window into a pre-Victorian group with no less doubt than Leslie Stephen and George Eliot—just less honesty.

Evangelicalism strove to erase the space between outward conformity and one's inner thoughts and life. John Wesley, a founder of British evangelicalism, argued that a person could have 'the *outside of a real Christian*' and yet not genuinely be a Christian. The exterior of the best of these non-Christians is remarkably impressive. She or he:

Does nothing which the gospel forbids. . . . he blesseth, and curseth not; he sweareth not at all . . . He not only avoids all actual adultery, fornication, and uncleanness, but every word or look that either directly or indirectly tends thereto . . . He abstains from 'wine wherein is excess'; from revellings and gluttony. . . . And if he suffer wrong, he avengeth not himself, neither returns evil for evil. . . . And in doing good he does not confine himself to cheap and easy offices of kindness, but labours and suffers for the profit of many . . . He reproves the wicked, instructs the ignorant, confirms the wavering, quickens the good, and comforts the afflicted. He labours to awaken those that sleep; to lead those whom God hath already awakened to the 'Foundation opened for sin and for uncleanness,' that they may wash therein and be clean; and to stir up those who are saved through faith, to adorn the gospel of Christ in all things. . . . He constantly frequents the house of God . . . behaves with seriousness and attention, in every part of that solemn service. More especially, when he approaches the table of the Lord, it is not with a light or careless behaviour, but with an air, gesture, and deportment which speaks nothing

[30] David Hume, *Dialogues Concerning Natural Religion*, ed. Norman Kemp Smith (Indianapolis, Ind.: Bobbs-Merrill Co., 1947), 40.

else but 'God be merciful to me a sinner!' To this, if we add the constant use of family prayer... [He or she is sincere in all this.] By sincerity, I mean, a real, inward principle of religion, from whence these outward actions flow. And, indeed, if we have not this, we have not heathen honesty... [31]

If that leaves you wondering what a person must possess in addition to all that to be a real Christian, then a 250-year-old evangelical provocation still works. This is not a mere gimmick, however. Wesley and the evangelical tradition as a whole set the bar very high for true Christianity. Being utterly, sincerely convinced of the absolute truth of the gospel was a mere preliminary: even decent pagans possessed that in regard to their own religion. A person who had internalized such a way of thinking learned that continuing with a life of worship while quietly doubting the claims on which it is based was not only of no spiritual benefit but was also a craven thing to do. As a teenager, George Eliot (Mary Ann Evans) was a fervent evangelical. As a young, single woman still living in her father's house, she decided that her doubts necessitated that she not even attend public worship, even though she knew that this would anger her father and create social embarrassment. Leslie Stephen was from a famous evangelical family going back to William Wilberforce and the days of the evangelical 'Clapham Sect'. He decided that his doubts required that he denounce his Anglican ordination, despite knowing that this might destroy his academic career. Wesley continually wished to drive people either to become perfect or near-perfect Christians or to realize that they were not Christians at all. In what one might view as a vision of the Victorian crisis of faith, Wesley prophesied that people would eventually give up on public worship altogether and any profession of the Christian faith if they were not Christian to their inmost core: 'in a century or two, the people of England will be fairly divided into real deists and real Christians. And I apprehend this would be no loss at all, but rather an advantage to the Christian cause.'[32] This high-stakes game bore fruit among the Victorians, with some people taking the path that moved decisively away from the Christian camp.

---

[31] Edward H. Sugden (ed.), *John Wesley's Fifty-Three Sermons* (Nashville, Tenn.: Abingdon Press, 1983), 30–3.

[32] Albert C. Outler (ed.), *John Wesley* (New York: Oxford University Press, 1964), 193.

Another stream of scholarship has charted plebeian unbelief in the nineteenth century. The most important scholar in this field has been Edward Royle. Of particular note are his two monographs that together cover the whole chronological range in detail, *Victorian Infidels: The Origins of the British Secularist Movement, 1791–1866* (1974) and *Radicals, Secularists and Republicans: Popular Freethought in Britain, 1866–1915* (1980).[33] These are wonderful, meticulously researched studies upon which I have drawn repeatedly in the course of this research project. Other studies followed them, such as Shirley A. Mullen's *Organized Freethought: The Religion of Unbelief in Victorian England* (1987).[34] A cursory glance at this material—coupled, especially but not only in older general studies, with crude statements about the Victorian working classes not generally being religious—has also allowed those not particularly interested in church history to imagine that unbelief was a much bigger part of the Victorian experience than it actually was. Of particular interest for this study is the pioneer work of Susan Budd. Budd's seminal article, 'The Loss of Faith: Reasons for Unbelief Among Members of the Secular Movement in England, 1850–1950', appeared in *Past & Present* in 1967.[35] A version of this article became chapter 5 in her monograph *Varieties of Unbelief: Atheists and Agnostics in English Society, 1850–1960* (1977).[36] Budd's study of Secularists used as its main primary source obituaries given in freethinking contexts. A by-product of this methodology was that it removed from the picture the Secularists who later returned to Christianity, as they, of course, did not receive freethinking obituaries. Yet, as this study will show, reconversions were a major reality in the Secularist movement. Budd even observes that the Secularist movement had a 'very high turnover of members', but implies that this was the result of a tendency toward

[33] Edward Royle, *Victorian Infidels: The Origins of the British Secularist Movement, 1791–1866* (Manchester: Manchester University Press, 1974); id., *Radicals, Secularists and Republicans: Popular Freethought in Britain, 1866–1915* (Manchester: Manchester University Press, 1980).

[34] Shirley A. Mullen, *Organized Freethought: The Religion of Unbelief in Victorian England* (New York: Garland Publishing, 1987).

[35] Susan Budd, 'The Loss of Faith: Reasons for Unbelief among Members of the Secular Movement in England, 1850–1950', *Past & Present*, 36 (Apr. 1967), 106–25.

[36] Id., *Varieties of Unbelief: Atheists and Agnostics in English Society, 1850–1960* (London: Heinemann, 1977).

apathy by many of the rank and file, without even considering the possibility that it might have resulted from erstwhile supporters changing their convictions.[37]

Joss Marsh's *Word Crimes: Blasphemy, Culture, and Literature in Nineteenth-Century England* (1998) marked a fruitful relocating of the traditional literary studies interest in Victorian doubt to the world of plebeian unbelievers.[38] The present study, *Crisis of Doubt*, in another way, likewise seeks to explore how this kind of transplanting might serve to refresh a somewhat tired area of scholarship. Marsh has transplanted the study of the literature of unbelief to a plebeian setting. I wish to transplant the use of intellectual religious biographies from social elites to popular radicals. At the same time as Marsh, David Nash was working on a similar project, *Blasphemy in Modern Britain: 1789 to the Present* (1999).[39] Again, this is not a call to bring such studies to an end: let there be more monographs on the Victorian crisis of faith, more studies of popular unbelief, and more literary analysis of the works of plebeian sceptics.

This book is not a study of the Victorian crisis of faith. Rather, it aims to uncover a new category, 'crisis of doubt'. A crisis of doubt may be discerned when a significant pattern can be found of erstwhile sceptics coming to find unbelief no longer intellectually convincing. As the loss of faith is the *telos* of the crisis-of-faith literature, the *telos* of this study is reconversion. A crisis can be resolved in the opposite direction as well, of course—with a person reaffirming their earlier commitment (every marital crisis, for example, does not end in divorce). Still, as none of the figures given chapters in Willey or Cockshut or other crisis-of-faith volumes resolved their crisis in favour of religion, so this study concentrates on reconverts. The Willey–Cockshut–Wilson template is retained but inverted: thus here also are chapter-length intellectual biographies offered as fascinating and telling case studies where a crisis of doubt is resolved by a reconversion. 'Reconvert' is used to indicate that these figures were religious before their commitment to Secularism (as also generally were the Secularist leaders who did not reconvert). The freethinkers

[37] Ibid. 100.   [38] Marsh, *Word Crimes*.

[39] David Nash, *Blasphemy in Modern Britain: 1789 to the Present* (Aldershot: Ashgate, 1999).

who receive chapter-length studies here returned to orthodox Christianity. The shape of these chapters has been influenced by the standard charges that were made against reconverts, such as that they had never been real freethinkers; that they were not very important to the movement; that they were loose cannons that the movement was better off without; that their reconversion had happened too suddenly to have intellectual integrity; and that their reconversion did not reflect their true intellectual convictions, but was rather prompted by an ulterior motive such as a desire for money or attention. The case studies move slow enough to provide the relevant evidence when weighing such charges. They also seek to explore carefully both the specific nature and content of the figure's unbelief and then the intellectual response they gave as a reconvert to these same critiques of faith. Having presented these main case studies in Chapters 2 through 8, Chapter 9 then discusses the extent and significance of reconversions, pointing the way toward the Appendix where a range of additional reconverts and other persons of interest in various ways are listed, some of whom moved out of religious scepticism and into other traditions such as Theosophy or Spiritualism. The location of this study is English nineteenth-century popular radicalism; its main focus is a cohort of Secularist leaders who reconverted. How this story might relate to or place in a new light the stories of a crisis of faith experienced by some Victorians from the social elite will be explored in the final chapter.

The story of Victorian Secularist leaders who reconverted is well worth telling. First, these figures are fascinating on their own terms, however representative or unrepresentative of their times and of wider trends they might be deemed to be. Second, as will be shown, the regaining of faith by Secularist leaders was a significant trend in the nineteenth century. Even for those interested only in popular unbelief, it is important that such a prominent pattern be recognized. In a wider frame, however, this study hopes to nuance, problematize, and, most of all, put back in perspective the Victorian crisis of faith. Many existing studies read as if—unless one was willing to be a hypocrite—'honest doubt' was the only possibility for a bright, reflective, and informed Victorian. This study seeks to highlight the remarkable intellectual cogency of the claims of Christianity in nineteenth-century Britain. Even those who had most imbibed the strongest critiques of faith—the same people who had given lectures and written as sceptics on German biblical criticism, theories of evolution, the impossibility of miracles, and much more—could find that, in the end, for them Christianity was more intellectually convincing than unbelief. These erstwhile sceptics experienced a crisis of doubt which was just as disruptive and just as driven by intellectual concerns as those who experienced a crisis of faith. The stories of figures such as Thomas Cooper, J. B. Bebbington, and Joseph Barker are also worth telling, also reveal something about what the Victorian period was like—even its intellectual history. Indeed, the loss-of-faith narrative is so powerful that crisis-of-doubt figures often are discussed in existing works as examples of blasphemers, deconverts, or unbelievers with their subsequent faith downplayed as insignificant—that is, insignificant to the overarching theme that has interested scholars. Sometimes their reconversion is not even acknowledged, or is erroneously painted as some sort of senile descent rather than what it actually was: another active phase of life in which they wrote books, gave lectures, and engaged in germane debates on issues of faith, doubt, and learning. Let those who accept volumes with chapters on figures such as J. A. Froude, F. W. Newman, and A. H. Clough also make room for these stories. Reconversion, however, is not being put forward as the new paradigm for '*the* pattern', to use Willey's phrase, but only as *a* pattern. The figures presented in this book were no less committed to truth, no less committed to the latest learning, and no less honest. They also tell us something important about the Victorian age as a whole. By reminding us of the intellectual vitality of Christianity and religion in the nineteenth century they serve as a necessary corrective to a distorted picture in which doubt is triumphant over all. Honest doubt is not the only model of the thinking Victorian; there was also honest faith. The Victorian crisis of faith is not the only story. There was also a crisis of doubt.

2

William Hone

William Hone (1780–1842) secures his place in history primarily as a waggish radical and a man of 'independence of mind' (to use one of his favourite self-descriptions) who was the defendant in some of the most celebrated trials of the first half of the nineteenth century.[1] In December 1817 Hone endured three trials on three consecutive days for publishing parodies, one of the Church of England Catechism (including the portions that include the Lord's Prayer and the Ten Commandments), one of the Church of England Litany, and one of the Athanasian Creed. At the first trial, Hone was charged with: 'printing and publishing a certain impious, profane, and scandalous libel on that part of our church service called the Catechism, with intent to excite impiety and irreligion in the minds of his Majesty's liege subjects, to ridicule and scandalise the Christian religion, and to bring into contempt the Catechism.'[2] For the third trial the form of words was 'an irreligious and profane libel... with intent to scandalise and bring into contempt the said Creed'.[3] Hone was not charged

---

[1] In the mid-nineteenth century Harriet Martineau wrote: 'Altogether the three trials of William Hone are amongst the most remarkable in our constitutional history. They produced more distinct effects upon the temper of the country than any public proceedings of that time. They taught the government a lesson which has never been forgotten... [The second trial] began a contest which is perhaps unparalleled in an English court of justice.... The triumph of the weak over the powerful was complete.' Harriet Martineau, *History of the Peace: Pictorial History of England during the Thirty Years' Peace 1816–1846*, new edn. (London: W. & R. Chambers, 1858), 60–2.

[2] *The Three Trials of William Hone, for publishing Three Parodies; viz.—the late John Wilkes's Catechism, the Political Litany, and the Sinecurist's Creed* (facsimile of London: William Hone, 1818; London: Freethought Publishing Co., 1880), 2.

[3] Ibid. 72, 140.

with the more serious offence of 'blasphemy', but as he was tried for disseminating words that were accused of being unacceptable from a religious perspective, his trials have rightly held a prominent place in discussions of blasphemy laws in Britain.[4] Moreover, Hone also takes his place in the history of freethought. Even an in-house history of British religious scepticism, J. M. Robertson's *A History of Freethought in the Nineteenth Century*, names Hone as one of a handful of key figures, if not *the* other key figure beside Richard Carlile, in the field of 'popular freethought propaganda' in the period prior to 1840.[5]

Hone was acquitted at all three trials, making him a popular hero, a radical David who had beaten a Goliath Tory government, a champion of the liberty of the press. Hone conducted his own defence entirely. Here is its substantive core: 'He never intended by these parodies to excite ridicule against the Christian religion...His intention was merely political.'[6] He was being prosecuted, Hone argued, because he had attacked the government and exposed it to ridicule. The bulk of his speeches in his own defence consisted of demonstrating that there was a long tradition of parodies of sacred texts, that many esteemed Christian ministers and leaders of respectable society had written parodies of portions of Scripture, and these had been published without even the possibility of prosecution ever being raised. The ridicule in such cases, as in his own case, was not directed toward the original text, but rather toward the subject of the alternative text. In short, he was not ridiculing the Bible or the Prayer Book, he was ridiculing the government: 'It was not written for a religious, but for a political purpose—to produce a laugh against the Ministers. He avowed that such was his object; nay, to laugh his Majesty's Ministers to scorn; he had laughed at them, and, ha! ha! ha! he laughed at them now, and he would laugh at them, as long as they

---

[4] Hone complained at his third trial that by Lord Sidmouth 'he had been most unjustly held out to the country as a blasphemer, although now persecuted by that minister only for a profane parody. This minister endeavoured in Parliament to stigmatise him for an offence which could not be even alleged against him before a jury.' Ibid. 168.

[5] J. M. Robertson, *A History of Freethought in the Nineteenth Century* (London: Watts & Co., 1929), 64, 304, n. 1.

[6] *Three Trials*, 126.

were laughing stocks!'⁷ Furthermore, Hone explained, charges were naturally enough not brought against some other biblical parodists (not least George Canning, a government minister at the time), because their efforts were in the service of conservative politics.

It is patently apparent that Hone's intention was purely political. The attorney-general, Sir Samuel Shepherd, averred of the first parody: 'It has nothing of a political tendency about it, but it is avowedly set off against the religion and worship of the Church of England, as established by Act of Parliament.'⁸ Even he, however, did not believe this—as his subsequent speeches made clear—and three separate juries certainly did not. Ironically, beside ruffled Tories and stodgy churchmen, it seems that only freethinkers are apt to suspect that the parodies did transgress a substantial religious boundary. Hypatia Bradlaugh Bonner, the daughter of Victorian Britain's most prominent atheist leader, Charles Bradlaugh, and a notable freethinking campaigner in her own right, claimed in her *Penalties Upon Opinion* that 'The publications for which Hone was indicted were political as well as "profane"', thereby apparently conceding that the Tory ministers were right in point of law and that Hone's assertions to the contrary were disingenuous.⁹ In a similar vein, J. M. Robertson argued: 'Before 1840 the popular freethought propaganda had been partly carried on under cover of Radicalism, as . . . in various publications of William Hone.'¹⁰ Likewise, the scholar David Nash, in what is a very fine study, nevertheless oddly speaks of Hone's 'blasphemy' and 'his blasphemous works', when even the government at the time did not go so far as to accuse Hone of blasphemy—never mind the fact that he was acquitted.¹¹ Hone's parodies were precisely what he always maintained they were, political squibs.

Nevertheless, as the purpose of this chapter is to explore Hone's religious thought, it is necessary to consider what the parodies, in an incidental way, may or may not reveal about his religious convictions

⁷ *Three Trials*, 162–3.   ⁸ Ibid. 2.

⁹ Hypatia Bradlaugh Bonner, *Penalties Upon Opinion* (London: Watts & Co., 1913), 89.

¹⁰ Robertson, *History*, 304.

¹¹ David Nash, *Blasphemy in Modern Britain: 1789 to the Present* (Aldershot: Ashgate, 1999), 80, 84.

at that time. Almost two centuries later, the parodies are still often quite funny. As is the nature of parodies, the punch of the humour comes precisely from already knowing the original text. Therefore, it seems highly likely that a section of deeply religious, orthodox, churchpeople have always been among the ones who have enjoyed Hone's quips the most. The prayer for the prince regent in Hone's Political Litany, for example—'defend him from battle and murder, and sudden death, and from fornication, and all other deadly sins'— evokes a smirk at the word 'fornication', due to the daring aptness of its insertion.[12] Far from this being an attack on Christian orthodoxy, it is a prophetic denunciation of immorality. Whether a joke is offensive or funny (or offensive and funny) is a subjective judgement. The bulk of Hone's best cracks would undoubtedly elicit a range of reactions from many orthodox hearers—then and now—from delight to disapprobation. The material on the Ten Commandments would probably amuse more than it would ruffle:

I thy Lord am a jealous Minister, and forbid familiarity of the Majority, with the Friends of the People, unto the third and fourth cousins of them that divide against me; and give places, and thousands and tens of thousands, to them that divide with me, and keep my Commandments. . . .
Thou shalt not call starving to death murder.[13]

Hone's parody of the Apostles' Creed, while undoubtedly delicious, might be more apt to make some orthodox Christians wonder whether they *ought* to enjoy it: 'I believe in George, the Regent Almighty. . . and in the present Ministry. . . they reascended the Treasury Benches, and sit at the right hand of a little man in a large wig; from whence they laugh at the petitions of the people who pray for Reform . . .'[14]

Many Christian ministers, including Anglican clergymen, publicly expressed their conviction that Hone was unjustly accused, and their joy at his acquittal. One of the best-documented of such figures, and one whose reactions seem widely representative, is the clergyman and prominent man of letters Samuel Parr (1745–1825). After the trial numerous people gave some £3,000 in total to a fund in Hone's aid. Many subscribed anonymously, some acknowledging explicitly that

---

[12] *Three Trials*, 81.   [13] Ibid. 9.   [14] Ibid. 4.

Hone was too notorious to support openly ('My name would ruin me'; 'I must not give you my name, but God bless you'), but Parr forthrightly put himself down on the subscription list: 'Samuel Parr (D.D.), who most seriously disapproves of all Parodies upon the hallowed language of Scripture, and the contents of the Prayer Book, but acquits Mr. Hone of intentional impiety, admires his talents and his fortitude, and applauds the good sense and integrity of his Juries.'[15] Two years after the trial, when Hone was busy compiling other people's parodies for a projected history of parody, Parr let his friend know what he thought was a joke too far: 'More particularly I entreat you from the best motives, and upon the best grounds, to spare all ludicrous representations of the Trinity.'[16] From this one can infer what part of Hone's 1817 parodies had made Parr most uncomfortable. In Hone's reworking of the Athanasian Creed, three prominent Tory ministers—Lord Eldon ('Old Bags'), Lord Castlereagh ('Derry Down Triangle'), and Lord Sidmouth ('the Doctor')—form a political trinity. Here is but a portion of it:

But the Ministry of Old Bags, of Derry Down Triangle, and of the Doctor is all one: the folly equal, the profusion co-eternal.

Such as Old Bags is, such is Derry Down Triangle: and such is the Doctor.

Old Bags a Mountebank, Derry Down Triangle a Mountebank: the Doctor a Mountebank.

Old Bags incomprehensible, Derry Down Triangle incomprehensible: the Doctor incomprehensible.

Old Bags a Humbug, Derry Down Triangle a Humbug: and the Doctor a Humbug. And yet they are not three Humbugs: but one Humbug.[17]

Many earnest, orthodox Christians took Parr's view that at least some sections of Hone's parodies would have been better left unsaid. Nonetheless, it was not at all clear to them whether his actions

---

[15] *Three Trials*, 243. The pagination is continuous in this reprinted volume, but this portion of it is from a facsimile of the following document: *Trial By Jury and the Liberty of the Press. The Proceedings at the Public Meeting, December 29, 1817, at the City of London Tavern, for the purpose of enabling William Hone to surmount the difficulties in which he has been placed by being selected by the ministers of the crown as the object of their persecution* (London: William Hone, 1818).

[16] Frederick W. Hackwood, *William Hone: His Life and Times* (1912; New York: Burt Franklin, n.d.), 216.

[17] *Three Trials*, 143–4.

were starkly sinful or merely not in the best of taste or a potential gift to genuine religious scoffers—and they certainly ought not to be deemed criminal. Numerous anonymous donors to Hone's fund identified themselves with phrases such as 'One who dislikes Parodies on Scripture, but is an Enemy to Persecution' and 'No Parodist, but an Admirer of the Man'.[18]

After he became an orthodox Christian and returned to habitual corporate worship in 1832, a short account of Hone's religious history was written by the namesake son of the prominent evangelical clergyman David Simpson (1745–99). Hone reprinted Simpson's account in one of his own publications for the benefit of those wishing to know 'something respecting myself', declaring that it 'was written by a very dear friend, who knows me intimately, and for the present it must suffice'.[19] In other words, Hone put it forward as an authorized account of his own spiritual journey. Here is Simpson's depiction of the religious state at the time of the parodies of 'Mr. William Hone, whose name, a few years ago, stood associated in the public mind, with profaneness and infidelity':

It is but justice to Mr. Hone to state, that the object of his parodies, was *political*, and that they were not composed *for the purpose* of bringing religion into contempt, although that was their unquestionable tendency.... if the promotion of infidelity did not enter into the plan of the parodies, yet, that no person could have aimed at a political object by such means, whose mind was not, at the time, under the complete influence either of infidelity, or indifference—of opposition to religion, or carelessness about it.[20]

It is not at all clear that the general assertion being made here ('no person') is sound. Hone had shown quite amply at his trial that numerous well-respected Christian leaders had written biblical parodies or similar topsy-turvy compositions (such as putting sacred

---

[18] Ibid. 240.
[19] William Hone (ed.), *The Early Life and Conversion of William Hone [Sr.] ... A Narrative Written By Himself* (London: T. Ward & Co., 1841), 46–8. Regrettably, Hone's entry in the *Oxford DNB* gives the impression that this is his own autobiography rather than that of his father: H. C. G. Matthew and Brian Harrison (eds.), *Oxford Dictionary of National Biography* (Oxford: Oxford University Press, 2004), xxvii. 906.
[20] Hone, *Early Life*, 46–7.

themes to worldly texts), including Martin Luther, Bishop Latimer, the great preacher Rowland Hill, the influential hymn-writer Isaac Watts, and Archdeacon Paley.

Perhaps what we have at work here is the principle, applicable in many different contexts, that only insiders are allowed to make fun of those things pertaining to the group. If one was in no doubt that Luther was seeking to build up and not tear down Christian orthodoxy, then a firm supporter of that faith could laugh at his biblical parody guiltlessly. If, however, it was suspected that a despiser of one's faith was the jester, then it would hardly do to join in the fun. So, leaving aside the parodies, what can be known of Hone's religious convictions in 1817? At his trial, he asserted: 'They were not to inquire whether he was a member of the Established Church or a Dissenter; it was enough that he professed to be a Christian; and he would be bold to say, that he made that profession with a reverence for the doctrines of Christianity which could not be exceeded by any person in that Court.'[21] The stakes were high—prison and his family left destitute if he lost the case—so it was important that he trod carefully. This statement seems to contain two points that invited his hearers to assume more than had been said. First, the opening sentence implies that he was a Dissenter. Jurymen were meant to respond by thinking that a good Congregationalist, for example, is just as much a solid Christian (if not more so) than a churchman. It is an evasion because the equation of 'member of the Established Church' versus the implied alternative, member of a Dissenting congregation, was a false one. Hone was actually not a member anywhere, and was not in the habit of attending public worship at all, and had not been for fifteen years.[22] His dissociation from organized Christianity was so absolute that when his daughter Emma was born in 1814, he did not even have her baptized, a standard cultural practice at that time even for those seemingly quite indifferent to religion (three children born after Emma, in

---

[21] *Three Trials*, 18.

[22] In addition to this chronology also according with several statements Hone made later in life, a letter dated 24 September 1802 from a friend of his joked that perhaps Hone was having trouble earning an income because 'Providence' was not interested in blessing someone who did not go to church. Hackwood, *William Hone*, 68.

1818, 1822, and 1825 respectively, were also not christened).[23] Second, his 'reverence for the doctrines of Christianity' begs the question what those doctrines are, leaving his hearers to assume that they were the theological positions set out in the ancient, ecumenical Christian creeds, while freeing Hone quietly to decide that, for example, although the vast majority of people professing to be Christians held to the Trinity as a major dogma of their faith, that this was in fact an untenable view and therefore had no part in his version of 'the doctrines of Christianity'. On the other hand, the evidence of the trial and his own statements in later years would not indicate that Hone was an atheist at that time: the Hone of 1817 was a theist and an admirer of Jesus Christ, but also someone who had no place in his life for organized religion.

It is impossible to reconstruct with as much accuracy as one would like the chronology of the events that influenced Hone's religious convictions over the course of his life. In later life he spoke or wrote of numerous formative incidents, passing phases, and specific beliefs or doubts, but when precisely they happened (including before or after his famous trials), or how long they lasted, is not always decipherable or coherently reconcilable. Hone's own account, as well as the judgements of his biographer and the authors of inspirational works on his religious life who knew him personally, all agree that, at the time of his trial, Hone's religious scepticism was less thoroughgoing than it had been at an earlier point in his life. From all the evidence, it seems that 'deist' is as good a one-word description of Hone's religious stance at the time of his trial as one can hope for. An alternative that has been offered, 'Unitarian', does not fit as well. All deists, of course, were Unitarians in the sense that they rejected the doctrine of the Trinity, but one obvious difference was that Unitarians still gathered for corporate worship, while deistic religion tended to dispense with that requirement. As Hone was living in London, and therefore would have been able to attend a Unitarian church, that is one indication that deism is a more fitting description of his religious stance. Indeed, he was friends with Robert Aspland, the prominent Unitarian minister. Aspland helped Hone gather sources

---

[23] Ibid. 318.

for preparing his defence, but one does not gain the sense that it ever occurred to either man that they might worship together in a Unitarian chapel or be denominational co-religionists.[24]

One dateable bit of evidence is that Hone later recalled that when he received word that he would be tried for his parodies he was then working on a book (which, in the end, was never published) that he refers to as his 'Extracts from the Bible'.[25] This project, it is safe to assume, is identical with that of an undated incident in his religious history when he came to study the New Testament with fresh respect after idly starting to read Jesus' Sermon on the Mount. He was out walking in the countryside and stopped randomly at a house to ask for a drink. The woman went out of the room to fetch it, leaving the Bible she had been reading open at that passage:

He said to himself, 'there is more in one verse here than in a whole page of the Greek philosophers,' which he had been reading.... The next morning... he... purchased a Testament, which he read carefully with pencil in hand, crossing out all the passages he could not believe. He then, with a pair of scissors, cut out the portions which *he could believe*, and pasted them into a book for his own use. He said to himself 'What a beautiful simple thing is christianity, but this Paul has wrought it up into a *philosophical system*.'[26]

Many of Hone's most successful published works, as he himself freely admitted, were similar cut-and-paste jobs. This project, then, seems identical in spirit to one that a leading American deist, Thomas Jefferson, had undertaken thirteen years earlier, producing the so-called 'Jefferson Bible', in which he removed the miraculous passages and other troublesome sections of the gospels and printed what remained.[27] Hone alluded to his 'Extracts from the Bible' in one of his trial speeches, couching it in the most reassuring terms as follows: 'He on all occasions made frequent use of the language of Scripture. That proceeded from his intimate acquaintance with it. He had ever

---

[24] R. Brook Aspland, *Memoir of the Life, Works and Correspondence, of the Rev. Robert Aspland, of Hackney* (London: Edward T. Whitfield, 1850), esp. 618–20.

[25] Hackwood, *William Hone*, 61.

[26] [Frances Rolleston], *Some Account of the Conversion from Atheism to Christianity of the late William Hone*, 2nd edn. (London: Francis and John Rivington, 1853), 20.

[27] Thomas Jefferson, *The Jefferson Bible: The Life and Morals of Jesus of Nazareth* (Boston: Beacon Press, 1989).

delighted to read its beautiful narrations. He had long been employed in preparing a publication on the Bible, and he hoped yet to finish it, and to give it to the world, notwithstanding he had been called a blasphemer'[28]—the discreetly made distinction tacit in that statement being that 'its beautiful narrations' is not a synonym for the Bible, but rather a reference to the wheat that was left once Hone had removed the chaff by deleting the numerous biblical passages that he found in some way problematic.

Having started with his spectacular moment of fame, it is useful at this point to examine Hone's religious life during his childhood, youth, and adult years prior to the trials. Hone's spiritual formation was profoundly influenced by the intense, experiential, judgemental, and narrow Christian faith of his father, William Hone, Sr. (1755–1831). The father, who worked as a clerk in a law firm, wrote a spiritual autobiography that was published after his death by his son. Hone Sr.'s evangelical conversion, which took place in 1778 or 1779, was as dramatic and archetypal as they come, complete with a prior life of defiant sinfulness, supernatural occurrences, and a depth of spiritual agony and awareness of coming damnation so dehabilitating that a nurse was called in to attend to him. The turning-point was as decisive as one could imagine: 'my bed room being filled with the glory of it, a light above the brightness of the sun; and at that instant there came forth an audible voice, saying, "Thy sins be forgiven thee".'[29] Thereafter, Hone Sr.'s narrative is peppered by a marked defensiveness regarding his own lack of education. He tells a whole string of anecdotes that make the point that his experiential piety has no need of being augmented by education or theological study (beside a direct devotional encounter with the one book needful, the Bible). Those who hinted to him that he might be able to preach and evangelize more effectively if he did some reading or studying were only thereby demonstrating how bankrupt their own spiritual lives were, a judgement that even falls with thunderous denunciations on some preachers within the pale of his own very tightly delineated religious boundaries, namely evangelical Calvinists in Lady Huntingdon's Connexion. This disparaging of learning is

---

[28] *Three Trials*, 175.　　[29] Hone, *Early Life*, 20.

underlined in the pejorative phrases he used to describe the ministry of educated servants of Christ, such as 'the enticing ways of preaching in the wisdom of man, by the arts of logic and rhetoric'.[30]

Upon moving to London when his namesake son was just 2 years old, Hone Sr. made the family place of worship the congregation gathered around William Huntington, a popular if highly eccentric evangelical Calvinist and polemicist.[31] Huntington too was a man with a strong conversion experience, scant formal education, and judgemental in outlook. Hone (Jr.), in his account of his own spiritual history (also left unpublished at his death), declared scathingly that Huntington was 'an illiterate man', a statement that cannot be accepted as literally true.[32] Rather, it should be taken as indicative of a temperament that the minister shared with Hone Sr.—both men had strong views on numerous subjects, but these opinions did not always fare well when compared with the knowledge of these topics that could be acquired by reading and other forms of ordinary investigation. In Hone's own telling of it, this discrepancy was central to his loss of faith.

Hone repeatedly told, in considerable detail, a story of how 'his father and his friends' (that is, the Huntington orbit) were given to denouncing John Wesley as a 'child of the devil'. When Hone was around 6 years old he was at his beloved dame-school teacher's deathbed when she was visited by the great Arminian Methodist leader himself. The boy was able to observe beyond all doubt that Wesley was actually a good, kind, and truly Christian man: 'from that hour I never believed anything my father said, or anything I heard at chapel. . . . and so I lost all confidence in my good father, and in all his religious friends, and so in all religion.'[33] Rather than take that concluding statement at face value, it would seem more probable to read this story as the best anecdote available for encapsulating a

---

[30] Hone, *Early Life*, 31.

[31] See Donald M. Lewis (ed.), *The Blackwell Dictionary of Evangelical Biography, 1730–1860* (Oxford: Blackwell, 1995), i. 586–7.

[32] Hackwood, *William Hone*, 28.

[33] Rolleston, *Some Account*, 10. J. E. Howard confirmed Rolleston's account, testifying that Hone had told him this same story: J. E. Howard, *Recollections of William Hone. Thirty Years an Atheist, Afterwards a Happy Christian* (London: Religious Tract Society, n.d), 6.

whole series of moments of discovery throughout Hone's upbringing that assertions made by the two pontificating authority figures in his life—his father and his minister—were wrong-headed.

Hone had an insatiable appetite for all the exotic facts and fantasies that ever made their way into print. He was taken out of school to study at home, and thus grew into a classic nineteenth-century plebeian autodidact intellectual. He reminisced in 1824: 'Prone to inquiry from my childhood . . . I had no one to direct or regulate me: all books that fell in my way, no matter on what subject, I read voraciously, and appetite increased with indulgence. . . . I got through a vast deal . . .'[34] His mother helped him acquire reading material that the head of the family might have deemed unsuitable. Destined to be an antiquarian book dealer, Hone bought his first old folio at the age of 11. He took his first job at the age of 13 as an office boy for a solicitor, but was 'deservedly dismissed' due to his tendency to engage in private reading whenever he was not being watched. Despite having been fairly warned by his employer that he must mend his ways, the temptation of a bookcase in the office filled with treasures he had yet to explore proved irresistible.[35] At home, the son did not always please the father. Hone Sr. punished the boy by ordering him to memorize a large portion of Scripture within a time period that the boy found unrealistic. This, on his own account, alienated him from the Bible. He would let his stern parent keep his one book, and settle for all the rest: 'My poor Father was not aware of the mischief fraught in me by this severity; from that time I regarded the Bible as a book of hopeless or heavy tasks.'[36] Frances Rolleston, Hone's neighbour and friend in later life, who wrote an edifying account of his conversion after his death, recounts that, despairing of his assignment, he threw the Bible down the stairs, vowing, 'when I am my own master I will never open you'.[37] His father gave him a copy of Bishop Watson's *Apology for the Bible* (a rebuttal of Thomas

---

[34] William Hone, *Aspersions Answered. An explanatory statement to the public at large, and to every reader of The Quarterly Review in particular* (London: William Hone, 1824), 54.

[35] Hackwood, *William Hone*, 47.

[36] Ibid. 42.

[37] Rolleston, *Some Account*, 8. Rolleston tends to serve as a foil for Hone scholars, leaving the impression that she was some pious but not very perceptive or intellectually

Paine's *Age of Reason*), but even though he thought Watson had largely proved his case, the book nevertheless had the unintended effect of awakening him to the possibility that the Bible itself was assailable.

At around the age of 16 Hone began to associate with and adopt the views of both religious sceptics and political radicals. In defiance of his father, he became a member of the London Corresponding Society, the centre of organized English plebeian political radicalism and restless, brewing, popular discontent. It is at this point that Hone was able to acquire intellectual resources for constructing an alternative worldview from that of orthodox Christianity. He tells of the influence of a new friend:

He was my elder by three years, well educated, and seducingly eloquent. He had settled to his own satisfaction that religion was a dream, from which those who dared to think for themselves would awake in astonishment at their delusion; that the human mind had been kept in darkness, and men held in slavery, but that the reign of superstition was over... My new friend told me this was the 'New Philosophy.'... I was in my sixteenth year when I became a convert to this wretch-making 'New Philosophy,' as it was then called... [38]

A polemical exposé of English 'infidel societies', focused heavily on the London Corresponding Society, was written in 1800. Preserving the language of that era, it also uses the term 'the new philosophy', applying it to the religious scepticism of figures such as Paine, Voltaire, Rousseau, and Volney.[39] The author, William Hamilton Reid (whose status as a controversialist must temper the weight we place on his evidence), while admitting that the London Corresponding Society included political radicals who were not infidels, nevertheless claimed that deism and atheism won the day in the movement

sophisticated church lady. A learned contemporary, however, discovered her to be 'an accomplished and extraordinary person, skilled in Hebrew, reads Syriac and Sanscrit, writes no despicable verse, draws, is enthusiastically attached to this mountain region with its local traditions'. Eustace E. Conder, *Josiah Conder: A Memoir* (London: John Snow, 1857), 345.

[38] Hackwood, *William Hone*, 51.

[39] William Hamilton Reid, *The Rise and Dissolution of the Infidel Societies in the Metropolis* (London: J. Hatchard, 1800): facsimile in Victor E. Neuburg, (ed.), *Literacy and Society* (London: Woburn, 1971), 4.

as a whole, and that the phrase 'he is no Christian' served as a glowing character-reference among some members of the Society.[40]

Hone attributed his loss of faith primarily to the influence of one book. He refused to supply its title, however, lest he poison others with his own tendency to seek out intriguing volumes of which he had heard tell. Hone's biographer, F. W. Hackwood, hazarded a guess: 'The reference is believed to be to the philosophy of Holcroft and Godwin.'[41] In fact, although it has not been hitherto named, enough clues are available for this decisive volume in Hone's intellectual history to be identified. It was Baron d'Holbach's *The System of Nature; or, The Laws of the Moral and Physical World*. This work was printed in London by G. Kearsley in 1797, with the authorship erroneously attributed to M. Mirabaud (who, unlike d'Holbach, was safely in his grave and therefore immune to recriminations). The book fits precisely Hone's description of it: 'This work was then publishing in sixpenny numbers, by Kearsley, a respectable bookseller in Fleet Street. It caught my imagination and it wrought upon me to believe, what its object was to prove, that in Nature there was nothing but Nature.'[42] To this evidence, we can add Rolleston's claim that the book that 'reduced him to a state of universal doubt and uncertainty' was 'a French work' (Mirabaud or the Parisian resident d'Holbach, rather than Godwin or Holcroft).[43] Moreover, Reid tells us that the book was heavily promoted by the London Corresponding Society:

their minds were prepared for this more popular performance, by the more learned and elaborate productions of Mirabaud's System of Nature, and Volney's Ruins of Empires: the latter, in point of style, is looked upon as the Hervey of the Deists; the former, as the Newton of the Atheists; and, as the System of Nature was translated by a person confined in Newgate as a patriot, and published in weekly numbers, its sale was pushed, from the joint motive of serving the Author, and the cause in which the London Corresponding Society were engaged.[44]

Likewise, Edward Royle notes that, in addition to Paine's *Age of Reason*, the London Corresponding Society was also responsible for print-runs of Volney's *Ruins of Empires*, d'Holbach's *System of*

---

[40] Reid, *Rise*, 9.   [41] Hackwood, *William Hone*, 54.   [42] Ibid. 54.
[43] Rolleston, *Some Account*, 77.   [44] Reid, *Rise*, 6.

Nature, and Northcote's *Life of David*.[45] Hone was 17 years old when Baron d'Holbach's *System of Nature*—this 'new philosophy', this latest thought in the field of religion—was coming fresh off a London press for the first time.

Joss Marsh, in her excellent book *Word Crimes*, claims that Rolleston's assertion (following Hone's own self-descriptions) that Hone was an atheist is 'an overstatement': 'He almost certainly never strayed beyond Deism, and probably leaned towards Unitarianism.'[46] Rolleston was certainly misguided in her efforts to take literally his apparent words to her, 'I was an Atheist thirty years'.[47] She was well aware that he also said that he was not an atheist at the time of his trial, leading her to the unlikely calculation that, upon discovering his father's opinion of John Wesley was ill-founded, he became an atheist at the age of 6. When Hone applied to become a member of the evangelical Weigh House congregation in 1834, he testified that he was returning 'after an estrangement of nearly thirty years' from a life of habitual corporate worship.[48] This is the thirty years—thirty years of unbelief, or (in a religious phrase then used) 'practical atheism'. Nevertheless, there are numerous more precise statements that Hone made that can be taken at face value as revealing that he did internalize the intellectual cogency of atheism for a season, albeit a much briefer one than thirty years. Most precisely, he records: 'For

[45]　Edward Royle, *Victorian Infidels: The Origins of the British Secularist Movement, 1791–1866* (Manchester: Manchester University Press, 1974), 29–30. The shelf-life of d'Holbach's *System of Nature* for English plebeian radicals is indicated by a copy of it held in the Vanderbilt University Library. It is inscribed 'George Julian Harney 1875' and annotated throughout by him. Cole claims that Harney shares with Ernest Jones 'the distinction of having been the first English Marxist': G. D. H. Cole, *Chartist Portraits* (1941; New York: Macmillan, 1965), 298. A list of the books in Harney's library has been published. It reveals that he also had two books by Hone, *The Political House That Jack Built* and *The Spirit of Despotism*. Margaret Hambrick, *A Chartist's Library* (London: Mansell Publishing, 1986).
[46]　Joss Marsh, *Word Crimes: Blasphemy, Culture, and Literature in Nineteenth-Century England* (Chicago: University of Chicago Press, 1998), 31.
[47]　Rolleston, *Some Account*, 27.
[48]　Hackwood, *William Hone*, 317. A letter Hone wrote in 1829 inviting a friend to come and spend a Sunday together at his house makes it apparent that corporate worship was not a part of the Hone family's Sunday routine: John Wardroper, *The World of William Hone: A New Look at the Romantic Age in Words and Pictures of the Day* (London: Shelfmark Books, 1997), 16.

a short time, in my early years, I was a believer in all unbelief.'[49] Hone wrote in 1841, 'the History of my Mind and Heart, my Scepticism, my Atheism, and God's final dealings with me, remains to be written'.[50] His 'scepticism' was the kind of religious opinions he held for most of those thirty years, but there was a time in the early years of that period when he believed that the arguments in favour of atheism were persuasive. Indeed, at one point he asserts that this period— what I am identifying as the period of atheism as opposed to scepticism—lasted for two years, which we can reckon as having been during his last few years as a teenager.[51]

This is where we are aided by uncovering that d'Holbach's *System of Nature* was the decisive work in this mental development, for that book was explicitly atheistic. J. M. Wheeler, in a reference-book of freethinkers published in 1889 which is careful to distinguish accurately gradations of scepticism, referred to the *System of Nature* as a 'textbook of atheistic philosophy'.[52] Hone's summary statement of the book's teaching was apt. Baron d'Holbach declared:

Let us, then, reconduct bewildered mortals to the altars of nature; let us destroy for them those chimaeras which their ignorant and disordered imagination has believed it was bound to elevate to her throne. Let us say to them, that there is nothing either above or beyond nature; let us teach them that nature is capable of producing, without any foreign aid, all those phenomena which they admire, all the benefits which they desire, as well as all the evils which they apprehend.[53]

The book even attacks the deist doctrines of the divine creation of the world, life after death, the realm of the spirit, and the existence of God. Indeed, the *System of Nature* condemns deism by name at length. However refined deists' views might be, they have taken a fatal wrong turn that leads inevitably on to 'superstition', 'fanaticism', and 'credulity'.[54] In short, deism must be rejected side by side with traditional religion: 'We see, then, that the DEISTS or THEISTS, have

---

[49] Hackwood, *William Hone*, 60.   [50] Hone, *Early Life*, 48.

[51] Hackwood, *William Hone*, 55.

[52] J. M. Wheeler, *A Biographical Dictionary of Freethinkers of All Ages and Nations* (London: Progressive Publishing Co., 1889), 174.

[53] [Paul H. T. d'Holbach], *The System of Nature; or, The Laws of the Moral and Physical World* (London: G. Kearsley, 1797), iii. 309.

[54] Ibid. 362.

no real motives to separate themselves from the superstitious, and
that it is impossible to fix the line of demarcation, which separates
them from the most credulous men, or from those who reason the
least upon the article of religion.... all theology is a mere fiction;
there are no degrees in falsehood, no more than in truth.'[55] Atheism
is the only rational viewpoint—people shrink from this conclusion
not for intellectual reasons, but rather simply because they cave in to
human weaknesses:

The repugnance, which the greater part of men shew for ATHEISM, perfectly
resembles the *horror of a vacuum*; they have occasion to believe something,
the mind cannot remain in suspense, above all, when they persuade themselves, that the thing interests them in a very lively manner, and then, rather
than believe nothing, they will believe every thing that shall be desired, and
will imagine that the most certain mode is to take part.[56]

If Hone was persuaded by this book, as he said he was for a season,
then he was indeed convinced by the intellectual claims of materialistic
atheism. Moreover, the editor's preface included a call to honest doubt:
'Truth speaks. Her voice can only be heard by those honest hearts
accustomed to reflection.'[57] The main body of the book reiterated this
call for the young Hone to be brave enough to follow reason wherever
it might lead, and to renounce his father's faith: 'There have been,
however, men of sufficient courage to resist the torrent of opinion and
delirium.... Thus, some thinkers had the temerity to shake off the
yoke which had been imposed upon them in their infancy.'[58] After a
couple of years, however, Hone found that he could no longer keep
faith with atheism. Another statement he made of his religious views
before his evangelical conversion is perhaps more representative of his
convictions throughout many of his years as a freethinker:

I should have conscientiously affirmed myself a Rational Christian. According to my comprehension of the Saviour's character, I admired it, and I
believed as much as I could of his Miracles. There was a glimmer of light in
my head, but no warmth in my heart. I conceived I could be quite religious
enough at home on Sunday... It was a maxim with me that 'Conduct is
Worship,' and to do what is right is all that God requires.[59]

[55] [Paul H. T. d'Holbach], *The System of Nature*, 370–2.
[56] Ibid. 366.   [57] Ibid. i. p. xi.   [58] Ibid. iii. 281.
[59] Hackwood, *William Hone*, 313–14.

For Hone for most of those thirty years, the doctrine of the Trinity was mere superstition and corporate worship was superfluous, but there was a God in heaven, and Jesus of Nazareth was a great example for humankind.

Although it is often quickly passed over by scholars, many religious people in Hone's own lifetime thought that his greatest attack on orthodoxy was not his parodies but rather his *Apocryphal New Testament* (1820).[60] Notable, formal responses by indignant orthodox Christians included an article in the July 1821 issue of the Tory *Quarterly Review* (as well as an answer to Hone's reply in the January 1824 issue); a published charge to the clergy of the archdeaconry of Derby by Samuel Butler; and a book on the inspiration of Scripture by Thomas Rennell that named Hone in its very title: *Proofs of Inspiration, or the Ground of Distinction between the New Testament and the Apocryphal Volume: occasioned by the recent publication of the Apocryphal New Testament by Hone* (1822). Hugh James Rose (1775– 1838), who wrote the anonymous article in the *Quarterly Review,* claimed that Hone was 'a wretch as contemptible as he is wicked', who represented 'the infidel party' and a 'revival of Toland's blasphemy'.[61] Butler argued that the foes of religion were now engaged in 'a more secret and insidious mode of attack', and that Hone's book was the most sinister of them all—it was a dissemination of poison, 'AN ENEMY HATH DONE THIS'.[62] The very first sentence of Rennell's volume was: 'Among the various attacks which have been made of late upon the Holy Scriptures, the most dangerous, perhaps is the publication of a volume, entitled, "The Apocryphal New Testament".'[63]

Indeed, Hone's own brother Joseph, a lawyer, was so convinced by these claims that this book revealed William to be an enemy of

---

[60] Marsh's *Word Crimes*, however, does give careful and illuminating attention to this controversy.

[61] *Quarterly Review,* 25: 50 (July 1821), 347–65.

[62] Samuel Butler, *The Genuine and Apocryphal Gospels compared. A Charge, delivered to the clergy of the Archdeaconry of Derby, at the Visitations at Derby and Chesterfield, June 6 & 7, 1822, and published at their request* (Shrewsbury: Wm. Eddowes, 1822), 7–8, 34.

[63] Thomas Rennell, *Proofs of Inspiration, or the Ground of Distinction between the New Testament and the Apocryphal Volume: occasioned by the recent publication of the Apocryphal New Testament by Hone* (London: F. C. & J. Rivington, 1822), p. i.

Christianity, that Hone's failure (for several years) to offer a rebuttal led Joseph to opt for a course of total estrangement from his older brother as a known infidel—a judgement that he had not made in regard to the parodies.[64] Hone once met a leading Baptist minister, Robert Hall, and took him to task for having lumped him together with the avowed infidel Richard Carlile. Hall, however, defended himself by arguing: 'it is not for your parodies I have so spoken of you; I care not for them; with regard to your trial, I thought you a persecuted man; it is for your re-publication of the Apocryphal Gospels.'[65] In Hone's own spiritual narrative as a reconvert (which was not finished, and was left unpublished until long after his death), he tellingly expressed no regrets for his parodies, but did offer an apology for his *Apocryphal New Testament*: 'And here I desire to state that I have long felt deep remorse for having produced that work. I have lived to experience that it is justly offensive to pious minds, and so is detestable to my own.'[66]

Hone's *Apocryphal New Testament* was an edited volume of various non-canonical documents from the early church period. Some of these writings were deemed to be unsound and the work of heretical groups by orthodox Christians; others were viewed as orthodox works by respected church fathers. On one level, Hone was simply making a scholarly contribution. Who could object to the mere dissemination of writings of historical value and interest? Moreover, the orthodox themselves regularly argued that encountering what they believed to be the patently inferior quality of these documents served by way of contrast to confirm the unique quality and worth of genuine Scripture. Such a claim might lead to the conclusion that Hone had done orthodoxy a service. Rennell, however, let slip his snobbish fear that (just like the jurors at Hone's trials?) the common people might not discern the appropriate conclusion on this matter. Therefore, part of Hone's offense was 'to publish them in a form peculiarly adapted for common reading and extensive circulation'.[67]

A major part of what made this publication objectionable, however, was the judgements and insinuations made in Hone's introductions and notes. The volume's very introduction began:

---

[64] Hone, *Aspersions Answered*, 10–11. [65] Rolleston, *Some Account*, 49.
[66] Hackwood, *William Hone*, 62. [67] Rennell, *Proofs*, p. i.

'After the writings contained in the New Testament were selected from the numerous Gospels and Epistles then in existence, what became of the Books that were rejected by the compilers?... It has been supposed by many that the volume was compiled by the first council of Nice [Nicaea, 325].'[68] This way of structuring the discussion was repeatedly denounced as being as invidious as it was erroneous. Hone himself admitted that even a fair-minded reviewer would be right to notice that his antipathy to the Council of Nicaea was clearly on display. That council was the decisive moment in church history when the doctrine of the Trinity was affirmed as essential to orthodox Christianity. Hone paints Arius, the heretical villain of the story in an orthodox telling of it, as a kind of heroic honest doubter persecuted by narrow-minded dogmatists. Indeed, Hone's anti-Trinitarian sentiments are repeatedly revealed in this work. Hone himself was forced to concede that, upon further investigation, the council made no pronouncements on the canon, and therefore it might well have been his preoccupation with anti-Trinitarianism that had led him astray on this point. Hone's critics, however, were making a much more fundamental objection: the very notion that a group of (unsavoury) bishops, like some kind of a literary prize jury, came together and threw some documents in a canonical pile and others in the non-canonical one was a fantasy. Moreover, it was a pernicious one. Rennell averred: 'From the question itself, it is intended that the reader should imagine the selection of the books contained in the New Testament to have been quite an arbitrary one, conducted according to the fancy or the caprice of the prelates assembled; a supposition that cannot fail to unsettle his mind as to the real authority of the sacred volume.'[69] Butler replied that the New Testament documents were not selected by a council, but rather collected in an organic way by the whole church: 'Such *collection* therefore, would be made by progressive additions of genuine and authorised books, not by *selections* of what appeared to be best.'[70] The *Quarterly Review* pointed out that the New Testament

---

[68] *The Apocryphal New Testament, Being all the Gospels, Epistles, and other pieces now extant attributed in the first four centuries to Jesus Christ, His Apostles, and their companions, and not included in the New Testament by its compilers*, 2nd edn. (London: William Hone, n.d. [c.1821; 1st edn., 1820]), p. iii.

[69] Rennell, *Proofs*, pp. vi–vii.   [70] Butler, *Genuine*, 15.

documents are the earlier ones, and they were generally quoted as authoritative by the earliest church fathers, while the documents in Hone's collection often had not even been written when the church was already using the documents in the New Testament as Scripture, and that some of them were never used approvingly by church fathers.

The other major offence of Hone's volume was that he set out the text of these apocryphal writings so that they had the visual appearance of the Bible, separating them into chapters and verses, using two columns of text per page, and generally adopting the typeface and other printer's choices used for the Authorized Version of the Bible. In other words, he deliberately made these writings *look* like Scripture. Hone was researching his projected 'History of Parody' when he stumbled into his *Apocryphal New Testament* project, and it is reasonable to infer that his mind gravitated toward these documents as the ultimate biblical parodies. To take a random example, here is a portion of the Gospel of Thomas (1:5–10) from Hone's edition:

5 But a certain Jew seeing the things which he was doing, namely, his forming clay into figures of sparrows on the sabbath day, went presently away, and told his father Joseph, and said,

6 Behold thy boy is playing by the river side, and has taken clay, and formed it into twelve sparrows, and profaneth the Sabbath.

7 Then Joseph came to the place were he was, and when he saw him, called to him, and said, Why doest thou that which it is not lawful to do on the Sabbath day?

8 Then Jesus clapping together the palms of his hands, called to the sparrows, and said to them: Go, fly away; and while ye live remember me.

9 So the sparrows fled away, making a noise.

10 The Jews seeing this, were astonished, and went away, and told their chief persons what a strange miracle they had seen wrought by Jesus.[71]

The echo of a whole series of texts familiar from the Bible is unmistakeable, yet this passage is essentially an arguably rather ludicrous story about a pre-adolescent with supernatural powers animating

---

[71] *Apocryphal New Testament*, 60–1. This is the infancy narrative Gospel of Thomas. What is usually meant when the Gospel of Thomas is referred to today is the Coptic-language Gnostic one—a document that was not available in Hone's day, a text of it having come to light only through the 1945 Nag Hammadi finds.

his toys. For Hone's critics this was crude material in contrast to the lofty narratives of genuine Scripture, but those who had read Paine's *Age of Reason* had been introduced to the contention that familiar biblical narratives are often no less ludicrous when examined objectively. It seems an inescapable conclusion that Hone was trying to destabilize the canon. He denied that he was implying that these documents were also Scripture. The real point, however, was surely that some portions of the canon were no more worthy of the stamp of divine authority than the Gospel of Thomas. Over a century later, the judgement of the English freethinking community was also that his parodies were not his greatest contribution to religious scepticism: 'Hone's most important service to popular culture was his issue of the *Apocryphal New Testament*, which, by co-ordinating work of the same kind, gave a fresh scientific basis to the popular criticism of the gospel history.'[72]

Hone's natural mode of self-expression was the wry, the ironic, the indirect. He seemed uncomfortable offering plain statements of his own beliefs, and parody was his favourite means of communication. Even when he felt passionately about political or social injustices, his contributions were not earnest denunciations, but rather apposite and biting parodies such as *The Political House That Jack Built* (1819) and *The Queen's Matromonial Ladder* (1819). The two major projects that he so wanted to write that were not arch and refracted in their tone and construction, his 'History of Parody' and his spiritual autobiography as a reconvert, he could never bring himself to finish, despite expending considerable labours on them.

In a curious interpersonal connection for the theme of this book, A. O. J. Cockshut has informed us that the nineteenth-century crisis of faith only reached this ironical stage in the lifetime of the grandson and namesake of one of Hone's critics, the novelist Samuel Butler (1835–1902). Cockshut averred, regarding Butler's satirical novel *Erewhon* (1872): 'Although all this is rather obvious stuff, it yet contained something new—not a new thought but a new tone. Instead of the high-mindedness of Mill and Arnold, instead of the fiery indignation of Bradlaugh and Huxley, we have a detached snigger. The agnostics of the high Victorian period could not sneer—they

---

[72] Robertson, *History*, 64.

cared too much.'[73] The agnostic author of *The Way of All Flesh* loved his dear old grandfather, and took upon himself to produce his double-decker *Life and Letters*. The ecclesiastical Samuel Butler had early in his ministry preached a sermon against the evangelicals and in favour of toleration and broad-mindedness entitled *Christian Liberty*, and his grandson chose to imagine that it was the key to his whole life and thought. Having given it a generous examination in its proper chronological place, he then returned to it at the very end of the book as a kind of theme song for the credits.[74] On the other hand, he never once mentions his grandfather's published charge—indeed, perhaps his only published charge—attacking Hone's *Apocryphal New Testament*. That this was a deliberate suppression is underlined by the younger Butler's hand-wringing at having been unable to track down for the benefit of his readers a charge the cleric incidentally mentioned he had once made recommending 'the adoption of stoves in churches': 'The charge above referred to does not appear to have been published. There is no copy in the British Museum, nor have I found it among Dr. Butler's private collection of his published charges and sermons, nor yet among his MSS.'[75] Having done the research for the book, the novelist then donated the originals of his grandfather's letters to the British Museum, taking the liberty, however, to destroy 'any letters the preservation of which might cause pain without serving any useful purpose'.[76] The clergyman's letters to Hone were ones that he found it desirable to destroy. The grandson published extracts from this correspondence, however, although they are so decontextualized—focused on the civilities that controversialists sometimes offer one another in private by way of compensation—that they can be read as if Butler was one of Hone's sympathizers rather than among his most outspoken public critics. One wonders to what extent the novelist recognized the Regency parodist as a plebeian thinker who had found his way more than a half-a-century earlier to the freethinking sensibility he was then striking.

[73] A. O. J. Cockshut, *The Unbelievers: English Agnostic Thought, 1840–1890* (London: Collins, 1964), 101.

[74] Samuel Butler, *The Life and Letters of Dr. Samuel Butler* (London: John Murray, 1896), ii. 372–3.

[75] Ibid. i. 206–7.   [76] Ibid. p. vi.

The one judgement that can be made with the most confidence about Hone's inner religious life and convictions is that for the last decade of his life he was a sincere, orthodox, evangelical Christian. A second clear judgement that can be made was that this final decade of evangelical orthodoxy represented a considerable change from Hone's prior convictions; in short, that it was the result of a religious conversion.[77] Hone's religious scepticism had been informed by some of the latest and most rigorous and advanced thinking in that vein. Having already examined that mental furniture, the task at hand now is to explore the intellectual contours of his return to orthodoxy. It is a premise of this study that, although it is certainly true that non-intellectual factors play a part in people's rejecting or accepting of beliefs, there is no good reason why a historian should assume that intellectual concerns are decisive when it comes to a loss of faith but inconsequential when it comes to the appropriation of religious convictions. Nevertheless, scholars often seem to form their narratives with some such notion at work. Joss Marsh, for example, confines her recounting of Hone's return to orthodoxy to this statement: 'The loss of a child, penury, and the severe illness of a favorite daughter in 1832 turned him back to Christianity.'[78] If one were to indulge in such lines of enquiry, one might find it far more significant that Hone's father had died recently, particularly as penury, illness, and other troubles had come his way before. My working premise, however, is that ideas do matter and that Hone's conversion cannot be reduced to purely non-intellectual factors, any more than his scepticism can by fully explained by such factors (such as defiance of his father). Hone was an avid reader with a vigorous mind, a plebeian intellectual, and these things can be said about him with equal truth both before and after his reconversion. Harriet Martineau's final judgement on Hone was that he was 'a gentle and innocuous hunter after all such reading as was never read'.[79] Hone aptly described himself in 1838 as 'an insatiable reader in search of truth'.[80] It is unlikely that he could come to a

---

[77] It is perhaps indicative of how uncomfortable or uncertain this terrain seems for many scholars that Joss Marsh felt the need to use scare quotes when referring to Hone's conversion. Even in the index, readers are reassured that 'conversion' is not a word the author would use in her own voice.

[78] Marsh, *Word Crimes*, 30.   [79] Martineau, *History*, 62.

[80] Hackwood, *William Hone*, 60.

position of faith by simply bypassing the intellectual issues at stake—
for Hone and figures like him there could be no deconversion or
reconversion without a real intellectual integration.

Several factors can be identified as prompting Hone's reassessment
of the case against materialistic atheism and (ultimately) for orthodoxy, factors that will recur in the stories of many of the other figures
discussed in this volume: disillusionment with the conduct of freethinkers; the inadequacy of materialism and the thoughts of classical
authors as a philosophy of life; experiences of the paranormal or
spirit realm; a fresh appreciation for the Bible; the character and
teaching of Jesus of Nazareth; and other reading material beside the
Bible. As we have already noted, Hone was persuaded by atheistic
materialism for no more than a couple years. His abandoning of this
position was his first crisis of doubt: 'For two years I speculated on
them as facts. At length it occurred to me to collect a few *evidences* of
the truth of their assertions. Vain were all my researches for a single
specimen of *proof*, and I began to doubt the verity of the New
Philosophy.'[81] To this was added his disillusionment at having met
one of his favourite sceptical authors—Hackwood makes a good case
that it was Godwin—and having been shocked to discover that his
grand, alternative philosophy was so impotent as a way of life that it
coexisted with a violent, ungovernable, irrational temper.[82] Furthermore, to anticipate a discussion that will come later, fresh investiga-
tions convinced him that his cherished substitutes for Christian
resources were intellectually inferior: the teaching of Jesus was
more profound than Plato's and the character of Christ was more
noble and instructive than that of Socrates. In 1824 he recorded his
intellectual journey up to that point: 'I wondered at the world and
myself, and theory after theory arose as the waves, weltering and
disappearing. Ardently seeking for truth ... it was by patient research
and painful process that I arrived at the clear evidence for the truth of
Christianity.'[83]

---

[81] Hackwood, *William Hone*, 55.

[82] Ibid. 55. The two men certainly knew each other, as Godwin wrote the letter of
reference needed for Hone to attain a reading ticket for the British Museum library:
Wardroper, *World*, 5.

[83] Hone, *Aspersions*, 66–7.

Hone was from a generation that came too early in the century to be influenced by the Spiritualist movement, as some plebeian radicals would be later on. Nevertheless, he also came to believe that materialism did not account for all human experience. Several witnesses, including both Frances Rolleston and J. E. Howard, testify that Hone found telling an occasion when he had an experience of foreknowledge regarding the contents of a house he had never been in. He concluded: 'There is something here which, on my principles, I cannot account for. There must be some power beyond matter.'[84] Delightfully, Rolleston felt a need to insist that Hone's experience *must* have been explicable in materialist terms, solving the riddle to her own satisfaction by postulating that he suffered from 'the phantasmagoria disease of the eyes'.[85] This firm believer in the Holy Ghost also would not tolerate Hone's testimony that he had seen ghosts. J. E. Howard, Hone's other devotional chronicler, also recounted the spooky story begrudgingly: 'I hesitate a little as to recording the circumstance, which to some persons would savour too much of the marvellous.'[86] However much he might have been out of step with the worldview of an evangelical Anglican such as Rolleston, Hone's openness to the spirit realm was also a trait of a succession of intellectuals engaged in popular social and political movements, from Robert Owen onwards.

Marsh is right that Hone also testified that he found his alternative philosophy of life an insufficient one in a time of trial: 'under the weight of sudden calamity, I needed powerful support; in the storm of my mind I turned to Rational Religion for help—it blew away from me, like a heap of chips in a hurricane.'[87] This, like a new openness to the realm of the spirit, is a kind of knowledge from experience in keeping in its own way with the scientific spirit of the Enlightenment. It is also only a prompt for reflection rather than a supplying of conclusions, analogous to an intellectual claiming that the reason why they became a Marxist, a democrat, or a feminist was because of a personal experience of suffering. Hone found the doctrines of orthodox Christianity a source of succour, but he could not make himself believe that they were true for that reason any more

---

[84] Howard, *Recollections*, 12.   [85] Rolleston, *Some Account*, 22.
[86] Howard, *Recollections*, 21.   [87] Hackwood, *William Hone*, 314.

than he could have decided to believe that the Tories were really working for the best interests of the masses simply because it would have been a more reassuring thought.

Perhaps the most important item informing Hone's reconversion was the Bible itself. Completely intertwined with it was a fresh encounter with the person and teachings of Jesus presented therein. A variety of stories have been preserved regarding Hone's return to Scripture. While they all tend to present themselves as *the* crucial turning-point, it seems more probable to imagine that they all reflect moments when the claims of the Bible suddenly seemed more compelling to him, an intellectual struggle in which a positive view of the worth of the Scriptures ultimately gained a permanent victory. Hone testified of the time of transition that when he tried to read the New Testament he often 'left off confusedly'.[88] The story has already been related of how he picked up the Bible that a woman had left: 'The impression made upon his mind was chiefly the richness of thought and condensation of matter and style. He said to himself, "There is more in one verse here than in a whole page of the Greek Philosophers," which he had been reading.'[89] This led on to a period of personal study of the New Testament, in which he was convinced by the beauty of what he discerned to be original Christianity as opposed to the theological system created by the apostle Paul.

Victorian evangelicals seemed to love a sentimental story in which Hone was deeply struck by a girl's unselfconscious assertion that she loved her Bible, and a religious tract was even produced that recounted the incident in verse.[90] It was also said that Hone began to study the New Testament in a new way as a response to the criticism that was made of his *Apocryphal New Testament*. One version of this story traced it to his conversation with the Baptist preacher Robert Hall.[91] It is clear that Hone's friendship with a Quaker, Mr Ball of Bristol, helped to facilitate his journey back to orthodoxy. Here is his son's account of his father's role in Hone's rediscovery of Scripture:

---

[88] Hackwood, *William Hone*, 314.   [89] Howard, *Recollections*, 21–2.
[90] *The Child and the Traveller. A True Story* (London: Paternoster Road, n.d.). A copy of this tract can be found in the William Hone Collection, Special Collections, Adelphi Universities Libraries, Garden City, New York.
[91] Rolleston, *Some Account*, 48.

further and more interesting conversation ensued, and my father asked Hone if he had ever attentively read the New Testament? Hone said he had, but confessed he might have done so with a mind prejudiced against its doctrine by the manifest hypocrisy of many who made great parade of reverence for its authority. My father affectionately pressed him to read it through once again, remembering that the hypocrisy of those who bore the name of Christians, or even their wickedness, could not be held by any sensible man as an argument against that truth... [92]

It is telling that this anecdote delineates the issue at stake in such a manner that it is the doubt which arises from blinding emotions, while the appeal to faith speaks of argument, truth, and reason.

A huge amount of unspecifiable reading material must have also played a significant part in Hone's intellectual journey back to ortho-dox Christianity. His perpetual reading must be kept in mind. A letter to Rolleston dated 23 January 1834, for example, reveals a constant discussion of books. He mentions, for example, that he was returning her 'Protestant Journal, Chr. Observer, Delusions [a book on Montanism], Baily on Inspiration, Stuart on the Trinity'.[93] This is not a portrait of a man with a purely emotional spirituality, but rather of someone filled with intellectual curiosity regarding the contours of Christian thought. Even as a reconvert, he was still fascinated with non-canonical works such as the Book of Enoch and the Ascension of Isaiah, and was eager to discuss with Rolleston what conclusions might be drawn from a study of them.[94]

One book was mentioned by Hone as particularly influential in his reconversion, Richard Cecil's *Remains*, a volume that included an account of the life of the evangelical clergyman.[95] It is no surprise that Hone would have found it engaging: Richard Cecil (1748–1810) was an ideal match for William Hone. Cecil, we are told in the *Remains*, although he had a childhood Christian faith, later became an unbeliever:

---

[92] Howard, *Recollections*, 14.

[93] William Hone to Frances Rolleston, 23 Jan. 1834. William Hone Collection, Special Collections, Adelphi University Libraries, Garden City, New York.

[94] Rolleston, *Some Account*, 68.

[95] Howard, *Recollections*, 13. Hone also mentions, as a lesser influence, a spiritual classic written by a seventeenth-century Scottish professor and divine, Henry Scou-gal's *Life of God in the Soul of Man*.

He was suffered to proceed to awful lengths in infidelity. The natural daring of his mind allowed him to do nothing by halves. Into whatever society he enlisted himself, he was its leader. He became even an apostle of infidelity—anxious to banish the scruples of more cautious minds and to carry them all lengths with his own. And he was too successful. In after-life he has met more than one of these converts, who have laughed at all his affectionate and earnest attempts to pull down the fabric erected too much by his own hands.[96]

The intellectual component in Cecil's reconversion narrative is strong. He claimed that: 'When I was sunk in the depths of infidelity, I was afraid to read any author who treated Christianity in a dispassionate, wise, and searching manner.' As to the best sceptical literature, 'I have read all the most astute and learned and serious infidel writers, and have been really surprised at their poverty'.[97]

Like Hone, Cecil was a bibliophile: his incessant study while at Oxford brought on a period of six months when his vision was seriously impaired. He became famed for his clarity and originality of thought, and for his knowledge of secular as well as religious subjects.[98] Cecil, a man of the same generation as William Huntington and William Hone Sr., though a leading evangelical preacher, was also an intellectual. His advice to young ministers was 'Go to your books'.[99] Despite opposition from fellow evangelicals, Cecil tells of how he insisted on preaching dispassionate, learned, cultured sermons as the minister at St John's Chapel, Bedford Row. A piece in the volume entitled 'On the Occasions of Enmity against Christianity' no doubt reminded Hone of his father and of Huntington:

Ignorance, in ministers, is an occasion of exciting enmity against Christianity. A man may betray ignorance on almost every subject except the way of salvation. But if others see him to be a fool off his ground, they will think him a fool on that ground. It is a great error to rail against human learning, so as to imply an undervaluing of knowledge.... *An ostentatious spirit* in a professor of religion does great injury—that giving out that he is some great one. Even a child will often detect this spirit ... [100]

---

[96] Josiah Pratt, *Remains of the Rev. Richard Cecil* (Boston: Samuel T. Armstrong, 1817), 15.

[97] Ibid. 16. [98] Ibid. 39. [99] Ibid. 51. [100] Ibid. 182–4.

Richard Cecil modelled a learned, cultured, sensible, evangelical Christianity that fully understood the latest sceptical critiques of faith, but was not convinced by them.

A final influence was the preaching that Hone heard. Rolleston records that, 'from a sermon of the missionary John Campbell, of Kingsland, he received the conviction of the divinity of Christ, that in Him "dwelt the fullness of the Godhead bodily".[101] This is a particularly illuminating incident, as it was not the decisive occasion of his conversion experience: he simply had a change of views regarding his Unitarian or deistic Christology by encountering an articulate, well-reasoned exposition of the orthodox view. The immediate cause of his conversion to Christian orthodoxy was an impromptu decision on New Year's Day, 1832, to go to the Weigh House chapel, where the Congregationalist Thomas Binney, who would become known throughout London and beyond as 'the great Dr Binney', was in the earlier years of his ministry. Hone testified: 'Through the Minister, Mr. Binney, a startling summons was delivered to me in the course of the sermon, and I came away with my mind disturbed, but deeply solemnized. I must be brief. In a very short time it pleased God to break down my self-will, and enable me to surrender my heart to Him.'[102] Even in that extract, one can observe that the road to Hone's heart ran through his mind.

It is worth underlining what did not change. It has already been emphasized that his intellectual curiosity did not abate. Hone's commitment throughout his adult life to political radicalism was another constant. Hone himself was emphatic on this point: 'Observe though God has changed my opinions and religion, I have not changed my politics.'[103] Indeed, letters of his from 1838 reveal that he was still so much a radical even as an ageing evangelical that he could not refrain from vehemently attacking even the Whigs, let alone the Tories.[104] Hackwood points out that Hone 'never repented' of his radical, stinging political attacks such as *The Political House That Jack Built*.[105]

---

[101] Rolleston, *Some Account*, 50.
[103] Rolleston, *Some Account*, 41.
[105] Hackwood, *William Hone*, 229.

[102] Hackwood, *William Hone*, 306.
[104] Ibid. 63, 66.

Hone's commitment to Christian orthodoxy during the last decade of his life—not a short period of time, it must be borne in mind—was public and unwavering. Binney wished to err on the side of a sure, solid, lasting, publicly attested conversion, and therefore it was not until 30 December 1834 that Hone was admitted as a member of the Weigh House congregation. Thirteen family members also joined the church on the same occasion. Of particular interest in this group was a 36-year-old son-in-law, Thomas Hemsley, who was baptized as well, as were he and his wife Fanny's three children (Hone's grandchildren). In other words, Fanny had found a husband who had never been baptized and who was not a churchgoer and did not have his children baptized. Nevertheless, Thomas Hemsley—a middle-aged man—was sufficiently impressed by Hone's conversion that he reversed his own habits of a lifetime and followed his father-in-law into the church.[106] Hone spent his last eight years of regular paid employment working as a sub-editor for the *Patriot* newspaper. As this paper represented both evangelical Christianity and the political radicalism of Nonconformists who were impatient with the Whigs, and as it was leavened by the genuine commitment to culture and learning of its editor, Josiah Conder (who had also been a bookseller), it was quite an apt fit.[107] In 1834, on his fifty-fourth birthday, William Hone penned a poem that encapsulated his testimony of Christian reconversion. This bit of verse impressed many of his religious contemporaries:

> The proudest heart that ever beat
> Hath been subdued in me.
> The wildest will that ever rose
> To scorn Thy Word, or aid Thy foes,
> Is quelled, my God, by Thee!
> Thy will, and not my will, be done,
> My heart be ever Thine!
> Confessing Thee, the mighty 'Word,'
> I hail Thee, Christ, my God, my Lord,
> And make Thy name my sign.[108]

---

[106] Hackwood, *William Hone*, 317–18.

[107] For the *Patriot* newspaper and Nonconformist political radicalism, see Timothy Larsen, *Friends of Religious Equality: Nonconformist Politics in Mid-Victorian England* (Woodbridge, Suffolk: Boydell, 1999).

[108] Rolleston, *Some Account*, 4.

He also delivered a sermon on at least one occasion. Preaching and devotional poetry are perhaps more than one should expect from a habitual satirist, and Rolleston prodded him in vain to go evangelizing among the deists. Having moved house, the Hone family were received into membership at the Tottenham Baptist Church on 1 November 1840.[109] When William Hone died on 6 November 1842, his Tottenham Baptist communion ticket was found in one of his pockets, as if to make explicit that at the time of his death he was a card-carrying Christian.

---

[109] It is not clear to what extent he adopted Baptist sentiments. Hackwood states: 'Though there is no record of his baptism there, Hone told the Rev. Davies that his antiquarian researches had convinced him that immersion was the original form of baptism.' As some churches have immersed infants, that is less than a statement in favour of believer's baptism. Hackwood, *William Hone*, 343–4.

3

Frederic Rowland Young

Frederic Rowland Young was born in 1826.[1] His father, 'Joseph Young, of Stoke Hills, Ipswich, and Diss, Norfolk', was already dead when his mother, Betsey Young, died on 9 March 1854 at the age of 64.[2] As a Secularist lecturer, Young was billed as someone who had once been 'an evangelical preacher'.[3] 'Preacher', of course, is a more modest claim than 'minister', and it is highly improbable that, in his pre-Secularist days, Young was ever anything more than a lay preacher. His earliest, extant (unpublished) letters are dated with '3 mo.' and '9 mo.' instead of March and September, indicating that he might have been raised as a Quaker.[4] Quakers did not have a full-time, professional ministry at all. It is a reasonable scenario that he gave exhortations in some Quaker meetings. A probable Quaker identity is underlined by the fact that the firm he worked for before joining the leading Secularist G. J. Holyoake was an operation owned and run by Quakers (alternatively, it is possible that workplace standards put him in the habit of dating his letters in the Quaker manner).[5] In 1874 Young claimed that he had not believed in the

---

[1] This information comes from the 1881 Census. I have accessed it through www.familysearch.org. I am grateful to the Church of Jesus Christ of Latter-day Saints for making this resource available.

[2] *Reasoner*, 12 Mar. 1854, p. 190.

[3] Ibid., 7 Sept. 1853, p. 157.

[4] Manchester, The Co-operative College Archives, Holyoake Papers, F. R. Young to G. J. Holyoake. The earliest one is dated 3 mo. 11, 1850. Quakers refrained from using the traditional names of the months and the days of the week, on the grounds that they were derived from pagan gods.

[5] Ransomes & Sims letterhead had the 'Mo.' printed on it in order to ensure that the date was given the Quaker way.

doctrines of the Trinity or the deity of Christ for twenty-seven years.[6] Therefore, his scepticism in regard to orthodox Christianity dated from 1847, when he was 21 years old.

The trail becomes clear in 1850. Young was then living in Diss, Norfolk. Some articles of his had been published in the *Ashton Times*. These had now been expanded into a book: *Chapters on Policy Versus Straightfowardness; or, Thoughts on the Political, Religious, and Literary World*. He was by this time already locating himself within popular freethinking networks. The book was tellingly published by James Watson, a freethinker who had twice been imprisoned for his radical offerings. Moreover, Young's book was announced in Holyoake's Secularist newspaper, the *Reasoner*. Along with information on his book came the additional announcement that Young was available to give lectures. Thirteen titles of addresses he was prepared to deliver were listed, ranging from 'The Life and Genius of Robert Burns' to 'Capital Punishment'. None of them were explicitly on a freethinking theme, the closest being 'Persecution for Opinions'.[7] On 11 March 1850 Young wrote to Holyoake inviting him to come to lecture at Diss. A 'few friends of progress' had agreed on how much money they could pay the leader of the Secularist movement, and Young hoped it would be sufficient for him to accept.[8]

In December 1852 Young announced in the *Reasoner* that he was seeking subscribers for his next publication. He was then living in Ipswich rather than Diss, and working at Ransomes & Sims, Manufacturers of Agricultural Works.[9] The book, which was indeed published in 1853, was entitled *Facts and Fancies; or, Random Sketches of Men, Women, and Principles*. It was apparently self-published. An introductory chapter was provided by James Spilling, who was later a frequent author and Swedenborgian, but was probably at this time still a religious sceptic.[10] This book had chapters similar in kind to those of his previously announced lectures, with an emphasis on studies of authors. Holyoake added that he would be happy to receive money from subscribers to pass on to Young, indicating good-will

---

[6] *Unitarian Herald*, 10 Sept. 1875, p. 300.   [7] *Reasoner*, 27 Nov. 1850, p. 91.

[8] Manchester, The Co-operative College Archives, Holyoake Papers, F. R. Young to G. J. Holyoake, 3 mo. 11, 1850.

[9] Ibid., F. R. Young to G. J. Holyoake, 29 Jan. 1853.

[10] For Spilling, see his entry in the Appendix.

and that they were in communication. The *Bucks Advertiser and Aylesbury News* praised the book as 'removed from the regions of orthodoxy beyond all doubt', and prophesied that the author 'will have to encounter a storm as long as he lives for having his name upon the title page of a book which utters his convictions without reservation'.[11] If that was to read more into the book than what the author had actually put in print, then it reveals all the more that Young was openly identified with the freethinking world.

In May 1853 Young contributed a review to the *Reasoner*.[12] By June 1853 he had emerged as a Secularist lecturer, taking up the standard themes in the repertoire of such a role. His first lecture in London was a Sunday evening one at the premier Secularist venue, the Hall of Science. It was an anti-Bible address: 'The Bible Doctrine of Woman, stated and examined.' Young's objective was to expose the Scriptures as wrong-headed on social issues: 'It is probable that the orthodox female portion of Mr. Young's audience were perplexed to reconcile their orthodoxy with their own sense of woman's rights and duties, as it was very clearly proved that both the Old and New Testaments accorded an *inferior* position to woman.'[13] Young revisited this theme a few months later in a *Reasoner* article, concluding, 'throughout the whole of the New Testament there is not one verse to favour the idea of the equality of the sexes, while marriage is treated as a disagreeable necessity'.[14]

In 1853 Holyoake hired Young to work for him full-time at his publishing company. The 20 July 1853 issue of the *Reasoner* announced: 'Mr. F. R. Young will be prepared any time after July to lecture for Secular and other Societies, not more than 200 miles from London. The Sunday and Monday of each week would be preferred, but exceptions can be made in special cases.'[15] His address was given as '3, Queen's Head Passage, Paternoster Road, London', that is, the business address of his employer, Holyoake & Company—premises shared, incidentally, with James Watson, the publisher of Young's first book. Young's third book, *Fireside Politics*, which was originally

---

[11] As reprinted in the *Reasoner*, 15 June 1853, p. 399.
[12] Ibid., 25 May 1853, pp. 330–1.
[13] Ibid., 1 June 1853, p. 347; 15 June 1853, p. 396.
[14] Ibid., 7 Sept. 1853, p. 154.
[15] Ibid., 20 July 1853, p. 87.

serialized in the *Political Examiner*, appeared in 1853, published jointly by Holyoake and James Watson.

In 1853 Young also became a founding member of the London Secular Society. At its first quarterly meeting he referred to 'the points at issue between Christians and Secularists'.[16] Such a bifurcation indicates that he did not consider himself a 'Christian' in any sense. He was a regular lecturer on Sundays, including Sunday mornings, for the London Secular Society at the Hall of Science. His 11 September 1853 Sunday evening lecture had him billed as an honest doubter who had lost his faith: 'The subject is "Confessions of a Convert from Theology to Secularism," which, from Mr. Young's former experiences as an evangelical preacher, will prove of special interest.'[17] He now had a new list of lectures he was prepared to give, and they were in the classic anti-Bible tradition of Secularist lecturing. Titles included one of particular interest, because he would later address this theme as a Christian minister: 'The Bible Doctrine of Prayer.'[18] Likewise, a report of a speech Young made at a London Secular Society meeting is worth quoting at length. Not only does it show his clear identification with the Secularist movement, it also puts him on record as rejecting doctrines that he would later find very important, such as human nature as fallen, the ministry of prayer, and the need for a saviour:

Mr. F. Rowland Young proposed 'That this meeting expresses its satisfaction with the Reports which have been submitted to it, and pledges itself to exertions to spread the principles of Secularism.'... Mr. Holyoake has wisely stated that 'Secularism meets the case of those who are outside of all the churches by condition, character, and conviction.' In this respect, it is valuable. There are a number of persons, young men especially, of enlarged intelligence and purity of conduct, who are unable to accept the teachings of theology on God, providence, prayer, hell, and human nature, and who, having been thus bereft of their former creed, can find no rest or food for their souls. Orthodoxy offers them its dry husks, but they now know that husks cannot afford strength or pleasure. In such a position Secularism meets them with promise and power. It... calls the mind from speculation on an incomprehensible being to a living observance of living facts. It

---

[16] Ibid., 27 July 1853, p. 58. [17] Ibid., 7 Sept. 1853, pp. 157–8.
[18] Ibid., 21 Sept. 1853, p. 186.

teaches that man's condition is not the result of some decree or power apart from himself, but that his sole dependence is in himself.[19]

By autumn 1853 Young was in full stride as a Secularist leader. Attention was being drawn to him in literally every issue of the *Reasoner*, sometimes in two or more separate items. It was quite common for Young to be one of only a handful of lecturers named as scheduled to speak in London or elsewhere in the country; his books would be advertised among just a half-dozen other titles. He was a member of a select group. In addition to speaking frequently for the London Secular Society at the Hall of Science, Young was also speaking in other places. His Sunday morning lecture at the Philpot Street Hall on 13 November was so popular that he was asked to repeat it again on a Sunday evening later in the month at the same venue (presumably the morning and evening attracted, as it were, different congregations).[20] In December Holyoake moved his business to 147 Fleet Street, as part of plans for its expansion. In the process of the move, Young fell and injured his ankle severely. Holyoake's cheerful complaint that he therefore had to do Young's work as well as his own indicates what Young's job description might have been: 'the mishap has converted me into a sort of industrial universalist—consisting of correspondent, clerk, shopman, superintendent of country parcels, and editor in the intervals, which are excessively few and far between.'[21] By the end of January 1854 Young had sufficiently recovered to lecture at the Hall of Science again. He spoke on a book by the freethinking H. N. Barnett (who later apparently also reconverted).[22] Moving beyond the London orbit, beginning in late February, Young gave a series of three lectures for the Northampton Secular Society. In March he spoke at the Secular Hall, Hackney Road, on 'The Excellencies and Defects of Secularism'.[23] When he spoke in Manchester, his theme was an explicitly anti-Christian one: 'A Few of the Advantages of Secularism over Christianity.'[24] In April, giving his address as 48 William Street North, Caledonia Road, Islington, London, he put forth his most

---

[19] *Reasoner*, 5 Oct. 1853, pp. 215–16.   [20] Ibid., 23 Nov. 1853, p. 345.
[21] Ibid., 14 Dec. 1853, p. 389.
[22] Ibid., 22 Jan. 1854, p. 63. For Barnett, see his entry in the Appendix.
[23] Ibid., 12 Mar. 1854, p. 191.   [24] Ibid., 19 Mar. 1854, p. 208.

aggressively sceptical list yet of lectures that he was prepared to give. The first of the 'theological' series was entitled, 'The Bible proved to be Self-contradictory and Unreliable', and the last was, 'Six Objections to Christianity'.[25] Young was a leader in the movement, and he was explicitly anti-Bible and anti-Christian.

On the other hand, although he was clearly a freethinker it is not clear that he ever went so far as to refuse to affirm any theological propositions. He had changed the title of his autobiographical lecture to 'The Confessions of a Convert from Theology to Eclecticism' rather than 'to Secularism'.[26] In a somewhat confused speech to the London Secular Society in mid-1854, although he admitted that over half of the Society's members were atheists, he declared for himself: 'There are some members of this Society who hold that God and immortality are fallacies, others that they are problems not yet solved, while a considerable number think that belief in God and a future life is a matter of consciousness, superior to, and independent of, all logical proof. With that latter I class myself.' He was a Secularist in the sense that he believed that secular resources were sufficient for humanity: 'There may be other sanctions for morality than those of human nature, utility, and intelligence, but these also are accessible and reliable sanctions.' He went on, however, to praise the nature of Secularism in a way that does not seem easily compatible with his superior consciousness of the divine: 'its God is law, its Bible nature, its worship labour, its motive and inspiration utility, its final appeal reason.'[27]

It was the utterance of a man in transition. His repositioning seems to have happened in a six-month period outside of the public limelight during the second half of 1854. In January 1855 the Unitarian newspaper the *Inquirer* ran the following announcement: 'Newbury. The Rev. F. R. Young has received and accepted an invitation from the congregation at Newbury to become their minister, and will enter upon his duties on Sunday next.'[28] The *Reasoner* reprinted this without comment. In its next issue appeared an advertisement for Young's latest book, *Hints How to Make Home Happy*.

[25] Ibid., 30 Apr. 1854, p. 304.   [26] Ibid.
[27] Ibid., 4 June 1854, pp. 369–71.
[28] *Inquirer*, 20 Jan. 1855, as repr. in the *Reasoner*, 11 Feb. 1855, p. 93.

The publisher was Edward Truelove—radical freethinker, Owenite, secretary to the freethinking John Street Institution, and publisher of Paine and Voltaire, with prison time yet to come. Publishing with Truelove, therefore, did not signal any kind of move away from James Watson due to a religious turn, but it might have represented some kind of weakening of his connection with the Holyoake–Watson axis. W. H. Johnson would later report that he saw Young while he was lecturing in Huddersfield in August 1854, and Young had told him that although Holyoake's company published the popular freethinking leader Robert Cooper, there was a culture at the firm of not fulfilling orders for his publications. In other words, a rival to Holyoake's supreme position of leadership in the popular freethinking movement was being kept down by disreputable means.[29] Young probably would not have said such a thing if his employment there was not already over or clearly coming to an end. In a preface dated December 1854, Young expressed a hope to write a book entitled *The Bible History and Doctrine of Woman*, so either he changed his views within a month or he had become a radical Unitarian who was still sceptical about the Bible.[30]

In a distorted echo of the way that it used to be, Young made it into his third issue of the *Reasoner* in a row with this:

Mr. Young's Lectures. The following curious notice will interest our readers: 'A course of nine sermons are being delivered in the Unitarian Chapel, Newbury, by the Rev. Federick Rowland Young, on the Closing Events in the Life of Christ... Mr. Young will avail himself of these opportunities to state his own views on the person and character of Christ, and the comprehensive designs of his mission.' *Inquirer*, Feb. 10, 1855.[31]

Although no report of these lectures appears to have survived, they represent the first round in what would become the dominant intellectual question that haunted Young for the rest of his life: 'What think ye of Christ?'[32] The response of the Secularist movement to

---

[29] *Reasoner*, 30 Nov. 1856, p. 175.

[30] Frederic Rowland Young, *Hints How To Make Home Happy* (London: Edward Truelove, 1854).

[31] *Reasoner*, 25 Feb. 1855, p. 125.

[32] Matt. 22: 42, a text that Young put on the title-page of his final and most sustained engagement with that question: Frederic Rowland Young, *Indirect Evidences in the New Testament for the Personal Divinity of Christ* (London: W. Stewart & Co., 1884).

Young's having drifted out of their camp was apparently confined to the adjective 'curious'.

Young ministered in Newbury for several years. He then accepted a call to the Vicarage Street (Unitarian) Chapel in Yeovil, a pastorate he held from 1857 to 1860.[33] In 1861 he moved to what would become his most sustained and significant place of Unitarian ministry, (New) Swindon, Wiltshire.[34] In 1874 the *North Wilts Herald* testified to the nature and success of Young's ministry in Swindon from its earliest days: 'Thirteen years since the church was opened, and the thoughtful discourses of Mr. Young—free from the conventionalities which are hebdomadally inflicted upon so many congregations—attracted large numbers who were interested in hearing the utterances of a man who spoke boldly and courageously, and who sought to introduce into the pulpit something of a work-a-day religion, and not mere Sunday talk.'[35] With his address given as Rose Cottage, Swindon, he was listed as a Unitarian minister in the *Unitarian Almanac* for a decade or more leading up to 1874.[36] Although he stayed in Swindon for as long as he stayed in the denomination, Young was considered, at least by some, as a fine catch in the Unitarian world: 'he received more than one invitation to take charge of a Unitarian congregation in other places, notably Wolverhampton, and at Chicago, Boston and New York, U.S.'[37]

Although Young repeatedly attacked 'Christianity' and the Bible as a freethinker, he does not seem to have addressed the question of his view of Jesus. The closest he came was arguing that Jesus' view of marriage was one of male privilege rather than gender equality, but that was in the service of a comprehensive survey of the New Testament rather than an expression of an interest in questions of Christology. In 1865 the Unitarian Society for the Diffusion of Christian

[33] George Eyre Evans, *Vestiges of Protestant Dissent* (Liverpool: F. & E. Gibbons, 1897), 181, 263.

[34] Young often used the contemporary phrase 'New Swindon' to describe the location of the church. 'New Swindon' referred to a new development a little to the north of the historic town that had been prompted by the building of the railway works. The distinction has not been retained, so for the sake of simplicity and clarity, simply 'Swindon' will be used hereafter.

[35] *North Wilts Herald*, as repr. in the *Inquirer*, 15 Aug. 1874.

[36] Information kindly provided to me by Alan Ruston.

[37] *North Wilts Herald*, as repr. in the *Inquirer*, 15 Aug. 1874.

Knowledge in Belfast published Young's most important statement on the issue of Christology as a Unitarian: *Our Lord Jesus Christ the Personal Revelation of God*. Young's self-imposed task in this tract was to position Jesus as not divine, on the one hand, but as more than just one of the prophets on the other. He is clearly by this time not the kind of Unitarian that was working on a fluid boundary-line with freethinkers. Young formally sidesteps the question of the exact nature of Scripture as a matter Christians dispute among themselves, but in practice he quotes Scripture often (albeit overwhelmingly the New Testament), and always on the assumption that it is saying something that is true; perhaps even that it is true because Scripture is saying it. His Unitarianism is unequivocal, a point that it is important to underline, as he would later move decisively away from the position articulated here: 'I would draw the conclusion that Jesus Christ is not Himself the very and eternal God, for He cannot be the Being whom He manifests. But while He is not Himself God, He is the Personal Revelation of God.'[38] Nevertheless, it is not right, in Young's view at that time, to think of Jesus merely as a Great Teacher or prophet:

Jesus came into this world to do something more than tell us about God. Had that been His only or chief mission, Moses, or David, or Isaiah, or Paul might have fulfilled it. . . . If He be not something more than a Teacher, a great Miracle-Worker, a Master, an Example, He does but take His place with the rest of earth's mighty ones, and I feel that in dealing with Him I am still dealing only with the human, and not with the divine.[39]

The revelation of God in Jesus was unique and accurate: 'whatever Christ is, God is.' One imagines that Young has Secularist interlocutors in mind when he says that this doctrine 'suffices the mightiest minds'. Toward the other end of the spectrum, he addresses orthodox opponents of Unitarians with the argument that the Christian church ought to rally together around this revelation 'instead of creeds'. Young was no longer a freethinker, but rather a devout denominational Unitarian who—far from trying to push the boundaries of

[38] F. R. Young, *Our Lord Jesus Christ the Personal Revelation of God* (Belfast: Depository of the Unitarian Society for the Diffusion of Christian Knowledge, 1865), 11.
[39] Ibid. 9, 11.

the denomination—was endeavouring to ensure that its faithful maintained a high view of Christ.

The period 1864 to 1874 was largely one of continuity for Young—faithful Unitarian ministry based in Swindon. In 1869 he can be glimpsed volunteering himself to perform a rite of healing through the laying on of hands on Sarah Jacob, the 'Welsh Fasting Girl', who would tragically die of starvation.[40] This is a fascinating vignette, as it reveals biblicist and supernaturalist strains that show just how theologically conservative for a Unitarian Young by then was. In 1870 his edited collection of *Five Hundred Hymns for the use of Free Christian Churches* was published. 'Free Christian' was a label preferred by some Unitarian congregations, including his own, and this volume may be taken as a contribution to the liturgical life and corporate worship of Unitarians.[41] Still, it contained numerous hymns written by or dear to evangelical orthodox Christians, including 'Come Thou Font of every blessing', 'Hark! The herald angels sing', 'There is a fountain, filled with blood', and 'When I survey the wondrous cross'.

In 1875 came a disruption. Young's theological instincts were creeping in a more conservative direction, while those of the Unitarian body as a whole were moving in a more liberal one. He was not happy with the extent of the theological liberalism of many of his co-religionists. In September 1875 Young announced his decision to withdraw from the denomination. It is important to read his rationale in his own words:

I am as much a Unitarian as I have been for some years; no more and no less. For the past twenty-seven years I have not believed, nor do I now believe, in the Tri-personality of God, or that the Lord Jesus Christ is himself the very and Eternal God; nor do I know of any so-called Trinitarian community which I could conscientiously join. But when I find the Unitarian body slowly but very surely committing itself to the position that Christ is only one of our great religious heroes, born under the 'law of sin and death' which presses upon all human beings, and that the death of Christ is being regarded as merely one more added to the roll of the world's martyrdoms; when I find our Lord's moral perfection and sinlessness not merely

---

[40] John Cule, *Wreath on the Crown: The Story of Sarah Jacob, the Welsh Fasting Girl* (Llandysul: Gomerian Press, 1967), 32.

[41] Frederic Rowland Young (ed.), *Five Hundred Hymns for the Use of Free Christian Churches* (London: E. T. Whitfield, 1870).

questioned, but in one form or other denied; and when the very existence and the personality of Satan are scouted as old world dogmas; when, in fact, as it seems to me, Unitarians are rapidly becoming simple Theists, while some of their ministers speak of Christ with no more reverence than they would accord to James Martineau, and give to Christ's words and commands no more authority than they would to those of that illustrious thinker and divine, I think it is time to pause and ask myself where I am. Accordingly I have done so, without hurry or carelessness, and have come to the conclusion that if I would be simply true to my own soul I must be contented to take a position outside the Unitarian body, and also outside all Trinitarian bodies—in fact, to stand alone. I say this with no desire to be smart or sensational, but my conscience is my own, and I dare not, if I would be true to its Lord, do other than I am now doing; while I claim for all those who differ from me all the liberty I claim for myself, and impute no evil and no ungenerous motives to others. . . . If . . . it should be said that I am on the verge of going over to the Trinitarians, and that it is merely a question of time I beg to say that I have no intention near or remote . . . I hold what are called High Arian views, which appear to me incompatible with free and friendly co-operation with Unitarians as they at present stand, and also with Trinitarians.[42]

This confession of faith was a long way from his old *Reasoner* self. Here he is explicitly affirming human fallenness, the sinlessness of Christ, and even an idea so ridiculous to nineteenth-century free-thinkers as a literal devil. The editor of the *Unitarian Herald* could see the distance that had grown up between the former Young and the new one as well, retorting that it is precisely Unitarian 'openness which enabled Mr. Young himself to come among us, for when 21 years ago, he passed—without an interval—from being a secularist lecturer to being a Unitarian minister, his views of the church could hardly have been very high!'[43] It was not his views on ecclesiology, however, but rather Christology that were decisive. 'What think ye of Christ?', was the paramount question, and Young was increasingly frustrated by the replies he was hearing in his own denomination. Having pulled himself and his congregation out of the Unitarian denomination, Young continued to serve as the minister at the Free Christian Church, Swindon, for at least two more years.

---

[42] *Inquirer*, 11 Sept. 1875; *Unitarian Herald*, 10 Sept. 1875, p. 300.
[43] *Unitarian Herald*, 10 Sept. 1875, p. 300.

In 1873 the popular freethinking lecturer George Sexton reconverted.[44] Young, who had made the same jump from freethinking
platform to Unitarian pulpit eighteen years earlier, invited Sexton to
come and preach at his church. Sexton was invited to deliver the
congregation's anniversary sermons, a task of honour, and his move
back into the orbit of organized Christianity was further underlined
by his receiving communion for the first time as a reconvert from
Young's hand.[45] The two men soon became fast friends and collab-
orators. It is not clear when Young became interested in Spiritualism.
A British Library catalogue entry has him as the founding editor of
the *Christian Spiritualist*, a periodical launched in 1871. This means
that his acceptance of Spiritualism would have pre-dated Sexton's
announcement in 1872 that he had been convinced by the evidence.
Sexton succeeded Young as editor in 1874. In September 1875 this
publication merged with the *Spiritual Magazine*, retaining the title of
the latter but the editor (Sexton) of the former. In the *Spiritual
Magazine* for 1876 can be found sermons by Young, notices that
Young and Sexton had exchanged pulpits, and, more to the point of
the *raison d'être* of the journal, reports of addresses that Young gave
to the Dalston Association of Enquirers into Spiritualism. From the
latter is extracted this statement of Young's own definition of Spiritualism and personal convictions:

I am, as you all know, a Spiritualist; that is to say, I am a believer in the
doctrine of immortality, demonstrated in the realm of the senses by certain
phenomena, generally described as Modern Spiritualism; and that the disembodied, or departed spirit can so avail himself of the material conditions
of our existence as to communicate with us who remain behind, and so
assure us that he still IS, as really as he WAS with us in bodily form. As I
understand it, any man who believes as much as this is a Spiritualist. His
creedal opinions and ecclesiastical relations neither make him a Spiritualist,
nor unfit him for being one. Personally speaking, I am a believer in the Lord
Jesus Christ, as the Son of God and the Saviour of the world, as man's Divine
Teacher and Master, from whose authority there lies no right of appeal; but I
am quite aware that the majority of Spiritualists do not occupy that position,
nor am I concerned at the present moment in dealing with any differences
between Spiritualists who are Christians and those who are not.[46]

[44] For Sexton, see Chap. 8.   [45] Young, *Indirect*, 106.
[46] *Spiritual Magazine* (1876), 97.

Another report in the *Spiritual Magazine* reveals that Young had moved into lecturing on Christian apologetics, that is, that he had gone from propagating religious scepticism in the early 1850s to combating it in the mid-1870s. Young gave a lecture series on 'Modern Unbelief' at his church and had arranged for Sexton to round off the series. Young's lectures, given one a week throughout January 1876, were: 'Modern Unbelief: its Nature, Varieties, and Extent', 'Some of the Causes of Modern Unbelief', 'Modern Unbelief considered as to some of its Consequences', and 'How should Modern Unbelief be treated?' The commentary expressed a sense that such work was of 'the greatest possible importance in this sceptical age, and will doubtless be productive of much good'.[47]

Having collaborated on the *Spiritual Magazine*, Young and Sexton found a further forum for their anti-sceptical energies when Sexton became, in 1880, the editor of the *Shield of Faith*: 'A Monthly Paper in Opposition to Infidelity.' This paper declared explicitly that it existed 'to direct our attacks mainly against the camp...which goes by the name of Secularism'.[48] Here we find ourselves in the rough-and-tumble world of the combative debates between Christian apologists and Secularist leaders. Polite Christians sometimes disapproved of the paper's blunt language and its willingness to air gossip and to substantiate its claim that Secularism led to immorality by repeating what might have best been left unsaid. Rattled freethinkers dubbed it the 'Shield of Filth'. The *Secular Review* for 7 July 1883 gave a lengthy reply to the contents of the latest issue of the *Shield of Faith*, endeavouring to show that 'it contains the most glaring specimens of misrepresentation and special pleading'.[49] Young likewise, by this time, must have thought that his erstwhile friend Holyoake was dangerously wrong to have joined in such an attack on the Secularist camp. It is, incidentally, mentioned that Young had lectured on behalf of the Hartlepool Christian Defence Association.[50] It is safe to assume that he spoke in various parts of the country on behalf of that association. Again, this was the precise inverse of the days when he would travel to speak for associations such as the Northampton

[47] *Spiritual Magazine* (1876), 89.   [48] *Shield of Faith* (Jan. 1880), 1.
[49] *Secular Review*, 7 July 1883, p. 10.   [50] *Shield of Faith* (Jan. 1880), 12.

Secular Society: the Christian Defence Association existed to combat religious scepticism.

Toward the end of its life Young was sharing some of the *Shield of Faith's* editorial work with Sexton. When the paper folded in early 1884, the *Secular Review* (in a piece written by Charles Watts) initially offered a touching tribute to Sexton as an honourable foe.[51] When Young placed an advertisement expressing a desire to sell the now defunct journal, the *Secular Review's* 'Saladin' (William Stewart Ross) was ready to have some fun:

In Deuteronomy, Moses writes an account of his own death . . . the *Shield of Faith* . . . excelled both Moses and Swift in its description of its own death, not only affording information as to *how* it died, but expatiating on *why* it died. That was certainly wonderful enough. It announced its own death; but now its assistant editor advertises its *corpse* for sale; for, seeing the journal is dead, in the name of the Styx, what else can he advertise for sale in regard to it?

. . . The *Shield* has been defunct quite, and, 'Lord, by this time *it* stinketh, for *it* hath been dead four *weeks*' (cf. John xi. 39). Nevertheless, who will buy the corpse from Dr. Young? By the way, that enterprising trader must have abbreviated his name. Written in full, his name cannot be simply Dr. Young, but must be Dr. Young-and-Green. The *Shield*, at least, tried to break the teeth of the Infidel; so, although the Sexton has mournfully rung the funeral chimes over it, the Most High, prevailed upon by earnest prayer, may, even yet, see that the journal is necessary to 'withstand the fiery darts of the wicked,' and to regalvanise the corpse, may send a shower of half-crowns down from heaven upon the pate of his servant, Dr. Young-and-Green. We shall see.[52]

Opposing infidelity was rarely a money-making venture.

A report in 1882 reveals that Young had gathered a congregation for 'Unsectarian Christian Services' that was meeting on Sundays at the Athenaeum, Camden Road.[53] By 1884 Young was ready to affirm doctrines that he had rejected thirty-seven years earlier and had stood apart from for most of his ministerial career, the deity of Christ and the Trinity. He now appears before the world as a doctor of divinity (Frederic Rowland Young, DD, or Dr Young). It is not clear

---

[51] *Secular Review*, 19 Jan. 1884, p. 33.   [52] Ibid., 9 Feb. 1884, p. 82.
[53] *Shield of Faith* (Jan. 1882), 22.

how this diploma was conferred, but Sexton had a knack for accumulating a wide assortment of degrees, and perhaps he was kind enough to point the way for a friend.[54] In 1884–6 Young served as the minister at Augustine Congregational Church, Reading.[55] He was clearly helping out a struggling congregation: the pastorate had been vacant since 1881. Young made an incidental comment in a volume in which he is identified as the minister of Augustine, that he had given some sermons to 'his own congregation at Reading' in 1882,[56] so it would seem that he was an interim preacher or pastor there for a couple of years before he was given a proper appointment (or before the Congregational Union was informed). After Young's resignation in 1886, the congregation decided there was no point in endeavouring to struggle on, dissolved itself, and amalgamated with a Congregational church on Castle Street. Perhaps being reluctant to give up his status as a minority of one, although Young was recognized as a minister who was serving a church in the Congregational Union, he never became an official Congregational minister himself. The fact that he had already become intellectually convinced by Trinitarian theology would have been a prerequisite of his being interested in Augustine Congregational Church and that congregation being willing to accept him.

In 1884 Young's magnum opus, *Indirect Evidences in the New Testament for the Personal Divinity of Christ*, was published. He had begun publishing parts of it in the *Shield of Faith* in 1881, confirming that he had been a Trinitarian for at least three years already. *Indirect Evidences* was a sustained defence of a doctrine that he had denied for most of his adult life, the deity of Jesus Christ. A common feature of nineteenth-century reconverts was that they were haunted by Jesus, and Young's book opens with a typical articulation of how large this issue came to loom in the minds of many reconverts: 'I happened to be one of an increasing number of persons who believe that almost, if not quite, all the great fundamental controversies of to-day must,

[54] For honorary degrees and dubious doctorates for sale, see Timothy Larsen, 'Honorary Doctorates and the Nonconformist Ministry in Nineteenth-Century England', in David Bebbington and Timothy Larsen (eds.), *Modern Christianity and Cultural Aspirations* (London: Sheffield Academic Press, 2003), 139–56.

[55] *Congregational Year Book* for 1885, 307; *Congregational Year Book* for 1886, 281.

[56] Young, *Indirect*, 136.

sooner or later, be determined by what we do really and truly believe about the person of Christ.'[57] If one did not already know Young's story, it would not be readily apparent from reading this volume that it represented a significant change of viewpoint for the author. In the light of knowledge of his past history, however, there are many telling phrases. He declares: 'Now, after a patient, continuous, prayerful, and, I am sure, independent study of the New Testament, carried on for many years, I am able to affirm unhesitatingly, not only that there are large numbers of *indirect* testimonies in those pages to the personal divinity of Christ, but that their very indirectness constitutes a large portion of their value.'[58] 'Now' indeed! Although that word could be read as a point of emphasis, as in 'Now let me tell you', it really is a marker of an intellectual journey that had, after a very slow passage, arrived at a new destination. Young claims that the classic 'proof texts' used to argue for or against Jesus' divinity 'will quite honestly bear any fair strain' which might be put on them: a concession that has embedded in it a tribute to the days when he, in good faith, read those biblical passages as teaching that Jesus was not God.

Young mentions the humanitarian view (i.e. that Jesus was only a human being), and the Swedenborgian view (which he does not define, but he probably has in mind Modalism), as alternatives to the orthodox view that he will endeavour to show in this volume is that of the New Testament writers. Young dismisses the more liberal wing of Unitarians as in no sense Christians and therefore irrelevant to this conversation. His foil therefore is his old co-religionists from the days when he found a home on the conservative wing of Unitarianism. He cites the Christological views of several 'Christian Unitarians'. A statement he heard the eminent Unitarian minister, Brooke Herford, make in a public address in 1873 serves for Young as a succinct expression of the Christology that he now finds to be inadequate and un-biblical: 'I tell you frankly that I believe Jesus was simply a man, a man born in honest wedlock.'[59]

It is not necessary to rehearse Young's methodological progression through the New Testament. It should be borne in mind, however, that the main burden of his work was to tease out what he believed to

---

[57] Ibid., p. ix.   [58] Ibid., p. x.   [59] Ibid. 1.

be the assumption that Jesus is God embedded in numerous Scriptural statements. As any former Secularist would be, he is aware of the potential intellectual problem for his project regarding the reliability of the Bible and the findings of modern biblical criticism. Although he explicitly rejects verbal infallibility and plenary inspiration, Young nevertheless contends that modern readers have a sufficient record of the words of Christ and the apostles to form sound judgements regarding what they believed on such a fundamental issue:

> The theory that has prevailed for so many ages, that 'the Holy Ghost guided the sacred penmen in every Alpha, every Omega, every Iota, they formed upon the scroll,' is gradually being given up by all scholars, orthodox and heterodox alike. But what remains after criticism has done its work most exactly and most honestly, does not take away from us, but leaves us intact such statements made by our Lord respecting Himself, and of Him by others, as cannot be made to harmonize with the humanitarian theory.[60]

Biblical criticism must not become a mask for indulging one's personal preferences without regard for an intellectually credible and consistent method: 'you may, in fact, pick and choose your way through these narratives, taking what is consistent with your notion, and rejecting all that is against it. But in doing so, you have, as a result, not the Christ which the four Evangelists have given us, but an eclectic Christ, the Christ of your own arbitrary making.'[61] Young had long left behind the anti-biblical stance he had held in the early 1850s, but his mind was alive to the critical issues involved in handling the Scriptures.

The entire work is dedicated to affirming the position that Jesus is God, and at several points in the book Young also affirms the doctrine of the Trinity. Here, in a passage which announces the stance he will defend, he articulates both positions:

> But if Jesus of Nazareth was the Son of God, not alone by office, but by nature; if He was, in deed and in truth, 'of one substance with the Father;' if, in other words, He was a Divine Being, if the Son and the Father are equal, if Jesus Christ was the incarnate Son of God, the God-Man, 'the Word made flesh,' an outward and visible manifestation of the invisible God; if the

60 Young, *Indirect*, 26.   61 Ibid.

Christian doctrine of the Trinity be the revelation of an eternal Father through an eternal Son, and that revelation brought home to our entire consciousness by an eternal Spirit,—then the position Christ occupies towards God, towards man, towards everything, is simply and absolutely unique, and as authoritative as it is unique.[62]

Repeatedly, Young expresses both his own and what he believes to be the Bible's view of the person of Jesus with the affirmation that the Son was 'of one substance with the Father'. One could not be more explicit. He is quoting the language of the Nicene Creed—words that were written precisely in order to rule out an Arian Christology, the very position that Young had reaffirmed as his own by name when he left the Unitarian denomination in 1874. Although he had no intention of becoming a Trinitarian at that time, intellectual trajectories can never be predicted with complete confidence. As to one eminently assailable point often affirmed by orthodox theologians from the early church fathers onwards, Young stoutly averred: 'To me, an impassible God is a simple monstrosity.'[63] It is important to reaffirm, however, that Young was now self-identifying as a Trinitarian, even if he was not interested in pinning down the details with great precision: 'I hold very cheaply the controversies which have been held for so many years, and are now being held, about what may be properly described as the 'Tri-personality' of God; but the doctrine of the Trinity is, nevertheless, a Christian doctrine, a truth which sums up within its own limits, and comprehends them all, all that man can need to know of God, and certainly all that God has revealed about Himself to man and for man.'[64]

Appendix II in Young's *Indirect Evidences in the New Testament for the Personal Divinity of Christ* was entitled 'The Philosophy of the Incarnation'. This was a condensed version of a series of sermons he had preached in his Congregational pulpit. His doctrinal position revealed in this text is also incompatible with what he believed as a Unitarian in his tract from 1865. Right from the start, he declares that what he means by the incarnation is what the anti-Arian Nicene Creed means. Nevertheless, as it is vital to recognize continuity as well as discontinuity over time in his intellectual life, what is striking about reading Young's 'Philosophy of the Incarnation' is how similar

---

[62] Ibid., p. xiii.   [63] Ibid. 29.   [64] Ibid. 61–2.

it is to his Unitarian *Our Lord Jesus Christ the Personal Revelation of God* (1865). It follows the same trajectory, beginning with the concept of a revelation of God, moving on to specific sources for this such as in the history and thought of the Jews, and culminating in Jesus Christ as the full and final divine revelation. It would be tedious to catalogue the various passages which parallel one another thought for thought in the two books, but here is one example:

the Jewish people... seem to me to have been 'raised up and set apart' by God to keep alive in their times, and hand down to their posterity, the great truths of God's Unity, Spirituality, and Holiness... (1865)

they were set apart and trained to receive and hand down through the ages the threefold doctrine of God's unity, holiness, and spirituality... (1884)[65]

Young was bringing from his intellectual storehouse treasures new and old.

Young was 60 years old when he resigned the pastorate of Augustine Congregational Church, Reading, in 1886. A few more telling clues can be gleaned from the preliminary pages of *Indirect Evidences*. First, there is an advance announcement of a book of his 'in preparation' entitled *The Word 'Christian'*. The final chapter might have been aimed at convincing those tempted by unbelief that there was no satisfactory alternative philosophy of life to live by: 'If I am not a Christian, what am I?' It does not seem that this book was ever published. Second, there is a notice of lectures that 'Dr. Young' is willing to deliver. He specifically names as possible groups that might be interested in his services YMCAs and Sunday School Unions (as well as Mutual Improvement Societies). Some of these proposed lectures are not on overtly religious themes, but rather cover subjects such as money. Others have a moralizing tone, but could well have been the title of a Secularist lecture: 'Why do some people get drunk?' His lecture 'The Unwritten Life of Christ' is another testimony to how reconverts were haunted by Jesus.[66] The most revealing lecture titles for the purpose at hand, however, are the ones that seem to suggest a direct refutation of his Secularist lectures. One can imagine

---

[65] Young, *Our Lord Jesus Christ*, 8–9; Young, *Indirect*, 124–5.

[66] It would seem to reflect the same impulse that prompted another reconvert, Joseph Barker, to write *Jesus: A Portrait* (Philadelphia: Methodist Episcopal Book Room, 1873). For Barker, see Chap. 6.

his 1884 'The Rationale of Prayer' as a kind of perfectly germane apologist response to his 1853 lecture 'The Bible Doctrine of Prayer'. Likewise, the material in his 1854 'The Bible proved to be Self-contradictory and Unreliable' undoubtedly informed his 1884 reply, 'Some of the Real Difficulties in the Way of a Right Understanding of the Bible'. Such themes demonstrate a commitment to face rather than evade the critical challenges raised by freethought.

The most intriguing thing about Young's *Indirect Evidences* beyond its actual substantive contents, however, is its publisher: W. Stewart & Co. This was a decidedly freethinking firm run by William Stewart Ross (1844–1906). Ross was the 'Saladin' of the *Secular Review* who had danced over the grave of the *Shield of Faith* and mocked Young as 'Dr. Young-and-Green'. Indeed, W. Stewart & Co. was also the publisher of the *Secular Review* and, in the same year it published Young's book, it also launched the *Agnostic Annual*. It is hard to know what might have been the rationale behind this strange alliance. For Ross, who was also publishing textbooks for those wishing to prepare to take London University examinations, it might have been a way of reassuring potential clients that he was not merely a freethinking publisher. For Young, it might have been an effective way to reach the audience that he thought was in most need of being persuaded that Jesus really was more than a man, in the same way that another reconvert, Thomas Cooper, was in the habit of advertising his Christian lectures in the *Reasoner*. Young was in dialogue with the Secularist community in one way or another for his entire adult life.

As will be shown in subsequent chapters, increasingly Secularists came to make a variety of standard charges—whether they fitted well or not—against reconverts: they were after Christian money; they had changed views too suddenly for it to have been an intellectually legitimate decision; they were obnoxious people who it was good to see go or who had never really been true freethinkers; they were seeking after notoriety. None of these charges ever seem to have been made against Young, but then none of them even remotely applied. There might have been some truth in saying that he never was a true Secularist, if that is defined narrowly to require agnosticism or atheism. Nevertheless, he was a vocal, active, and founding member of the London Secular Society, an employee at the movement's national headquarters, Holyoake's firm, and a ubiquitous

presence in the *Reasoner*. He himself had lectured as a 'convert to
Secularism'. He may always have been a theist of some sort (the
record is not clear on that point), but he was explicitly anti-Bible
and anti-Christian and had given voice and leadership to the cause.
There is certainly no evidence that Young was after money. Quite
to the contrary, he must have ended up being either a man of private
means (perhaps with the death of his mother in 1854) or someone
who gained a comfortable living from some secular profession. He
boasted in 1874 that he had 'never received one penny of salary' from
his congregation in Swindon, despite being their minister for thirteen
years.[67] He repeatedly turned down offers from large and more
significant Unitarian congregations. When Young, on a Christian
Defence Association speaking tour in Co. Durham, was taunted by
local Secularists with the claim that Sexton owed the atheist leader
Charles Bradlaugh £50 for some unresolved transaction from his
freethinking days, Young's response was to immediately put £100 of
his own money in a special bank account, guaranteeing that Sexton's
alleged debt would be paid out of his own pocket if Bradlaugh
confirmed that it was indeed owed him.[68] A man who ministers for
free, and who has £100 to hand which he is willing to part with in
order to vindicate the honour of a friend, would seem to be a man of
independent means. There is a hint that Young personally contributed substantially to the fund for a new church building for his
Swindon congregation. It is probable that his own funds underwrote
some of his various publishing adventures. He certainly was not
involved in the *Shield of Faith* as a way of generating revenue.
Young was not tailoring his beliefs to pecuniary opportunities.

As to a suddenness that betrays that one is not accepting new
conclusions on the basis of rigorous, critical reflection, one might be
able to see something unseemly in emerging as a Unitarian minister
six months after one was a Secularist lecturer. Nevertheless, six
months is a decent period of reflection for any change of thinking
patterns. Young had signalled that he was on the theistic wing of the
movement as a Secularist, and he did make the shortest jump to the
most congenial version of organized Christianity, the more liberal

[67] *Unitarian Herald*, 17 Sept. 1875, p. 308.
[68] *Shield of Faith* (Jan. 1880), 12.

wing of the Unitarian movement. Liberal Unitarians and Secularists not infrequently collaborated. From landing in liberal Unitarianism in late 1854, he then steadily moved at the markedly measured pace of a decade per change: a decade later, in 1864, he had made it to the conservative wing of the Unitarian movement; another decade on, in 1874, he had become sufficiently theologically conservative to no longer want to identify with the Unitarian denomination; given ten more years, by 1884, he was an orthodox Trinitarian serving a Congregational church.

Finally, least of all was Young someone hankering after the drama of conversion, hungry for notoriety and intent on making a sensation. Ironically, to the extent that he ever did, the only time he went in for such sensationalism was when he had himself billed, under the title 'Confessions of a Convert from Theology to Secularism', as a freethinker. He quietly assumed his Unitarian identity without any public statement that he had renounced the Secularists or had some kind of conversion experience. When he left the Unitarians, he deflated all possibility of his making a splash in the orthodox camp by firmly declaring that he was still a Unitarian theologically. When he finally became a Trinitarian, he did so quietly again, taking up the task of articulating the credibility of that viewpoint without advertising himself as a convert. Frederic Rowland Young's theological opinions may have been right or wrong. They certainly changed over time. Nevertheless, he held them all—however contradictory they might have been—each in turn with intellectual integrity for the simple reason that, in all phases of his life, he was genuinely persuaded by the convictions he publicly espoused. He never shrank from thought, from reading and hearing what learned and reflective people of other persuasions believed, from argument, from critical enquiry, from the quest for knowledge and truth.

4

Thomas Cooper

In March 1843 Thomas Cooper (1805–92) was sentenced to two years imprisonment for seditious conspiracy. He spent this time in Stafford jail, where he was not a model prisoner. His surly disposition was sufficiently intimidating that, when Cooper's resolve was patent, his jailers were apt to back down and let him have his way. He was violent; he was a vandal; he was disruptive; he accosted any non-incarcerated person he could scheme to reach—on one occasion reducing the prison chaplain to a pathetic, cowering heap of fear. All this unruly behaviour was directed toward improving the terms and conditions of his life there. On 17 May 1843 Cooper managed to scribble an illicit note and have it delivered to a friend on the outside: 'They are murdering me! Skilly, potatoes—rotten ones, too—and blue bread . . . to live on. I am sure I was nearly mad yesterday, and could not forbear shouting "Murder." No books—no writing! My poor wife, I fear is dead, for they will not tell me a syllable! For God's sake alarm—alarm! This is a stolen letter. They will not let me petition.'[1] It was characteristic of Cooper to include along with a starvation diet and the feared death of his beloved Susanna (who had been ill when he went into prison), being deprived of books as evidence of cruel and inhumane treatment. He could not live by bread alone, even if it was not blue.

The prison governor was no match for the physical-force Chartist, and Cooper gained all the privileges he most prized: a better diet (the

---

[1] Robert J. Conklin, *Thomas Cooper, the Chartist (1805–1892)* (Manila: University of the Philippines Press, 1935), 200. For a recent, scholarly biographical sketch that emphasizes Cooper's religious history, see Timothy Larsen (ed.), *Biographical Dictionary of Evangelicals* (Leicester: Inter-Varsity Press, 2003), 158–60.

authorities even acquiesced to Cooper's judgement that coffee was essential to his good health), freedom to write letters, especially to his wife (who recovered), books to read, and the right to compose his own book-length manuscripts.

Cooper's prison reading was solid and voluminous. Old favourites were revisited. He reread Gibbon's *Decline and Fall of the Roman Empire*, a text seminal for English freethinkers. He read Virgil in Latin. He read Shakespeare, Milton, and Shelley (another favourite for sceptics). He became obsessed with studying the Hebrew language, and composed a teach-yourself-Hebrew primer for possible publication, *Hebrew for the Million; or, the way to acquire a language without a master*.[2] His main project, however, was an epic poem in Spenserian stanzas with the arresting title *The Purgatory of Suicides*. Published in 1845, it was 346 pages of classical allusions in the service of radical politics.[3] A former shoemaker with scant formal education declaiming formal verse, with a cast of characters including Sappho, Marc Antony, Nero, Lycurgus, Brutus, Ajax Telamon, Hannibal, Oedipus, and Demosthenes, was a wonder to behold for the great and good of Victorian society. Cooper's 'Prison-Rhyme' was praised by a range of men of letters, not least Benjamin Disraeli, Charles Kingsley, Charles Dickens, and Thomas Carlyle. Although primarily political and social commentary, the poem also reflected Cooper's religious scepticism and his disaffection with organized Christianity. For example:

> I say not that there is no God: but that
> *I know not*. Dost *thou* know, or dost thou guess?—
> Why should I ask thee, priest? Darkness hath sat
> With Light on Nature,—Woe with Happiness,—
> Since human worms crawled from their languageless
> Imperfect embryons, and by signs essayed
> To picture their first thoughts. 'Tis but excess
> Of folly to attempt the great charade
> To solve; and yet the irking wish must be obeyed!—[4]

---

[2] Conklin, *Thomas Cooper*, 211. Publishers, however, were not convinced that the millions desired to learn Hebrew, and the volume never made it into print.

[3] For a recent analysis of this work, see Stephanie Kuduk, 'Sedition, Chartism, and Epic Poetry in Thomas Cooper's *The Purgatory of the Suicides*', *Victorian Poetry*, 39: 2 (Summer 2001), 165–85.

[4] Thomas Cooper, *The Purgatory of Suicides. A Prison-Rhyme* (London: Jeremiah How, 1845), 191.

When Judas Iscariot appears—the Bible's most notorious contribution to this poetical procession of history and literature's most memorial suicides—he identifies Cooper as a 'proud unbeliever'. Hone's nemesis, Castlereagh, is identified as of the same ilk as Judas.[5]

Cooper was born on 20 March 1805 in Leicester. His widowed mother raised him in Gainsborough, toiling as a dyer in order to eke out a modest existence for the two of them. The heading for one early page of his autobiography reads 'Starvation and the Tax-Gatherer'.[6] Cooper's exceptional mental abilities were evident from an early age. Local lore had it that at the age of 3 not only was he already reading himself, but that his dame-school teacher had set him to work teaching a 7-year-old boy his letters. Cooper's celebrated autobiography is heavily laced with the bibliography of his mental development. The chapter that covers his life between the ages of 9 and 11 begins: 'The happiest hours of all I had in early years were spent alone, and with books.'[7] From 11 to 15 he attended a day school free of charge, on the understanding that he would act as a teacher's assistant, tutoring the younger children. The titles of books tumble on in his narrative. At the age of 13 he was enthralled by Byron. Later in his teens he read classic freethinking texts such as Volney's *Ruins of Empires* and Voltaire's *Philosophical Dictionary*. This material had to vie with a heavy consumption of Christian literature, including Samuel Clarke's *Demonstration of the Being and Attributes of God* and Lord Lyttelton's *Conversion of St Paul*. Cooper, in what must have been a boast leavened with an apology, claimed: 'Mine has been almost entirely self-education, all the way through life.'[8]

Cooper's struggles with faith and doubt, perhaps like many people's, were a mixture of intellectual considerations with numerous other influences, including emotions; his varying relationship to organized Christianity and organized freethought and with various Christian and sceptical leaders; and his social and political experiences and beliefs. At the age of 14 he experienced an intense evangelical conversion through the missionary efforts of Primitive

---

[5] Cooper, *Purgatory*, 94.

[6] Thomas Cooper, *The Life of Thomas Cooper* (1872; Leicester: Leicester University Press, 1971), 26.

[7] Ibid. 22.   [8] Ibid. 43.

Methodists. This revivalist sect, however, greeted his reading habits with disapprobation—a censure he, in turn, would not abide: 'My mind rebelled completely now.'[9] He ended up joining the Wesleyans instead. In 1820 he embarked upon his first vocation by becoming apprentice to a shoemaker. His obsessive studying habits on the margins of his days led to a breakdown when he was 22 years old. The following year he decided to integrate his love of learning with his quest for an income by becoming a schoolmaster in Gainsborough. His school would naturally serve his own milieu, the lower classes. After getting off to a good start, Cooper was disillusioned to learn that parents baulked at his assumption that Latin should be an essential component of the curriculum—and that the children agreed with their elders on this point.

Meanwhile, Cooper also became a 'local preacher' (that is, a lay preacher as opposed to a full-time minister) with the Wesleyans. His ministry was popular and electric:

I had soon larger congregations than any other local preacher in the circuit; and grew into request for anniversary sermons in the surrounding circuits. I threw my whole heart and soul into my preaching; and the effects were often of a rememberable kind. Shouts of praise from believers often overpowered my voice . . . not seldom, sobs and tears foreshowed what kind of work there would be for the prayer-leaders when the sermon was over.[10]

Cooper was too clever, too brash, too confrontational, and too popular for a carefree life. He organized opposition to their mediocre Methodist superintendent who, in turn, used his influence to keep Cooper down.[11] Cooper's solution was to move to Lincoln, but the Gainsborough superintendent sent a bad report of him on to Cooper's new circuit. He therefore clashed with his new superintendent as well, leading Cooper to withdraw altogether from Wesleyanism in bitterness. Cooper was always susceptible to strong arguments both for and against Christianity, and—just as the positive emotions of a revivalistic atmosphere helped to tip the balance one way—so now these negative emotions reinforced sceptical habits: 'It soured

---

[9] Ibid. 39.   [10] Ibid. 90.
[11] Cooper does not identify the superintendent in his autobiography, but he is named as Benjamin Williams in a local newspaper's report of one of his speeches: *Bradford Review*, 15 May 1852.

my own mind against religious professors, and raised within me a wrong, rebellious spirit. My mind grew angry whenever I thought of my ill-treatment; and I soon left off my habit of attendance on public worship.'[12]

He also changed vocations once again, this time moving into journalism. This led on to a relocation to London where he went to hear such celebrated freethinkers speak as W. J. Fox and Robert Owen. A decisive turn of events came when he returned to the Midlands in order to work for the *Leicestershire Mercury*. Cooper was sent to report on a Chartist meeting, and he was won over to the cause by what he heard there. In the industrialized town of Leicester, Cooper encountered widespread, desperate poverty the like of which he had never met before, especially the heart-wrenching plight of stocking weavers. This experience would add fuel to both his political radicalism and his religious scepticism. If there was a god, could such suffering also exist, he wondered? Questions of theodicy were a central component of his religious scepticism.

Cooper wrested control of the Leicester Chartists and built them into a powerhouse for the movement as a whole. His political activism had quickly lost him his position with the *Leicestershire Mercury*, and so he became a full-time political organizer and self-employed editor of Chartist publications. Blending his love of learning with his new militarism, he called his Chartists 'the Shakespearean Brigade'.[13] He dubbed himself their 'General'. By July 1842 Cooper had built them up into a formidable group of 2,300 members.[14] Moreover, he was passionately committed to physical-force Chartism, the most defiant of all the brands, and to Feargus O'Connor, the most fiery of all the national leaders. It would be reasonable to surmise that during this period of his life Cooper would have supported the use of violence, if and when it appeared that the attempt might have had a reasonable chance of success. He was certainly willing to lead a mob in attacks on the supporters of various candidates during election times. In the Chartist movement

---

[12] Cooper, *Life*, 101.

[13] This name came from the Shakespearean Room that they then met in, but as Cooper went on to stage a Shakespeare play at a Chartist benefit it is clear that he liked the substantive resonance of this name.

[14] Conklin, *Thomas Cooper*, 115.

as a whole, Cooper was a major force with which to reckon. Although boasting, he was also not far from the truth when he wrote, in December 1842: 'I wield, in spite of my poverty, a more powerful influence than any Chartist in England except our chief [O'Connor]. My "Shakesperean Brigade" numbers nearly three thousand, and it is more completely under the sway of my "enthusiasm" (you have selected the right word) than is the association in any other town under the influence of any single man.'[15]

In August 1842 Cooper was on his way as a delegate to the Chartist convention to be held in Manchester, when he stopped to give political speeches in Hanley, where workers were engaged in a desperate general strike. On the first day Cooper preached a political sermon on the text 'Thou shalt do no murder', which—by offering a litany of legislation that was murderous in its effects on the lower orders— worked the crowd up into a fury against the government. On the following day, after he had given another speech, a large number of strikers turned into a violent mob, whose activities included burning down the homes of several of their perceived enemies, including the Hanley parsonage. It was estimated that they had done £12,000-worth of property damage.[16] These are the events that led to Cooper's time in prison. In March 1843, at the age of 38, he was convicted of seditious conspiracy and given a sentence of two years.

Cooper's religious scepticism deepened while he was in prison. His sense of the weight of human suffering was more existentially intense than ever before, and he could not see his way to squaring this reality with the notion of a good and all-powerful God. Moreover, Feargus O'Connor—who apparently had become jealous of Cooper— attacked him. The two men fell out, and Cooper, who seems to have had his fill of the perils of direct action, drifted away from the Chartist movement. Instead, he ended up finding in popular, organized free-thought a new movement in which to centre his identity and invest his talents. Cooper's source of income at this stage in his life was as a freethinking lecturer, a career he pursued with tremendous success from 1846 to 1855. In 1847 and 1848 Cooper was also W. J. Fox's choice as someone to do pulpit supply at his renowned freethinking South Place Chapel when Fox himself was ill or attending to

---

[15] Ibid. 167.   [16] Ibid. 142.

parliamentary duties.[17] Cooper was a favourite speaker at all the main popular freethinking halls in London. Even the sceptical journal, the *Investigator*, in an article in 1857 that sought to discredit Cooper, was forced to concede that he had been 'for several years the most popular lecturer on Free Inquiry in the metropolis, and always commanding crowded audiences'.[18] Cooper also entered into a lifelong friendship with the premier Secularist leader, George Jacob Holyoake, editor of the *Reasoner*. During Cooper's freethought lecturing phase, Holyoake himself affirmed that Cooper was 'incomparably the most attractive of all our metropolitan lecturers'.[19] Indeed, Cooper was so popular that he was able to attract a Sunday morning as well as Sunday evening Secularist audience, even though previous efforts by other speakers to hold meetings at that time had been unsuccessful.[20]

Cooper made a thorough study of the most controversial work of biblical criticism then emanating from Germany, *Leben Jesu*, a book by D. F. Strauss that George Eliot translated into English as *The Life of Jesus Critically Examined* (1846). Strauss's book sent shock-waves through Christian Britain, and this work became the dominant intellectual influence that shaped the contours of Cooper's unbelief. It was *the* book of biblical criticism to engage with at that time— recent, scholarly, and formidable—and Cooper's attentiveness to it shows how committed he was to encountering the latest thought. Indeed, his rigorous study of this long and detailed work can be contrasted with the widespread failure of the social elite to combine their denunciations of Strauss with a careful reading of his book. The Christian world latched onto Henry Roger's ostensible refutation of Strauss in his article in the October 1849 issue of the *Edinburgh Review*: 'Reason and Faith; their Claims and Conflicts.'[21] Roger's essay went through eight impressions. Nevertheless, it is readily apparent that Rogers had not bothered actually to read the book in question![22] The *British Quarterly Review*, in a fifty-eight page review

---

[17] Amsterdam, Internationaal Instituut Voor Sociale Geschidenis, Coll. Cooper, W. J. Fox to Thomas Cooper, 21 May 1847 and 14 Dec. 1848.

[18] *Investigator*, May 1857, p. 22.   [19] Conklin, *Thomas Cooper*, 374.

[20] Ibid. 319.   [21] *Edinburgh Review*, 90: 182 (Oct. 1849), 293–356.

[22] I discuss this in more detail elsewhere: Timothy Larsen, *Contested Christianity: The Political and Social Contexts of Victorian Theology*, (Waco, Tex.: Baylor University Press, 2004), chap. 4.

of Strauss's work, confined its comments exclusively to the book's introduction and conclusion.[23] The *Inquirer* declared its intention to review it but, after several embarrassing months of delay published a review of, quite literally, Strauss's first sentence![24] The clergyman Charles Kingsley spoke anxiously about how essential it was that someone answer Strauss, but he apparently did not feel up to the task himself, nor did he find a willing challenger elsewhere.[25] All of this is in marked contrast to Cooper, who digested the book page by page, and made its arguments and evidence his own.

Strauss was a professional scholar, who had been trained at the University of Tübingen. His *Leben Jesu* was an attack on the two ways of handling the stories in the four gospels that had been dominant. Strauss was confident that the old orthodox way, which affirmed, notably, that Jesus had indeed performed genuine miracles, was no longer tenable. For Strauss, supernatural claims were ruled out a priori as unscientific. On the other hand, he was equally opposed to rationalist interpretations. Rationalist scholars had endeavoured to show that the gospel stories were based on events in Jesus' life that were, in fact, entirely natural: these incidents had simply been misunderstood as supernatural. For example, when Jesus declared that someone with leprosy was healed and that they should show themselves to the priests, he was not instantly, miraculously healing the person but rather merely giving a sound medical diagnosis that, although the skin was still disfigured, the disease was no longer active or contagious. Strauss went systematically through all of the gospel narratives, from Jesus' conception to his resurrection, arguing that neither the orthodox nor the rationalist readings were satisfactory. In place of them, he offered a third interpretive approach, a 'mythical' view. For Strauss, the gospel accounts were generated by the expectations that the Jews had regarding what the Messiah would be like. These expectations gave rise to suitable stories about Jesus that corresponded to them. For example, the Jews anticipated that the Messiah, as an even greater figure than the prophets, would perform

[23] *British Quarterly Review*, 5 (1847), 206–64.
[24] *Inquirer*, 3 Oct. 1846, pp. 628–9.
[25] F. E. Kingsley, *Charles Kingsley: His Letters and Memories of His Life* (London: Macmillan, 1901), i. 94–5.

feats that equalled or surpassed those recorded regarding the ministries of the prophets of old. As Scripture recounted that the prophet
Elisha had healed someone with leprosy, supernaturally multiplied
food supplies, and raised someone from the dead, it was only fitting
that the Messiah's ministry would also be marked by such miraculous
works, and tales therefore arose that were in line with these expectations. Therefore, Strauss's work was particularly radical in the sense
that it undercut the historicity of the gospel narratives far more
thoroughly than even the rationalists had done. The telling point
for Cooper, however, was not the anti-rationalist critique, but rather
the anti-supernaturalist one.

As a reconvert, Cooper identified Strauss's work as the most
decisive intellectual factor in his move into unbelief:

Nor did I, after my release from imprisonment, yield helplessly to atheistic
reasonings. They would arise in my mind, perforce of old habit; but I did not
settle down in them. I never proclaimed blank atheism in my public
teaching. And I feel certain that I should have broken away from unbelief
altogether, had I not fastened on Strauss, and become his entire convert. I
read and re-read, and analysed, the translation in three volumes, published
by the Brothers Chapman: the translation begun by Charles Hennell, and
finished by the authoress of 'Adam Bede.' I became fast bound in the net of
Strauss; and at one time would have eagerly helped to bind all in his net: nor
did I feel thoroughly able to break its pernicious meshes, or get out of it,
myself, for twelve years.[26]

This retrospective self-assessment agrees with the abundant evidence
that has survived from Cooper's freethinking years. Cooper gained
much attention in plebeian sceptical circles by a series of lectures that
he gave popularizing Strauss's arguments: 'Critical Exegesis of Gospel
History, on the basis of Strauss's "Leben Jesu"'. During the period
1848–50 he gave this series as Sunday evening lectures at the two
most important popular freethinking halls in London, the Literary
Institution, John Street, Tottenham Court Road, and the Hall of
Science, City Road. They were so well received that he was encouraged to publish them, and did so in 1850 in his own short-lived
*Cooper's Journal: or, unfettered thinker and plain speaker for Truth,
Freedom, and Progress.* Cooper wrote an introductory note that he

26 Cooper, *Life,* 262–3.

affixed immediately beneath the title of the first lecture as a disclaimer. As it captures so well the extent and limits of his unbelief, it is worth quoting at length:

All who are afraid of thinking, and who dread that the People should think, on the most important of all subjects, will censure me for the publication of these discourses. Let none of these, however, misrepresent my motives. I yield to none in fervent admiration and love for the character of Christ. Under all changes of opinion, his moral beauty has ever kept its throne in my heart and mind, as the most worshipful of all portraitures of goodness. I seek to multiply, not to lessen, the number of his true disciples. . . . I am anxious to aid the preservation, in some minds at least, of continued and purified attachment to the substance of Christianity, while its shadows are being dispelled. I know no higher teaching than Christ's: I acknowledge none. But his religion no longer commends itself to me by mysterious or miraculous sanctions. I hold it to be the most perfect version of the Religion of Humanity; and for that reason, desire to see it divested of all legendary incrustations that may prevent its reception with sincere and earnest thinkers. The great work of Strauss assisted me much in coming to a clear and determined conclusion respecting the source of the corruptions in the real history of Christ . . . [27]

In short, Cooper continued to admire the character and teaching of Jesus while rejecting all the miraculous claims made by orthodox Christians.

It will be more useful for the purposes at hand to highlight those aspects of these lectures that bring out Cooper's own distinctive voice, but it must be borne in mind that much of their contents are, in fact, a faithful representation of Strauss's work. Cooper declares his frank admiration for 'the powerful analytical mind of Strauss'.[28] Cooper is also candid in his rejection of all the supernatural elements, not exempting the resurrection of Christ itself: 'we cannot believe it ever took place.'[29] He makes much of the observation that the gospel accounts do not even claim that anyone witnessed the resurrection itself, but rather only the empty tomb and post-burial visions of Jesus, which can be taken to have been nothing more than mere internal impressions. As for Christ's ascension, the

---

[27] *Cooper's Journal: or, unfettered thinker and plain speaker for Truth, Freedom, and Progress*, 1 (London: James Watson, 1850; repr. New York: Augustus M. Kelley, 1970), 8.
[28] Ibid. 12.   [29] Ibid. 460.

notion is downright risible: '*Up into heaven!* The old childish ideas of
a substantial heaven about the blue air!'[30] A distinctive contribution
of Cooper's is his passionate attack on the very concept of substitutionary atonement:

Why, is it the pouring out of a red fluid, which has been formed by the
digestion of bread and meat and vegetables, that can alone satisfy an Infinite
Existence for transgression, not of the being who suffers, but of the other
unnumbered millions of the world? If thy brother had offended thee would
not thy nature feel it to be more noble to forgive freely, without a human
slaughter? And do you really form to yourself a God for worship with a less
exalted nature than your own?[31]

Traditional Christian teaching on eternal punishment is also condemned. Doctrines of Scripture that speak of the Bible's inspiration,
especially its 'plenary' inspiration, are attacked throughout. On the
positive side, 'Reason' is extolled as humanity's surest guide. Cooper
hopes that his hearers are 'true disciples of Reason'.[32] He is proud to
be distinguished by the name 'freethinker'. He is devoid of 'any belief
in orthodoxy'.[33] Most rich for the wider theme of this study, as was
typical of Victorian popular freethinkers, Cooper asserted in his
sceptical phase that it was questionable whether there was any such
thing as honest faith—an intellectual orthodox believer who had
genuinely weighed the issues: 'Excuse me, one moment, when I say
to you that I wonder how any man can hold by orthodoxy when he
has once dared to think for himself.'[34] What was left, then, of the life
of Jesus? It is a truism that the pictures of Christ that emerge
from attempts to pen critical lives of Jesus have generally been self-
portraits. Cooper's Jesus was a plebeian autodidact of extraordinary
intellectual abilities, whose work as a carpenter eventually and inevitably was replaced by his work as a champion of the poor.

No member of the cultural elite at that time, or anyone else in
Britain for that matter, was offering such a sustained, sympathetic
engagement with this seminal text. If in 1850 any Britons wished to
have a serious encounter with the latest modern biblical criticism,
they would have been better off going to hear Cooper lecture than

---

[30] *Cooper's Journal: or, unfettered thinker and plain speaker for Truth, Freedom, and Progress*, 1 (London: James Watson, 1850; repr. New York: Augustus M. Kelley, 1970), 459.
[31] Ibid. 345.   [32] Ibid. 301.   [33] Ibid. 351.   [34] Ibid. 317.

attending any British university. As will be shown in Chapter 7, Cooper's dissemination of Strauss's thought was instrumental in the loss of faith of J. B. Bebbington. The clergyman and author Charles Kingsley was rattled by such effective work. He wrote an alarmed letter to J. M. Ludlow in 1850:

But there is something which weighs awfully on my mind,—the first number of Cooper's Journal, which he sent me the other day. Here is a man of immense influence, openly preaching Straussism to the workmen, and in a fair, honest, manly way, which must tell. Who will answer him? Who will answer Strauss? . . . To me it is awfully pressing. If the priests of the Lord are wanting to the cause now?—woe to us![35]

Cooper's freethinking orations ranged over many subjects. He often gave lectures extolling the lives and thought of seminal religious sceptics such as Thomas Paine, P. B. Shelley, Voltaire, Rousseau, Woolston, Bolingbroke, Godwin, and others. Cooper preferred the label 'freethinker' to Secularist but, not wishing to be misconstrued, he insisted in 1853 that this was more a semantic preference than an expression of a more substantive difference: 'My friend Mr. Holyoake and myself accord very nearly on what is called theology. I make this avowal openly.'[36] And so life went on for Cooper for some years. He continued to be involved in various efforts in popular radical politics as well, but his main identity was as a popular freethinker. Another short-lived editing venture of his during this period, the *Plain Speaker*, a weekly penny periodical devoted to radical politics that ran for the first half of 1849, was filled with open letters to Tory leaders berating them for their attitudes. Cooper was in contact with the Italian revolutionary Giuseppe Mazzini, whom he admired greatly, and was a member of the People's International League.

Before focusing on the specific questions precipitating Cooper's crisis of doubt, it is worth being reminded that Cooper belongs in the premier league when it comes to being a voracious reader and a greedy collector of knowledge. His lectures on secular as opposed to Secularist themes during these same freethinking years are staggering in their range. He spoke against the taking of human life. He lectured

---

[35] Kingsley, *Charles Kingsley*, i. 194.
[36] G. J. Holyoake, *Trial of Theism* (London: Holyoake & Co., 1858), 5; Conklin, *Thomas Cooper*, 393.

on European political developments and on injustice in Ireland. He lectured on the life and genius of Milton, of Burns, of Shakespeare, of Byron, and others. He gave a ten-lecture series on the history of Greece and seventeen lectures on the history of Rome. He gave addresses on Cromwell and the Commonwealth, on the French Revolution, on George Washington. He gave an eight-lecture series on Napoleon, and four on the duke of Wellington, while Nelson was covered in two. He gave fifty-one lectures on the history of England. He did a series on seven schools of painters: Italian, Dutch, Flemish, Spanish, French, and English. He gave six addresses on Russian history. He lectured on musicians, including Handel, Haydn, Mozart, Mendelssohn, and Beethoven. His lectures on discoverers and explorers included Columbus, Newton, Cortez, and Pizarro. He helped his hearers understand Mohammed and Swedenborg. He lectured on slavery, on the national debt, on the age of chivalry, injustice in Poland, the gypsies, the conquests of Alexander the Great, on ancient Egypt. He informed his audiences regarding the histories of Italy, Switzerland, and Hungary. He lectured on the philosophy of Bacon and Locke. His efforts to educate his hearers in a range of sciences included addresses on vegetation, astronomy, geology, and natural history. This, moreover, is not even close to an exhaustive list of the specific subjects that he addressed. Cooper commented in a matter-of-fact tone: 'The reading which was necessary in order to enable me to deal with such a variety of themes, and to render my lectures attractive to crowds of intelligent hearers, was, of course very great. At John Street, especially, I was surrounded by scores of the really *élite* of the working classes.'[37] As had been the case with Hone, Cooper found the British Museum library an inestimable boon.

Having been liberated from the seemingly insoluble intellectual difficulties of orthodox Christianity, after spending years as a leading thinker in organized freethought, Cooper slowly began to develop a growing conviction that a sceptical outlook had limitations and apparent intellectual impasses and contradictions of its own. His own recollections as a reconvert highlighted the basis of morality as the crucial intellectual problem he found could not be solved to his satisfaction from a Secularist point of view. From May to November

[37] Cooper, *Life*, 346.

1855 Cooper was not based in his London freethinking circles, but rather was on a national tour lecturing on the Crimean War, and he identified that period as a time in which he began to re-evaluate his core beliefs:

But the six months' absence had wrought a signal change in me. I felt as if all my old work were done, and yet I knew not how to begin a new work. My heart and mind were deeply uneasy, and I could hardly define the uneasiness. I felt sure my life for years had been wrong. I had taught morals, and taught them strictly; but the questioning within, that would arise, day by day, and hour by hour, made my heart ache. 'Why should man be moral? Why cannot he quench the sense of accountability? and why have you not taught your fellowmen that they are answerable to the Divine Moral Governor, and must appear before Him in a future state, and receive their reward or punishment?'

It was not a conviction of the truth of Christianity, of the reality of the Miracles and Resurrection, or of the Divinity of Christ, that had worked the change in me. I was overwhelmed with a sense of guilt in having omitted to teach the right foundation of morals. I had taught morals as a means of securing and increasing men's happiness here ... [38]

Reports in local newspapers of Cooper's speeches from the late 1850s add even more precision to the contours of his crisis of doubt. The thought of Robert Owen loomed large in British plebeian freethinking circles at that time. Many of the leaders of the movement, not least Holyoake, had spent some time early in their careers as Owenite lecturers. Even Charles Bradlaugh, the apostle of atheism who would lead the movement in the 1880s, was deeply influenced by Owen's thought, and proudly recalled that he was called upon to read the speech that the octogenarian Owen had written for, as it turned out, his last birthday in 1858, thus implying that the elder statesman's mantle had fallen on the young 'Iconoclast'.[39] Owen taught a form of environmental determinism. Strictly speaking, in Owenite thought people should not be blamed for what they do, although they might be punished as a way of changing their environment and thereby altering their behaviour. As Cooper began to reflect on this worldview, he came to see it as an alarmingly deficient basis for morality.

[38] Ibid. 352–3.
[39] Hypatia Bradlaugh Bonner, *Charles Bradlaugh* (London: T. Fisher Unwin, 1895), i. 78.

A report of one of his speeches in 1858 from the *Norfolk News* highlights this aspect of the story:

In explanation of his turn to Christianity, he gave an account of the mental process which commenced about two and a half years ago, and which had its origin in the circumstance that he took as the subject of one of his Sunday evening lectures, in London, a work written by Robert Owen in advocacy of the doctrine that man is a creature of circumstances, undeserving of either blame or praise for bad or virtuous deeds. In thinking upon these views, and discussing the word 'duty' in relation thereto, he reflected that as he had a conviction that there were such things as right and wrong, this must be the consequence of a moral sense, and if so, then there must be a moral governor. Having thus gained an inch of solid ground, he clung to the hope thus stirred up within him with a resolute grasp...[40]

On 13 January 1856 Cooper was scheduled to lecture on 'Sweden and the Swedes' at the Hall of Science, London. Instead, he dramatically declared his belief in 'the existence of the Divine Moral Governor, and the fact that we should have to give up our account to Him, and receive His sentence, in a future state'.[41] From the available evidence, it does not seem that Cooper had ever categorically denied these things, although he had wondered aloud in more than one freethinking speech if the problem of suffering indicated that there was no God or, should God exist, that perhaps God was immoral. It is important to realize that Cooper's affirmations on this mid-January Sunday evening fell far short of orthodox Christianity and well within the bounds of what many leading freethinkers had also believed. Thomas Paine, at the very start of his *Age of Reason*—that seminal text for British plebeian religious scepticism all the way to the end of the nineteenth century—had also acknowledged that he believed in God and that he possessed a 'hope for happiness beyond this life'.[42] On the other hand, Paine's comment was a line of affirmation before a book full of denunciation. Cooper was making a

---

[40] *Norfolk News*, 10 Apr. 1858.

[41] Cooper, *Life*, 353. In his private ledger of his speaking engagements, Cooper wrote: 'Subject was "Sweden"—but I could not talk about it—& made Confession of my change.' Lincoln, Lincoln Central Library, Local Studies, Thomas Cooper Mss, Ms. 5060.

[42] Thomas Paine, *The Age of Reason* (1795–96; The Thinker's Library; London: Watts & Co., 1938), 1.

portentous move from an emphasis upon what religious falsehoods it was his duty to dispel, to an emphasis upon what religious truths it was his duty to disseminate.

Perhaps the real intellectual problem here was that the old deism had come to seem more and more untenable to nearly everyone. Bishop Butler's reputation was high in the mid-Victorian period, and many people were satisfied with his argument in the *Analogy of Religion* (1736) that it was not possible to defend natural religion and reject revealed religion, as the critiques which are claimed to be sufficient against the latter also apply to the former. In the mid-nineteenth century it seemed to many as if one now needed to believe either less or more than Paine had done. Cooper therefore set out to see if it might be possible for him to believe more, all that he knew of modern critical thought notwithstanding. It was a slow and perplexing process, fraught with confusion and uncertainty. It is rare in any context—of political thought, for example, no less than religious—to catch a glimpse of a public figure's mind when it is truly in transition. It is a great gift to this study, therefore, that a series of letters from Cooper to Charles Kingsley have survived in which Cooper was precisely at the point in which his old sceptical thought had come to seem bankrupt, but orthodox Christianity had not yet come to seem intellectually credible. Here is a poignant letter dated 15 February 1856:

In mentioning Lange's 'Leben Jesu'—you have touched a sore chord in me. Ah, my friend, what shall I do with Strauss? He is the stern impassable stone which next lies in my path. My heart is with Christ—has always been with him. I have maintained his beauty, with tears, amidst the scoffs of these 'reasoners'; have told them openly, again & again, of the shock of disgust & pain with which I read [Francis William] Newman's shuddering attack on Christ's character;—but the jeer has always been cast back 'Have you not yourself shown us that the greater part of the so-called Gospels is legend?'

How shall I get to Christ as my Saviour? That is what my heart yearns for; but my reason cannot get there.... I would give worlds—I had almost said I would live ten years in Hell—so that I could, with reason & heart, find the saving Christ again. Does Lange really answer Strauss? I fear not.[43]

---

[43] Amsterdam, Internationaal Instituut Voor Sociale Geschiedenis, Coll. Cooper, Thomas Cooper to Charles Kingsley, 15 Feb. 1856.

It might be tempting to use this quotation as grounds for dismissing Cooper as someone who wanted to believe and therefore would find a way to believe. Such glibness, however, does not give full weight to the real intellectual work that must be done by any honest and reflective person, however much they are emotionally attracted to faith or doubt, or, for that matter, any hitherto rejected political, social, or philosophical viewpoint. Cooper was in deadly earnest—he was self-aware enough to know that he wanted to believe, but he was also scrupulous enough not to let such a desire trump the substantial intellectual challenges that had to be faced squarely. He was not posturing in public, but rather wrestling in private. Kingsley understood this, and therefore he offered, not a pious homily or an emotional appeal, but rather a weighty academic tome. Johann Lange was a leading German theologian and scholar. When Strauss was forced out of his academic post at Zurich, it was given to Lange instead. Lange therefore wrote his own scholarly and critical, but less radical, *Leben Jesu*, as a corrective to Strauss. Lange's *Leben Jesu* would not be translated into English until 1864. Most Oxbridge dons would not have been up to the task of reading Lange in German, but Kingsley was confident that 'the self-educated shoemaker' was.[44]

His longing to believe notwithstanding, over four months later Cooper was still working his way through the critical issues with no sense that any particular outcome was inevitable: 'I read the New Testament, and will read it—but how often it all looks like a bundle of fables! Shall I ever come to read it with a feeling of the solid reality of what I read? . . . Can you tell me what to do—anything that will help me to Christ? Him I want. If the Four Gospels be half legends I still want him. . . . But how is it, then, that I am still so full of doubts?'[45] The faith he would finally possess would be as honest as any Victorian's doubt ever was. The intellectual heavy lifting having finally all been done, Cooper at last reported to Kingsley on 1 April 1857—well over a year after the first transitional letter quoted above—that he was ready to take up a public Christian identity.[46]

---

[44] 'Self-educated shoemaker' was a self-description: Cooper, *Purgatory*, p. viii.

[45] Amsterdam, Internationaal Instituut Voor Sociale Geschiedenis, Coll. Cooper, Thomas Cooper to Charles Kingsley, 22 June 1856.

[46] Ibid., Thomas Cooper to Charles Kingsley, 1 Apr. 1857.

Cooper was genuinely taken aback by how forcefully many of his erstwhile sceptical friends attacked him as a reconvert. He seems to have thought that they would recognize that he was a man of intellectual integrity and agree to disagree civilly, perhaps even amicably. Holyoake did respond with civility, and the two remained lifelong friends. Even Holyoake, however, would refer to Cooper's reconversion with patronizing claims that Cooper, although sincere, was always apt to be led by his emotions rather than his intellect.[47] Not unlike a Calvinist, holding to the doctrine of the perseverance of the saints, arguing that a lapsed Christian *ipso facto* must have never been a real one, Holyoake and other freethinkers like him needed to question whether Cooper ever had grasped the intellectual case for doubt, as it seemed a matter of doctrine with them that such insight, once seen, could never again be denied in good conscience. Such a retrospective view, of course, is belied by the way that Holyoake had so heavily praised Cooper's sceptical writings and lectures. Particularly ironic, given his own future reconversion, was Joseph Barker's striking of this pose. In an article in the *Reasoner* tellingly entitled, 'Mr. Thomas Cooper—Remarks on his reputed conversion', he wrote: 'I confess I cannot conceive how a sane man, of average intellect, and reasonably acquainted with the facts of the case, can, after having been once freed from early Christian prejudice, ever become again a believer in the truth and supernatural origin of the Bible or Christianity.'[48] In another publication, Barker took Holyoake's line that Cooper would appear to have been a man of emotion rather than thought, in explicit contrast to himself (who was therefore immune to reconversion):

His change might be the result of passion, rather than of argument; and his return to Christianity may be the result of the subsidence of passion. If reason had little to do with his conversion from Christianity, no wonder if it had little to do with his after changes.... I should like to have an opportunity of comparing the history of Thomas Cooper with my own history. Has he any hopes, I wonder, of converting such men as you and me?[49]

---

[47] See e.g. *Norfolk News*, 8 May 1858.
[48] *Reasoner*, 15 Aug. 1858. For Joseph Barker, see Chap. 6.
[49] Joseph Barker, *Confessions of Joseph Barker, a Convert from Christianity* (London: Holyoake and Co., 1858), 15–16.

It was indeed possible to hope that even Barker himself would reconvert, as Chapter 6 will show. Moreover, this assessment of Cooper's ability can be contrasted with a private letter Barker wrote to Holyoake in 1853, that is, when Cooper was still a freethinker in good standing, in which he singled out Cooper's articles for praise.[50]

Worse abuse by far, however, was heaped on Cooper by the militantly sceptical journal the *London Investigator.* Cooper, as we have seen, actually had a prolonged and uncertain period of transition. It was a stock view of popular freethinkers that all Christian conversions were 'sudden' and therefore not the fruit of reflection. The journal initially attempted to make this charge stick, adding for good measure the innuendo that this was a case of feigned faith in a search for worldly advantages: 'we have a right to inquire what has led to the change, and so *suddenly.* Sincere conviction of our error on great questions is rarely effected *in a week.* . . . Experience proves that *policy* and not sincerity lies at the foundation of such humiliating exhibitions, more *especially when the change is from an unfashionable to a fashionable creed.'*[51]* Actually, Cooper had thrown away a perfectly good source of income for no prospects whatsoever. After four desperate months of unemployment, he ended up in low-paying work as a mere copyist of bureaucratic letters—a demeaning step down in life that he would have to continue to endure for nearly two years. Holyoake, ever fair, admitted that his reconversion had not been to Cooper's financial advantage. The attacks continued in subsequent issues of the *Investigator.* Over a year-and-a-half later it printed this broadside:

the majority do not hesitate to say that he is a bit of a hypocrite, and that a love of bread and cheese had great influence in his conversion. . . . we yet question the sincerity of his conversion. No man who has once dared to think for himself; who has had the courage to strip the Bible of all its traditional awe, and to look upon it merely as a book; and who, having set himself carefully to examine it, has discovered in it contradictions and absurdities such as no author of average discrimination would be guilty of, a system of morals which the greatest sinner of us all would blush to own,

---

[50] Joseph Barker to G. J. Holyoake, 22 Feb. 1853 (Millwood, Knox Co., Ohio), George Jacob Holyoake Correspondence Collection, The Co-operative College Archives, Manchester, GJHCC 562.

[51] *London Investigator* (Jan. 1857), 342.

and a series of doctrines against which human reason revolts—would have the audacity to maintain that this book was the word of God, that these morals he would have us practise, and these doctrines believe, and that the whole was necessary to our salvation.... To conclude, we believe that Thomas Cooper is in a great measure insane, and we are sorry for it.[52]

Here in one article is the charge of hypocrisy combined with the *ipso facto* argument that a true reconvert is an intellectual impossibility. The final blow, the charge of insanity, although by far the most abusive, does not cohere with what has gone before, and seems to be a tacit concession that Cooper was sincere after all; that he seemed genuinely to believe what, from a plebeian sceptic's point of view, no sane person who had carefully examined the evidence ought to be able to believe.[53]

Although Cooper did not arrive at a settled conviction that he could believe in and defend orthodox Christianity with intellectual integrity until April 1857, after a six months' break from lecturing, he had already started to make good on his pledge of January 1856 to attempt to inculcate what religious truth he could. Cooper's own handwritten manuscripts of some of his lectures have survived. These reveal what care he put into them—they are full texts that unfold a well-thought-out argument in fluent prose—not mere memory prompts for a largely extemporaneous explanation. Some of his lectures as a reconvert have attached to them texts from lectures he had given as a sceptic, from which he planned to retrieve useful knowledge on natural history and other themes. On Sunday evening, 21 September 1856, Cooper spoke at the Hall of Science, London, on the theme of 'The Being, Power, & Wisdom of God: the Design Argument re-stated: selections of striking instances of Design'.[54] Once again, it should be emphasized that such a title is not evidence of an orthodox Christian faith—a deist could also have taken up this same theme. Nevertheless, Cooper begins by anticipating some

---

[52] *Investigator*, 1 Aug. 1858, p. 75.

[53] At Cooper's death, the popular radical and freethinker George Julian Harney set the record straight in an obituary: 'His mental changes...from ultra-scepticism to evangelical Christianity were startling. But he was always sincere...His renunciations and adoptions were without ulterior aim of acquiring power, place, or pay.' *Newcastle Weekly Chronicle*, 23 July 1892.

[54] Lincolnshire Archives, Lincoln, Thomas Cooper, Misc. Don. 2 Bapt. 2, no. 7.

sneers, if not rage, as well as demands that he explain the reasons why
he had doubted these things in the past. He then launched into a list
of prompts for religious doubt: (1) 'the greatest cause of Scepticism is
the bad example of religious professors'; (2) 'Another cause of
Scepticism—and especially with the young is the forbidding of Free
Enquiry.... That system of forbidding Free Enquiry will have to be
given up, I am very sure, if religious truth is to be maintained'; (3)
'Oppression... I used to tell the manufacturers that their chimneys
were monuments to Atheism'; (4) 'the whole question of the Existence of Moral Evil & Physical Pain in the Universe. I hold this to be
the greatest difficulty for the Thinker. I have often told you that I felt
it to be so'; (5) 'By the spread of science, we have become acquainted
with the physical or secondary causes of a great many natural phenomena. A class of philosophers has arisen who profess Materialism.'
This last point becomes the launching-pad for exploring the scientific evidence in order to advance the argument from design, but the
whole list is not only autobiographical, but also indicative that
Cooper would be a Christian apologist who did not brush past real
objections and set up straw figures to knock down. He knew whereof
he spoke.

Moreover, if Cooper was willing to brave the ill-feeling of plebeian
sceptics, he was also not afraid to say things that many orthodox
Christians would have deemed heretical. He also refused to dodge the
most difficult challenges. On 12 October 1856 he tackled one of the
issues that had always vexed him the most: 'The Questions of Suffering in the Universe, of the system of Prey among Animals, and the
existence of Moral Evil, examined; and reconciled with the doctrine
of God's existence, wisdom, and goodness.'[55] It might be said that
Cooper's answers on these questions are no more or less convincing
than those generally offered. He certainly tackles the issue with an
admirable thoroughness and forthrightness. He has a particular flair
for highlighting telling features of the natural world, from the nerves
of insects to the knees of camels. He also declares that he does not
believe in a doctrine of endless punishment, and he could not
reconcile such a view with a belief in divine goodness. In his lecture
on the following Sunday evening he denied the doctrine of divine

[55] Lincolnshire Archives, Lincoln, Thomas Cooper, Misc. Don. 2 Bapt. 2, no. 14.

impassibility and affirmed the ultimate universal restoration of all things (that is, that everyone will eventually receive salvation).

During autumn 1856, therefore, Cooper had continued his career as a popular lecturer while focusing the theme of his orations exclusively upon religious apologetics. During 1857 he would continue these efforts from an explicitly orthodox Christian stance, and he would spend the rest of his life working as, to use his own self-description, a 'Lecturer in Defence of Christianity'.[56] Cooper would tour the country indomitably well into his late seventies and beyond. He typically arrived in some provincial town, delivered a series of lectures all week long in a hall, and then preached in the morning, afternoon, and again in the evening at some Nonconformist chapel. For example, on Monday to Saturday, 23–8 March 1863, Cooper lectured in Leeds on the following themes: Astronomy; Replies to Objections—A priori and Moral Arguments—and Future States; Pentateuch and Colenso; Origin of Christianity; Miracles of Christ; Internal Evidences. Then, on the Sunday, 29 March, he preached at the General Baptist chapel in the morning and evening, while delivering a sermon at a (Particular) Baptist chapel in the afternoon.[57] Having come back to the Christian faith, Cooper also set his mind to reflecting on denominational distinctions, a process that resulted in his being baptized as a believer in a General Baptist chapel in Leicester on Whit Sunday, 1859. Holyoake could not resist a jab at this, and also insinuated the charge of suddenness: 'His last conversion was very undignified. He might be said to have leaped off the Freethought platform, splash into a Baptist dipping-pool.'[58] Cooper was an evangelical General Baptist, with many pulpits from a wide variety of denominations open to him, for the rest of his life. When the data in the two large ledgers Cooper kept is tabulated, it reveals that in his Christian apologist phase alone he delivered 4,292 lectures and preached 2,568 sermons. These efforts were made in 545 different cities, towns, or other distinct localities from Inverness to

[56] This is how he described himself on his wife Susanna's gravestone, which in due course became his as well. Lincoln, Lincolnshire Archives, 'Canwick Old Cemetery', M.I.S., grave location: T(b)137.

[57] Lincoln, Lincoln Central Library, Local Studies, Thomas Cooper Mss., Ms. 5059.

[58] G. J. Holyoake, *Thomas Cooper Delineated as Convert and Controversialist: A Companion to his Missionary Wanderings* (London: Austin Holyoake, 1861), 8.

Jersey.[59] Moreover, London, for example, would count as just one of these 545, even though dozens of different venues are listed there, from Sussex Hall, Milton Hall, and the Hall of Science, to Spurgeon's Metropolitan Tabernacle, the YMCA, and the Friends' Meeting House. Cooper frequently advertised his forthcoming lectures in the *Reasoner*.[60]

The *Investigator* was wide of the mark when it asserted that Cooper was in it for what material advantages he could accrue, even if one takes the long view of his career. There is much that could be said against Cooper's character: a good case could be made for charges such as that he was egotistical, boastful, stubborn, hot-headed, and thin-skinned. Never in his whole life, however, did Cooper ever prioritize his own material welfare. His lectures as a Christian apologist did not make him prosper. Rather, he lived anxiously from week to week, never even sure that his speaking-related expenses would not be greater than his income. In plebeian freethinking circles it was standard practice to charge an entrance fee for lectures, but as a Christian apologist Cooper insisted on free admittance, being more concerned with the lives that he could influence than the money he could make. He took voluntary collections and sold his books and hoped for the best. He even guarded against the temptation to skew his itinerary towards more prosperous communities. He was also large-hearted, and received and responded favourably to more than his share of begging letters. Indeed, in 1881 Holyoake was so moved by the fact that Cooper's hard work and advanced years were accompanied by continuing impecuniosity that he successfully appealed to Gladstone to secure for him a civil pension, thereby knowingly squashing a campaign for himself to receive such a boon, despite his own genuine needs. The statesman of Secularism wrote to the Grand Old Man: 'There is Mr. Thomas Cooper, much older than myself, who from the days of his political imprisonment forty years ago until now has been an honest and brave teacher of working people. I found him lately in Lincoln, going out in his 76th year to preach Christianity to which he is devoted, in inclement weather,

---

[59] Lincoln, Lincoln Central Library, Local Studies, Thomas Cooper Mss. 5059 and 5060.
[60] See e.g. *Reasoner*, 1 Mar. 1865, p. 12.

because his slender income is too small for his needs.'[61] Although it was certainly true that Cooper literally could not afford to retire, it also must be emphasized that he was driven to preach by a sense of duty. In April 1864 Cooper gave a lecture series in Bedford, and his ledger contains a revealing comment regarding Sunday 24 April which, on a normal arrangement, ought also to have been spent in Bunyan's town: 'My friends could not get me a chapel to preach in! So I went back to London for my first Sunday's holiday since I began to preach again. But, may God forgive me! I will never spend another Sunday so miserably in idleness—as long as I can preach.'[62] It was the practice at that time to give such civil pensions in an annual lump sum, but special provision was made to divide Cooper's into smaller payments made three times a year, as he would otherwise have been tempted to give away too much of it to those whom he deemed worse off than himself, taking no thought for the morrow.

So Cooper toured the country giving lectures in the service of Christian apologetics. He also wrote numerous books, most of them being versions of his Christian lectures. The first of these, *The Bridge of History Over the Gulf of Time* (1871), was by far his most successful publication from all the phases of his life.[63] In 1885, when he published his last book, the advertisements at the back showed this work had sold 24,000 copies, whilst his *Life*, which had been originally published in the same year, came in second with 14,000 copies. It is therefore worth emphasizing that the current view, that Cooper's *Life* is his most interesting work and his apologetic efforts are the least interesting, does not appear to have been shared by the reading public in the late Victorian period.[64] Cooper did not strive for originality in his apologetic work, and freely gave credit to the

---

[61] Conklin, *Thomas Cooper*, 460–1. Even more extraordinarily, Holyoake often ran pieces in his Secularist journals enthusiastically praising Cooper's apologetic writings and his dedication to his Christian ministry. See e.g. *Reasoner*, Feb. 1871, p. 25; May 1872, pp. 242–3.

[62] Lincoln, Lincoln Central Library, Local Studies, Thomas Cooper Mss., Ms. 5059.

[63] Conklin's work obscures this point by a copying error which turned sales of 14,000 copies of the *Life* into 'forty' thousand: *Thomas Cooper*, 438.

[64] For example, John Saville has written, '[Cooper] wrote and published a great deal of fundamentalist theology, now all unreadable; and the only book that has continued to be read is the *Life* which . . . has continued to be read widely. It deserves to be.' Thomas Cooper, *The Life of Thomas Cooper*, with an introduction by John Saville (Leicester: Leicester University Press, 1971), 24–5.

authors whose arguments he was popularizing. The *Bridge of History*, however, is not only his most successful volume, but also his most original one. Furthermore, it is the volume that had as its main task refuting Strauss, thus indicating that the self-educated shoemaker had indeed been left to do that intellectual heavy lifting on his own.

The *Bridge of History* begins by first addressing the sun (god) theory before moving on to address Strauss's mythical theory. The sun theory argues that ancient cultures were apt to create gods that personified the sun: for example, Krishna for the Hindus, Osiris for the Egyptians, and Phoebus Apollo for the Greeks. In like manner, Jesus is a manifestation of this same tendency. In short, Jesus was not a historical figure at all. While it might initially appear that Cooper is just setting up an easy target to knock down, this level of scepticism actually had significant credence in Victorian plebeian freethinking circles. The sun theory was disseminated in a popular text in that world, Volney's *Ruins of Empires*. It was a view held by a leading London popular sceptic in the first half of the century, Robert Taylor (1784–1844), the so-called 'devil's chaplain', and popularized in his influential book the *Diegesis* (1828), its very title being a sort of unflinching pun on its thesis. A decade after Cooper published his *Bridge of History*, a new catalogue of books published by Bradlaugh's and Annie Besant's Freethought Publishing Company, included not only both Volney's *Ruins of Empires* and Taylor's *Diegesis*, but also lesser-known titles of the same ilk, T. E. Partridge, *On the Connection of Christianity with Solar Worship* and John Stuart Glennie, *Isis and Osiris, or the Origin of Christianity*, the latter having first been published only in 1878. As a young sceptic, Bradlaugh wrote his own manuscript of biblical criticism in 1850 in which he acknowledged that the existence of Jesus could be proven. By 1854, however, he was no longer willing to concede this point and added a correction: 'I would not defend the existence of Jesus as a man at all'.[65] In 1884, Bradlaugh published a tract of his entitled, *Who Was Jesus Christ?* Here is the penultimate paragraph: 'Who was Christ? born of a virgin. So was Chrishna, the Hindoo god incarnate. The story of Chrishna is identical in many respects with that of Jesus. The story of Chrishna was current long prior to the birth of Jesus.

---

[65] Bonner, *Bradlaugh*, i. 22.

The story of Chrishna is believed by the inhabitants of Hindostan and disbelieved by the English, who say it is a myth, a fable. We add that both are equally true, and that both are equally false.'[66] The sun theory was no straw figure in this milieu.

The conceit signalled in the title of Cooper's *Bridge of History Over the Gulf of Time* was a retrospective tour from the present, back century by century to the time-period when Jesus was said to have lived. This structure gives Cooper a chance to download some of his useful knowledge regarding European history, while making the point that there was no period at which this sun fable could have been invented, whereas there is a continuous record of affirming the historical existence of Jesus, from the days when eyewitnesses would have been still alive to comment on the matter up to the present. When discussing King Alfred, Cooper was led on from words about English freedom to praise a favourable remark by Gladstone on franchise extension that had warmed 'the heart of the old Chartist prisoner'.[67] Having dealt with the sun theory, he then moved on to the more subtle mythical theory of Strauss, adding for good measure the more recent, less-than-orthodox life of Jesus by Ernest Renan.

Cooper's summary of the gist of Strauss's argument, that Christianity exists as a world force today because 'a weak fanatical woman first imagined she saw Jesus in the garden where his sepulchre was', did actually put a finger on Strauss's unmistakeable sexism—a feature that more highbrow critics seem to have overlooked.[68] The bulk of Cooper's response is a combination of the early evidence regarding the gospels and their authors, combined with a close reading of the gospels themselves—one that points toward their veracity rather than away from it, as Strauss's work had done. Strauss had claimed that the four gospels were all anonymous. Cooper countered that they have always had authors affixed to them, Matthew, Mark, Luke, and

---

[66] 'Iconoclast' [Charles Bradlaugh], *Who Was Jesus Christ?* The copy I have has no publisher and no date. The earliest copy listed on WorldCat is dated 1884, but it is possible that that is a reprint as Bradlaugh's use of his nom de plume tended to be earlier in his career.

[67] Thomas Cooper, *The Bridge of History Over the Gulf of Time* (London: Hodder & Stoughton, 1871), 43.

[68] Ibid. 80.

John—these are not fanciful medieval additions but the testimony of the earliest church fathers. The authorship of the gospels is just as certain as that of any ancient document, he averred. No one goes around denying that Julius Caesar wrote the *Commentaries on the Gallic War*, yet the evidence is no greater. He then proceeds to attempt to demonstrate congruence between the biographical details of the four gospel writers as given by the early Christian writers and the gospels identified with them.

Cooper particularly excels with the second gospel, which, following early church tradition, he claims Mark based on the preaching of the apostle Peter. Taking the account of Christ calming the storm, he shows how Mark alone mentions that the Lord was asleep on 'a pillow', which moreover, Cooper says, should have been translated from the Greek as 'the pillow', a detail which only Peter would mention because he fondly remembered that 'he had always provided a pillow for his dear Master's head, in his own boat, and most likely, had not one himself'.[69] The original language is very important to Cooper, and he repeatedly insists that working-men who wish to take sides in these controversies ought to be intellectually serious enough to learn Greek. Cooper goes on to show that Mark provides the most precise statement about the cock crowing as a sign of Peter denying Christ, and that whilst other gospels merely say that Peter wept, Mark says, 'When he thought thereon, he wept', thus indicating that this gospel writer had heard him speak of his thoughts. Mark's habit of using the word 'immediately' betrays the 'phrase and manner of an energetic speaker'.[70] Peter was preaching in Rome, and this explains why Mark's gospel includes explanations of Jewish customs which, if written in Jerusalem, would have been 'like carrying coals to Newcastle'. A case is made for the traditional authors of the other gospels as well. For example, Luke, who is said to have been a doctor, does not deny that the woman with the issue of blood could not be healed by her physicians but, in contrast to Mark, he does not admit that her condition grew worse under their care: 'he will not let his profession down.'[71] Clearly, Cooper had not retreated from intellectual enquiry into a private realm of merely emotional piety, but rather was making

---

[69] Cooper, *Bridge*, 110.   [70] Ibid. 114.   [71] Ibid. 127.

a bona fide and thoroughgoing attempt to counter well-reasoned sceptical criticism with well-reasoned believing criticism.

Cooper, in contrast to Holyoake (let alone more scoffing sceptics), had always expressed his admiration for the 'moral beauty' of Jesus. Even in *Purgatory of Suicides*, after a clear-eyed poetic nod to the sun-god theory, complete with references not only to Osiris, Isis, and Apollo but also to a whole pantheon of lesser-known deities, he still could not resist going on to testify: 'I love the Galilean:—Lord and Christ | Such goodness I could own... | I love the sweet and simple narrative,—| With all its childlike earnestness... | I would the tale were true.'[72] Cooper eventually came to see this as an apologetic point in its own right, and one that answered Strauss as well as even adding credibility to a belief in miracles. In a move we will see replicated in the cases of Joseph Barker and George Sexton, Cooper came to the conviction that the portrait of Jesus given in the four gospels was too good not to be true: 'Gradually, the strong conviction grew within me that the perfectly holy and spotless character of Christ itself was a miracle, and the greatest of all miracles.'[73] Or again: 'While thus intent on convincing myself and others that there was nothing above humanity in the moral perfection of Christ, and that science and mental progress would eventually bring in the reign of such moral perfection, I did not perfectly succeed in convincing myself. Every fresh glance at the pure spirituality of the New Testament teaching threw me back...'[74] The compelling nature of the figure of Jesus of Nazareth was a major influence on the reconverts.

The *Bridge of History* was the first of five volumes which his publisher called 'Thomas Cooper's Christian Evidence Series'. The others were: *God, the Soul and a Future State* (1873), *The Verity of Christ's Resurrection from the Dead* (1875), *The Verity and Value of the Miracles of Christ* (1876), and *Evolution, the Stone Book, and the Mosaic Record of Creation* (1878). The last of these volumes, although treating the issue of perhaps greatest interest to some readers today, was the most peripheral in terms of Cooper's own sense of the themes of greatest importance for apologetics; hence its appearing

---

[72] Cooper, *Purgatory*, 90.
[73] Thomas Cooper, *The Verity and Value of the Miracles of Christ* (London: Hodder & Stoughton, 1876), 167.
[74] Cooper, *Life*, 365.

last after the more urgent and weighty issues had received due attention. The first thing which needs to be said is that not only did Cooper formulate his apologetics in a pre-Darwinian intellectual environment, but he also (like many others) evaluated and rejected theories of evolution during those earlier years. In one of his 1856 lectures he criticized 'the school of Lamarcks [*sic*], the French Naturalist', which has 'striven to restore the old exploded Greek doctrine of appetencies or desires'.[75] He also had already made a careful reading of that 'Victorian sensation' of evolutionary advocacy, *Vestiges of the Natural History of Creation* (1844).[76] Nevertheless, although Cooper was already set on an apologetic tack from which he would not be deflected, and approached the debate somewhat with the air of a man who thinks he has heard it all before and already answered it, he still made a serious effort to tackle this new intellectual challenge. In 1878, when he was 73, Cooper wrote playfully to his friend, Mr Whitwell: 'So: you are reading periodicals,—while I am toiling through big books—Haeckel—& other monsters! I am determined to know what they all say, & to know it thoroughly. I have just gone through Lyell's 'Principles of Geology' for the 2nd time. Many parts of it are delightful reading.'[77]

Cooper's volume on evolution and geology endeavoured to offer a historical summary of the books which were considered landmarks in these fields, and his more argumentative sections are filled with references to an array of thinkers. In addition to mentioning the ideas

---

[75] Lincoln, Lincoln Archives, Misc. Don. 2 Baptist 2, item 7, Thomas Cooper, 'The Being, Power, & Wisdom of God: the Design Argument restated: selection of striking instances of Design', City-Road [Hall of Science, London], 21 Sept. 1856.

[76] Cooper relates his encounter with this work soon after its publication in his *Evolution, the Stone Book, and the Mosaic Record of Creation* (London: Hodder & Stoughton, 1878), 11. He attached to his 1856 lectures old notes from past lectures of a purely scientific nature. One has a reference to a page from *Vestiges* to cite: Lincolnshire Archives, Misc. Don. 2 Baptist 2, item 14, 'The Providence of God: Proofs of the continued action of God in the Universe: importance & salutariness of the doctrine of Providence', City Road [Hall of Science, London], 19 Oct. 1856.

[77] Lincolnshire Archives, Misc. Don. 2 Baptist 3, item 7, Cooper to Mr Whitwell, 5 Aug. 1878. The reception of *Vestiges* has now been given as thorough and as insightful a study as one could ever hope for in regards to almost any book (perhaps it is resonant with themes in this study to observe that the author himself notes that only the reading of the Bible has apparently been treated in more depth): James A. Secord, *Victorian Sensation: The Extraordinary Publication, Reception, and Secret Authorship of 'Vestiges of the Natural History of Creation'* (Chicago: University of Chicago Press, 2000).

of the major British contributors to the current debate—Darwin, Lyell, Wallace, Huxley, Tyndall, and Spencer—he alludes to the American, Asa Gray; the Germans Haeckel, Virchow, Nageli and Carl Vogt (as well as Goethe); and the Frenchmen Lamarck, De Maillet, Geoffroy St-Hilaire, and Boucher de Perthes. Beside praising the older science of Cuvier, Linnaeus, Buckland, Sedgwick, and their heirs, Sir Roderick Murchison and Dr Whewell, one of his main lines of attack is to argue that Darwin has unreasonably demanded 'unlimited time' for his evolutionary process.[78] Cooper, whilst accepting a much older earth than some traditional readings of the Bible would allow, and giving his approval to 'the Nebular or Cosmical theory of Laplace' (a view that some orthodox thinkers found incompatible with their faith),[79] nevertheless argues that the existing geological evidence clearly indicated that the earth was not as old as Darwin needed for his theory to be viable, citing the work of Helmholtz, Sir William Thomson, and Professors Croll and Tait in support of this judgement.

In short, Cooper primarily criticized Darwinism by appealing to the authority of other scientific opinions rather than that of revelation. The need for such an attempt to be made, however, and its inclusion in a series of apologetic writings indicated his belief that this theory could undermine some people's commitment to orthodox Christianity. One reason for this conviction was that it was becoming clearer that Darwin's theory was a threat to Cooper's cherished argument from design. One almost gains the impression that he found it hard to imagine an orthodox Christian denying this argument, thus thereby virtually turning it into a doctrine and creating an ironic situation in which an apologetic has to be developed in order to defend an apologetic.[80]

His central objection was the extent to which Darwin's theory denied the uniqueness of the human race, and the destructive implications this was felt to have in the field of moral philosophy. In Cooper's last book, a collection of essays on everything from industrial strikes to Handel's *Messiah* entitled *Thoughts at Fourscore and*

---

[78] Cooper, *Evolution*, 16.

[79] For Christian suspicion of the nebular hypothesis, see Alieen Fyfe, *Science and Salvation: Evangelical Popular Science Publishing in Victorian Britain* (Chicago: University of Chicago Press, 2004), 232–4.

[80] Cooper, *Evolution*, 2–3.

Earlier, he included an essay on 'Charles Darwin, and the fallacies of evolution' and another one on 'The Origin of Man'. His comments on Darwin himself are gracious, claiming that he was 'undoubtedly, a benefactor to his race', and taking several paragraphs to describe his personal virtues before going on to critique his theory. Cooper's main argument was that there is a huge gulf between humans and apes. The differences he perceived between the two species he catalogues in detail, ending with what in his view is the most crucial one, humanity's possession of a moral and spiritual nature.[81] This is telling, as the moral argument was the one that Cooper himself found the most decisive, and therefore he is arguably engaging with Darwinism primarily as a way of protecting his greater concern regarding the basis of morality and the existence of a Moral Governor that can be inferred from an awareness of moral law. In the other essay he promotes the more noble views of humanity articulated by Max Müller.[82] Moreover, Cooper had read Strauss's last book, *The Old Faith and the New*, which was published in London in 1874, and the connection between evolution and unbelief was surely reinforced in his mind by seeing his rejected master abandoning Christianity altogether and replacing it with Darwinian thought.[83] Even the freethinking phase of Cooper's life might have helped to reinforce these intellectual instincts: he was deeply rooted in the culture of self-help, which was in turn grounded in an emphasis on human dignity. When he was still a freethinker he commended the learning of classical languages to working-class men: 'It will give you the key to unlock a grand treasury of thought—the most valuable riches to every man who does not pride himself on being merely an animal.'[84]

The argument from design was undoubtedly attractive to Cooper personally. A major outlet for his enormous intellectual curiosity was the natural world. As a boy Cooper 'often longed to know the names

---

[81] Thomas Cooper, *Thoughts at Fourscore and Earlier* (London: Hodder, 1885), 132–62.

[82] Ibid. 322–34.

[83] Thomas Cooper, *The Verity of Christ's Resurrection from the Dead* (London: Hodder & Stoughton, 1875), 29; D. F. Strauss, *The Old Faith and the New* (London: Asher & Co., 1874).

[84] Thomas Cooper, *Eight Letters to the Young Men of the Working-Classes* (London: J. Watson, 1851), 13.

of flowers, which none could tell'.[85] His wife Susanna shared this passion. Some correspondence between the Coopers and their horticultural friend Mr Whitwell has survived. It reveals the avid and systematic way in which the couple collected plants. Cooper begins yet another request for a coveted cutting with the words, 'My dear blue-stocking will <u>not</u> be content'.[86] The natural world never failed to delight him, and Cooper, as a Christian, instinctively felt that this wonder should provoke praise for the Creator. This personal sense of the fitting nature of the argument from design dovetailed with Cooper's not unrealistic assessment that it was a mode of thinking which it was not easy for freethinkers to dismiss. Despite the widespread assumption today that the Darwinian theory of evolution stripped William Paley's argument of its force, this impression was not quickly made. When Cooper debated with Bradlaugh in 1864 (five years after Darwin's *On the Origin of the Species* had been published), not only was he still using the argument from design, but Bradlaugh himself made no reference to theories of evolution in his attempt to refute it. Instead, like Holyoake and Barker, he expounded a philosophical response which was not obviously more compelling than Paley's logic.[87] In this case, Bradlaugh claimed that the argument was based on a false analogy, because it is 'impossible to reason from design of that which is already existing, and thus to prove the creation of that which before did not exist'.[88] The argument from design was also the apologetic approach that offered the most scope for inserting large sections of 'useful knowledge' regarding natural history, anatomy and the like, a bonus that popular audiences appreciated, and one that was in keeping with Cooper's own delight in learning.

Although Cooper viewed the argument from design as the most effective one he had to offer, the one which most satisfied his own mind was the moral argument. This line of thought was central to Cooper's own intellectual history, and took a prominent place in the

---

[85] Cooper, *Life*, 19.

[86] Lincolnshire Archives, Misc. Don. 2 Baptist 3, Cooper to Mr Whitwell, 21 Aug. 1873.

[87] John Kent also made this point in regard to the Bradlaugh–Brewin Grant debate in 1875: *From Darwin to Blatchford: The Role of Darwinism in Christian Apologetic, 1875–1910* (London: Dr Williams's Trust, 1966).

[88] *Discussion between Mr. Thomas Cooper and Mr. C. Bradlaugh* (1864 debate; London: Freethought Publishing Co., 1883), esp. 9.

worldview which he developed. He had answered Strauss by using Christ's perfect moral nature as a door leading into the whole realm of orthodox Christology, and he believed that the existence of a moral nature in human beings functioned in a similar way on the more general issue of theism. Cooper challenged his audience to think about their own moral nature: 'How come you to have it? There is but one possible answer:—Because it has been given to you by the Moral Governor to Whom you are responsible. Your very possession of the Moral Nature proves His existence. And it was the conviction of the great thinker, Immanuel Kant, that it is the strongest and most undeniable of all the proofs of God's existence.'[89] Cooper was deeply impressed by the moral argument. He was still teaching it in his last book, recalling as an octogenarian that it was this argument which had conquered his unbelief all those years ago.[90]

Cooper's apologetic efforts largely consisted of popularizing the various lines of argument which had already been well established by others. Although he appeals to Kant's authority to bolster the moral argument, he was not deterred by the fact (assuming he recognized it) that 'the great thinker' believed that more traditional apologetic arguments lacked force. Cooper placed the moral argument side by side with the classic a priori argument and the argument from design as a trilogy of proofs of God's existence. Holyoake ridiculed this the-more-the-merrier approach in a pamphlet he wrote on Cooper's lectures as 'a companion to his missionary wanderings'. Holyoake claimed that his old friend had 'opened a theological Curiosity Shop', noting, 'A priori, à posteriori arguments, abandoned even by the Evangelical Alliance, Mr. Cooper galvanises and sets in motion again'.[91] Undeterred, Cooper persisted in this approach in his book *God, the Soul and a Future State*.

The a priori argument was, in Cooper's hands, a mixture of philosophy, logic, common-sense assertions, and the occasional suspiciously sharp turn in the argument. The section of his book which outlines it is indebted, as he freely acknowledged, to a contemporary

[89] Thomas Cooper, *God, the Soul, and a Future State* (London: Hodder & Stoughton, 1875), 99.

[90] Cooper, *Thoughts*, 352–65.

[91] Holyoake, *Thomas Cooper*, 5.

work, W. H. Gillespie's *The Argument, a Priori, for the Being and Attributes of the Lord God* (1833).[92] On the existence of an afterlife, he uses various approaches, including another look at what having a moral nature implies, but his favourite and perhaps most original argument is an endearing reflection of the man. Cooper, the self-educated shoemaker whose obsessive studying habits led to a physical breakdown, suggested that the desire within a human being to know ever more was a clue to a nature designed for immortality:

And do we not all know that the more we learn to know, the more we thirst to know? It is only sheer ignorance that has no desire for knowledge.... Is the wisdom of God so abortive as to make a being of boundless desires for knowledge, only at the end of a few years to put him out of existence?... The Progressive Nature of Man—if I use the most circumspect language—is a strong *presumptive* argument for a Future Life for Man.[93]

Cooper's Christian-evidence writings are littered with references to a wide range of authors, from apologists to sceptics, from scientists to poets. This is well illustrated by his volume on miracles. Originality is not the aim, but rather exposing people from the working classes to the ideas of the cogent books and great minds which have taken the orthodox view. He freely remarks after popularizing one argument, 'I would not have you suppose that this is any discovery of mine'.[94] Although he also refers to items published recently, one of his main approaches is to claim that the current sceptical objections had all been raised and answered in the eighteenth century. He identifies the works of 'the Old English Freethinkers': notably, Shaftesbury's *Characteristics*, Clount's *The Oracle of Reason*, Tindal's *Christianity as Old as the Creation*, Woolston's *Discourses*, and Hume's *Essay on Miracles*.[95] As he had lectured on the thought of these men as a freethinker, he was engaging with ideas that were still considered alive and cogent in the world of popular scepticism. Cooper also lists those who endeavoured to answer them, authors who together comprise a 'library of "Apologetics"': Bentley, Samuel Clarke, Boyle, Stillingfleet, Locke, Leslie, Chandler, Hugh Farmer, Campbell, Gilbert West, Lord Lyttelton, Lardner, Leland, Ray,

---

[92] Cooper, *God*, 16. Cooper corresponded with Gillespie: Thomas Cooper and Robert Taylor, *A Calm Inquiry into the Nature of Deity* (London: Farrah, 1864), 35.
[93] Cooper, *God*, 172.   [94] Id., *Miracles*, 55.   [95] Ibid. 43–7.

Derham, Smallbrook, Sherlock, Bishop Watson, and of course, Paley and Butler.[96] Cooper then makes this appeal: 'Let me earnestly recommend young working men to read their books, which take up all the objections to Miracles current in their times, and which fully answer those objections.'[97] For good measure, Cooper notes that a contemporary freethinker, John Stuart Mill, had also criticized Hume's argument.[98] He also praises Prebendary Row's *The Supernatural in the New Testament*, Ralph Wardlaw's *On Miracles* (1852), and James Mozley's 1865 Bampton Lectures. The various arguments of these works are popularized, strung together into an unfolding argument, and leavened with Cooper's own ideas, opinions, and illustrations.

Cooper's own intellectual curiosity rings out in his *God, the Soul and a Future State* in his references to various works of secular learning, from Aristotle's *History of Animals* to Sir Astley Cooper's *Lectures on the Principles of Surgery*. Abandoning all apologetic purposes, he even printed as an appendix an extract from a work by the medical pioneer William Harvey, just in case his illustration had aroused interest in a particular theme of anatomy.[99] Cooper does cite Huxley's *Lay Sermons* (1870) and criticize such thinkers as Hume, Spinoza, and Darwin, but many of his targets are from his own milieu of popular radicalism: Holyoake, Robert Owen, a Sheffield Socialist, Richard Otley, and various unnamed people whom he had heard make contributions to discussions.

Cooper's crisis of doubt was real. Like other figures in this study, he became convinced that the sceptical method he had been using was too fine a filter: what made it through it was not sufficient to live on. As John Henry Newman argued in *An Essay in Aid of a Grammar of Assent* (1870), Cooper came to believe that he knew more than he could prove by the procrustean standards of Enlightenment rationalism. This was true in the field of ethics no less than religion. Nevertheless, like Newman, his solution was not to retreat from

---

[96] For an examination of Butler's place in Victorian intellectual history, see Jane Garnett, 'Bishop Butler and the *Zeitgeist*: Butler and the Development of Christian Moral Philosophy in Victorian Britain', in Christopher Cunliffe (ed.), *Joseph Butler's Moral and Religious Thought: Tercentenary Essays* (Oxford: Clarendon Press, 1992), 63–96.
[97] Cooper, *Miracles*, 46.   [98] Ibid. 47–56.   [99] Cooper, *God*, 106–8.

reason but to have—or so at least they believed—a more reasonable view regarding what it could achieve and what counted as reason. Cooper therefore could speak poignantly about how a sceptical point of view led him both to a crisis of doubt and a chastened view of the role of apologetics:

Common as it is for writers on the Evidences to assert, that it needs but the employment of their ordinary powers of understanding for men to become convinced of the Truth of Christianity, I believe that that is not true . . . I find that I must receive many things for solid truth which I cannot reason out, logically . . . I cannot live in a world of cold negations. It is a wonder to me that other men can live in such a world. But I do not condemn them for it. I only wish that they felt the satisfaction, the happiness, the thankfulness that I feel in receiving Christianity.[100]

Moreover, Cooper's mature Christian faith was not a slavish acceptance of conventional views in orthodox circles. His intellectual enquiries had led him to see that certain positions were incorrect. Cooper denied a literal six-day creation, admitted that the earth was millions of years old, and occasionally even seemed to concede the possibility that the theory of evolution might be valid for forms of life below the human.[101] He censured Christians who stirred up interest in the possibility of Christ's second coming being imminent.[102] Cooper candidly admitted that his studies had convinced him that the ending of Mark's gospel given in the Authorized Version did not belong to the original document.[103] He confessed that he thought the biblical accounts of Christ's temptation in the wilderness might be merely 'a parabolic description of His own mental conflict'.[104] On the doctrine of Scripture, he writes, in a way similar to what would become Joseph Barker's final view: 'Whatever may be pronounced, at some future period of the Church's history, to be the *true* theory of inspiration (for, although eighteen centuries have passed away, the Christian Church, as yet, has *not* pronounced what is the *true* theory), it will be a theory which admits the fact

---

[100] Id., *Miracles*, 169–70.
[101] Id., *Evolution*, 91, 109, 123, 130; id., *Thoughts*, 132–62.
[102] Id., *Bridge*, 157–8.
[103] Id., *Resurrection*, 83.
[104] Id., *Miracles*, 165.

that *verbal* inspiration does not characterize every part of the Scriptures...'[105] Most of these judgements were a direct tribute to his attentiveness to the evidence that Secularists used to attack views sometimes espoused by orthodox Christians.

To conclude, it cannot be said that Cooper never felt the full weight of sceptical objections to religious faith. It cannot be said that he was not keeping up with his reading, that an honest encounter with the thought of Darwin, Huxley, Hume, Paine, Strauss, or some such author would have made orthodox Christian belief irrevocably untenable for him. This was said, of course, but such claims were only wishful thinking or propaganda from freethinking controversialists. Cooper came to doubt his doubts, and to find ways to answer rather than evade the then current intellectual objections to Christian thought. This is what is meant by honest faith.

[105] Id., *Bridge*, 103–4. A volume of sermons by Cooper which was published in 1880 was praised as likely to do sceptical readers much good by the Evangelical Alliance's journal, but with the warning that the reviewer was not 'guaranteeing the strict theological accuracy of every doctrinal statement contained in these discourses': *Evangelical Christendom*, 1 Jan. 1881, p. 21. I am grateful to Todd Thompson for discovering this review for me.

5

John Henry Gordon

John Henry Gordon was born on 19 July 1838 in St Luke's, London. His father, John Gordon, was a schoolteacher for the British and Foreign School Society. His parents were members of a Congregational (or Independent) church. J. H. Gordon was taught the Lord's Prayer by his mother as a child, and went on to be the 'quickest boy' and the teacher's favourite in his Sunday-school class, graduating to 'best hope of the Senior Bible-class', and finally emerging as a Sunday-school teacher himself.[1] At the age of 19 Gordon gave his address as 12 Etterby Street, Stanwix, Carlisle, which was also the parental home.[2] Gordon first had sceptical thoughts about the Bible as a teenager, but initially overcame them. He went to work for a period at 'a distant commercial city', and had a renewed encounter with unbelief: 'I read sceptical books.' He then lost his faith. This scepticism 'German transcendentalism had first nurtured, and English unbelief strengthened and completed'.[3]

By the age of 19 Gordon was ready to join forces more decisively with organized unbelief. He was reading with admiration G. J. Holyoake's Secularist newspaper the *Reasoner*, and he aspired to be a contributor. He sent Holyoake an article that appeared on the front

[1] J. H. Gordon, *The Public Statement of Mr. J. H. Gordon, (Late Lecturer to the Leeds Secular Society,) with reference to his repudiation of secular principles, and his adoption of the Christian faith. [Delivered in the Music Hall, Leeds, on Tuesday, August 5th, 1862. The Rev. G. W. Conder in the Chair.]* (Leeds: J. Hamer, 1862), 5–6, 27. Information on his pre-Carlisle life comes from research kindly done for me by Stephen White of the Carlisle Library and from Gordon's obituary: *Baptist Magazine* (Dec. 1878), 547–54.
[2] Manchester, The Co-operative College Archives, Holyoake House, Holyoake Papers, J. H. Gordon to G. J Holyoake, 16 Dec. 1857.
[3] Gordon, *Public Statement*, 6.

page of the 30 December 1857 issue, 'Clericalism in Carlisle'. The contributor was identified with the *nom de plume* 'B.B.B.'[4] The article was a gossipy piece. Washington Wilks, editor of the *Carlisle Examiner* was a well-respected local figure and a popular speaker. Wilks had therefore not unnaturally been asked by the Carlisle branch of the YMCA to give an address. A local clergyman, the Revd B. A. Marshall, however, had privately insisted that the invitation be withdrawn. Marshall threatened to dissociate himself from the Carlisle YMCA if Wilks was allowed to speak, and let it be known that he was confident that the bishop and the dean would also follow his principled example. The dean and bishop were both decided evangelicals, who had been appointed only the year before, in 1856. The bishop, Henry Montagu Villiers (1813–61), was the first of Palmerston's evangelical appointments to the episcopal bench.[5] The dean, Francis Close (1792–1882), was a resolute campaigner for righteousness.[6] Gordon speculated in his article that Marshall was a front-man, acting on the orders of Close. At his death in 1874, a sympathetic local obituary testified that Marshall was 'as stern and unyielding as a Covenanter wherever the truth of Christ was concerned'.[7] It is reasonable to surmise that these recent ecclesiastical appointments had led to a more combative atmosphere in Carlisle, as committed evangelicals sought to implement their agenda and some non-evangelicals chafed against their efforts. This anticlerical article by Gordon was a fascinating debut, as he would eventually travel full circle in a more specific way by deciding that his polemical tendencies could be confined to annoying stodgy Anglican clergymen.

Gordon was well placed to pick up this piece of local gossip, as Wilks was his employer. In January 1858 Gordon wrote to Holyoake from the office of the *Carlisle Examiner and North Western Advertiser* on official letterhead, noting that he was on the editorial staff there, and therefore it would be inappropriate for him to write letters to the

⁴ *Reasoner*, 30 Dec. 1857, 'Clericalism in Carlisle'.

⁵ For Palmerston's evangelical appointments, see Nigel Scotland, *'Good and Proper Men': Lord Palmerston and the Bench of Bishops* (Cambridge: James Clarke, 2000).

⁶ For Villiers and Close as evangelicals, see their entries in Donald M. Lewis (ed.), *The Blackwell Dictionary of Evangelical Biography 1730–1860* (Oxford: Blackwell, 1995).

⁷ *Carlisle Patriot*, 6 June 1874, 'Death of the Rev. B. A. Marshall'.

local press concerning Wilks.[8] Gordon's initial career was in the newspaper business.

'Clericalism in Carlisle' had delicious effects for Gordon. Wilks had been pleased with the article, whoever its author might have been. A disgruntled letter was written in response by 'A Clergyman' that was published in the *Carlisle Patriot*.[9] Gordon wrote to Holyoake claiming excitedly that the 'affair is causing considerable sensation here'.[10] He suggested that he could ghost-write a letter in response to the clergyman that would be signed by Holyoake. He was also ready to say more about 'Clericalism in Carlisle' in print. He had discovered, for example, that Marshall had not subscribed to a relief fund, even though he had been appointed to its committee.

Thus was launched Gordon's freethinking career. More articles for the *Reasoner* followed. Gordon seems to have quickly decided that he would rather have the personal credit, and was quite happy to throw off the cloak of anonymity. Holyoake, however, appears to have liked the 'B.B.B.' pen-name perhaps because it reminded the Secularist world that Gordon had made his reputation through his journal. When a separately published essay of Gordon's appeared in 1861 from Holyoake's publishing firm, the author was identified as 'John Henry Gordon, Better known as B. B. B. of the REASONER', and it was quite common for him to be referred to in *Reasoner* reports, in what one imagines was a sort of compromise between them, as 'J. H. Gordon, B.B.B.'.[11]

In March 1859 'B.B.B.' can be found receiving a present of books and a congratulatory address from the Edinburgh Secular Society for his service to them as their secretary, during which time he had 're-established' that society, 'now in a prosperous condition by his endeavours'.[12] B.B.B. spoke in February 1860 at the Sheffield Secular Society's Hall of Science on 'The Gospel according to

[8] Manchester, The Co-operative College Archives, Holyoake House, Holyoake Papers, J. H. Gordon to G. J Holyoake, 15 Jan. 1858.

[9] *Carlisle Patriot*, 16 Jan. 1858, 'A Few Words of Caution'.

[10] Manchester, The Co-operative College Archives, Holyoake House, Holyoake Papers, J. H. Gordon to G. J. Holyoake, 19 Jan. 1858.

[11] John Henry Gordon, *The Exodus of the Priests: A Secularist's Dream of Better Times*, Essays by the Way:—No. 1, Series 1861 (London: Holyoake & Co., 1861). For an example of a report, see *Reasoner Gazette*, 25 Nov. 1860, p. 191.

[12] *Reasoner*, 27 Mar. 1859, p. 103.

Secularism'.[13] The Secularist movement needed to replenish its stock
of leaders, and in such a climate Gordon was anointed as an emerging golden boy. Charles Bradlaugh ('Iconoclast'), who would later
emerge as the most prominent atheist in the movement, was also just
starting out in 1860. He was clearly more prominent than Gordon,
but Bradlaugh was also five years older. Gordon was a mere 22 years
old when he was recognized as one of the eight national leaders of the
Secularist movement by an invitation to speak at the historic Castle
Hill meeting in August 1860.[14] Joseph Barker was 54, and Holyoake
and Robert Cooper were in their forties: Gordon was the youngest of
them, and he, Bradlaugh, and John Watts were the three men in their
twenties who represented the surging vitality of the movement. There
were some 5,000 people in attendance, and Gordon, callow speaker
that he was, did not come across as a confident orator. Nevertheless,
the *Reasoner*'s report was encouraging, on the grounds that Gordon
was the promise of the future.[15]

He was soon lecturing often and with flair. Only two weeks later
the *Reasoner* did not need to make allowances for Gordon's performance at the Shipley Glen meeting: 'Mr. J. H. Gordon spoke very
usefully and clearly.'[16] The lecturing opportunities started coming
fast. He was working in Manchester for an unnamed firm not
associated with the Secularist movement, and living at 34 Cottenham
Street, Ardwick, Manchester. He took as his motto something that
might pass for playing with language by twenty-first century post-
modern scholars, '*In Fidelity*'. In October 1860 Gordon announced
no fewer than twenty-six lectures that he was prepared to deliver.[17]
The first thirteen were a series on Secularism, beginning with 'What
is Secularism?' Gordon had an irrepressible urge to appropriate
religious terminology. Thus we have title after title of this ilk: 'Secularism, the "Pure Religion and Undefiled"' and 'Secularism, the only
Revivalism'. Lectures 14–26 were labelled as a miscellaneous series.
They were the ones in which anti-Christian polemics were overtly on

---

[13] *Reasoner Gazette*, 26 Feb. 1860, p. 35.
[14] For the significance of the Castle Hill meeting as a unique show of Secularist
strength, see Edward Royle, *Victorian Infidels: The Origins of the British Secularist
Movement, 1791–1866* (Manchester: Manchester University Press, 1974), 190. (Not all
of the speakers invited were able to attend.)
[15] *Reasoner*, 12 Aug. 1860, p. 263.   [16] Ibid. 26 Aug. 1860, p. 276.
[17] Ibid. 28 Oct. 1860, p. 352.

offer. The least subtle is 'Why I hate Christianity'. One in the classic anti-Bible tradition is 'The Bible-God, "the Chief of Sinners"'. Gordon would carve out a place for himself as one of the more abusive and blunt anti-Christian lecturers. The last lecture title actually undersold its contents: 'It Is Finished! Thoughts suggested by the biography (as written by four of his friends) of that old Hebrew martyr, Jesus of Nazareth.' A sympathetic report from some-one who heard this lecture revealed that Gordon first dismissed the supernatural elements in the gospel narratives as unhistorical, and from what was left deduced that Jesus was 'fanatical and even insane', and therefore 'as such should have been confined, not crucified'.[18] That was strong meat even by unabashed anti-Christian standards.

Events began to move quickly. Gordon reported in a November 1860 letter that his burgeoning freethinking work had caused his employer to dismiss him. He hinted that a prejudice against religious scepticism might have been the motivation, thus securing for himself a faint glow of martyrdom: 'I have been told that I cannot attend to *other* things and my work here; fault has been found with the latter; and I speedily leave them.'[19] He announced that he would pursue a career as a Secularist lecturer. In no time, he was successfully finding engagements on the northern Secularist circuit. Liverpool Secularists, for example, liked what he had to offer: 'Mr. Gordon has an impres-sive manner of delivery, a very pretty action, and, for a young speaker and a young man, possesses many of the elements of success.'[20]

The next step in earning one's place as a battle-hardened leader in the popular freethinking world was the major gladiatorial debate. The great debate of Gordon's freethinking period was with the Revd David King (1819–94), the leading minister of his generation in the British Churches of Christ.[21] B.B.B. announced that he would affirm 'that, while the Gospel according to Saints Matthew, Mark, Luke, and John, is neither the "Gospel of Salvation" or the "Gospel of Peace," the Gospel according to Secularism is both'.[22] Crucially for later

---

[18] *Reasoner Gazette*, 25 Nov. 1860, p. 190.
[19] *Reasoner*, 18 Nov. 1860, p. 376.
[20] Ibid. 30 Dec. 1860, p. 423. (Report of his lectures on Sunday, 2 December.)
[21] David M. Thompson, *Let Sects and Parties Fall: A Short History of the Association of Churches of Christ in Great Britain and Ireland* (Birmingham: Berean Press, 1980).
[22] *Reasoner Gazette*, 25 Nov. 1860, p. 191.

developments, King countered that in order to prepare to hold a debate on such a subject, he would need to be given in advance an exposition of what Gordon meant by Secularism. Gordon acquiesced to this request by supplying King with Holyoake's *Principles of Secularism*. The debate took place in Birmingham on 10–12 December 1860. A transcript was never published; one wonders if this might have partly been because Gordon's bluntness made such a prospect distasteful to King and risky for a publisher. A decade later Bradlaugh debated with King on exactly the same theme, 'Christianity v. Secularism', and the transcript of that discussion was published.[23] When Gordon reconverted, Bradlaugh argued (after the fact) that Gordon's emotive style had not been welcome. The *National Reformer*'s 'Iconoclast' wrote in an open letter to the *Reasoner*'s B.B.B.: 'You have in your lectures chosen coarse titles where more befitting ones could, without difficulty, have been found.'[24] Bradlaugh also reminded him that in his debate with King, Gordon had referred to Jesus as 'a bastard'. Whether despite or because of such an unsparing approach, Birmingham Secularists seemed genuinely pleased with how Gordon performed in the debate. Further endorsing Gordon as a national Secularist leader, they resolved: 'the Committee hereby unanimously express their approval of Mr. Gordon's conduct and advocacy in the late discussion, and that they consider him entitled to the confidence of the Secular body, and that the same be published in the *Reasoner* and *Reformer*.'[25]

On the heels of this came the most extraordinary opportunity. For the first time, a British Secularist society felt that it was up to the financial challenge of hiring a full-time lecturer. Secularist societies often functioned like churches, and this was a classic breakthrough toward, as it were, becoming a congregation with a full-time minister.[26] It is a sure sign of his high standing at that time that Gordon

[23] David King and Charles Bradlaugh, *Christianity v. Secularism: report of a public discussion between David King and Charles Bradlaugh, held in the Co-operative Hall, Bury, Lancashire, September, 27, 28, 29, and 30, October 25 and 26, 1870* (Birmingham: D. King, 1870).

[24] *National Reformer*, 2 Aug. 1862, 'To John Henry Gordon, of Leeds'.

[25] *Reasoner Gazette*, 23 Dec. 1860, p. 207.

[26] Shirley A. Mullen, *Organized Freethought: The Religion of Unbelief in Victorian England* (New York: Garland Publishing, 1987).

was chosen for this honour. Ever one to play with religious language, he announced his appointment with the terminology that a Dissenting minister would have used:

Secular friends generally, and personal friends in particular, will rejoice to learn that I have received a 'call' from the Leeds Secular Society to become resident lecturer there ... I would that other societies adopted the course of that one which, in this matter, at any rate, *leads* off right bravely. For myself, I shall enter upon my duties in a spirit of entire consecration to the great cause of which I shall thus become, in the very centre of its centre of progress, the honoured and trusted representative.[27]

Meanwhile, Gordon wrote *The Exodus of the Priests: A Secularist's Dream of Better Times* (1861). It was published by Holyoake's firm, and Holyoake's endorsement of him was printed at the back: 'We consider that it will be a great advantage to Secular views if B.B.B. becomes a frequent speaker on the platform.'[28] Gordon observed that he would like the book to be the first of a series, but only if it was a commercial success.[29] Although it is possible that others followed promptly of which no trace has been found, it seems more probable that the series did not progress as planned. After settling in at Leeds, however, something more did appear: the *Counsellor* reported in October 1861 that Gordon had published *Fifty Bible Falsehoods: An Inconcordance*, but no copy of it appears to have survived.[30]

Consistent with Gordon's debut, *The Exodus of the Priest* is a deeply anticlerical piece. Seven figures are cited in the text, and only one of these is cited twice: Thomas Cooper. Cooper was well established as a reconvert by this time, but the anticlericalism of his *The Purgatory of Suicides* continued to feed Gordon's imagination. The other notes include two freethinkers, G. H. Lewes, and Henry N. Barnett, the minister at the freethinking South Place Chapel, who also apparently went on to reconvert.[31]

The conceit of *The Exodus of the Priests* is a dream of the future. In his dream, Gordon visits Britain 'hence one hundred years': that is to say, in 1960. He finds a utopia. Some of his remarks are delightfully prescient: 'the people built their houses larger and their streets

---

[27] *Reasoner*, 23 Dec. 1860, p. 416.   [28] Gordon, *Exodus*, [13].
[29] Ibid., [i].   [30] *Counsellor* (Oct. 1861), 15.
[31] For Barnett, see his entry in the Appendix.

wider.'[32] Phyiscal health is pervasive. The reason for this was that the British had forsaken spiritual remedies and theological speculations and, instead, concentrated exclusively on practical, attainable knowledge: 'Thus, instead, of praying God not to send fever among them, the people took care not to breed it in their midst.'[33] Secularism versus Christianity is presented as a kind of zero-sum game. All spiritual activity necessarily takes away from physical improvements: 'Instead of busying themselves in thought upon matters far beyond their ken, I saw the people busy with more useful and more sober studies. How to better their life on earth,—better it every way,—this was the theme on which they thought, not how to better themselves after life.'[34] The people were as greatly improved in their moral condition as in their physical. Tellingly, there were no ' "licensed" boozing-kens';[35] Gordon's 1960 is clearly one in which people are no longer damaging their health through drunkenness. Equally telling is his assertion that incentives through fear of hell or reward in heaven had been removed. People did what was right simply because it was right.

How is this remarkable transformation to be accounted for? Gordon discovered the key was that people had learned to get along without priests. The world that has been dismissed is one in which 'a fat bishop stops to tie up a rich vestment'.[36] There is one incidental attack on Christology, when Gordon observes that the people no longer wanted to be ruled by either priests or a 'fancied son of God'.[37] Along with the priests had gone the Bible. The Scriptures and the clergy had been the forces that had been hitherto holding back such an idyllic condition.[38] Gordon sees in his vision 'a band of students' find one of the few remaining copies of the Bible, and their response is, 'after musing on its monstrous "old wives' fables," long laughing at the folly of their sires.'[39] On the one hand, we might take that as a semi-autobiographical note regarding the teenage Gordon sneering at the beliefs of his orthodox seniors such as the Revd B. A. Marshall. On the other, it can be seen as a bit of false bravado: a futuristic fantasy when the Bible could be dismissed lightly. More revealing is an odd scene that comes later in the piece, in which Gordon sees this

---

[32] Gordon, *Exodus*, 2.   [33] Ibid.   [34] Ibid. 5.   [35] Ibid. 2.
[36] Ibid. 11.   [37] Ibid.   [38] Ibid. 10.   [39] Ibid.

new age being ushered in by a massive, public Bible-burning demonstration, at which he hears the joyful shouting of the participants:
'With the charred pages of "the unholy Bible," blown away, also, is
the curse that made the book a bane,—gone are the ministers that
did its bidding. Had it been safe to chain the book up, as once upon a
time it had been, perhaps that had been done again; but, knowing
that unsafe, the people burnt it.'[40] This is an astonishing tribute to his
visceral sense of the Bible's power.

During his trial period, Gordon decided to stir things up with
some sensationalism. He advertised his lectures with confrontational
placards. One found particularly objectionable by some included the
following warning: 'In consequences of the gross obscenity and vile
immorality of the quotations to be made from "The Holy Bible," (!)
ladies are respectfully requested not to attend these lectures.'[41] Such a
provocative approach not only outraged local clergymen, but also led
to a public rebuke from Holyoake in the *Reasoner*. In this article,
Holyoake affirmed again that Gordon was a man of ability, who 'has
qualities that ought to command respectful attention from the public', but he also called upon him to steer clear of 'vulgarity'.[42] In
response, the committee of the Leeds Secular Society defiantly supported their young, brash lecturer: 'this Committee not only approve
the kind of advocacy adopted by Mr. Gordon, but take upon themselves the responsibility thereof, and recommend their lecturer to the
increased confidence and support of the Society, as well as of the
cause generally.'[43] It even went so far as to remark: 'That, in consequence of the great improbability of the same, Mr. Holyoake has no
reason to be jealous of any prosecution that he may be anticipating in
Leeds.' This was unfair. Holyoake was sincerely trying to move the
movement away from the old, abusive freethinking advocacy to a
Secularism that was commendable to respectable society. Nevertheless, whether Holyoake liked it or not, throughout the nineteenth-
century popular freethinkers would increase their reputations by
pushing the boundaries in ways that would seem ill-advised to
some. Holyoake wanted the movement to go beyond this stage, but
that was only an aspiration: Bradlaugh would go on to offend some

---

[40] Ibid. 11.   [41] *Reasoner*, 10 Feb. 1861, p. 82.   [42] Ibid. 81–3.
[43] Ibid., 17 Feb. 1861, p. 107.

while winning the loyalty of many others, and G. W. Foote pursued what Holyoake disdained as 'the "sensation" line' in the early 1880s, and also thereby became a hero for many.[44]

The arrangement at Leeds went well. Gordon married, and by mid-July 1862 was living with his 'young' wife and 'one little child' at 44 Wilks Street, New Wortley, Leeds.[45] Gordon passed his trial period, and was given a one-year contract that was in due course renewed for another year. Everyone would understand that a long-term arrangement might be expected, just as it would have been for a Dissenting minister at that stage. In a year-and-a-half Gordon had taken a Secularist congregation of forty members and built it up to one of 140: an encouraging rate of growth by the standards of any denomination or movement. He was a success story illustrating what organization, energy, and commitment could achieve for the cause. B.B.B. had given 120 lectures to the Leeds Secular Society. He also found ways to speak to Secularists in other places. For example, in June 1861 he spoke to the Bramley Secular Society on 'Bible Lies and Bible Liars!'[46] A decisive event was when Gordon was invited to give a series of lectures in April 1862 at the South London Secular Society. J. B. Bebbington's *Propagandist* was polite, but cool, regarding Gordon in London. The coolness, however, may be read as a back-handed tribute to Gordon's status as a key national leader, and one who was—his rebuke notwithstanding—in the Holyoake camp. The *Propagandist* had been sniping at Holyoake in print as a way to carve out a share of the popular freethinking market for itself. Conversely, some Secularists, including Holyoake, were suspicious of Bebbington's key contributor, William Maccall, because he was a pantheist rather than an atheist. Therefore, with the aid of a little jealousy, the *Propagandist* provides a unique witness to just how unequivocally Holyoake had asserted, just a few months before his reconversion, Gordon's credentials as *the* bona fide voice of British Secularism:

The next opportunity for a fling occurred on Mr. Holyoake's taking the chair for a lecture delivered by Mr. Gordon, of Leeds, at the Hall of Science.

---

[44] *Reasoner*, 10 Feb. 1861, p. 82: for Foote, see David Nash, *Blasphemy in Modern Britain: 1789 to the Present* (Aldershot: Ashgate, 1999), chap. 4.

[45] Gordon, *Public Statement*, 23, 20; *Secular World*, 1 Aug. 1862, p. 117.

[46] *National Reformer*, 1 June 1861.

Mr. Holyoake dilated at length on the fact that Mr. Gordon was the first person who had occupied an 'official position' among the Secularists. He then complained that people occupied *that* platform, who came, no one knew whence—who went, no one knew whither—a sneer that if not intended for Mr. Maccall was not intended for any one—and recommended that none but 'official' and 'recognised' lecturers should occupy *our* platforms.[47]

A reporter for the *Propagandist* (probably either Maccall or Bebbington) heard Gordon speak at the South London Secular Society on 'The Christian Devil'. The reporter expressed a wish that it had been a learned discourse on the latest findings in the history of religions, rather than a polemical, knockabout display of populist sarcasm. It should also be added that the *Propagandist* was positioning itself as the journal that was bringing a new level of erudition to the movement. It had 'the comparative history of Religions' as one of its declared subject matters, and Maccall would himself give a lecture on the 'History of the Devil' along these lines.[48] Nevertheless, despite an instinct to keep a rival from receiving too much credit, the *Propagandist* also conceded that Gordon was a very effective public speaker.[49]

Gordon's reconversion to orthodox Christianity took place in mid-July 1862. He endeavoured to explain himself in a public lecture at the Music Hall, Leeds, on 5 August 1862 (although angry Secularists drowned him out and the effort had to be abandoned) that was then turned into a published document: *The Public Statement of Mr. J. H. Gordon, (Late Lecturer to the Leeds Secular Society,) with reference to his repudiation of secular principles, and his adoption of the Christian faith* (1862). Hitherto this chapter has relied as much as possible on documents that were created before Gordon's reconversion when explaining his beliefs and work from that period. This material may now be augmented with Gordon's own statement as a reconvert of the planks of his sceptical thinking:

---

[47] *Propagandist*, 31 May 1862, p. 25.
[48] Ibid., 3 May 1862, p. 1; 2 Aug. 1862, p. 62. It should be noticed that the *Propagandist* also reviewed Bradlaugh's performance in a debate and condemned him as well for being populist and superficial rather than more erudite and up-to-date: 4 Oct. 1862, pp. 81–3.
[49] Ibid., 3 May 1862, p. 15.

First, I concluded that the book called 'the Holy Bible' was not a divine revelation....

Second, I concluded that the Bible-God did not exist. He seemed, to my mind, such a horrible incarnation of everything foul and false, such a monstrous monster...

Third, I concluded that there was no reason for supposing, much less for believing, that *any* God existed....

Fourth, I concluded that there was no reason for supposing, much less for believing, that there was any other nature in man than that of his physical, or material, frame....

Fifth, and finally, I concluded that there was no reason for supposing, much less for believing, that there was any other life for man than that of this present, or earthly, existence.[50]

It should be observed that Washington Wilks, Gordon's original employer, also spoke from Secularist platforms.[51] It is probable that Wilks was a sort of intellectual role-model in Gordon's move into religious scepticism.

The immediate trigger for Gordon's reconversion was the visit of his mother, who dragged him along to Belgrave (Congregational) Chapel to hear its eminent minister, George William Conder (1821–74), preach on Sunday morning, 13 July 1862. Conder was a very different kind of minister from the Revd B. A. Marshall. He was a radical in politics, a resolute Dissenter, and a sworn foe of church establishments who could have said a hearty 'amen' to an outburst against clericalism. Conder was also bright, well educated, and cultured. Gordon found Conder's sermon both impressive and strikingly on target. The text came from John's gospel, where Jesus replies to the request 'shew us the Father, and it sufficeth us' with the words 'He that hath seen me hath seen the Father':

First and foremost, then, I was favourably impressed with the candid and truthful manner in which the preacher stated, with all its force of plausibility, as, also, with all its rare sincerity, the case of the Atheist, and, by so doing, my own exact position. There was no under-stating, there was no over-stating, no ridicule, no jest,—on the contrary, there was the chivalrous statement of an opponent's case, the wise comprehension of it, in noble

---

[50] Gordon, *Public Statement.*

[51] For Washington Wilks speaking at London freethinking halls, see *Secular World,* 10 May 1862, 'Freethought and Secular Societies'; *Propagandist,* 3 May 1862, p. 15.

justice, and in conscious strength. 'The Atheist,' said the preacher, 'acknow-
ledges power, beauty, use, wonder, grandeur, mystery, in the world of life
around him; but he does not see God there. "Show me the Father," he says,
"let the Father show himself, and I will instantly bow down before him, in
devoutest worship and profoundest humility."' It was this, I say,—this
wondrous statement of my own real position; so wondrous, indeed, that,
although Mr. Conder did not know of my presence, I could have sworn
almost that he preached the sermon for me, and to me, and at me!—it was
this, I say, in addition to my current dissatisfaction with Unbelief, that won
me over to the possibility of a reception of those truths the statement of
which was yet to come. Besides, I could not help asking myself the suggestive
question:—How is it that this man, evidently sincere and earnest, of greater
age and experience than myself, and of wider culture, too,—how is it that
this man, knowing the full force of my case, does not join issue with me in
the conclusion to which I come?[52]

An intense crisis of doubt ensued. Gordon struggled against the
emerging faith: 'Out upon the thought, said I; but, then, the thought
would not go out! It persisted in remaining in; and although I
summoned whole hosts of unbelieving arguments to my aid, it
seemed as if they had lost the element of their power, and as if, in
the presence of something far greater and grander, they were
unworthy of notice and regard.'[53] He preached a fiery sceptical sermon
that night—delighting his unbelieving congregation, but not succeeding in convincing himself. He wrote a confidential letter to
Conder telling him that he had been thrown off balance by his
sermon and, if he was to go forward to faith, would need answers
'to meet the thousand-and-one unbelieving difficulties that beset my
path'.[54] Conder, however, had left town for the week, and during
those days Gordon eventually made his own intellectual break-
throughs that led him to conclude that, although both faith and
scepticism were assailable, he now found the weight of truth on the
side of faith. He met with Conder as a callow convert, and then
immediately wrote a letter of resignation to the Leeds Secular Society.
    A less immediate trigger than Conder's sermon had been Gordon's
time spent in April with freethinkers in London. In his telling of it at
least, Gordon's coming for the first time to the centre of English

---

[52] Gordon, *Public Statement*, 17.   [53] Ibid. 18.   [54] Ibid. 20.

freethought from the Secularist culture of the north had a disillu-
sioning effect, something akin to the earnest monk Martin Luther's
trip to Rome. Gordon found the movement in a terrible state of
internal sniping, and hinted that he had discovered that some of the
key leaders of the movement were living immoral lives. Whether or
not Gordon was in possession of any additional gossip, it was inevitable that those most loyal to the movement at its centre would have
been at that time debating incessantly among themselves regarding
Bradlaugh's recent decision to champion George Drysdale's *Elements
of Social Science; or, Physical, Sexual, and Natural Religion*. The vast
majority of Secularists viewed this volume as advocating sexual
promiscuity, and therefore immoral.[55] Joseph Barker had parted
ways with Bradlaugh over it nine months before Gordon's trip, and
the fall-out was continuing. Far from defending Drysdale's work,
Holyoake attempted to quarantine it by referring to it in his reply to
Gordon as 'a hateful book which an enemy may have written, and
which the great majority of Secularists repudiate as much as Mr.
Barker'.[56] A couple of years later Holyoake was still trying to undo the
damage done: 'A book has been circulated which no woman in a
bookseller's shop could hand to a customer without a blush...no
one is sure that the author does not hold seduction to be a physio-
logical virtue. An enemy might have written the book—no enemy
ever could do the harm it has done. As far as we are concerned, we
have kept Secularism free from the scandal of complicity with it.'[57]
Gordon's point, however, was not whether or not individual Secularists approved or disapproved of extramarital sexual activity, but
rather whether or not Secularism provided the intellectual resources
for making such moral judgements. Gordon came to the alarming
conclusion that Secularism did not necessitate any particular moral

[55] The *Propagandist* read it as teaching 'in the language of its author, that change
and variety in love is natural' and 'a scheme of promiscuous intercourse': 6 Sept.
1862, p. 74.

[56] Leeds Secular Society, *The Converted Lecturer, or, Mr. Gordon's Repudiation of
Secular Principles Examined* (Leeds: B. Summersgill, 1862), 14. Gordon reported that
he had forced Holyoake to admit that he had authored this piece: J. H. Gordon, *Helps
to Belief; or Essays by the Way. No. 4. Just-What-You-Like-Ism. A brief explanation of
Mr. G. J. Holyoake's 'Principles of Secularism Briefly Explained.'* (Leeds: J. Hamer,
1863), 86.

[57] *Reasoner*, 1 June 1864, 'An Interval'.

convictions at all. The Leeds Secular Society affirmed three principles which it existed to promote, the second of which was: 'that natural morality is practically sufficient for the guidance of this life.'[58] Having undergone a crisis of doubt, this was precisely what Gordon no longer believed:

> I questioned myself, day after day, and week after week, until, in good time, I clearly saw that, however virtuous and worthy might be the lives of the great mass of those professing Secularists who knew next to nothing about Secularism, *the man who reduced Secularism to its logical conclusions, the man who practised the philosophy of its precepts, was a man who could justify any action it was his pleasure to commit, and who, under cover of that justification, could make any action pleasing in his sight!*... True... I had frequently prepared and delivered whole passages of moral inculcation... but... that recollection only tended to show me that, as a Secularist, I had no more business, or right, to rank such inculcation under the head of a lecture on Secularism than I had to rank it under the head of a lecture on Hydrostatics...[59]

Gordon denounced Secularism as 'just-what-you-like-ism', that is, as a system in which one could justify any action that was deemed desirable, and he wrote a whole pamphlet expounding this theme in June 1863.[60] In it, he argued that the only authority that Secularists recognized was 'self', and that was a recipe for immoral self-indulgence: 'men and women must have guidance, control, a standard of right and wrong, a something to quicken and culture all that is good within them, and a something to neutralise and destroy all that is depraved and gross. Any system, however, that throws a man back upon himself, and bids him seek all direction and guidance there, is not the system wanted; and Secularism, or Just-what-you-like-ism, is such a system.'[61] Fascinatingly, *Just-What-You-Like-Ism* takes the form of an attack on Holyoake's *Principles of Secularism Briefly Examined*. Although put forward as the official statement of the movement's aims, its 'Bible' as it were, Gordon found it to be a totally inadequate guide for living. One wonders if he thought David King had the better side of the argument when he had himself

---

[58] *Counsellor* (Nov. 1861), 'Code of Rules of the Leeds Secular Society'.
[59] Gordon, *Public Statement*, 13–15.   [60] Gordon, *Just-What-You-Like-Ism*.
[61] Ibid. 93.

put Holyoake's book up as the authorized Secularist target for a Christian to shoot at, while he, in turn, attacked the Scriptures. Gordon's *Just-What-You-Like-Ism* is a kind of redeployment of the anti-Bible strategies of popular radicals, complete with pedantic and ungenerous close readings. Gordon begins by observing that there are only 1,713 lines in Holyoake's pamphlet. Then he systematically whittles down this number. For example, 394 of these lines are quotations, many of them from orthodox writers or the Bible itself. Many of them are merely about organizational matters rather than principles—and so on. From today's perspective, it is a rather grating approach. Nevertheless, the intellectual point is a sincere one: Gordon had come to see the Secularist movement as a sort of carping opposition party which had no alternative vision, solutions, or positive way forward to offer. Holyoake was well aware of this concern and was actively working to make Secularism something constructive, but Gordon no longer thought this project could succeed.

The other intellectual breakthrough that Gordon describes as fundamental to his Christian conversion was a realization that an oppressive commitment to reason, too narrowly construed, had led him to preclude realities that were actually justifiable. 'Mere logic' was too ruthless a filter; it did not let in much that was true. He came to replace it with a wider criterion, 'the standpoint of the entire Consciousness': 'Down went my reason to its own proper place and level,—it had had a long period of prideful usurpation,—and up came my Inner Consciousness ... Mark you, I had accepted nothing contrary to my reason, nor had I accepted anything which required the undue subjection of my reason; but I had accepted many things to which my reason could not rise ...'[62] With the gatekeeper of 'mere logic' removed, he was able to replace unbelief, 'cold and cheerless as an iceberg', with a Christian belief that answered 'to the highest wants of human life ... distinctively and instinctively appealing to the stillest, but deepest, voices of man's nature'.[63]

Bradlaugh immediately challenged Gordon to a debate,[64] but the latter pleaded that he was not yet a strong enough Christian to defend his new position in public combat. With endearing

---

[62] Gordon, *Public Statement*, 24–5.   [63] Ibid. 31.
[64] *National Reformer*, 2 Aug. 1862, 'To John Henry Gordon, of Leeds'.

candour, he even acknowledged that he still felt the force of sceptical objections:

> I can tell you how, ever and anon, my old unbelieving arguments come back upon me, and that with fearful force... Indeed, I tell you candidly that it would be a fatal mistake to suppose that a change of mind, such as that through which I have just passed, can, all at once, pervade the life of the convert.... For me, therefore, to stand upon a public platform, and, thus early, to advocate, or discuss, those things which I have only just come to know, would be, in very truth, as pretentious as my past advocacy has been, and almost as mistaken. On the contrary, I must permit myself,—and this, with His help, I hope to do,—to outgrow the Past of unbelief, and grow into the Present of belief, more thoroughly and assured.[65]

He gave his 'Public Statement' (or tried to at any rate) and had had it published because the members of the Leeds Secular Society in particular had a right to an explanation of his change of views.

Gordon did, however, publish several works of apologetics, under the general title *Helps to Belief* (1863). He counted his *Public Statement* (published in 1862) as the first of these, and *Just-What-You-Like-Ism* was the fourth. The second essay in the series was entitled *Earnest Appeal to Secularists*, and was dated 21 February 1863, that is, seven months after his Christian conversion. In it, he argued that true freethinkers should have an open mind about the claims of Christianity as well. He implored them to distinguish between Christianity itself and the sometimes discreditable behaviour of people who might claim to be Christians. It is irrational 'to condemn Christianity because of offences which, instead of sanctioning, it condemns'.[66] He appealed to them to look to the wants of their own nature, and to give Christianity a fair trial. Perhaps with a nod to the continuing fall-out from Bradlaugh's support for Drysdale's book, he observed: 'I know, indeed, that large numbers of you are far from being satisfied with the party, so-called to which you belong.'[67]

Corroborations of Christianity: a short series of commonly-received disproofs shown to be a convincing series of positive proofs was the third

---

[65] Gordon, *Public Statement*, 29–30.

[66] J. H. Gordon, *Helps to Belief; or, Essays by the Way, No. 2—Earnest Appeal to Secularists. No. 3.—Corroborations of Christianity* (Leeds: J. Hamer, 1863), 37 (the pagination is continuous across both essays).

[67] Gordon, *Earnest Appeal*, 46.

essay in the series. In this piece Gordon took arguments used by
Secularists against Christianity and endeavoured to demonstrate that
they actually were evidence in its favour. Secularists, for example,
claimed that people often convert to Christianity in the face of
sickness, misfortune, or death, implying thereby that it was a matter
of emotional duress rather than rational enquiry. Gordon countered
that such times in life were actually 'when men are best able, and
most ready, to realise their actual position as men'.[68] Much of this
essay is taken up with the question of errors in the Bible. Bradlaugh
wondered if Gordon had found answers for all of his *Fifty Bible
Falsehoods* and 'all difficulties' of the text.[69] Gordon, however, maintained that he now realized that a prejudicial frame of mind caused
Secularists to manufacture biblical discrepancies. He laughed at
himself for having once pressed home as a contradiction the fact
that Exodus 12:40 speaks of the Israelites being in Egypt for 430 years,
while Acts 7:6 refers to 400 years (a criticism, incidentally, that
Bradlaugh persisted in using).[70] The Bible's verisimilitude was only
reinforced by the discovery of the existence of some discrepancies in
the text, Gordon argued. When inventing a story, one is careful to
keep it consistent, but 'a number of simple witnesses to the truth'
often have details in their various accounts that seem irreconcilable.
Furthermore, every great culture's distilled proverbial wisdom contains prima facie contradictory statements for the simple reason that
reality is complex. In short, the former lecturer for the Leeds Secular
Society testified, arguments that he once thought were decisive
against Christianity he now viewed as evidence in its favour.

To return to the immediate aftermath of Gordon's conversion,
Secularist leaders, as one could predict, immediately sought to discredit him. There were five responses that were reflexively made
against almost any reconvert by their erstwhile freethinking com-
rades: that the change had happened too suddenly to be intellectually
credible; that they were insincere; that they were seeking pecuniary
advantages; that they had proven themselves to be an unworthy ally

---

[68] Gordon, *Corroborations*, 53.

[69] *National Reformer*, 2 Aug. 1862, 'To John Henry Gordon, of Leeds'.

[70] Gordon, *Corroborations*, 56; Charles Bradlaugh, *The Bible: What It Is* (London:
Austin, 1870), 14; Timothy Larsen, *Contested Christianity: The Political and Social
Contexts of Victorian Theology* (Waco, Tex.: Baylor University Press, 2004), 106.

and it was good to see them go; and that they had never been a true freethinker or had not been very important to the movement. Naturally, some of these charges fit some cases better than others, but they tended to be all initially tried on for size with a new reconvert. Gordon's conversion was a rather short process, and therefore the 'suddenness' charge is a reasonable one to make in his case. Nevertheless, it is telling that Bradlaugh's response before hearing any of the facts of the case was to write in his public letter to Gordon: 'probably your conversion has been very sudden.'[71] The 'probably' betrays the predisposition to assume this was always the case. Once the facts were out, Holyoake was on delightfully good form with this point, sounding almost like a son of the Puritans bemoaning modern piety: 'Conversion...used to be a serious and protracted affair of time, of doubt, of remorse, of agony, of obvious contrition, of gradual change of thought and of life. Now it is an affair of a week. It can be got up to order. A converted soul is now turned off the modern lathes of Christianity as round, as smooth, as polished, as perfected, and as promptly as the latest machine by Haberzettel, or Sharp and Roberts could accomplish it.'[72]

As to the other charges, some effort was made to downplay how important Gordon had been to the movement. The *Propagandist* was in the best position to do this, because it had been annoyed at how Holyoake had stressed Gordon's uniquely official status. Its article on Gordon's conversion was entitled, 'Much Ado About Nothing'. 'Mr. Gordon is a very small personage indeed', it pronounced dismissively.[73] This pose was somewhat undermined, however, by the fact that, having ended the article with the words, 'really the affair is not worth further notice', even the *Propagandist* itself could not resist coming back to the story.[74] Holyoake himself tried to weaken the claim that Gordon was in the only official position in the movement, despite having been the primary promoter of such a notion. Holyoake rather pathetically pointed to the fact that the Sunday Institute, Philadelphia, also employed a resident lecturer.[75]

[71] *National Reformer*, 2 Aug. 1862, 'To John Henry Gordon, of Leeds'.
[72] Leeds Secular Society, *Converted Lecturer*, 5.
[73] *Propagandist*, 2 Aug. 1862, pp. 55–6.
[74] Ibid., 6 Sept. 1862, p. 73.
[75] Leeds Secular Society, *Converted Lecturer*, 9.

The standard charge that all reconverts must be motivated by a
desire to gain Christian money and resources was also made, despite
the fact that Gordon, unlike virtually all other Secularist lecturers,
had a secure Secularist salary and a contract that had just been
renewed. P. Newsome wrote an article on Gordon's Christian conversion for the *National Reformer* in which he declared that he had
made this change 'probably because there is less fodder in the fold of
Secularism than in the fold of Christ'.[76] Once again, we have that
revealing word 'probably'. Newsome reprinted a short and perfectly
straightforward and innocuous letter that Gordon wrote to the
Christian ministers of Leeds, informing them that he had accepted
Christianity and resigned his position. Gordon had sent them all a
circular as a Secularist lecturer—presumably putting out a standing
challenge to debate any local Christian minister—and he therefore
now felt it was his duty to inform them of his change of views and
rescind the prior missive. Nevertheless, Newsome was determined to
read this announcement as a quest for income, adding for good
measure the corollary standard assumption that Gordon was disingenuous: 'After this "petition" to the clergy and "advertisement" to
the public, that he is "to let," I have no doubt he will meet with that
encouragement he deserves; and that the thing might answer. Let
those think John Henry Gordon in his new character honest and
sincere that will, it is more than I am willing, at present, to admit.' He
was in no sense, 'to let', however, and such a status would have been a
retrograde step from a salaried position. Holyoake also made a half-
hearted attempt at the pecuniary-necessity charge by attempting to
magnify a recommendation by some members of the board of the
Leeds Secular Society that Gordon tone down his tirades into a hint
that his position might have been less secure than it seemed.[77] As
Holyoake was writing anonymously on behalf of the Leeds Secular
Society, however, if there was merit to such an argument it could
have been made much stronger as a simple report of the direction in
which the committee had been heading, or at least of the convictions
of some of its members at the time. As it was, Holyoake could not
report that even a single member of the committee had so much as

---

[76] *National Reformer*, 2 Aug. 1862, 'Mr. Gordon A "Christian Brother." '
[77] Gordon, *Converted Lecturer*, 23.

privately entertained the idea that the society might be better off without Gordon as its lecturer.

The main response by freethinkers to Gordon's reconversion was to claim that he had been a liability and therefore it was a relief to see him go. Holyoake's *Secular World* printed Gordon's letter announcing his reconversion in full in a piece headlined 'Fortunate Conversion of Mr. Gordon'.[78] The letter was introduced with the words, 'We read with great satisfaction the following letter', and was followed with the words, 'We hope this is true'. The reason given for such a judgement was, 'if Mr. Gordon preaches Christianity with the extravagance he did Secularism, he will be a better Secular missionary than he ever has been'. Gordon was dismissed as having been too inflammatory a proponent of the freethinking cause. At the centre of this charge was the fact that the Leeds Secular Society committee had vetoed three titles for lectures of his that Gordon wanted to advertise on placards: 'The Bloody Word of God', 'What shall I do to be Damned?', and 'Bible Lies and Bible Liars'.[79] The second, of course, was a witty inversion of a standard biblical text for evangelistic sermons, 'What must I do to be saved?' (Acts 16:30). Fascinatingly, in 1882 G. W. Foote's *Freethinker* helped to establish its credentials as a heroic champion of the cause by running an article with that very same title.[80] 'Iconoclast' also took this tack in the *National Reformer*, cataloguing a series of statements Gordon had made that he deemed counter-productive in their gratuitous offensiveness. Gordon once claimed that Jesus was a thief, as he 'used to help himself to other people's jackasses'. Gordon also had brushed aside 'the immaculate conception' (by which, in the context of Victorian shibboleths, must have been meant the doctrine of the virgin birth of Christ rather than Mariology) as a 'vulgar tale'.[81] No doubt some of the more senior leaders in the movement did think that Gordon said some imprudent things occasionally, and we have seen that Holyoake even went so far as to rebuke him in print. Still, the movement in general, and

---

[78] *Secular World*, 1 Aug. 1862, 'Fortunate Conversion of Mr. Gordon'.

[79] Ibid., 1 Dec. 1862, 'Extraordinary Sale at Belgrave Chapel'; Leeds Secular Society, *Converted Lecturer*, 8.

[80] David Nash, *Blasphemy in Modern Britain: 1789 to the Present* (Aldershot: Ashgate, 1999), 129.

[81] *National Reformer*, 2 Aug. 1862, 'To John Henry Gordon, of Leeds'.

Holyoake in particular, had chosen to continue to stand by him and promote him. As we have seen, just months before Gordon's change of views Holyoake was on record endorsing him to the point of exciting jealousy. No one claimed that Gordon's approach had suddenly become unduly crude in the few months leading up to his conversion, and some of Bradlaugh's evidence for this charge came from B.B.B.'s debate with King back in 1860. It is indisputable that John Henry Gordon was a major Secularist leader in good standing at the time of his reconversion.

As with so many reconverts, Gordon came to the conviction that he was called to be a Christian minister. He wisely concluded that he would need to be taught before he could teach, and therefore entered a training programme at Cavendish College, Manchester, an institution founded and led by the Congregational minister Joseph Parker, who would later become the celebrated pastor of City Temple, London.[82] Gordon was reconnecting with the denomination of his youth and that of his guide back to the land of faith, G. W. Conder. Still, intellectual honesty sometimes disrupts a smooth path ahead, as this study amply shows. In the course of his theological studies Gordon became convinced that it was inappropriate to baptize infants. He had to abandon the contacts he had built up and find his way into a new denominational context—not the move of someone with his eye on lucre. Gordon was baptized as a believer by a leading Baptist minister in Manchester, Alexander MacLaren. Gordon built up a reputation as a preacher and was called to be the pastor of Astley Bridge Baptist Church in Lancashire. His ministry there was a success, and he gained some additional good-will by also giving popular lectures. In 1865 he accepted a call to a Baptist church in Darlington, and settled in that town thereafter.

In 1870, when King debated with Bradlaugh, he not surprisingly made much of Gordon's reconversion, quoting his *Public Statement*

---

[82] The details about Gordon in this paragraph are based on two obituaries written by 'H.D.B.': *Baptist Handbook* (1879), 311–12; *Baptist Magazine* (1878), 547–54. 'H.D.B.' was almost certainly the Baptist minister Henry David Brown (1844–1906). Brown became a Baptist minister in Darlington in 1874, and therefore presumably was Gordon's successor when he moved from the full-time pastorate to itinerant lecturing for the Liberation Society.

at length.[83] In 1873–4 we find him billed as 'Pastor Gordon' of Darlington, and engaging in an epistolary debate with an Anglican clergyman on the issue of church establishments.[84] Gordon gained public attention in Darlington on the issue of disestablishment. Local clergymen had arranged to give a series of lectures in defence of the state church. Gordon reportedly gave a reply that was so devastating that the rest of the series was abandoned. The clergymen regrouped and decided to bring in outside talent, the Revd Dr Massingham. Gordon took him on as well, in a packed town-hall: 'On that occasion Mr. Gordon achieved a signal victory, and his enthusiastic friends presented him with a valuable timepiece and a purse of one hundred sovereigns.'[85] This was a foreshadowing of his final career.

In 1874 Gordon published *Thoughts for the Million; or Buds, Blossoms, and Berries.*[86] The book is a list of 1,000 original sayings and pithy thoughts. It is hard to imagine who might enjoy reading them today, but it is not unreasonable to assume that some Victorians found them thought-provoking and pleasing. Some of these sayings had originally appeared in a leading Baptist journal, the *Freeman*, others in C. H. Spurgeon's *Sword and Trowel*. The latter were in a series Gordon entitled, 'Free-thoughts', the perfect mirror-image response to his freethinking 'In Fidelity'. A pre-eminent American minister, Henry Ward Beecher, praised Gordon's aphorisms in the *Christian Union*, underlining the fact that they might have been deemed striking in their day. Many of them explicitly address doubt and doubters. Number 934 arguably reflects the seasoned life perspective of a reconvert: 'The garments of truth, as we are obliged to wear them (in sizes, that is, to suit us), are like children's pinafores, and consist, very largely, of certain deep hems, or tucks, which may be let out, as we grow older, and, though looking new, are not new— except to our visible experiences.'[87] Gordon had been seeking to publish some of these sayings as early as 1865, and when a selection

---

[83] King and Bradlaugh, *Christianity v. Secularism,* 47–9.

[84] S. G. Potter and J. H. Gordon, *'Church and State.' Controversy between the Rev. S. G. Potter, D.D., and 'Pastor Gordon,' in fourteen letters* (London: W. Macintosh, 1874).

[85] *Baptist Handbook* (1879), 311.

[86] John Henry Gordon, *Thoughts for the Million; or, Buds, Blossoms, and Berries* (London: Haughton & Co., 1874).

[87] Gordon, *Thoughts,* 143.

first appeared in the *Freeman* in 1869 he expressed a hope that, if readers welcomed them, they would make 'an invalid pastor' feel 'not altogether useless'.[88] On at least one occasion, in 1876, Gordon was identified in the press as 'author of "Thoughts for the Million", &c.'.[89]

Gordon recovered from whatever made him an invalid in 1869. Before addressing the final stage of his career, it will be useful to tell of some occasional debates and of his end. In the winter of 1875 Gordon gave a series of anti-Unitarian lectures in Darlington's townhall: 'The hold he continued to maintain on the public was then very apparent, for the hall was crowded night after night.'[90] Sometime during the second half of 1876 Gordon accepted Bradlaugh's challenge to a debate: he was a mature Christian now, who knew his mind on the matter and how to argue it. The debate was on atheism and took place in Darlington: 'The two opposite camps once more mustered their adherents in great force, so that this debate proved one of the most memorable of his many conflicts.'[91] There was no shorthand reporter, and therefore no transcript.[92] Gordon's health was clearly deteriorating in the first months of 1878: in the classic Victorian manner this is put down to overwork. Gordon decided that he needed a change of pace and scene to recover, and determined on a trip to America. His condition worsened as the voyage progressed, and he died in mid-passage on 10 March 1878. The last thing he wrote on the ship was 'of a devotional character'. He was 40 years old, and left behind his wife and their six children. Gordon's funeral was attended by representations from a variety of Christian organizations. A fund of £1,100 was raised in order to assist his family.

Let us end, however, with John Henry Gordon the brash polemicist in action. In 1876 he can be found as a full-time lecturer for the Liberation Society. The Society's primary objective was to see the Church of England disestablished, and it was waging a heated controversy with those churchmen who deeply feared and bitterly

---

[88] Gordon, *Thoughts*, [iii].

[89] In the *Nottingham and Midland Counties Express*, as reprinted in the *Nonconformist*, 1 Nov. 1876, p. 1079.

[90] *Baptist Magazine* (Dec. 1878), 550.

[91] Ibid.

[92] Hypatia Bradlaugh Bonner, *Charles Bradlaugh: His Life and Work* (London: T. Fisher Unwin, 1895), ii. 47.

resented this assault. Gordon needed the capacity to withstand the hatred of an opposing group that was also a prerequisite of the Secularist cause. A natural joy in iconoclasm and polemics would also serve him in good stead. As he toured the country, his meetings not infrequently provoked violent clashes.

A report of some comments he made at a meeting on 18 December 1876 in Torquay capture well the contours of his work: 'The lecturer was bound to say that his experience of Liberation meetings, and it averaged five or six meetings a week, was that a great many of their meetings were packed with roughs... Why, he was there, the survivor of half a hundred broken-up meetings; and he had been met much more by the argument of force than the force of argument.'[93] Ample examples may be found from just the four months leading up to that statement. Reminiscent of Bradlaugh's itinerancy experiences, in Ashby de la Zouch 'Mr. Gordon appeared on the green, every place of meeting having been emphatically refused'.[94] At Long Eaton, Derbyshire, the platform was stormed and Gordon's supporters 'literally dragged him out by a door behind, and into the graveyard', to spare him from assault. At Failsworth, near Manchester, the meeting was successfully broken up by a massive infusion of the air with cayenne pepper: 'in a few minutes everybody in the place was coughing, some persons very violently.'[95] In Darlington it was a firecracker.[96] The meeting was rescheduled, and did complete its programme with the help of the attendance of the superintendant of police and several officers, but nevertheless: 'Mr. Gordon had to be guarded to his cab, in a back street, which took a roundabout way home.'[97] In Egremont, Cumberland, he was threatened by Orangemen, but the meeting was saved by the police being called for and arriving promptly.[98] Gordon had an 'uproarious' meeting in Southport, at which his audience was packed with churchmen determined to keep him from speaking. Eventually the platform was stormed. In

[93] *Nonconformist*, 28 Dec. 1876, 'Mr. Gordon At Torquay'.
[94] Ibid., 27 Sept. 1876, 'Mr. Gordon Again in Leicestershire'.
[95] Ibid., 31 Oct. 1876, 'Mr. Gordon in Derbyshire' (also includes the Failsworth report).
[96] Ibid., 25 Oct. 1876, 'The Disestablishment Movement'.
[97] Ibid., 1 Nov. 1876, 'The Disestablishment Movement'.
[98] Ibid., 8 Nov. 1876, 'Mr. Gordon's Lectures'.

a deft piece of anticlerical writing, the *Nonconformist* reported: 'One rev. gentlemen, whose fine condition said much for the excellent pastures of the Establishment, pressed on with the recklessness which despair sometimes inspires.' Once again, the police had to be called for to restore order.[99]

Gordon was now in complete accord with an orthodox branch of English Christianity, Dissenters such as Congregationalists (his parent's and Conder's denomination), Baptists (his own), and others. The Liberation Society was supported by many leading evangelical Nonconformist ministers, including the most popular preacher of the age, C. H. Spurgeon. Indeed, G. W. Conder was a very strong and active supporter.[100] On the other hand, the Secularist movement also thought that Gordon was by this time back on the side of the right in a significant way. The *Secular Chronicle* ran as its lead story in its 31 December 1876 issue an article on Gordon entitled 'An Old Acquaintance', written by Francis Neale. It is useful to present in detail this remarkably glowing report of his Liberation Society work:

The Rev. J. H. Gordon, once upon a time, considered himself to be a Secular lecturer. He was a speaker not altogether devoid of ability, and judging from what he is now, he might have done Secularism good service had he remained with us . . .

The other week, a lecturer, engaged by the Society for the Liberation of Religion from State Patronage and Control, visited Newcastle-under-Lyne, to deliver a lecture in the Town Hall against the State Church. Much to my surprise, the lecturer turned out to be none other but our old acquaintance, Mr. Gordon. Since 1862, he seems to have improved intellectually, and in justice to him it may be said that his Liberation lectures at Newcastle, and subsequently at Longton, Tunstall, Chesterton and Silverdale were exceedingly good. They were well calculated to arouse the indifferent, though perhaps they were too outspoken to conciliate or persuade Churchmen. If Mr. Gordon confines himself to this kind of work, he will have the sympathy of all true friends of progress. So far as his Newcastle lecture is concerned, an 'old inhabitant' of the borough informs me that there has not been so stormy a meeting in Newcastle for years. An infuriated cleric brought to

---

[99] *Nonconformist*, 22 Nov. 1876, 'The Disestablishment Movement: Uproarious Meeting at Southport'.

[100] For Conder and the Liberation Society, see Timothy Larsen, *Friends of Religious Equality: Nonconformist Politics in Mid-Victorian England* (Woodbridge, Suffolk: Boydell, 1999).

the meeting about twenty sturdy forgemen from Knutton, and the noise they created was something terrific.[101]

In other words, Gordon was just as forceful as a public agitator at the end of his career as he had been toward the beginning: he was still 'too outspoken' for some; he was still arousing fury; he was still marshalling all the facts and taking no prisoners. 'Since 1862, he seems to have improved intellectually' may be taken as a statement that he had a keen mind that he was not neglecting, something that a less biased witness might credit as equally true in all phases of his adult life, whether arguing for or against Christianity, for or against Secularism. With his Liberation Society work, he was in many ways keeping faith with the anticlericalism that had launched him into the world of organized unbelief. He was still attacking figures like the Revd B. A. Marshall. As a Liberation Society lecturer he could go with the grain of his polemical, confrontational, baiting, iconoclastic, and anticlerical tendencies even after he had shed a Secularist mentality. John Henry Gordon's own combative temperament, as well as his intellectual rigour and honesty, were on display both when he was a Secularist leader and when he was a Christian minister.

---

[101] *Secular Chronicle*, 31 Dec. 1876, 'An Old Acquaintance'. A Baptist author, one might say, returned the compliment by acknowledging that as a Secularist spokesman Gordon had possessed a 'mastery of repartee, which gave him many advantages over his opponents'. *Baptist Handbook* (1879), 311.

6

Joseph Barker

Although he would later come to accept the possibility of communication with disembodied spirits, at the age of 40 Joseph Barker (1806–75) certainly did not believe in seeing fairies. In Barker's midlife autobiography, the pixies are conjured up merely to evoke the unlearned environs of his youth which he had to overcome by the force of his commitment to self-education: 'My parents were both believers in witchcraft and fairies, as well as in some other superstitions.'[1] He was born in Bramley, a town near Leeds, on 11 May 1806. His father was in the militia and totally illiterate when he married his mother. His father settled into employment in the woollen industry, and Barker grew up 'in extreme poverty', the fifth of eleven children.[2] Barker's father did teach himself to read and write, but the world of learning opened no wider. His parents were deeply religious Methodists, but not analytical thinkers: 'They knew nothing of theology, nothing of controversy.'[3] Barker's formal schooling came from the Sunday school. As a child he was a firm believer in Christianity, but his enquiring mind was also already on display. When his mother would rebuke him for bad behaviour, he was apt to vex her by 'asking puzzling questions about religion, and speaking as if I entertained doubts with respect to some of its doctrines'.[4]

Barker's mental culture was rising above his context, a point he drives home haughtily by displaying for purposes of ridicule

---

[1] J. T. Barker (ed.), *The Life of Joseph Barker, Written by Himself* (London: Hodder & Stoughton, 1880), 19–21. I am citing from this source for convenience, but it should be noted that this portion of it is a faithful republication of a source written and printed before his reconversion: [Joseph Barker], *The History and Confessions of a Man, as put forth by Himself* (Wortley: J. Barker, 1846).
[2] Barker, *Life*, 28. [3] Ibid. 14. [4] Ibid. 39.

infelicitous phrases that he had heard working-class people use in public prayer.[5] Likewise, Barker, though writing at the age of 40, took juvenile delight in recounting examples of incompetent preaching that he had heard, sometimes even supplying the name of the speaker.[6]

In his 1846 autobiography, after the chapter on 'Religious Experience' comes one, as if as a sort of antidote, on 'Books and Reading'.[7] Reading material was hard to come by, but he was thirsty for secular as well as religious knowledge.[8] Around the age of 16, Barker took on the task of learning Greek and Latin in order to open up further vistas of reading and knowledge.[9] He was working twelve to sixteen hours a day as a wool-spinner, but contrived to read whenever possible.

Some kind, educated Methodist preachers in the area also agreed to tutor him, loaned him books, and alerted him to important authors (including his first encounter with Shakespeare). This scholarly mentoring Barker eloquently described as a kind of conversion experience:

I felt as if I had risen from the rank of nothingness to that of being: I felt as if I really was a man, or destined to be one, and as if the world had not been made in vain. I felt as if I had been an outcast from the world before, an outcast from the world of thoughtful, intellectual, honourable men, and as if I was now admitted within its circle. It was, in fact, a new era in my history; it was like the commencement of a new life to me, or of a new feeling of life.[10]

Ill-health—Barker indicates it was brought on by excessive studying—began to interfere with his work, and therefore his father allowed him to go to a school run by a Methodist in Leeds. Here whole libraries were greedily consumed, including Wesley's fifty-volume 'Christian Library'. As to classical learning, the Latin authors

---

[5] Ibid. 49.
[6] Ibid. 121.
[7] Barker, *History and Confessions*, 116 (for chapter title).
[8] Barker, *Life*, 56.
[9] For the wider context of this theme of plebeian reading, see a stimulating study that includes Barker in its large cast: Jonathan Rose, *The Intellectual Life of the British Working Classes* (New Haven: Yale University Press, 2001).
[10] Barker, *Life*, 73.

mentioned by name are Virgil, Ovid, Horace, Cicero, Florus, Justin, Sallust, Livy, Tacitus, and Seneca.

Barker was an earnest Christian—marked out as more gifted than his peers—and he was soon launched upon a preaching ministry. The first step was a kind of local Methodist mutual improvement society for young men who wanted to practise the art of sermonizing. Barker greatly impressed this aspiring band with a gruesome oration on eternal torment. He then worked his way up the system, first being acknowledged as an exhorter and being sent to carry God's word to out-of-the-way places, and then graduating to the rank of local preacher on trial. His trial sermon, however, was written under the influence of Grotius's *The Truth of the Christian Religion*. Its erudition aroused the suspicions of the adjudicating ministers, and he was not approved at that time. His next trial sermon was much plainer, but it did have a speculative passage that was considered not quite sound. Barker was accepted this time, albeit on the understanding that he would think again about that dubious point. He was on his way to the status of travelling preacher, but he was also chafing against the Wesleyan leadership, finding it restricting both in its practical power and in the tight way that it delineated certain doctrinal boundaries.

Barker then encountered the Methodist New Connexion. He was attracted to its claim to represent 'the rights and liberties of the people', while simultaneously gaining a growing conviction that Wesleyan polity 'seemed all unscriptural and tyrannical'.[11] One also suspects that Barker had surmised that he had blotted his copy-book with the Wesleyan leadership, and needed a fresh start if he was to get on. The new denomination accepted him in 1828 and he became a travelling preacher with them. His relationships with his superiors were not always easy here, either. Barker's view was that the superintendents were apt to be jealous of the young preachers, and no doubt the superintendents deemed rising ministers such as Barker to be arrogant, reckless, and lacking in deference. Barker clashed with his superintendent when he was stationed at Newcastle under Lyme.

---

[11] Barker, *Life*, 103–4. For the New Connexion, see Timothy Larsen, *Contested Christianity: The Political and Social Contexts of Victorian Theology* (Waco, Tex.: Baylor University Press, 2004), 133–43.

He irritated the superintendent to the point that he went so far as to have Barker's rooms secretly searched for anything that might discredit him. The best he could come up with was reading material that did not seem particularly in line with the learning necessary for the calling of a Methodist preacher, 'the works of Lord Byron and the works of Shakespeare'.[12]

Barker was a powerful personality, with an active mind and great energy. He was continually throwing himself into new causes and controversies. Throughout his life he had the capacity to gather disciples and inspire followers. He was also a compelling speaker. Though considerably younger than the denomination's official leaders, Barker became one of the most popular ministers in the New Connexion. When he was scheduled to preach, the congregations were significantly larger than usual. He was sought after to be the speaker at special events. Barker was assigned to Blyth for the year 1831–2, and doubled the size of the society there in that year. For the rest of that decade, when it came time to assign new circuits Barker was a prize to be vied for.

One of Barker's causes in the 1830s was refuting the anti-Christian views of infidels, especially Owenite reformers, who were also the popular champions of Socialism as well as religious scepticism at the time. At one point in his early career he had a neighbour who was an atheist. This man lent him a copy of the *Republican*, a journal by the most prominent plebeian sceptical leader of the time, Richard Carlile.[13] This neighbour also agreed to hear Barker preach if he would attempt a refutation of atheism. Barker brushed up on his apologetics and duly delivered the requested sermon. While he was stationed in Sheffield in 1833–5 Carlile himself came to lecture there. Barker penned a refutation, *Carlile's Logic*. Barker's real fame as an anti-Socialist debater came once he moved to Gateshead in 1839. He took on the local Socialist society in Newcastle upon Tyne in well-attended debates: 'The news of these meetings ran quickly through the country, and I was invited to lecture on Christianity and Socialism in all the principal towns in the North of England.'[14]

---

[12] Barker, *Life*, 116–17.
[13] For Carlile, see his entry in the Appendix.
[14] Barker, *Life*, 249, 251.

A debate that Barker had with the Owenite lecturer Lloyd Jones (who apparently later himself reconverted), at Oldham in February 1839, can serve to indicate his thinking at that time.[15] Barker set as a condition: 'That in the debate nothing shall be taken for Christianity but the system of Jesus Christ, as laid down in the New Testament.'[16] This is telling, as Barker's growing anti-creedal biblicism would soon lead him down a path with surprising twists. Jones argued that Christianity led to persecution. As well as putting forward the rejection of persecution as the teaching of the Bible, Barker also argued from world experience, claiming that America and England were both the countries where the New Testament was most widely read and obeyed and the ones most free of persecution: 'The sect called Quakers attend more, perhaps, to the spirit and precepts of the Gospel', and there are no persecuting members of the Society of Friends.[17] When Jones denounced the intolerance of the bishops at the Council of Nicaea—the architects of orthodox doctrine— Barker cheerfully agreed with him, even denying that they were real Christians.[18] Most tellingly, in the light of his later views, Barker was willing to assert a high view of biblical inspiration: 'there are no such things as discrepancies in the Gospel from beginning to end. . . . I am prepared to prove the statement at a proper time,— that the New Testament contains no discrepancies; but that its teachings, from end to end, are all in perfect agreement.'[19] Even more strongly: 'Indeed, there was a time when I looked at Christianity as it is misrepresented by infidels and false pretenders to Christianity, and I had almost turned infidel myself; but, thank God, I went to the fountain head; I read the New Testament. . . The New Testament has truth without any mixture of error for its contents . . .'[20]

---

[15] For Lloyd Jones as a reconvert, see his entry in the Appendix.
[16] *The Influence of Christianity. Report of the Public Discussion which took place at Oldham, . . . February 19th and 20th, 1839, between the Rev. J. Barker . . . and Mr. Lloyd Jones, Of Manchester, Social Missionary* (Manchester: Cave & Sever, 1839), 4.
[17] Ibid. 20.
[18] Ibid. 34.
[19] Ibid. 44.
[20] Ibid. 116–17.

As to the intellectual strength of sceptical thought, Barker averred:

I have read the objections of Porphyry, of Celsus, of Julian, of Hobbes, of Toland, of Tindal, of Blount, of Woolston, of Hume, of Gibbon, of Burdon, of Paine, of Voltaire, of Rousseau, of Diderot, of Helvetius, of Carlile, of Taylor, of Owen, of Lloyd Jones, and of Haslam, and they are all alike. Arguments there are none; but false accusations, bold and extravagant statements, without truth or foundation, there are in abundance.[21]

Far from Christianity being opposed to an enquiring mind, Barker asserted: 'I have proved that the Gospel is a system of liberty throughout; that it does not forbid free inquiry, but commands it; that it requires no blind faith, but such only as has truth and proper evidence to rest upon.'[22] Moreover, Barker counter-charged that Socialism promoted immorality—blaming 'the prevalence of prostitution' on 'the filthy working of infidel and licentious principles'— and claiming that 'all that the Socialists ever propose to do is to form you into a community, and furnish you with animal and sensual indulgences'.[23] He also told stories of leading sceptics who had abandoned their wives, taken mistresses, and the like. Barker's concern for morality is evident throughout the debate. He also argued that Christians are better able to face death, and that Christianity had advanced the cause of equality for women. Barker would keep these outcomes as litmus tests throughout his life, whether arguing that Christianity passed or failed when judged by these standards.

Meanwhile, Barker's growing popularity as a controversialist was only fuelling his tendency to defy denominational authorities and shibboleths. It began to trouble him that the word 'Trinity' does not occur in Scripture. His moralism seemed to chafe against the standard evangelical expositions of such doctrines as justification by faith, original sin, and the atonement. He commented later, whether recalling naivety or feigning it: 'I had no idea I could be a heretic or heterodox so long as I kept so plainly to Scripture and common sense.'[24] At the denomination's annual conference he objected to the theological claims that newborns were 'guilty' and to the assumption that 'persons'—the traditional term—was an appropriate word to

---

[21] Ibid. 59–60.   [22] Ibid. 206.
[23] Ibid. 118–19.   [24] Barker, *Life*, 142.

use when discussing the Father, Son, and Holy Spirit.[25] Barker often returned to the theme of liberty, and it was quite clear that no one was going to tell him what to think.

The issue that provoked the final showdown was Barker's rejection of the rite of baptism, after reading Thomas Clarkson's *Portraiture of Quakerism*. Barker convinced some parents who wanted him to baptize their children that a blessing ceremony in which both the use of water and the Trinitarian formula were eliminated was all that was required. More than one minister was present when he performed this alternative rite, and loyal followers of his gave candid reports, confident in the knowledge that because he had done it, it must have been right.[26] When asked to justify his actions, Barker simply responded with defiance, leading to his expulsion from the New Connexion in 1841.[27] Barker's popularity was so high that this turn of events led to the most serious crisis in the denomination's history: 4,348 members and twenty-nine societies left the New Connexion in protest, perhaps as much as one-third of the entire body.[28] Many of these held together for a season as a sort of sect, coming to be known by outsiders as the Barkerites and by insiders as Christian Brethren. A prominent New Connexion minister, William Cooke, held a public debate with Barker in 1843.[29]

What was Barker to do now? A man who could command that kind of a following would have no problem forming his own movement, but whither would he lead them? He based his ministry in the renegade New Connexion congregation in Newcastle upon Tyne. Here, with the aid of some Quaker and some (so-called) Plymouth Brethren ideas, he gave free reign to implementing biblical literalism, however extreme a literalist approach to New Testament dictates might appear. Barker gave up taking a salary, opting for the

---

[25] Joseph Barker to Thomas Allin, 16 July 1840. Joseph Barker Papers. John Rylands University Library of Manchester.

[26] See the letters in the file, 'Joseph Barker case: Barker refuses to baptize with water'. John Rylands University Library of Manchester.

[27] For his theological rationale, see Joseph Barker, *Water Baptism: A letter to Thomas Allin, corresponding member of the Annual Committee of the Methodist New Connexion* (Newcastle: J. Blackwell, 1841).

[28] Donald M. Lewis (ed.), *The Blackwell Dictionary of Evangelical Biography, 1730–1860* (Oxford: Blackwell, 1995), i. 60.

[29] For Cooke, see his entry in ibid. 251.

precarious way of living by faith.[30] Insurance, saving-plans, and the like were not in accord with taking no thought for the morrow.[31] Charity was dispensed so freely that the congregation became a magnet for spongers. Years later Barker would use as an argument against the Bible that, if taken seriously, it would lead one to behave in such ill-judged ways. Key Quakers supported him in his peace advocacy, and this led on to sympathetic contacts with Unitarians, including preaching in Unitarian chapels and adopting Unitarian views. Barker was poised to reposition himself in a more explicitly heterodox direction.

Having put all his eggs in the biblicist basket, Barker's enquiring mind then began to examine the Scriptures more critically. Early cracks can be seen in his tract, *The Inspiration of the Sacred Scriptures* (*c*.1845). His moralism led him to deny that the Song of Solomon—a 'thoroughly earthly and carnal' book—was God's word.[32] Moving on to the New Testament, Barker eliminated from it the Book of Revelation, the moral objection to it being that it manifested a spirit of vengeance. This new critical boldness was given a much more developed treatment in his *A Review of the Bible* (1848). Barker was still a defender of the Bible in general terms, but he believed by that time that it was his duty to point out the portions of the Bible that contain errors. Barker viewed himself as a fearless enquirer after truth, bravely going wherever honest reflection might lead. The Old Testament is found to contain numerous passages that are so unseemly that they would have been, at the very least, better left unrecorded. Barker's prudery is, in this case, true to stereotypes of the Victorians. The Bible, in his view, is also filled with unscientific pronouncements, and anthropomorphic statements that depict the Almighty in an unworthy manner. The New Testament is condemned for the

---

[30] Timothy Larsen, ' "Living by Faith": A Short History of Brethren Practice', *Emmaus Journal*, 12: 2 (Winter 2003), 277–315.

[31] Barker scarcely ever had a thought that he did not rush into print. This mental phase, like all his others, left a string of tracts in its wake. For these views, see Joseph Barker, *The Duty of Christians to Provide for their Poor Members, and the impropriety of professing Christians connecting themselves with benefit societies, rechabite societies, life insurances, loan funds, or with any societies founded on worldly principles* (Newcastle: J. Blackwell, n.d.).

[32] Joseph Barker, *The Inspiration of the Sacred Scriptures* (Newcastle upon Tyne: J. Barker, n.d. [*c*.1845]), 1.

passages that advocate support for the authorities, although these were neatly quarantined as interpolations by later hands. The fact that the advice is bad is a good enough reason for the assumption that it is not apostolic: 'Like most religious forgeries, it proves its evil origin by its want of universal adaption to the circumstances of mankind. The passage appears to us to have been forged by some advocate of civil and political tyranny, in some such days as the days of Constantine.'[33]

The Bible is also found to fall short on the issue of women's rights. New Testament passages are also set aside due to their apparent acceptance of the institution of slavery. Barker later claimed that his move away from a high view of Scripture was partially induced by arguments made to him by the American radical abolitionist Henry C. Wright, who lived in Europe for several years in the mid-1840s. Although he was in favour of the Bible in general terms, Barker also condemned it for giving 'countenance and support to the notion of Spiritualism'.[34] Curiously, within a decade he would be a supporter of Spiritualism, but unequivocally and rancorously anti-Bible. At this moment, however, Barker's restless mind thought it had found a permanent habitation. Some souls might have their faith shaken by an admission that there were errors in the Bible, 'but I shall . . . place the faith of man on such a foundation, that no one will be able to shake it afterwards'.[35] In only a few years, however, this prophecy would prove false, even in his own case. Although he did not know it, Barker's Christian faith was draining away altogether: 'Down this incline I gradually slid, till I reached at last the land of doubt and unbelief. My descent was very slow. It took me several years to pass from the more moderate to the more extravagant forms of Unitarianism.'[36]

In 1846, with the aid of Unitarian financial backers, he began his own publishing company at Wortley, near Leeds. In that same year Barker also took up radical politics. With his remarkable capacity for emerging as a leader in a cause as soon as he adopted it, Barker

---

[33] [Joseph Barker], *A Review of the Bible* (London: J. Watson; Wortley: J. Barker, 1848) 54.

[34] Ibid. 83.

[35] Ibid. 90–1.

[36] Barker, *Life*, 282.

quickly became one of the most powerful advocates of Chartism in the north of England, as Stephen Roberts has shown.[37] From 1848 until 1851 Barker edited a cheaply priced journal, *The People*. The paper blended radical politics with affirmations of natural religion, bitter denunciations of traditional Christianity, and discussions of emigration to America.[38] Events began to move fast in 1848: Barker was elected a Leeds town councillor, he was sent by Leeds Chartists to the National Convention of Chartists in London, and he was even 'elected' MP for Bolton by popular acclaim at the hustings, though he never proceeded to the actual poll. Most of all, in a government crackdown on Chartist leaders Barker was arrested and charged with sedition and conspiracy. It did not bode well for him when a man who distributed *The People* was sentenced to two years imprisonment for circulating seditious literature—nor when Barker's solicitor advised him to plead guilty. He stood firm, however, and eventually the charges against him were dropped. Nevertheless, it was hard to see how political radicalism could make much advance in 1850s England, the 'Age of Equipoise'.[39] In 1851, having pointed the way to his readers for several years, Barker and his family emigrated to America. His phase as a political leader had by then stalled, and Barker was in search of fresh causes and opportunities.

In America Barker joined the radical abolitionists. As they were often more pronounced in their religious scepticism than he was, Barker found that he continued to move in that direction. He took up farming in Ohio, but combined it with platform work and writing, emerging as a leading anti-Bible speaker. Already in November 1852 he organized a freethinking Bible Convention in Salem, Ohio, at which Henry C. Wright played a prominent part.[40] Its resolutions included that 'the Bible therefore is not a book of divine

---

[37] Stephen Roberts, 'Joseph Barker and the Radical Cause, 1848–1851', *Publications of the Thoresby Society: The Leeds Historical Society: Miscellany*, 2nd ser., vol. 1 for 1990 (1991), 59–73. See also Joseph O. Baylen and Norbert J. Gossman (eds.), *Biographical Dictionary of Modern British Radicals: Volume 2: 1830–1870* (Brighton: Harvester Press, 1984), 38–41.

[38] e.g. *The People*, 1: 16, p. 121. (Barker did not date issues of the journal, but a letter was published in this one dated 27 Aug. 1848.)

[39] W. L. Burn gave this label to the mid-Victorian period beginning in 1852: W. L. Burn, *The Age of Equipoise* (London: Unwin University Books, 1964).

[40] *Reasoner*, 1 June 1853, pp. 340–2.

authority—that its testimony is not decisive as to the truth or falsehood of any principle, or the goodness or badness of any practice'. The 'prevailing notion' of the Bible as a divine authority, on the other hand, 'is not only altogether erroneous, but exceedingly mischievous'.[41] Barker's speech on this occasion laid stress, among other themes, on the fallibility—indeed culpability—of the Bible's translators.[42] Whatever might be imagined regarding some pristine original of which we have no flawless copy, today's Bible is filled with errors and self-contradictory.[43] His openness to new causes is on display in a section praising vegetarianism. Most of all, Barker denounced the Bible's advice regarding submission to rulers, praising instead those radical political heroes who resisted tyranny. The peroration even took a swipe at the core teaching of Jesus as presented in the gospels, terrain he had left alone hitherto: 'Even the boasted teachings of the sermon on the Mount will be found, on many points, to be either vague and meaningless, or false and dangerous.'[44] Barker was not far now from the Secularist kingdom.[45]

George Jacob Holyoake was the clear leader of English Secularism at that time. Barker therefore wrote to him on 22 February 1853 in order to build new bridges. Some repentance was needed, as Holyoake had been a loyal Owenite in the 1830s when Barker was making his reputation by denouncing Socialists abusively. Barker asked Holyoake to make public his realization that in his former work as a controversialist he had done Owen and the Socialists an injustice. We catch a glimpse of Barker's mind in transition: he supports Secularism as a practical policy that one's time should be spent on pursuing secular goals, but as he still hopes there is an afterlife he does not accept Secularism as a philosophy; he thinks some form of Socialism is necessary, but needs more light before committing himself to any particular scheme. The most telling

---

[41] Joseph Barker, *The Popular Imperfections of the Bible. A Speech delivered by Mr. Joseph Barker, President of the Bible Convention in Salem, U.S.* (London: Holyoake & Co., 1854), 4.

[42] Ibid. 8.

[43] Ibid. 13.

[44] Ibid. 24.

[45] I have analysed Barker's anti-Bible arguments more fully elsewhere: Larsen, *Contested Christianity*, chap. 6.

passage, however, was the introduction to these concessions and caveats:

I must add, that I am not yet an Atheist, a secularist or socialist, in the sense in which I understand those words. I confess I know nothing of God, but as he is revealed in his works. With me the word God stands for the unseen cause of all natural phenomenon. I attribute to God no quality but what seems necessary to account for what I see in nature. My Jewish and Christian notions of God all are gone, except so far as they appear to be utterances of nature. Still, I lean to the belief that under all natural appearances lives a great and infinite being, in whom the powers, the intelligences and beatitudes of all things originate and in whom they all reside.[46]

In short, he was a deist. Still, the word 'yet' was a revealing one—he was 'not yet an Atheist'.

In December 1853 Barker began giving anti-Bible lectures at the Sunday Institute, Philadelphia. He also issued a challenge to debate to Philadelphia's clergymen. They duly picked their champion, Joseph Berg, a Dutch Reformed minister. The result was Barker's most important debate as a freethinker in America: eight nights in January 1854 on 'the origin, authority, and tendency of the Bible'.[47] Despite an entrance fee of 12½ cents, the hall was filled with up to 2,500 people every evening. Barker began with a speech chronicling instances when the biblical portrait of the Almighty appears to be an unworthy one: for example, God is depicted as 'limited in knowledge', because a 'passage represents him as putting the rainbow in the clouds, to aid his memory'.[48] As he moved on to a moral critique, the rhetoric became strident: 'No book can give the Deity a darker character than this. None can throw out against him more atrocious blasphemies.'[49] Of course, other passages present a more refined view of the Almighty, but that only proves that the Bible is filled with contradictions.[50] The Scriptures, he averred, support slavery, the

---

[46] Joseph Barker to G. J. Holyoake, 22 Feb. 1853, Millwood, Knox Co., Ohio, GJHCC 562, George Jacob Holyoake Correspondence Collection, The Co-operative College Archives, Manchester.

[47] *Great Discussion on the Origin, Authority, & Tendency of the Bible, between Rev. J. F. Berg, D.D., of Philadelphia, and Joseph Barker, of Ohio* (Stoke-on-Trent: George Turner, 1854).

[48] Ibid. 8.

[49] Ibid. 12.

[50] Ibid. 16.

subjugation of women, parental cruelty, and polygamy. In a complete reversal of the correlation he had made as a Methodist minister, Barker argued: 'In the history of the world, there are ten hundred years that are known as *the dark ages*. They were the ages when the Bible men reigned supreme.'[51]

Although the advantage of Barker's deism was that it allowed him to employ the arresting technique of critiquing the Bible itself as blasphemous, Berg goaded him with the observation that the God of natural revelation was subject to the same criticisms. If biblical slaughters show that the God of the Old Testament is cruel, do not modern-day plagues and natural disasters expose Barker's God of providence to the same charge? Such taunts might have eventually caused Barker to wonder whether atheism might not be a more intellectually coherent position.

In subsequent evenings Barker's plebeian sense of self-culture and self-reliance came to the fore. He rejected the evangelical gospel as antithetical to self-help and morality. The doctrines of justification by faith and forgiveness for the repentant were inducements to immorality, and therefore themselves immoral. Barker also testified to his loss of faith:

The deceitfulness and dishonesty of leading believers, and distinguished writers in defence of the Bible and Orthodox forms of theology, destroyed my faith in them. My opinions were, consequently, modified. New discoveries of priestly fraud, forced upon me by reading, observation and experience, modified my opinions still more. I saw, at length, how my youthful mind had been abused. I inquired into the grounds of my early faith, and found that it rested on a false foundation. I renounced my errors as fast as I detected them.[52]

Barker's fervent desire to unmask the Bible sometimes led to rather strained lines of attack. Here he is on the consequences of the Fall: 'The earth bears thorns and thistles, but where is the proof that they are a curse? There is none. There is proof that they are blessings.'[53] On the other hand, Barker could also eloquently present the case for

---

[51] *Great Discussion on the Origin, Authority, & Tendency of the Bible, between Rev. J. F. Berg, D.D., of Philadelphia, and Joseph Barker, of Ohio* (Stoke-on-Trent: George Turner, 1854) 27.

[52] Ibid. 67.   [53] Ibid. 69.

freethought. He argued that sceptics were generally more moral than Christians. He presented himself as a moral exemplar, taking enormous pride in being a teetotaller. The Bible, on the other hand, is an inadequate moral guide because it only condemns drunkenness, not drinking. From Mosheim's *Institutes of Ecclesiastical History* he had learned that Christians defend their positions by the use of pious frauds.

Barker's rise in America as a freethinking leader of national prominence is clearly revealed by the honour conferred upon him of presiding at the freethinking Hartford Bible Convention, Hartford, Connecticut, 2–5 June 1854. Samuel Putnam, in his *400 Years of Freethought*, made much of this convention as a landmark event in the history of organized freethought. Moreover, the convention was not Barker's initiative, but rather that of the leading Spiritualist, Andrew Jackson Davis. Davis, unlike some Spiritualists, was anti-Christian. An array of leading sceptics, abolitionists, Spiritualists, and women's rights advocates were also there, including Amy Post, Stephen S. Foster, Henry C. Wright, and William Lloyd Garrison. It was a significant marker of the esteem in which he was held that Barker was elected president in such company. Indeed, Putnam was so impressed with Barker's speeches on this occasion—he 'poured forth some magnificent arguments, deep and scholarly'—that he quoted him repeatedly, despite this meaning that he then had to address the fact that Barker had subsequently reconverted.[54]

Having triumphed in America, Barker then made a trip to England to capitalize there on his new status as a sceptical leader. Having already built up a relationship with Holyoake, he wrote a flattering letter to the editor of the *London Investigator*, Robert Cooper, praising his anti-Bible vade-mecum, *The Infidel's Textbook*, as well as his sceptical journal.[55] The *Reasoner* so reported his arrival as to indicate that Barker had the blessing of the most respected American freethinking minds: 'Mr. Lloyd Garrison and Theodore Parker saw Mr. Barker on the eve of his leaving.'[56]

---

[54] Samuel P. Putnam, *400 Years of Freethought* (New York: Truth Seeker Co., 1894), 519–25.

[55] *London Investigator* (Aug. 1854), 68.

[56] *Reasoner*, 4 June 1854, p. 379. For Theodore Parker, see Dean Grodzins, *American Heretic: Theodore Parker and Transcendentalism* (Chapel Hill, NC: University of North Carolina Press, 2002).

In August 1854 Barker delivered a series of anti-Bible lectures at the Adelphi Theatre in Sheffield. Of particular interest for future developments is his assertion that freethinkers affirmed a more moral view of marriage than the Bible did. Indeed, he was so strait-laced that he even condemned the Scriptures for failing to prohibit 'unrestrained indulgence in sexual pleasures among married people'.[57] Barker testified that Secularists were more committed to teetotalism than Christians. The Bible was also faulted for not forbidding gambling. As to his former polemical works as a minister: 'I have proved that I was greatly in error. I am astonished at some of the assertions in my former writings. . . . It seems a mystery, at times, how I could be so foolish as to utter some of the things which I find in my earlier writings. Yet there they are. And I uttered them in all sincerity.'[58]

Bitter, hyperbolic statements were now in order: 'I will undertake to prove that there is not a book on earth . . . that favours to a greater extent immorality and crime, or that favours it more strongly, than the Bible does.'[59] And on the orthodox community: 'Christians lie more than others; and Christians of the orthodox stamp most of all.'[60] Moreover, Barker's deity was no longer omnipotent: 'If people suffer undeserved calamities, we suppose it is because the God of nature cannot help it.'[61] One wonders why he did not entertain the equally logical supposition that the God of nature was lacking in perfect goodness rather than perfect power. Another possible deduction—that the God of nature did not exist—was yet to come.

On 17–19 January 1855 Barker had a debate at the Lyceum, Stockport, with John Bowes, editor of the *Truth Promoter*. Bowes began by expressing his hope that Barker would reconvert: 'I should be glad if I could bring Mr. Barker back to that Bible he once so ably advocated. . . . I should be glad if Mr. Barker would embrace that religion which he now pretends to destroy, but which before he so ably preached.'[62] Barker was ready by this time to denounce Jesus

---

[57] Joseph Barker, *Seven Lectures on the Supernatural Origin & Divine Authority of the Bible* (Stoke-on-Trent: George Turner, 1854), 41.

[58] Ibid. 84. [59] Ibid. 38. [60] Ibid. 85. [61] Ibid. 87.

[62] *The Report of the Public Discussion, at Stockport, between Mr. John Bowes . . . and Mr. Joseph Barker, . . . 'Are the Scriptures of the Old & New Testaments of Supernatural Origin and Divine Authority; Are the Doctrines contained therein Conducive to Morality and Virtue?'* (London: R. Bulman, 1855), 5.

unequivocally: 'Christ had the most serious defects. So far from loving all mankind he cares for none but the Jews. So far from exceeding all others, I am greatly mistaken if I cannot find in William Penn, Thos. Paine, John Finch, and Robert Owen incalculably more perfect characters than in Jesus.... I see nothing in Jesus's character, he was an exceedingly ignorant, conceited, and narrow-minded man.'[63]

Just a couple of days after this encounter came Barker's most significant public debate on this visit: ten nights in Halifax sparring with Brewin Grant, a Congregational controversialist. Grant was up for high-hearted cut-and-thrust as much as Barker. Barker's textual criticism looked more and more pedantic as Grant forced him to concede that, as the original autographs do not exist for almost any works, his argument would equally preclude statements that Shakespeare, Locke, or virtually any other author had said anything. When pressed on his deistic views, Barker replied: 'If the God of Nature does not do all he can for the welfare of his creatures, the God of Nature is to blame; he is not so good as many good men.'[64] Such a concession would presumably make it that much harder for Barker to employ in the future his argument that the Bible portrayed the Almighty in blasphemous ways.

Barker asserted the superiority of classical over biblical learning.[65] He recounted the lives of various figures from ancient Greece and Rome, arguing that they were morally superior to those of biblical heroes. Barker put succinctly and winsomely what might be taken as the creed of popular freethought: 'We receive no book as a master; we keep ourselves free. We believe in progress.'[66] His old views were largely right (for example, he was always an abolitionist); he was only wrong in asserting that the Bible was in accord with them. Barker disparaged Jesus at length. He was even unmoved by Christ's passion: 'we see nothing peculiarly courageous or noble in his demeanour.'[67] A particular hostage to fortune was his argument against the efficacy

[63] Ibid. 77.
[64] *Origin and Authority of the Bible. Report of the Public Discussion between Joseph Barker, Esq., and the Rev. Brewin Grant, B.A., Held at Halifax on Ten Nights... 1855* (Glasgow: Robert Stark, n.d. [1855]), 99.
[65] Ibid. 149.
[66] Ibid. 249.
[67] Ibid. 352.

of prayer: Christians were praying for his conversion, but that would never happen.[68] Barker did allude to issues regarding composition, authorship, and dating of the biblical documents that corresponded to the theories of the emerging discipline of higher criticism.[69]

From Grant's perspective, Barker's God of nature had already been exploded by apologists such as Bishop Butler: 'The deist must therefore continue to slip down his sliding scale of faith, and give up God together with the Bible . . . as a deist, he must either prove that no such evils exist in nature as he finds in the Bible, or else become a plain blank atheist.'[70] It is fitting for the purpose of this study, however, to end this account of their duel with high rhetoric from Barker making the claim that religious doubt was the mark of intellectual honesty: 'The reason why some become infidels sooner than others is, that they have clearer heads and better hearts; that they have a greater love of truth, a more eager desire to know it, more zeal and perseverance in seeking it, more honesty in embracing it, more courage in avowing it . . .'[71]

In addition to his debates, Barker delivered 153 lectures in Britain during this visit.[72] In late 1855 or early 1856, having returned to America by then, it was falsely announced in Britain that Barker had died. This bit of misinformation provides a unique way of glimpsing how high he stood in the esteem of the popular freethinking community at that time. The *London Investigator* eulogized:

We are overwhelmed with grief on receipt of the startling and melancholy intelligence of the sudden death of the ablest man who has risen from the working classes since the time of Cobbett. . . . He has fallen a signal martyr to liberty. Take him all in all we may never see his like again in our generation. Freethinking has sustained an irreparable loss. In exposition he was unrivalled, and in controversy invincible. His friends and admirers were legion.[73]

---

[68] *Origin and Authority*, 368.

[69] For an exposition of this theme, see Larsen, *Contested Christianity*, chap. 6.

[70] *Origin and Authority*, 380. For Butler and nineteenth-century thought, see Jane Garnett, 'Bishop Butler and the *Zeitgeist*: Butler and the Development of Christian Moral Philosophy in Victorian Britain', in Christopher Cunliffe (ed.), *Joseph Butler's Moral and Religious Thought: Tercentenary Essays* (Oxford: Clarendon Press, 1992), 63–96.

[71] *Origin and Authority*, 422.

[72] *Reasoner*, 30 Sept. 1855, p. 209.

[73] *London Investigator* (Jan. 1856), 149.

A similar marker of his ascent to the highest ring of the leadership of popular freethought in Britain is his inclusion in *Half-Hours with the Freethinkers*. This was a serial edited by Charles Bradlaugh, who would emerge as the most important British atheist leader, William Harral Johnson, and John Watts.[74] Twenty-five lives were recounted, stretching chronologically all the way back to Epicurus. Most of them were from the seventeenth and eighteenth centuries, including Voltaire, Spinoza, and Hume. To Barker, however, was given the unique honour of being the only living figure included in the collection. Here is a portion of his tribute:

In any work, purporting to be a record of Freethinkers, the name of Joseph Barker cannot be omitted. We find in him, from the commencement of his public life till the present time, an ardent desire for, and a determination to achieve, freedom of thought and expression on all subjects appertaining to theology, politics, and sociology. Possessing a vigorous intellect, a constitution naturally strong, great oratorical ability, and an unrivalled command of the Saxon language, he has made himself a power among each party with whom the transitionary state of his mind has brought him in contact. . . . he became a Methodist preacher, belonging to the Old Connexion, the New Connexion, and then advancing to Unitarianism, ultimately arriving at the climax of Freethought, in which he is now so distinguished an advocate.[75]

On his return to America, Barker decided to move his family to Omaha. The Nebraska Territory had just been opened for settlement on 30 May 1854, so Barker had taken on the task of taming a remote wilderness. He had moved at least once before in Ohio. This was partly the result of persecution for infidelity's sake, partly due to the fact that his natural self-assertion did not make him a valued neighbour. Starting a new in the wilds of Nebraska was not easy, but it paid off as a long-term financial strategy: on last report, there still is a Barker building in Omaha, and the Barker dynasty is still thriving in the state's largest city.[76] In 1857 Barker went on an infidel lecturing

[74] For William Harral Johnson, see his entry in the Appendix.
[75] The issue on Barker appeared on 15 Aug. 1857: J. Watts, 'Iconoclast' [Charles Bradlaugh], and A. Collins [William Harral Johnson] (eds.), *Half-Hours with the Freethinkers* (London: Holyoake & Co., 1857), 169–76. The copy I examined was the one that belongs to the London Library and had once been owned by Leslie Stephen.
[76] Information provided by the Douglas County Historical Society, Omaha, Nebraska.

tour, ending up with an eight-month contract to give the Sunday sermon to a Secularist congregation in Philadelphia. Having completed that engagement, he was offered another such contract to begin some months hence. Barker spent the interim reunited with his family in Nebraska, and then lectured in Philadelphia for two additional months before heading home again, leaving despite his contract having six more months to run.

Barker announced that he had become an atheist in 1858. He offered his public testimony to Holyoake, in a document dated 22 July 1858, *Confessions of Joseph Barker, A Convert from Christianity*:

Of higher beings than man, and of other states of existence than the present, I know nothing: I believe nothing. The last remnants of my old religious faith are gone. The doctrine of a personal God, and of a future life, appear to me to rest on no proof. I look in vain for anything in nature or in history to justify a belief in them. I am compelled to regard them as the offspring, not of the understanding, but of the imagination and affections.... My old religious and clerical associates warned me, when I refused to be bound by their creeds, and resolved to investigate the foundations of the common theology for myself, that I should become an Atheist. And so I have in the common acceptation of the word.... Yet I have come, at length, by slow degrees, after a thousand struggles, and with infinite reluctance, to the conclusion, that a personal God and an immortal life are fictions of the human mind.... One thing is certain: I have no desire to be a Christian again.... Atheism, or pure unmixed Naturalism, alone accords with what we know of the present state and the past history of the universe.[77]

Barker was convinced that to side with freethought was to side with the tide of history: 'it seems plain to me that pure Naturalism is the creed—if I may call it a creed—and pure Secularism the religion or the morality, to which the more thoughtful among men are all tending.'[78] He had read F. W. Newman's account of his move away from orthodoxy, *Phases of Faith* (1850), with delight, seeing in it 'the history of progress'.[79] Barker had become an atheist by sheer, hard, intellectual graft, by honest doubt at its most courageous:

---

[77] Joseph Barker, *Confessions of Joseph Barker, A Convert from Christianity* (London: Holyoake & Co., 1858), 3–5, 14.

[78] Ibid. 5.

[79] Ibid. 14.

Nothing but evidence, almighty and irresistible evidence, besetting me continually, presenting itself at every turn, could so completely have changed my views... Still, inquiry forced me into heresy further and further every year, and it has at length brought me to the extreme of infidelity.... What a history the history of my mind has been! What a diversity of phases of faith it has presented; and what a diversity of positions I have been forced to occupy.[80]

It had been a history of progress, however. Therefore, barring a tragic loss of his mental powers through a descent into senility, it was absurd to imagine that he might reconvert: 'So completely does the old belief appear to be without foundation in truth or fact, so utterly worthless do all the pretended evidences of a divine or super-human origin appear— so numerous and decisive are the proofs of an imperfect human origin, that it seems an impossibility that I should ever be capable of a re-conversion, except in case of such a change as turns the man into a child again.'[81] He offered the terse dictum: 'All religion is immoral.'[82]

Barker followed that up with a *Reasoner* article, 'Mr. Thomas Cooper—Remarks on his reputed conversion'. Cooper's reconversion came as a blow to Secularists, and must have hit Barker particularly hard. Stephen Roberts has observed that Cooper was 'the Chartist he most admired'.[83] When Barker became reconciled with Holyoake in 1853, he explicitly mentioned Cooper's articles when declaring his appreciation for the contents of the *Reasoner*.[84] What was one then to make of Cooper's return to orthodoxy? Barker averred that it was inexplicable as an intellectually honest move: 'I confess I cannot conceive how a sane man, of average intellect, and reasonably acquainted with the facts of the case, can, after having been once freed from early Christian prejudice, ever become again a believer in the truth and supernatural origin of the Bible or Christianity.'[85] There was no doubt that Cooper was claiming to have undergone a Christian conversion. The 'reputed' in Barker's title was there

[80] Ibid. 14–15.
[81] Ibid. 15–16.
[82] Ibid. 9.
[83] Roberts, 'Joseph Barker', 60.
[84] Joseph Barker to G. J. Holyoake, 22 Feb. 1853. GJHCC 562, George Jacob Holyoake Correspondence Collection, The Co-operative College Archives, Manchester.
[85] Joseph Barker, 'Mr. Thomas Cooper—Remarks on his reputed conversion', *Reasoner*, 15 Aug. 1858.

to carry the innuendo that a real conversion—a genuine mental development from scepticism to orthodoxy—was literally an impossibility. In order to expose Cooper's presumed wilful evasions of the truth, Barker repeatedly expressed his desire to debate with him: a prospect that Barker would relish less as it came closer.

No longer excited about either farming or being a Secularist lecturer in Philadelphia, Barker made the decision to move back to England, leaving on 11 January 1860. In a farewell letter to his American friends, he offered his approbation for all forces that were opposed to 'the Orthodox churches' (or 'the plague of Christianity'), whether Spiritualists, Hicksite Quakers, Progressive Friends, Parkerites, New-School Unitarians, or Universalists.[86] He had himself 'witnessed phenomena of late' that made the claims of Spiritualism compelling.[87] The *Reasoner* printed a list of fifty-two subjects that Barker was prepared to lecture on. The title of one was 'Books and Reading', and—beside the numerous lectures attacking religion—his autodidactic education was on display in lectures such as 'Lord Brougham's *Political Philosophy*'.[88]

Barker was welcomed with open arms by the British popular freethinking community. A plan was afoot in sceptical circles to launch a major newspaper with Bradlaugh as the editor. The prospectus said that its 'present platform, of theological advocacy, will be that of antagonism to every known religious system', and 'Iconoclast' was always happy to take the more succinct option of calling it an atheistic paper.[89] As Barker was back on the scene, he was named by the committee as a co-editor. After both men were dead, Bradlaugh's daughter recalled:

The arrangements for the paper were completed, and announcements concerning it made, when Mr Joseph Barker returned to England from America. His coming was heralded by a flourish of trumpets—literary triumphs, that is—receptions were arranged to welcome him, and there was evidently a widespread notion that Joseph Barker was a very great man indeed. It is difficult for us to-day, having before us his whole public career, with its

---

[86] Joseph Barker, 'Mr. Thomas Cooper—Remarks on his reputed conversion', *Reasoner*, 19 Feb. 1860, pp. 61–3.

[87] Ibid. 63.

[88] Ibid. 60–1.

[89] David Tribe, *President Charles Bradlaugh, M.P.* (London: Elek Books, 1971), 67.

kaleidoscopic changes of front, to realise the enthusiasm which his name provoked in 1860. But be that as it may, it is quite evident that at that time his reputation stood high amongst English Freethinkers....[90]

Moreover, Barker received first billing, with the masthead reading 'Edited by Joseph Barker and "Iconoclast" '; he wrote the leader and was responsible for all the articles in the first half of the paper. The *National Reformer* would be the most important popular freethinking paper in Britain for the next thirty years.

Being back in England also meant that Cooper could accept Barker's two-year-old challenge to a debate. Brewin Grant had complained that the anti-Bible lecturer would only debate with him if Barker was able to set all the conditions. Cooper now turned the tables on him, insisting that Barker's task in the debate would be to defend the atheistic and materialist statements he had made. Cooper wrote to a friend on 24 February 1860: 'Negotiations are going on between Bradford friends & Joseph Barker, with a view to bring him to a debate on the Being of God & other preliminary subjects. If he will consent to debate those subjects I shall be glad to meet him; but if he will only consent to debate the claims of the Bible—I shall not meet him, just to give him an opportunity of degrading Christ and the Scriptures.'[91] This tactic was savvy enough to rattle Barker's sons, George and Joseph Barker Jr. The namesake son wrote to his father:

George thinks Holyoake wishes to use you as the 'Infidel Champion' of his Secularist Sect. You are to do the Theological Debating part of the Work, while he will take the High political part ... He seems wishful to aid Cooper in forcing you to commit yourself to Atheism, to make it out that you do deny a future state and a God or Creator and are an acknowledged Atheist by that unfortunate letter of 'Confessions'. However, I think you can easily get over it. You really don't deny anything; you only deny a present belief from present data. So I take it after a careful perusal. You can get over it if you have to 'confess' again, George thinks. He does devoutly hope you will not take what he calls the insane ground that there is no God and No Future State. It must be very plain to all quick-witted people, I think, that Cooper wants to force you into a very untenable position, so as to be able to escape what he

---

[90] Hypatia Bradlaugh Bonner, *Charles Bradlaugh: His Life and Work* (London: T. Fisher Unwin, 1895), i. 121.

[91] Thomas Cooper to James Andrew, 24 Feb. 1860. I own this letter.

knows will be a complete and dreadful defeat if he is obliged to prove that the Bible is of divine origin. But Holyoake evidently wishes to aid him in making it out that you do take the ultra & foolish Atheistical ground. If you write anything on this subject, be sure you send us a copy as we are anxious to see how you get out of this scrape.[92]

The debate ran for six nights in September 1860 at the St George's Hall, Bradford. It was Barker's task to defend the following statement:

That it is foolish and presumptuous to deny the existence of God and the reality of a future state; and yet, not anything in nature or in history justifies a belief in them; a personal God and an immortal life are fictions of the human mind,—there are nowhere any signs or proofs of God and immortality, but everywhere proofs to the contrary; a personal God, the maker, or even the governor of the world, and a future life of eternal blessedness for mankind are great absurdities; the doctrine of an all-perfect God is both palpably false and infinitely immoral; and the only rational and the only moral doctrine is Atheism.[93]

Barker began defensively, repudiating both the wording of the statement and the very subjects themselves. Cooper replied that all the sentences in the proposition were direct quotations from Barker. Cooper wanted to know what Barker had meant by them. Barker was hankering after his old bag of tricks: 'My wish was to discuss the question of the divine authority of the Bible.'[94]

Barker went on to outline the classic argument that the existence of evil was proof that an all-perfect deity could not exist. Many have found this argument compelling and unanswerable, and Cooper's tepid reply was simply an attempt to minimize the extent of the reality of evil. Cooper's wondering if death is really an evil is curiously reminiscent of Barker's defences of thorns and thistles in his

---

[92] Joseph Barker, Jr. to Joseph Barker, 4 Apr. 1860. Joseph Barker Collection, Douglas County Historical Society, Omaha, Nebraska. I am working from a typed transcript of the original letter, presumably made some years ago by the Historical Society. It contains several spelling errors, and as I am not sure if they are in the original letter or reflect an inability to decipher it (or a simple typing error), I have corrected them. Notably, Holyoake is spelled 'Holoyoak'.

[93] *The Belief in a Personal God and a Future Life. Six Nights' Discussion between Thomas Cooper and Joseph Barker, held in St. George's Hall, Bradford, September, 1860* (London: Ward & Co., n.d.), 3–4.

[94] Ibid. 5.

polemics against Genesis. Barker responded to Cooper's use of the argument from design not with Darwin's book from the year before, but rather with a somewhat strained argument that design implies weakness because one designs to get over a limitation; after all, 'necessity is the mother of invention'.[95] Barker presented religion as the enemy of plebeian self-help: 'It may be more agreeable to some to believe in an all-good God taking care of them, than to believe in taking care of themselves.'[96] Cooper argued that as intelligence cannot come from non-intelligence we must have an intelligent Creator. Barker said that the human race might be eternal, or perhaps there is a way that we have not yet discerned that inanimate matter could produce intelligent life. When Barker mentioned Darwin later in the debate, Cooper pointed out that it was not a theory of the origin of life, but only of the generating of species from other living creatures: 'Suppose all that Darwen [*sic*] says were true—suppose that some part of the development theory were true, still you would be unable to account for the commencement of any life whatever on the globe unless you trace it to God.'[97] Barker astutely retorted, to use a later parlance, that this was a God-of-the-gaps theory: 'Mr. Cooper says they have done as good as to find out all the causes at once, and that it is God: that is the explanation of everything they don't understand—it is the name for ignorance—that's all.'[98]

Barker repeatedly referred to the thought of Baden Powell, apparently drawing on his contribution to *Essays and Reviews*. This reveals that Barker was keeping up with his reading, as that volume had been published less than six months earlier, and the controversy surrounding its more liberal approach to theological matters would not really heat up until the provocative review of it in the following month's issue of the *Westminster Review* (October 1860). Barker received cheers from the crowd when he quoted a speech Cooper had made against the design argument when he had been a freethinking

---

[95] Ibid. 39. Later in the debate he brought in Darwin together with Baden Powell as two men pointing the way toward a non-supernatural explanation, pp. 69–70.

[96] Ibid. 26–7.

[97] Ibid. 72. Darwin is misspelled 'Darwen' throughout this section, whether Barker or Cooper is being quoted. In later speeches, the name is spelled correctly for both speakers.

[98] Ibid. 73.

lecturer. It is indicative of how firmly Secularists believed that there was no honest road back to faith from such reasoned scepticism, that this prompted someone to shout out from the crowd that Cooper was a hypocrite. Barker himself accused Cooper of having reconverted because he could not pay the cost of standing for an unpopular truth.[99] Cooper outmanoeuvred Barker on the popular issue of radical politics. He denounced Barker for having condemned the militant abolitionist John Brown, and for failing to give unequivocal support to the Italian patriot Giuseppe Garibaldi. Perhaps these differences can be traced to the fact that Cooper had been a physical-force Chartist, while Barker had stopped at moral force; Cooper had gone to prison, while Barker had gone to America. The debate became more and more acrimonious, with both speakers frequently interrupting one another. Barker opted to quote long extracts. Cooper goaded him that he was just trying to run the clock out. On the intervention of the umpire and a vote of the audience, Barker was eventually pressured into addressing Cooper's anti-materialist arguments. Barker then offered a cogent reply that even Cooper acknowledged was germane, claiming that everything put forward as evidence of the human spirit was just the activity of the brain, and that Cooper's reasoning would serve just as well to prove that a dog had an immortal soul.

The last lecture that Barker gave as a sceptic was, fittingly, a classic anti-Bible polemic in which he catalogued the reasons why the story of Noah's ark should be dismissed as incredible. It appeared as a tract stamped 17 September 1863. In it, the main scientific source that Barker used as a foil to a literalist reading of Genesis was the writings of Edward Hitchcock (1793–1864), a leading American geologist. As to Noah procuring the animals, Barker observed that this must have been 'a wild-goose chase indeed'.[100]

Barker's reconversion to orthodox Christianity was a gradual process that began to become a publicly visible one during 1863. By that time he had been estranged from the main block of organized atheists for two years. He had left the *National Reformer* in August 1861, convinced that Bradlaugh was promoting immorality. In that year

---

99   Ibid. 155.
100 Joseph Barker, *Noah's Ark* (London: Barker & Co., 1863), 9.

Bradlaugh had began championing George Drysdale's *Elements of Social Science; or, Physical, Sexual, and Natural Religion,* a work that was ground-breaking in Victorian England for its willingness to provide information on methods of birth control. Moreover, certain statements in it were read, even by many leading freethinkers such as Holyoake, as promoting sexual promiscuity. Barker's own sceptical contributions to the *National Reformer* were as moralizing as any stereotype of Victorian Christians. In just one article, for example, he not only advocated teetotalism, but also denounced gambling, tobacco, and even theatregoing.[101] Barker was a strict moralist his whole life. He had argued for years that sceptics were more moral than Christians, but he would later reassess that judgement. Having fallen out with Bradlaugh and, with him, the main body of plebeian atheists, he established his own journal, *Barker's Review.* Barker's place at the very pinnacle of the British popular freethinking movement is amply confirmed by the fact that Holyoake flattered the Secularist community by crediting it with having been able to endure the loss of Barker without being utterly destroyed: 'In our party Mr. Barker was given the place of honour, power, and leadership. A person in this position in any other party, acting as Mr. Barker has done, would have broken it up.'[102]

During 1862 Barker also became the minister for a Secularist congregation in Burnley. He preached morality, and there began to re-evaluate the cases for the Bible, Christ, and Christianity. He re-established contact with his old New Connexion sparring-partner, William Cooke, in August 1862. In their private correspondence one can glimpse Barker in transition. On 17 September 1862 he wrote to Cooke:

You will at least see that . . . your old friend . . . is still nearer to you than to the enemies of morality. I suppose it is impossible for me ever to be orthodox; but I have infinitely more sympathy with you than with men who take pleasure in arguing against a great, good God and a blessed immortality, and who war with church and religion because they find them standing in the way of vicious license. My heart is entirely with you and with all ministers of religion, whose work it is to strengthen men's faith in God

[101] *National Reformer,* 1 Sept. 1860, pp. 2–3.
[102] *Counsellor* (Dec. 1861), 'One Paper and One Party'.

and immortality... Though I do not believe in the Divine Authority of the Bible... I place a high value on the Bible, and have much to say in favour, and very little against, the character and tendency of Christianity.... If I came inside a church that could allow me to hold and voice my present views on certain more speculative points I should have the greatest pleasure in preaching much of what I find in the Law and the Prophets, in the Psalms and in the Proverbs, and still more of what I find in the Gospels and the Epistles.... a large experience and much thought have worked considerable changes in my views on several important subjects, I freely acknowledge.... And after all I have said in maintenance of my views against what I call the extremes of orthodoxy, I do most sincerely believe that the teachings and character of Jesus have been for many ages... and for many ages to come will be beyond the teaching and character of any other man.[103]

This letter is telling in that, despite the remarkable movement that he has made, Barker is nevertheless still unable to affirm either the divinity of Christ or the divine authority of the Bible. It is not unlike his 'I am not yet an atheist' letter.

Nine months later we have another interim report to Cooke:

It is the case, that for some years my mind has been returning from its wanderings, moving sometimes steadily and sometimes not so steadily towards Christ and Christianity, as its centre and its rest. The horrible principles of license on the side of unbelief, as well as the darkness and dreariness of unbelief itself, repelled me on the one hand, and the beauty and purity and tenderness of Christ's moral teachings and character, and the bright and cheering doctrines of his Gospel with regard to God and immortality, attracted me on the other. At length my spirit appears to have reached, or nearly reached, its home and resting-place.... The change in my views and feelings has been accelerated by my determination, some two years ago, to search out and make known to my hearers and readers all that was true and good in the Bible, the Church, and the religion of Christ.... I am resolved that no one shall ever be able, after my death, to quote me as an authority in favour of a cheerless, Godless, demoralising, de-humanising system of unbelief.[104]

Barker observed later with regard to this correspondence, 'Those letters are the only record of the changing phases of my belief for

---

[103] Joseph Barker to William Cooke, 17 Sept. 1862. Joseph Barker Papers, John Rylands University Library of Manchester.
[104] Joseph Barker to William Cooke, 4 July 1863. Ibid.

the time commencing in Augt 1862 and ending Augt 1864'.[105] This would indicate that by Barker's own reckoning it took two years for him to move across a spectrum from a fresh openness to discovering value in Christianity to a full belief in the claims of orthodoxy. Indeed, as late as 20 February 1864 he apparently still had not reached a solid conviction that the orthodox view of the atonement was defensible.[106]

On the other hand, Barker had been steadily signalling his growing appreciation of Christianity for some time. In May 1863 he declared, in a funeral oration: 'The religion of Jesus is substantially true and divine; and, thus far, I declare myself a Christian.'[107] Again, this is carefully worded so as to fall short of affirming either that Jesus himself was divine, or that his teaching as recorded in the gospels is entirely true. On 8 November 1863 Barker preached a sermon at a secular venue on the text 'I am not ashamed of the Gospel of Christ'. It was a passionate statement that Christianity was superior to unbelief, but not an exposition of the precise doctrines that he had come to affirm.[108] His *Barker's Review* evolved into a forum for advocating the cause of Christianity. One lead article was entitled 'Christianity the Best Secularism'.[109] Barker had even worked his way around on the issue of the atonement, confidently launching into a defence of it in response to a sceptical correspondent with the words: 'The doctrine is in harmony with nature. We see vicarious suffering, and salvation by vicarious suffering, everywhere.'[110]

This was no deathbed conversion. Barker had a full decade of active Christian work ahead of him. He wrote much in that period, both defending the intellectual credibility of orthodox doctrines and explaining the reasons for his reconversion. His growing conviction that the cause of Christian morality was, after all, safer in the hands of Christians has already been mentioned. There are, of course,

---

[105] Joseph Barker to William Cooke, 22 Mar. 1866. Ibid.

[106] Joseph Barker to William Cooke, 20 Feb. 1864. Ibid.

[107] Joseph Barker, *Teachings of Experience, or, lessons I have learned on my way through life* (London: E. W. Allen, 1885), 135.

[108] Joseph Barker, *'I am not ashamed of the Gospel of Christ.' A Sermon preached by Mr. Joseph Barker, in the Athenaeum, Sunderland, on Sunday Evening, November 8th, 1863* (Newcastle upon Tyne: J. G. Forster 1863).

[109] *Barker's Review*, 12 Dec. 1863, p. 257.

[110] Ibid., 19 Dec. 1863, p. 268.

non-intellectual factors, as there presumably always are when dealing with human beings. One could tell Barker's story, for example, by simply saying that he had burnt his bridges with the atheist community, and must have been looking around for another movement in which his talents and training could be put to use. The point is not that this is untrue, but that the whole truth cannot be collapsed into such an explanation. Indeed, it was part of the polemics of both sides in the Victorian popular freethought–orthodox controversy to accuse the other of being motivated by non-intellectual factors. Infidels routinely accused reconverts of seeking some kind of pecuniary advantage. Orthodox controversialists, on the other hand, regularly argued that people became unbelievers because of a desire to live an immoral life. It would be unwise to imagine either that such motivations never occurred or that they always were the root of the matter. Barker himself, as a reconvert, gave great weight to the following explanation when accounting for his own previous loss of faith: he had felt mistreated by the New Connexion leadership, this led to bitterness toward Christian ministers that grew like a cancer into hostility toward the church in general, then Christianity itself, and finally even callousness toward Christ. Again, the point is not that this is not true, but that it is inadequate. Whatever other factors might come into play, for strong, inquisitive, well-read minds believing or disbelieving something is not merely a matter of willpower; it takes authentic intellectual labour.

Therefore, as ought to be expected, Barker's path back to orthodox was littered with books:

I had sunk below the level of ancient Paganism, and the books which I read on my first awakening to a consciousness that I was wrong, were Pagan works. I read much in Plato and Aristotle, Cicero and Seneca . . . The works of Epictetus, with the comments of Simplicius, proved exceedingly profitable. I then read the writings of Theodore Parker, Dr. Channing, and some of the works of Dr. Priestley, and got good from all. . . . I read Shakespeare freely, and Pope; and then Thompson, and Goldsmith, and Young, and Cowper, and Tennyson, and several other of our poets. Then came the writings of Burke, and Penn, and Wesley, of Robert Hall, and of Dr. Cooke, and of Mr. Newton; with Carlyle, and Paley, and Grotius. . . . Still later I read Augustine's *Confessions*, Montalembert's *Monks of the West*, and everything I could find to illustrate the history of Christianity. . . . I also read the

writings of Chalmers, Whewell, and Lord Brougham on natural theology...
Ecce Homo delighted me exceedingly. I read it a dozen times. I studied it, and
it did me a great deal of good. It both strengthened my faith in Christ,
and increased my love to Him.[111]

There is a basic verisimilitude to this account; many of the authors
listed are suggestive. The Unitarian voices of Parker, Channing, and
Priestley would have been a natural staging post on such a journey.
Ecce Homo, written by Sir John Seeley and published anonymously in
1865, was a book that some orthodox Christians condemned for
retreating from the deity of Christ, but that would serve for Barker
as a way of renewing a belief that Jesus' character was worthy of the
highest admiration.[112] Augustine's *Confessions* is the story of a formidable intellectual who thought his way further and further from
his mother's Christian faith—becoming a prominent advocate of a
rival movement—before finally thinking his way back to the conclusion that Christian orthodoxy appeared to be a more compelling
worldview after all.

Barker was candid enough to acknowledge that Spiritualism,
although not approved of in orthodox guide-books, was nonetheless an
oasis that many whose terminus was to be orthodoxy had found
reviving along the way. Point number fourteen on his own inventory
of causes of his reconversion was: 'Spiritualism had something to do
with my conversion.'[113] In another book, Barker recalled: 'As I travelled to and fro in America, fulfilling my lecturing engagements,
I met with a number of persons who had been converted, by means
of spiritualism, from utter infidelity, to a belief in God and a future
life.... I was satisfied that there was more in this wonderful universe
than could be accounted for on the coarse materialistic principles of
Atheism.'[114] Spiritualism was, of course, a more-or-less acceptable
option in popular freethinking circles in both America and Britain,
not least through the lead that had been given by a patriarch of popular
anti-Christian rationalism, Robert Owen. Even Holyoake's Secularist

[111] Barker, *Teachings*, 176–7.
[112] For *Ecce Homo*, see Daniel L. Pals, *The Victorian 'Lives' of Jesus* (San Antonio:
Trinity University Press, 1982).
[113] Barker, *Teachings*, 26.
[114] Joseph Barker, *Modern Skepticism: A journey through the land of doubt and back
again. A Life Story* (Philadelphia: Smith, English, & Co., 1874), 370, 375.

press printed Spiritualist titles. For some, Spiritualism also ended up adding fresh credibility to orthodox versions of spiritual realities.

Barker testified that he came to find materialistic atheism was merely destructive, and therefore not really a philosophy of life at all. It offered no basis for morality and no resources for facing suffering and death. Unlike Christianity, it did not inspire its adherents to practical work for helping humanity, such as establishing schools. More and more, he felt the tyranny of its procrustean logic:

Negative criticism, pulling things to pieces with a view to find faults . . . tends to cause doubt about every thing. It eats out of one the very soul of truth, of love, and of faith. . . . The Cartesian system of reasoning, which begins by calling in question every thing, and which refuses to believe anything without formal proof, is essentially vicious. The man who adopts it and carries it out thoroughly, must necessarily become an infidel, not only in religion, but in morals and philosophy. . . . This vicious system I adopted, and it hastened my fall into unbelief as a matter of course. Not one of all the most important things on earth admits of proof in this formal way. You cannot prove your own existence in this way. You cannot prove the existence of the universe. You cannot prove the existence of God. You cannot prove that there are such things as vice and virtue, good and evil.[115]

Fascinatingly, Barker partially attributed his own ungracious, fault-finding temperament to the hazards of an autodidactic ascent: 'And I was too critical, too pugnacious, too controversial. I was too much in the habit of looking for defects in what I heard and read . . . Considering that I was to a great extent self-taught, that much that I learned I learned after I had become almost a man, this perhaps was natural; but it was a disadvantage.'[116]

Eventually he realized that no ideology was unassailable. Traditional orthodox theology had its vulnerable points it was true, but if pure biblicism removed some of them it created others. Deism alleviated different difficulties, but as a halfway house it was exposed as inconsistent from both sides. Likewise, materialistic atheism was just as much open to charges of untenable extremism from reasonable voices in the sensible middle as was old-fashioned orthodoxy.

---

[115] Joseph Barker, *Modern Skepticism: A journey through the land of doubt and back again. A Life Story* (Philadelphia: Smith, English, & Co., 1874), 284–5.
[116] Ibid. 161.

Ideological warfare with good, well-read, reasoning people was therefore unavoidable, no matter where one stood on the spectrum. Barker mused ruefully:

When I commenced my career of religious exploration, I expected I should get rid of all difficulties, and that I should reach a region at last where all would be light; where there would be no more harassing or perplexing mysteries. . . . But when one difficulty was disposed of, another made its appearance, and in some cases several. And when I got outside the religion of Christ, more difficulties than ever made their appearance, and difficulties often of a more appalling character.[117]

In his mature view, the old external evidences such as the argument from fulfilled prophecy essentially conceded an advantage to sceptics by working within their too narrowly delineated boundaries: 'I may add, that the evidences which had most to do in convincing me of the truth and divinity of Christianity, were the internal ones. I was influenced more by moral and spiritual, than by historical and critical considerations.'[118] Just as Spiritualism could overcome a tired rationalism and Romanticism could counteract the sterility of the Enlightenment, so internal evidences could reach the places that external ones neglected.

A significant part of what this meant for Barker was the fresh conviction that instincts, feelings, sensibilities, and affections were germane when weighing the truthfulness of a proposition. He decided that his moral instincts, for example, were truer guides than seemingly irrefutable cold logic in the service of such propositions as that there is no logical reason to believe that lying is wrong or fidelity in marriage a virtue. Moreover, such guides pointed toward realities that the scientific method could not reveal:

Man has something within him which inclines him, impels him, constrains him to believe the same great doctrines which the Bible teaches. We instinctively believe in God, in duty, and in immortality,—in responsibility, in good and ill desert, and in rewards and punishments. The Bible finds the germs of these great beliefs in men's hearts; it goes on the supposition that they are there; and instead of trying to put them there, seeks only to develope [*sic*] them and call them into vigorous activity.[119]

---

[117] Ibid. 324.
[118] Barker, *Teachings*, 171.
[119] Joseph Barker, *The Bible, Its Great Worth and Divine Origin* (Philadelphia: Methodist Episcopal Room, 1873), 26.

It is the kind of plot-twist that an astute reader might have already predicted that Barker credited the Bible for his return to orthodoxy: 'the Bible, and especially the story of Christ, was the principal instrument of my conversion.'[120] One of his lists of reading material that aided his reconversion ended with the assertion: 'The book, however, that did me most good was the Bible.'[121] In his time of re-evaluation at Burnley, he set himself the task of reading the gospels, not as a polemicist looking for a weak point to exploit, but as a fair-minded person wishing to discover anything good to be gained there. He found a surprisingly large amount. The argument from internal evidences could therefore even establish the divine origin of the Bible: 'The proof, then, that the Scriptures are inspired of God is, their adaption to answer those great and desirable ends—to meet the moral and spiritual wants of men and Christians. These marks, these signs, these proofs of divine inspiration the Scriptures have; and that is enough.'[122]

In the end, however, the Bible was simply the vessel: the reality was Jesus Christ. When he spoke of the Bible he meant the gospels and when he spoke of the gospels he meant Jesus. The main conclusion that Barker derived from his fresh Bible reading was thus: 'I found Jesus Himself to be the most beautiful and exalted of all charac-ters.'[123] His statement that the Bible was the principal instrument in his conversion immediately clarifies itself as a Christological encoun-ter: 'that which melted my heart; that which won my infinite admir-ation; that which filled me with unspeakable love and gratitude; that which made me a Christian and a Christian believer, was Christ Himself.'[124] Barker's writings as a reconvert are filled with pages extolling the character of Christ; this theme will re-emerge repeatedly even in the same book, as if he could not get away from it. Barker eventually wrote *Jesus: A Portrait* (1873). It contained thirty-six chapters, taking a variety of tacks, including one entitled 'Jesus—Objections', which explicitly answered many, if not all, of the criti-cisms of the Nazarene that he had raised as a freethinker. Most chapters were straightforward tributes to Christ's admirable actions and attitudes, such as 'Jesus was kind to the poor', 'Jesus and woman',

---

[120] Barker, *Teachings*, 171.   [121] Ibid. 177.   [122] Ibid. 247.
[123] Ibid. 153–4.   [124] Ibid. 171.

and 'Jesus as a reformer'.[125] Barker ultimately came to the conviction that the Jesus revealed in the gospels was literally too good not to be true:

The story of Christ's life is its own evidence,—it proves its own truth. It could have no other origin than a real life; and no other life could have given birth to it but such a life as that of Christ. To have forged such a life, in such a country, and in such an age, would have been impossible. . . . it is impossible it should be a fiction. . . . as impossible as for a red Indian, a hundred years ago, to have forged the history of this nineteenth century, with all its inventions, discoveries, reforms and revolutions . . . There was nothing that could have suggested such a character as that of Jesus either to Jew or Gentile, but the character itself. There was nothing that could have produced such a story as that of the Gospels, but a real life answering to the story. There was nothing in the prevailing sentiments of the age, nothing in the religious sects of those times, nothing in the theologies, nothing in the philosophies, nothing in the books, nothing in the traditions, nothing in the teachers, nothing even in the desires, the expectations, or the dreams of the time to give birth to such histories as those of the Gospels. . . . The writers of the Gospels did not understand the kind of life they were writing. . . . Their books prove that the story of Jesus, if we may so speak, wrote itself,—that his character . . . photographed itself, through their almost unconscious instrumentality. . . . If the Gospel story had not been true, it never could have been at all. The *written* life, demonstrates the *real* life. And if Jesus really lived,— and if the account we have of him in the Gospels is substantially true, then Christianity and the Bible are divine.[126]

Whether or not one is convinced by this thesis, it is not an intellectual evasion. It is rather an argument that meets head-on the most formidable alternative to an orthodox view that had been proposed in Barker's lifetime, the mythical theory of Strauss's *Leben Jesu*.[127]

Barker did not merely arrive back where he had started; he knew the place differently. He did not simply regress to his youthful faith; intellectually, he was orthodox in a way he had not been before. This

[125] Joseph Barker, *Jesus: A Portrait* (Philadelphia: Methodist Episcopal Book Room, 1873).

[126] Barker, *The Bible*, 31–5.

[127] For the reception of Strauss's work in Britain, see Larsen, *Contested Christianity*, chap. 4.

is seen most clearly in his mature doctrine of Scripture. Barker returned to the view that the Bible was divinely inspired, but not to his earlier formulation of that doctrine. He would never say as a reconvert what he had said in his debate with Lloyd Jones: 'the New Testament contains no discrepancies.' His mature doctrine of Scripture was one that would have accorded with the liberal evangelical position of A. S. Peake, a leading biblical scholar of the early twentieth century: the Scriptures are vehicles of divine revelation, but they are not infallible.[128] It was obvious that there were some discrepancies, errors, and contradictions; this must be conceded: 'I accept plain facts. To deny them is to fight against God.'[129] The old orthodox articulation of the doctrine was untenable, but that did not mean that the doctrine itself was discredited: 'Many of the things I said about the Bible in my debate with Dr. Berg were true; but they amounted to nothing. Dr. Berg thought they were serious charges, and that if they were not refuted, they would destroy the credit and power of the Book. He was mistaken.... The sun has spots, but they neither disprove its value nor its divine origin.'[130] More than that, the documents that comprise the Bible were unquestionably coloured by the misconceptions of the ages when they were written. Peter rightly says that the biblical authors were divinely inspired (2 Peter 1: 20–1). However: 'He does not say that the holy men, when moved by the Holy Spirit, would cease to be men, or even be free from all the imperfections or misconceptions of their age and nation, and speak as if they had become at once perfect in the knowledge of natural philosophy, or of common history, or even on every point pertaining to religion.'[131]

---

[128] Peake held the Rylands Chair of Biblical Criticism and Exegesis at the University of Manchester. Curiously, Barker and Peake both wrote books that endeavoured to demonstrate how valuing the Scriptures highly could be combined with accepting modern biblical criticism, with remarkably similar titles: Barker's *The Bible, Its Great Worth and Divine Origin* (1873) and Peake's *The Bible, Its Origin, Its Significance, and Its Abiding Worth* (London: Hodder & Stoughton, 1913). For Peake, see John T. Wilkinson, *Arthur Samuel Peake: A Biography* (London: Epworth Press, 1971); Timothy Larsen, 'A. S. Peake, the Free Churches, and Modern Biblical Criticism', *Bulletin of the John Rylands University Library of Manchester*, 86: 3 (forthcoming).

[129] Barker, *Modern Skepticism*, 12.

[130] Ibid. 301.

[131] Ibid. 213.

In his transitional stage, Barker had taken more to heart the force of the challenge to find a better book with which to replace the Bible. He then reached a position not unlike Churchill's epigrammatic assessment of democracy: the Bible is the worst guide-book for life and morals, except for all the others. Barker's appreciation would grow yet further. Always an advocate of women's rights, he came back to the view that the Bible was sound on this issue: 'It has awakened an interest in woman not known in pagan lands, and has converted her from a slave, a drudge, or a toy, into...the equal of man.'[132] He finally decided that the Bible was to be lauded extravagantly, albeit judiciously: 'I do not believe it possible to praise the Bible too highly; but nothing is easier than to praise it unwisely, untruly. You cannot love or prize the Bible too much; but you may err as to what constitutes its worth.'[133] His liberal evangelical view included an acceptance of the findings of the emerging discipline of biblical criticism. It was wrongheaded to insist that books of the Bible were 'written by certain men, and at certain times, and no others'.[134] The divine origin of the Bible was affirmed by its according with our best instincts and deepest affections, and by its utility: 'But there is a practical perfection, a perfection of *usefulness*, in both [Nature and the Bible]; a perfection of adaptation to the accomplishment of the highest and most desirable objects: and that is enough.'[135] Indeed, the analogy with nature was an important one in his thinking on this matter. Mountains are even more wondrous and beautiful because they are not shaped as perfect cones. The fact that our air is not pure oxygen only adds to its utility. The Bible is glorious for what it is, even though it does not fully meet scientific standards of perfection by which we might choose to measure it.

Barker spent the last ten years of his life expounding and defending orthodox Christianity in lectures and writings in both Britain and America. He engaged in controversy with the Unitarians.[136] He chose Primitive Methodism as his denominational identity. Joseph Barker

---

[132] Barker, *The Bible*, 20.
[133] Id., *Modern Skepticism*, 209.
[134] Id., *The Bible*, 51–2.
[135] Id., *Modern Skepticism*, 369.
[136] Joseph Barker, *Unitarianism: What claims has it to respect and favour? A Lecture* (n.p., n.d. [probably 1866]).

died on his farm in Omaha, Nebraska, on 15 September 1875. Holyoake acknowledged the rigour of his estranged comrade's intellectual efforts, 'He left the adherents of every opinion that he espoused a legacy of exposition and denunciation which no other man contributed in his time.'[137] Given the Victorian obsession with deathbed pronouncements, Barker took pains to establish beyond all doubt that he had died in the faith. The month before he died he sent a written testimony of his continuing commitment to orthodox Christianity to William Cooke in England. A few days before his death, Barker dictated a last statement of faith to his lawyer and two additional witnesses:

I feel that I am approaching my end, and desire that you should receive my last words and be witness to them. I wish you to witness that I am in my right mind, and fully understand what I have just been doing; and, dying, that I die in the firm and full belief in Jesus Christ, and in the faith and love of His religion as revealed in His life and works, as described in the New Testament; that I have an abiding faith in and love of God, as God is revealed to us by His Son Jesus Christ, and I die trusting in God's infinite love and mercy, and in full faith of a future and better life. I am sorry for my past errors; but during the last years of my life I have striven to undo the harm I did, by doing all I was able to serve God, by showing the beauty and wisdom of the religion of His Son Jesus Christ. I wish you to write down and witness this my last confession of faith, that there may be no doubt about it.[138]

---

[137] *Secular Chronicle*, 31 Oct. 1875, p. 205.
[138] *Methodist New Connexion Magazine* (Dec. 1875), 759–60.

7

John Bagnall Bebbington

John Bagnall Bebbington was a working-man from the Potteries who was rooted deep in Staffordshire soil. His very middle name was a tribute to a local place-name.[1] When he gave a public statement explaining his reconversion, the atheistic *National Reformer* was so determined to discredit him in every conceivable way that it even claimed that his address was 'marred' by 'the broad provincial sound' of his regional accent.[2] His parents were Baptists from Burslem. He was born there in 1832.[3] His father died at the age of 25. Bebbington was therefore sent off to spend his boyhood with a kind and pious relative in a small village somewhere in the area around Burslem. This relative—who regretted not having received much education himself—attentively ensured by way of compensation that Bebbington gained the best education circumstances could allow.

Bebbington and his guardian inevitably attended the Primitive Methodist chapel, as it was the only place of worship in the village. It generally depended upon the ministrations of laymen. Young Bebbington's more than run-of-the-mill learning allowed him to see the limitations of his spiritual leaders. 'Fresh from earthenware or china manufactory', their preparation for preaching consisted more in purity of heart than study: 'they often made mistakes, fell into blunders. Their theology was not of a scholastic kind, their explanation of difficult biblical passages not always judicious. As

---

[1] Bagnall is a village a little north-east of Stoke-on-Trent.
[2] *National Reformer*, 22 Aug. 1863, 'The New Convert'.
[3] He gives his age as 49 in the 1881 Census. Information from this census may be accessed at www.familysearch.org. I am grateful to the Church of Jesus Christ of Latter-day Saints for providing this service.

I grew up I perceived this, and thereupon the mocking spirit took possession of me; gradually, very gradually, I gave myself up to derision. I began to feel proud that I knew better than these men.'[4] This is, of course, to evoke his perspective as a reconvert. Such a retrospective view is all we have to rely on until his own Secularist voice emerges in the contemporary record, beginning in 1853. What we find in the press from his freethinking days does tally, however, with his autobiographical reflections as a reconvert. It is, therefore, reasonable to accept the factual aspects of his reconvert autobiographical account as substantially accurate, while bearing in mind that the interpretation is influenced by his later commitments. The life-story of the pre-eminent leader of organized atheism in the second half of the nineteenth century, Charles Bradlaugh, was similarly founded on his clash with his parish priest when he was preparing for confirmation.[5] If Bebbington had not reconverted, we would presumably still have this story of seeing through Primitive Methodist preachers, only not as a tale of 'pride' but rather as one of his first courageous steps on the road to reason. Indeed, we do have a more general reflection in the heroic vein that Bebbington made as a leader of freethought: 'Many years ago the hollowness of the theologies flashed upon me—even before my boyhood had passed the revolt began.'[6]

Bebbington was a Sunday-school teacher. At the same time, he was also increasingly interested in sceptical literature. Even as a self-censorious reconvert, one can still hear bubbling up in his account a charming and eloquent witness to a common person's uncommon thirst for knowledge:

I soon began to seek for books to serve as an armory for weapons to puzzle with. By degrees I lost faith, and suspected that Paine and Volney—for to these writers had I gone—might be really right. At length I heard the name of Mirabaud: I travelled eight miles to procure the famous 'System of Nature,' commonly attributed to Mirabaud, really by D'Holbach. It was late on Saturday night when I set out to return home with this treasure.

---

[4] J. B. Bebbington, *Why I Was An Atheist, and Why I Am Now A Christian*, 2nd edn. (London: H. J. Tresidder, n.d. [1865]), 5.

[5] Hypatia Bradlaugh Bonner, *Charles Bradlaugh: His Life and Work* (London: T. Fisher Unwin, 1895), i. 7–24.

[6] *Propagandist*, 6 Sept. 1862, p. 75.

I was disappointed that I could not begin to read it as I walked along; I managed to cut it open with a knife even as I journeyed in the darkness. I devoured that book. I yielded myself up to the dangerous eloquence of the Frenchman. From that moment I was lost. Faith in God, in immortality, was gone. A God-forsaken apostate, I had accepted the creed of despair.[7]

D'Holbach, Paine, and Volney locate Bebbington in a radical free-thinking tradition stemming from the eighteenth century. Such material seemed irrefutable: the representatives of Christian thought in his life at that time, Bebbington reiterated, 'were utterly incapable' of 'dealing with my difficulties'.

In his late teenage years Bebbington gave up on the Primitive Methodists and started attending the Baptist chapel in Burslem. This was the family chapel. His father was buried there, his mother had continued to worship there after his father's death, and his guardian relative had served at one time as a deacon and trustee there. Bebbington became a Sunday-school teacher there as well. He reminisced regarding this place of worship: 'The preaching was of a much higher order than that to which I had been accustomed, but it came too late. I listened for years to the ministrations of the Rev. William Barker.'[8] William Barker was a minister in Burslem in 1849–53.[9] Fascinatingly, another major intellectual influence was Cooper's popularization of Strauss's *Leben Jesu*. If eighteenth-century deists provided the foundation, Bebbington was by this period becoming very much up-to-date, encountering some of the latest and most scientifically and philosophically rigorous sceptical ideas:

After teaching the children to read the Bible in the school on Sundays, I went home to devour the 'Exegesis of Strauss,' which Thomas Cooper was then engaged in publishing. From *Cooper's Journal* I culled out arguments with which to puzzle Mr. Barker in his Bible Class. Finally, I withdrew altogether from chapel attendance; I walked about the fields on Sundays, sketching the trees and cottages, and muttering very fine things about nature, destiny, humanity, and the godless millenium [*sic*].[10]

---

[7] Bebbington, *Why*, 5.
[8] Ibid. 6.
[9] W. T. Whitley, *Baptists of North-West England, 1649–1913* (London: Kingsgate Press, 1913).
[10] Bebbington, *Why*, 6.

As the contents of both d'Holbach's *System of Nature* and Strauss's *Leben Jesu* have already been discussed in previous chapters, they do not need to be rehearsed here. Bebbington's abandonment of chapel life could not have happened earlier than 1850 nor later than the first half of 1853.

In his account of this period as a reconvert, Bebbington then became in his free time a sort of Secularist lay evangelist. He would challenge open-air preachers. Like an evangelical distributing tracts, he would send copies of Holyoake's *Reasoner* to local ministers. It is at this point that Bebbington's autobiographical narrative as a reconvert can begin to be correlated with contemporary Secularist sources. As an ex-Secularist, Bebbington recalled his efforts to reach Christian ministers with freethinking ideas: 'I attended their chapels and churches in hopes to hear allusions to myself, or the *Reasoner*, from their pulpits.'[11] This can be overlaid with a report that was published in the 3 August 1853 issue of the *Reasoner*, in which Bebbington testified that he had heard the Wesleyan minister in Burslem preach.[12] As Bebbington was never an adherent at a Wesleyan church, his presence there was in all probability an example of his acting as a self-appointed Secularist spy.

At this point, in August 1853, Bebbington clearly emerges in the sources as the leader of the Secularist cause in Burslem. Ironically, the visit of Berwin Grant on an anti-infidel mission had succeeded in both making visible a hitherto unorganized sceptical segment of the local population and in galvanizing it into action. The rector, the Revd C. Herbert, became alarmed by the strength of freethought in his parish. He called for a public discussion between the two sides. Bebbington had hoped that the national leader of Secularism, G. J. Holyoake, could represent the cause of freethought. He even went so far as to accuse Herbert of having deliberately scheduled the meeting at a time when he knew that the editor of the *Reasoner* would not be available, complaining: 'Through this procedure, one or two working men stood there to defend Secularism against the whole of the paid clergy of Burslem.'[13] Whatever hope Bebbington

---

11 Bebbington, *Why*, 6.
12 *Reasoner*, 3 Aug. 1853, pp. 77–8.
13 Ibid., 10 Aug. 1853, 'The Local Convention in Burslem'.

had nurtured that there might be two Secularist advocates rather than one proved ill-founded. In the end, several people spoke on the side of faith (including a Mormon), but John Bagnall Bebbington was the only person to give voice to the sceptical point of view. He began with anti-Bible attacks:

Mr. Bebbington referred to the precepts in the sermon on the Mount, which commanded no thought to be taken for the morrow, &c., showing the practical consequences of such commands being acted upon. The people, when Jesus had ended his strange address, were 'astonished at his doctrine' which he taught, and he thought they had very good reason for being astonished. . . . He referred to the commands 'Resist not evil,' 'If a man take thy cloak, let him have they coat also,' &c.—such teaching as Volney justly remarked, 'emboldens the wicked by impunity, and degrades the virtuous by the servility to which it reduces them.'

Mr. Bebbington begged the rector to take up the Pentateuch, and read of the horrors which were perpetrated (he would not dare to contradict it) at the command of the God he worshipped. . . . All the Secularists wanted was the morality of the precepts and doctrines [of the Bible] defended. If they could be shown to be moral, they would accept them without miracles or prophecies to support them.[14]

The reference to Volney also corresponds to his later account of his intellectual influences. Bebbington then went on to discuss 'the futility of prayer', a topic that was not a particular focus for most Secularist leaders, but one which became a recurring theme for him. He attacked the morality of the belief that a notorious criminal could secure salvation through a deathbed conversion. One orthodox disputant expressed a wish that Christians knew their Bibles as well as Bebbington knew his Holyoake! This is a not-insignificant comment, as a testimony both to his capacity to imbibe learning, and to his devotion to Holyoake, a figure whom Bebbington would assail when he had reached his prime as a Secularist leader.

Someone complained that Bebbington had merely attacked faith rather than expounding the positive strengths of Secularism. He replied that he was willing to have another discussion with that theme as the subject under consideration. Then a Mr Smith, who would seem to have been a zealous layman, put himself forward as

---

[14] Ibid. 83.

defender of the faith. Even Bebbington wondered if a recognized minister might not be better suited for this task, but Smith secured the position by persistence or default. The match led to a decisive victory for Bebbington. The *Potteries Telegraph*, doing its best to protect the cause of Christ, refused to print what either party said or even summarize their arguments. It hoped that the community would only learn one thing from the debate: 'We may, however, suggest the importance of a wiser selection of a champion to defend the important interests, and enforce the superior claims of Christianity in any future public discussion.'[15] The positive side of Secularism, in Bebbington's reckoning, was based on a zero-sum game view of reality. This allowed him to expound his theme of 'the inutility of prayer'. Christians trust in aid from heaven, which is a dangerous distraction from the practical work that needs to be done: 'If men were going to sea, they had better learn to swim than to pray.'[16] Smith testified about receiving a job in answer to prayer, and Bebbington rejoined with an anecdote about how he had recently secured a good position straightaway without praying. Tellingly, his love of learning coming out, he also set up a contrasting choice between great literature and evangelical preaching: 'Mr. B. then went into an exposition of the motives which Secularism would present against the commission of crime, saying, that an intelligent perusal of Macbeth would be of more use than a thousand sermons on never-ending fire, which might be obviated by repentance at the last.'[17] John Bagnall Bebbington had emerged as a local Secularist leader.

Around this time, Bebbington organized local sceptics into a Burslem Secular Society. For a while this went well: 'The society progressed, and all appeared prosperous'.[18] At some point in the 1850s, however, it was dissolved due to ill-fated over-ambition. A major Secularist leader (presumably Holyoake) was brought in to give a series of lectures. The wider community was not tempted by this attraction, and the society was unable to ride out the deflating effect of a failed crusade and the resulting substantial debt incurred.

[15] *Potteries Telegraph*, 13 Aug. 1853, as reprinted in *Reasoner*, 14 Sept. 1853, p. 165.
[16] *Reasoner*, 14 Sept. 1853, p. 166.
[17] Ibid., 167.
[18] Bebbington, *Why*, 7.

In the end, the society simply disbanded. Although the Burslem Secular Society did not continue to prosper, Bebbington himself did. Having begun as a journeyman potter, he rose in the mid-1850s to being an employer himself. In May 1857 Bebbington displayed courageous honest doubt at its finest. A whole series of valuable items had been stolen from his business by an employee. The matter came before the police court in Hanley. When instructed to take the oath before giving his evidence, Bebbington informed the court that he regarded 'the oath as a civil, and not as a religious ceremony'.[19] The clerk helped the magistrate grasp the point of this distinction by offering this translation: 'He does not believe the Scriptures.' Whereupon, the magistrate became alarmed, dismissed the case, and ordered that the police return the stolen goods to the thief's house! Despite such injustice, Bebbington prospered to the point of emerging as a patron of the Secularist cause who had significant amounts of disposable income to donate to disseminating freethinking ideas.

In mid-1857 Bebbington moved to London. This change provided the scope for him successfully to make the transition to a national leader in the Secularist movement. He was contributing to the *Reasoner*, and developing a reputation for bringing a scholarly approach to the advocacy of popular freethought. On the other hand, Bebbington seemed to delight in transferring his evangelistic and heckling duties to a wider scene. He made a habit of spending part of his time sparring with the open-air preachers at King's Cross Railway Station.[20] He joined the National Sunday League, moving the first resolution in November 1857 calling for Sunday opening for national institutions.[21] He also became a regular lecturer at leading metropolitan freethinking venues. In October 1857 he spoke at the London Secular Society on 'God in History not recognised by Science'. Holyoake chaired the meeting. Bebbington's persistent interest in debunking the notion of prayer was expressed on this occasion through an attack on 'the theology of the fast day'.[22]

---

[19] *Reasoner*, 31 May 1857, p. 87.
[20] Ibid., 15 July 1857, 'Street Sceptics'.
[21] Ibid., 11 Nov. 1857, p. 259.
[22] Ibid., 28 Oct. 1857, 'London Secular Society'.

Bebbington also went into publishing—clearly not as a way of making money but rather of serving the cause. With his address given as 8 Exeter Change, Strand, WC, he published a book by James Robertson that defended Holyoake against the accusations of another freethinker, Robert Cooper.[23] Bebbington became a popular lecturer on the London freethinking circuit. He delighted the East London Secular Institute with his ability to combine in the same address substantial scholarship that satisfied the more refined with populist jibes and humour that gratified the less sophisticated. His lecture on that occasion was on the 'Doctrine of Special Providence', yet another rebuttal to the expectation of receiving answers to prayers.[24] Bebbington's elevation into the elite circle of Secularist leaders was given formal expression when he was elected the founding chairman of the Temple Secular Society. Named after the Temple district of London, it was established to fill the gap which had been left when the London Secular Society relocated to Hoxton. Its postal address was given as 147 Fleet Street, that is, Holyoake's firm, signalling the Secularist patriarch's approval of the scheme. The Temple Secular Society met every Sunday morning. In other words, it was a kind of Secularist church, with its own congregation and with Bebbington as its minister or presiding elder. John Watts was elected secretary—who, as he did not reconvert, is now an incomparably better-known name in the memory of the movement—but at that time Bebbington was given the office of pre-eminence.[25]

An impressive display of antiquarian erudition, originally published in the *Reasoner*, became Bebbington's book *Freethought Biographies, a series of sketches of the Lives and Writings of the most remarkable British Freethinkers* (1858). It was published by Holyoake's firm. Rehearsing the charges made against heretics of old was actually a rather clever way to air ideas that still just might have provoked a blasphemy trial if care was not taken as to how they were expressed. Of the very first figure discussed, Matthew Hamont,

[23] James Robertson, *Secularists and their Slanders: or, the 'Investigator' Investigated. Mr. Holyoake and his assailants, their defeat, and the votes of confidence in Fleet Street House, from Manchester and Elsewhere* (London: J. B. Bebbington, n.d. [c.1857]).

[24] *Reasoner*, 5 May 1858, 'East London Secular Institute'.

[25] Ibid., 19 May 1858, 'The Temple Secular Society'.

executed in 1579, we are told that he was charged with believing and teaching:

That the new Testament and Gospell of Christ are but mere foolishnesses—a story of men, or rather a meere fable....

That Christ is not God, nor the Sauiour of the world, but a meere man, a sinfull man, and an abominable Idoll.

That all they that worship him are abominable Idolaters, and that Christ did not rise againe from death to life by the power of his Godhead, neither that he did ascend into heauen.[26]

His commentary on Reginald Scot (d. 1599) prompted Bebbington himself to denounce the Bible directly, lest the lesson be lost on anyone:

That respectable old superstition, for which, it is generally acknowledged, we are indebted to the Holy Scriptures—witchcraft, sorcery, and demoniacal possession, as, indeed, on the whole of the European continent, flourished with a great degree of energy in England in the sixteenth and seventeenth centuries.... With the Bible in their hands, and appealing to it for their justification, the number of their victims from first to last has been calculated to exceed *four thousand* persons. With the progress of experimental science these delusions lost their hold over the minds of men—positive science proved a safer guide than the Bible.[27]

There is a long entry on the playwright Christopher Marlowe (1564–93), Bebbington being convinced beyond all doubt that 'his heterodoxy took the extreme form of Atheism'.[28] Bebbington hopefully infers from Shakespeare's willingness on one occasion to quote Marlowe that from this might be deduced that England's greatest dramatist was in sympathy with the atheist's sceptical opinions. *Freethought Biographies* was a genuinely learned work. As will become clear, Bebbington was positioning himself as a Secularist leader who wanted to see the movement display a deeper commitment to scholarship.

In March 1859 Bebbington filled in as lecturer at the South London Institute when Holyoake was prevented by illness from

---

[26] J. B. Bebbington, *Freethought Biographies, a series of sketches of the Lives and Writings of the most remarkable British Freethinkers*, reprinted from the *Reasoner* (London: Holyoake & Co., 1858), 1.

[27] Ibid. 22.

[28] Ibid. 8.

fulfilling his engagement. Remarkably, Bebbington agreed to speak on the theme that had been announced, the historical evidences for Christianity, indicating both his strong general base of knowledge and also his confidence as a public speaker and intellectual leader.[29] When a fund was started to acquire a Secularist meeting hall in central London, Bebbington came second on the list of key donors with a £5 contribution (£10 topped the list).[30] In May 1860 Bebbington contributed a fascinating article on Secularism to the *Reasoner*. He was optimistic that their cause was destined to triumph. Even orthodox ministers were steadily altering their doctrines as freethinkers demonstrated that they were untenable. These changes were all the more secure because they were gradual rather than sudden. He tellingly averred that 'Secularism aspires to present a complete philosophy of life'.[31] It was only a matter of time for this philosophy to be worked out systematically. Secularism would nurture the highest intellectual development. Apart from any theology, morality would also successfully arise from Secularism. In order for this to happen, however, the old faith had to be swept away: 'It is evident at once to the most superficial inquirer, that Secularism and Christianity are in the outset irreconcilably opposed.' The undermining of the kind of confidence and the assumptions expressed in this article are standard components of a Victorian crisis of doubt.

In 1860 Bebbington made a significant contribution to popular freethought by editing, publishing, and financing inexpensive editions of David Hume's essays. The *Reasoner* declared that Bebbington's name was a guarantee that the editing would be meticulous. It argued that a familiarity with Hume's thought was essential for everyone serious about considering the claims of scepticism. Bebbington was naturally offering readers the celebrated 'Essays on Miracles'. Beyond it, however, were also lesser-known essays that the *Reasoner* testified were of immense value: 'the one on Providence, for instance, which has never been reprinted.'[32] Bebbington later

---

[29] *Reasoner*, 27 Mar. 1859, p. 103.

[30] Ibid., 10 July 1859, p. 223.

[31] Ibid., 6 May 1860, pp. 148–9.

[32] Ibid. 147. Bebbington did not put himself on the title-page as the editor, making his editions difficult to track. I have only been able to see the title-page for the following: David Hume, *An Essay on Miracles* (London: J. B. Bebbington, n.d.).

claimed that he invested almost £200 in reprinting Hume, the majority of which he did not recoup.[33] To put it another way, he parted with more money for the sake of disseminating Hume's thought than most people in Britain at that time earned in a year.

Bebbington also went on a Secularist lecturing tour with John Watts in 1860. Holyoake hosted a soirée as a way of sending them out with fanfare, and boasted that the demand for Secularist lecturing was then increasing and that a team tour marked a level of activity that had not been reached for some time. Bebbington advertised six lectures that he was prepared to deliver, including 'Christian Morality incomplete and unreliable' and 'The Literature of Freethought'.[34] In August, Bebbington and his co-labourer, John Watts, were among the eight national leaders of the Secularist movement identified by the invitations extended by the historic Castle Hill meeting (though Bebbington was not able to accept).[35] Lending a hand to Bradlaugh as well as Holyoake, Bebbington was also serving the movement by writing uncredited material for the *National Reformer*.[36]

Bebbington's most ambitious contribution to the literature of freethought began in May 1862, when he founded and began editing his own journal, the *Propagandist and Theological, Social, and Political Review*. Bebbington saw it as an opportunity to elevate the literary standard and level of scholarship of the movement. A month or so earlier Bebbington had made the acquaintance of William Maccall, an erudite, freethinking Scot who would serve as the journal's key contributor. Bebbington could provide the financial backing, take care of the editing and publishing, and add his own literary and scholarly gifts to its pages. The hope was that it would become financially self-sustaining, but when that did not happen it stopped publication in mid-October. Still, it was a wonder to behold while it lasted. Maccall would offer a lead article of high literary quality for almost every issue. He would also provide translations of continental sceptics. Maccall had a proven track record in this area;

---

[33] *Propagandist*, 6 Sept. 1862, p. 75.
[34] *Reasoner*, 6 May 1860, p. 146.
[35] Ibid., 12 Aug. 1860, p. 262.
[36] *Propagandist*, 6 Sept. 1862, p. 78.

notably, his translation of a treatise by Spinoza had been published by Holyoake's firm in 1854.[37] The *Propagandist* successfully executed this plan. Perhaps most impressively, the paper offered a steady stream of translations of the German materialist philosopher Ludwig Büchner's *Kraft und Stoff* (a different English translation was later published as a book with the title *Force and Matter*). Büchner was only 38 years old in 1862, and his book had appeared only seven years earlier, in 1855. An English translation would not be published as a book for another two years (London: Trübner & Co., 1864). Oxbridge minds searching for the latest sceptical thought of the highest calibre would have done well to supplement the *Westminster Review* with the *Propagandist*. Bebbington's journal also contained snippets from and translations of works which referred to or interacted with the thought of an even more important Ludwig, the brilliant and seminal critic of Christianity, Feuerbach. There were translations from other German writers, as well as a range of French authors. There was an extraordinarily wide range of Swedish literature on offer, presumably capitalizing on Maccall's mastery of that language. On one occasion there was also a Danish translation. The journal prided itself on filling its pages primarily with either original compositions or the first English translations of continental material. It also offered a long selection from Charles Hennell's *An Inquiry Concerning the Origin of Christianity* (1838), the volume that precipitated George Eliot's crisis of faith.[38] There was an article on Baron d'Holbach, recounting the story of his life, his thought, and the misattributing of his *System of Nature* to Mirabaud.[39] Bebbington's journal was raising the literary quality of popular freethinking advocacy.

On the other hand, the *Propagandist* had no wish to be a refined alternative to hard-hitting Secularist attacks. Once again, Bebbington showed his flair for combining the credibility of a scholar with the populism of a street-fighter. He declared bluntly that his journal was designed to be 'thoroughly outspoken and anti-Christian'.[40] He

[37] Benedictus de Spinoza, *A Treatise on Politics*, ed. William Maccall (London: Holyoake, 1854).

[38] *Propagandist*, 5 July 1862, pp. 42–4.

[39] Ibid., 2 Aug. 1862, pp. 60–1.

[40] Ibid., 6 Sept. 1862, p. 78.

blasted Christianity as 'the fruitful parent of ten thousand immoralities and miseries'.[41] Bebbington tore into the Bible and Christianity unceremoniously:

The *New Testament* commands us to renounce the world, and become as pilgrims journeying to some better land—to crush that passion which is one of the strongest necessities of our nature, remembering with Origen that 'men have made themselves eunuchs for the kingdom of heaven's sake'—in short, to completely crush the Natural man in order to live for Christ. Now I—J. B. Bebbington... [believe] that this said teaching of the *New Testament* is a damnable heresy against Nature, and therefore to be combatted and crushed.... I make a stern and uncompromising declaration of war against Christianism—I brand it as denying and shamelessly blaspheming the authority of Nature.[42]

Readers were informed that if the apostle Paul were to tell his story of encountering the risen Christ today people would conclude that 'a screw had got loose or fallen out'.[43] Jesus is referred to as 'the malefactor of Palestine'.[44] And so it goes on. Bebbington also made good on his pugilistic pledge: 'We are going to be violent, and very violent too. We are going to be personal, and very personal.'[45]

Much is revealed in the pages of the *Propagandist* regarding Bebbington's work in the Secularist cause more generally, and of his own sceptical thinking. He gave a lecture at the Hall of Science, London, on the 'Human Origin of the Hebrew Scriptures'.[46] Unlike the kind of superficial discrepancy-chasing that Bradlaugh too often engaged in, this lecture revealed a significant encounter with the lines of thought important to the emerging discipline of biblical criticism, reflecting, for example, on the 'Elohistic and Jehovistic' strains in the Pentateuch. He cannily rounded off this learned lecture with knock-down rhetoric: 'In conclusion Mr. Bebbington said it was almost a humiliation at this day seriously to be discussing the question of the human or divine origin of the books of Moses. But their deadly practical influence rendered it necessary that the rottenness of the claims made for them should be exposed.' The *National Reformer* ran an unusually

---

[41] Ibid., 3 May 1862, p. 10.   [42] Ibid., 31 May 1862, p. 19.
[43] Ibid. 29.   [44] Ibid., 5 July 1862, p. 34.
[45] Ibid., 31 May 1862, p. 26.   [46] Ibid. 30.

effusive report by the secretary of the Liverpool Secular Society regarding a lecture Bebbington gave for them. Most unlike themselves, the Liverpudlian freethinkers found that they repeatedly interrupted the editor of the *Propagandist* with spontaneous applause. He was a rare, if not singular, example of a speaker who highly pleased everyone in their society; he was 'a pioneer among the foremost in the ranks of freeman'.[47] In September and October Bebbington went on a speaking tour to the north of England and Scotland, speaking at the Eclectic Institute in Glasgow, among other places. His lecture-titles included 'The Doctrine of the Fall of Man', 'The Character and Teaching of Christ', 'The Age and Authorship of the Pentateuch', and 'The God of the Bible'.[48] In 1862 Bebbington was ranked among the handful of the most prominent and respected national leaders of the popular freethinking movement in Britain.

That handful of leaders was not marked by harmonious good-fellowship and mutual respect. The first issue of the *Propagandist* contained an attack on the hero of Bebbington's early days in the movement, Holyoake. Over the course of the journal's life this attack became focused on the allegation that Holyoake had taken the free-will offerings of Secularists in order to set up a Reasoner Company and then had given up on the project without ever trying. It is difficult to discern the weight of various factors prompting this attack, and in any event, this dispute is not germane to the theme at hand. It is possible that Bebbington was partially motivated by a simple desire to carve out a market share for his journal both by tempting readers with punchy material and by attempting to draw them away from a rival publication by diminishing their respect for its editor. What is fascinating about the original attack is that Bebbington, as a freethinker himself, criticized Holyoake for precisely what he—and other reconverts—would identify as a fundamental weakness of the entire Secularist movement, the extinguishing of the truths of the heart through an oppressive, clinical logic. It must be read for its full resonance with his later statements to be appreciated:

---

[47] *National Reformer* report, as repr. in the *Propagandist*, 2 Aug. 1862, p. 63.
[48] *Propagandist*, 2 Oct. 1862, p. 89.

The head is there, but the heart is wanting. . . . A boast has been made that he is 'impassive.' Here is the key to his whole character. Impassive as marble he certainly is; it would be difficult to find a man with less of feeling in his nature. A plaster bust would be as easily excited to passion as Mr. Holyoake. While listening to him you are painfully conscious of the utter absence of that earnestness which can only arise from deep feeling. The idea of a God seems to him illogical; he, therefore, in the coldest and most methodical manner flings a syllogism at it. But when did he ever seem deeply stirred with a passionate sense of the wrongs which have been inflicted on humanity in the name of God? . . . Absent, too, is the imaginative faculty . . . [in his writings there is] never the spontaneous welling up of a rich, finely attuned, and sympathetic nature. We have revealed to us exactly the man who would sit down to Shakespere's *Tempest*, and, instead of rioting in its glorious poesy, call for a map that he might trace out the site of Prospero's island. He would never forgive the writer of the *Winter's Tale* for making Bohemia a seaport . . . Mr. Holyoake was once deeply engaged in mathematical pursuits—when he abandoned those he sadly mistook his vocation. He might have taken rank among the Babbages of his day; he could scarcely have manufactured a calculating machine more cold and passionless than himself.[49]

With the exception of the single line about wrongs committed in the name of God, that passage could have been written by almost any reconvert as a description of their view of the sceptical tradition as a whole.

The *Propagandist*'s relationship to Bradlaugh was more complex. It was consistently opposed to Bradlaugh's decision to disseminate Drysdale's *Elements of Social Science*, dismissing that book unequivocally as 'beastly and abominable' and its theories of sexual morality as 'in every respect unnatural and disgusting'.[50] Nevertheless, it also began by praising Bradlaugh and, when it was becoming clearer that the *Propagandist* might not achieve a self-sustaining financial situation, Bebbington even proposed merging forces with him. He apparently envisioned himself playing a kind of co-editor role at the *National Reformer*, like the one that Joseph Barker had vacated.[51] Bradlaugh declined this offer in a most gracious manner, and put out

49 Ibid., 3 May 1862, p. 2.
50 Ibid., 2 Aug. 1862, p. 58; 6 Sept. 1862, p. 74.
51 Ibid., 6 Sept. 1862, p. 78.

a hand of friendship to a co-belligerent. Any possibility of a merger having been ruled out, Bebbington apparently felt free to criticize 'Iconoclast' as well. Once again, as in his critique of Holyoake, there is a remarkable foreshadowing of thoughts and events to come. Extraordinarily, at this exact moment Bradlaugh engaged in a debate on 'Christianity and Secularism' with Bebbington's former minister (who had subsequently moved to a congregation in Blackfriars), the Revd William Barker. Bebbington's substantial review of the debate was his lead story in the 4 October 1862 issue of the *Propagandist*. Not terribly surprisingly, Bebbington chided Bradlaugh for populism at the expense of learning, just as the journal had done with Gordon's London lecture. More intriguingly, the piece expounds in forthright language several points that reconverts were also apt to make. First, 'Bradlaugh could never get beyond the exposition of a discrepancy'.[52] He was incapable of engaging any wider theme. At one point, the audience actually laughed uproariously at Bradlaugh's apparent inability to grasp the difference between the question of the possibility of a divine revelation per se, and the issue of whether or not the Bible was one. Moreover, according to the *Propagandist*, even if Bradlaugh must confine himself to an attack on the Bible, he did so in a superficial way, devoid of any sign of the latest scholarly research. An agreed theme for a portion of the debate was for the editor of the *National Reformer* to propound Secularist morality, and this, in Bebbington's telling of it, he was simply unable to do: 'When Mr. Bradlaugh attempts to expound principles he lamentably fails. On this evening Secular morality grew terribly indistinct before he had proceeded for five minutes in his opening speech. Ere a quarter of an hour had elapsed he was deeply engaged in an attack on Christian morality... Secular morality made a very poor appearance this evening.' Even as a freethinker, Bebbington knew that he was witnessing a supposed philosophy of life that was offering only mere negations.

More remarkable still is Bebbington's frank praise for the Revd William Barker's speeches. In this encounter, according to the editor of the *Propagandist*, the orthodox Christian was revealed to be the more 'logical', the more 'philosophical', the more rational of the pair:

52 *Propagandist*, 4 Oct. 1862, p. 81.

'Of the two disputants, Mr. Barker displayed by far the greater power of reasoning.'⁵³ The contrast was painful:

from beginning to end [Barker's] speeches were argument of some kind. Mr. Bradlaugh is the very opposite of all this; he attempts to reason but seldom. He is at a standstill when he is taken away from the discrepancies, and contradictions, and scientific blunders in the Old Testament, and the cruel and vindictive phase of the character of the God of the Bible. These things, however irrelevantly, were made to do duty on every evening.

This was a poor showing, Bebbington fretted. Popular freethought was going to have to become more cultured, more learned, more rational. If the impression is left that Bradlaugh's performance was 'the best thing that can be said on behalf of unbelief, then there is infinite harm'. In another article, Bebbington had also expressed his anxiety that popular scepticism lagged far behind the intellectual calibre of orthodox Christianity. Although clearly puffing up the need for the *Propagandist*, he was in earnest: 'We have never yet had a periodical that displayed half the ability of the *Christian Cabinet*, the lowest and the trashiest of penny christian prints.... Do our opponents despise or underrate training and culture? No, the churches are too wise in their generation for this.'⁵⁴ The actual decision to reconvert was not yet even on the horizon, but Bebbington was already becoming aware of the issues he would eventually cite as reasons for that change.

Bebbington announced his reconversion in July 1863. He stated simply, in a short letter, that he was returning to the faith of his youth, and that he would give reasons for this change in due course. Having lived through the reconversions of figures such as Cooper, Gordon, and Barker, Bebbington knew what to expect. This initial letter, printed in the *National Reformer*, showed that he had braced himself for the onslaught: 'I have no request for mercy or consideration to prefer [proffer]: I am even prepared to meet the usual imputations of insincerity and idiocy.'⁵⁵ His fears were not ill-founded. Even the most preposterous charge was made: John Childs, a leading-light of the Leeds Secular Society, insinuated that

---

⁵³ Ibid. 81–2.
⁵⁴ Ibid., 6 Sept. 1862, p. 74.
⁵⁵ *National Reformer*, 25 July 1863, p. 6.

'mercenary motives' were at the root of his change.[56] Bebbington's superabundant financial circumstances, not to say track record as a generous benefactor, made this so implausible that it never went beyond vague insinuations from the sidelines. Bebbington protested that John Watts had 'ascribed to me dirty motives for the change, in the dirtiest possible manner', but did not reveal what they were.[57] The *National Reformer* opted for the charge that Bebbington hoped to create a 'sensation'.[58] It largely confined itself, however, to the more legitimate task in such polemical warfare of denouncing his 'blundering statement' as 'illogical and opposed to reason'. As with Gordon's conversion, Bradlaugh immediately challenged Bebbington to a debate.

Holyoake, then editing the *Secular World*, was disarmed by Bebbington's decision to use a portion of his statement to retract in the most handsome manner his attacks on him, to assert categorically that he now knew that Holyoake had never done anything dishonest with donated monies, and to express deep regret at his violent language against him. This resulted in the editor being inclined to let Bebbington off on the standard charge of being disingenuous: 'The impression [his statement] gives is one of thoughtfulness and possible sincerity.'[59] (Still, the word 'possible' betrays how unnatural it was for a Secularist to make such a concession to a reconvert.) On the other hand, the potter from Staffordshire could not evade the 'suddenness' charge by manufacturing a long period of unease: 'He talks of years of "speechless agony" endured. Wonderful has been the success with which he disguised it!' At his best, Holyoake could playfully work the theme of a stark and suspiciously rapid change of views: 'the author has taken a great leap and landed himself uneasily and dangerously amid the crags of the New Testament. If spiritual vaulting were as serious as physical there would be occasion for the Queen to interfere to limit these displays of new converts.' Thus the popular freethinking movement parted with yet another of its erstwhile national leaders.

---

[56] Bebbington, *Why*, 28.
[57] Ibid. 28.
[58] *National Reformer*, 22 Aug. 1863, 'The New Convert'.
[59] *Secular World*, 1 Oct. 1863, 'Mr. Bebbington's Statement'.

Bebbington gave a public statement explaining his change of views in August 1863. This address was separately published as *Why I Was An Atheist, and Why I Am Now A Christian.* William Barker—his former minister, and the man of reason whom he thought, by way of contrast, had revealed the unconstructive superficiality of Bradlaugh's thought—was in the chair. Barker testified on Bebbington's behalf:

From an intimate knowledge of Mr. Bebbington in his youthful days, and from an anxious observance of his subsequent course as a Sceptic and Atheist, I feel myself in a position to express most confidently my belief in his sincerity...He was sincere as a Sceptic too, and must have made sacrifices for infidelity which are not always characteristic of the course of its advocates and abettors. And I believe his testimony to his Christian enlightenment and strong faith in the old writers of the Gospel, to be a sincere and truthful expression of honest overpowering conviction...[60]

Barker also revealed that there had been an extensive private correspondence between him and his old acquaintance from Burslem, and asserted that anyone who read it would be even more convinced of Bebbington's sincerity. This observation had the added advantage of helping to mitigate the 'suddenness' charge. In Bebbington's own account, his crisis of doubt had begun when he was on his Scottish freethinking lecturing tour in September and October 1862. Again, it was important in this polemical context to trace a gradual process: 'While on this tour I experienced the first faint glimmering of thoughts which have since germinated and borne fruit, which have worked a complete revolution in my convictions, in my whole being.'[61] At that time, the thought would come to him that he was on a 'gloomy errand'; that he was travelling a long way and going to laborious efforts just to disabuse people of hopes that they cherished which he thought did not have sufficient warrant. There were a couple of weeks or more in which he was scheduled to speak only on the Sunday, and thus was at a loose end for days. This time for reflection launched him on a process of re-examining the foundations of his unbelief. Although he was being very well received—enthusiastic reports of his tour were printed in the

---

[60] Bebbington, *Why*, [2].   [61] Ibid. 8.

National Reformer—Bebbington withdrew from the public arena to wrestle with these issues in earnest. There was, therefore, a substantial period of eight months (from mid-October 1862 to late July 1863) between his self-imposed retirement from Secularist advocacy and the announcement of his reconversion.

There is no need to rehearse here his account of his loss of faith. It is worthwhile, however, to give the list of the sceptical books that were his 'chief inspiration': d'Holbach's *System of Nature*, Hume's works, Hennell's *An Inquiry Concerning the Origin of Christianity*, Mackay's *Progress of the Intellect*, and Strauss's *The Life of Jesus Critically Examined*. Bebbington's statement is full of suggestive lines of thought, but it will suffice to concentrate here on two efforts that he makes to answer specific arguments he had been persuaded by as a sceptic, and then go on to present the alternative frame of mind that he wished to defend as a reasoning believer. As he journeyed into scepticism, the only argument for the existence of God that he thought had any force was the argument from design. At first he overcame it, with the aid of Holyoake's *Paley Refuted in his own Words*. He eventually saw through this work, however, concluding that there was more philosophical depth and merit in Paley's argument than in Holyoake's objection to it. In his statement, this leads Bebbington into a rebuke of Secularists who too often take Holyoake's word for things and do not bother to read what is said on the subject by those holding an opposing point of view. Bebbington claimed that the intellectual case against Holyoake's position is overwhelming, referring seekers after the truth to Henry Townley's replies to the sceptic Henry Batchelor's *The Logic of Atheism* and James Buchanan's *Modern Atheism*.[62]

Having dispensed with Holyoake, Bebbington, as a sceptic, was then persuaded by Hume's observation that the argument from design did not lead all the way to what was meant by the term 'God' (notably, an infinite, all powerful being). At most, as Bebbington interpreted Hume's account, the argument established only the

---

[62] Henry Townley and G. J. Holyoake, *Report of a public discussion carried on by Henry Townley and George Jacob Holyoake* (London: Ward, 1852); Henry Batchelor, *The Logic of Atheism* (London: Judd & Glas, 1858); James Buchanan, *Modern Atheism* (Boston: Gould & Lincoln, 1857).

existence of a powerful being, who might nevertheless be finite, limited in power, and fallible. As a reconvert, Bebbington was still convinced by Hume's critique on this point. What changed was that he now did with Hume what the Scottish philosophy had done with the argument from design—he demarcated his achievement as strictly limited. Bebbington came to see the argument from design as a stepping-stone that he had illogically refused to make use of. Hume had said that it only got one so far, but Bebbington chided himself for having been unwilling even to go that far. Bebbington then went on to argue that Almighty God was a much more rational inference from the argument from design than that of a limited, but powerful creator being: 'The supposition of an endless series of finite beings I knew to be endless nonsense . . . Go back as far as we will, we must at last repose in self-existence. That self-existence is GOD.'[63] In this manner, the intellectual case against theism collapsed, in Bebbington's mind.

Next came the case against Christianity in particular. Bebbington, as a reconvert, reconstructs (perhaps a little too neatly) his freethinking point of view on the faith of his childhood thus: Christians claim that their religion should be taken seriously because it is validated by miracles; Hume has demonstrated that no such validation is possible; *ergo*, there is no reason to take seriously the claims of Christianity. As he thought his way back to faith, Bebbington came to reject the reasoning of Hume's essay on miracles. He concluded that Hume's argument had 'a fundamental fallacy'; the Scottish philosopher was 'guilty of a *petitio principii*'. Moreover, Hume did not take into account the fact that Christian miracles were not on par with mere idle wonders but rather were supported by 'antecedent probability'. Hume had not factored in the 'moral aspects of the question'.[64] Despite all that, Bebbington's primary response was to deny the premise of his sceptical syllogism. Miracles did not validate the Christian message, but rather only played a kind of advertising role. He had been helped to see this by the writings of Thomas Arnold and by Richard Trench's *Notes on the Miracles of Our Lord* (1846). Having sidestepped his syllogism, he was then ready to investigate Christianity in order to discover what inherent worth it

---

[63] Bebbington, *Why*, 15.   [64] Ibid. 18–19, 22.

might have. What he discovered was that the Christian faith was self-authenticating: 'I commenced, then, for the first time in my life, seriously to examine the doctrines of Christianity apart from any consideration of miraculous evidence. And I saw in Christianity a complete adaptation to the moral condition, to the needs and requirements of humanity, so complete that in itself it was almost sufficient to stamp Christianity as divine.'[65] This line of argument merged with the earlier acceptance of the existence of God. If there is a Moral Governor, then human beings, as sinners, are guilty in God's sight. The Christian atonement is fitted to meet this human need. Reason and philosophy can only explore the contours of reality. They lack the power to 'cure a soul diseased'. Bebbington found this balm in the power of the cross.

The overriding theme of Bebbington's statement was that humanity possessed truths that were stifled by an exclusive reliance on a narrowly conceived rationalism:

Human consciousness and logic I now found to run parallel. I discovered that all along I had been starving one part of my nature—cultivating a thin, weak, penury soul. My heart had longed after God. I had repressed its longings, in obedience to the dictates of a diseased logic; I had only to give my heart fair play—a sounder logic I found to confirm and justify its promptings.... Down from the far, far ages, from the infancy of the world and of the human race, comes a voice from the heart of humanity.... it speaks of God. And we are asked to believe that the great heart of humanity lies—has always lied! It does not lie, it has not lied. God exists ...[66]

Secularists do not understand this, he observed, in language that closely parallels his critique of Holyoake as a freethinker: 'There is one quality that I have remarked in every atheist—at least every contented atheist—that I have met with. This is a predominance of intellect, a penury of feeling.... They are cold and passionless... They are as impassive as marble.'[67] For himself, Bebbington was quite willing to acknowledge that this had been an emotionally intense process for him. He was ready to defend his views as reasonable—he had not renounced 'reason' or 'common sense'—but he was not some passionless, detached investigator.

---

[65] Bebbington, *Why*, 20.   [66] Ibid. 15–17.   [67] Ibid. 17.

As with so many other reconverts, Bebbington also asserted that Secularism was unable to produce a viable morality on its own: 'Natural morality, when asked for a test to distinguish between right and wrong, is obliged to mutter that very ugly word—utility. ...by what canon of natural morality is a man to be called on to prefer the good of the greater number to his own good, when the two clash? But once recognise the law within, and it will speak irresistibly of duty, devotion...'[68] Holyoake retorted that if people cannot find a way to be virtuous as sceptics, it was indeed better that they went over to the church.[69]

A few more suggestive, if incidental, comments will round off this exposition of Bebbington's statement. He mentions somewhat apologetically that he did not pray until well into this time of transition. That detail correlates with his persistent attacks as a freethinker on the idea of prayer. Perhaps most fascinating of all are the concessions that demonstrate how his views were different from what they might have been if he had remained an orthodox Christian throughout his life. He rejected dismissively Christians who regale freethinkers with tales about unbelievers dying in agony. Rather, he testified candidly: 'I have seen the atheist die in peace.'[70] Arguably departing altogether from the traditional Christian orthodoxy of his day on this point, Bebbington held out hope that even those who die atheists might still benefit from the 'boundless mercy' of God. After all, deprived as they were of a full-orbed human consciousness, perhaps their unbelief will be viewed as a symptom of this impairment, and therefore as not culpable.

A few weeks after his public statement—on 3 September 1863— Bebbington was baptized as a believer by William Barker. Writing exactly a month later, on 3 October, Barker coyly indicated that he would support Bebbington if he decided to pursue some form of Christian ministry. He did not choose to do so. Having come back to the faith of his childhood and the denominational identity of his parents, Bebbington also returned to the landscape and vocation of his youth. In 1866 he was living in Hanley. He reappears at that time

---

[68] Ibid. 24.
[69] *Secular World*, 1 Oct. 1863, 'Mr. Bebbington's Statement'.
[70] Bebbington, *Why*, 31.

as a political radical, writing a blistering attack on a local Tory, William Evans. Because of his opposition to the Reform Bill, Bebbington identified Evans as a 'Judas' who had betrayed 'the working class with a kiss'.[71] After that Bebbington seems to have settled down to a quiet life. The 1881 census has him as a potter living in Stoke-on-Trent.[72] Living with him and his wife Eliza was a son, John, born in 1859 when they were living in London, a daughter, Eliza, born when they were in Hanley, and another son, Frederick. In *Why I Was An Atheist and Why I Am Now A Christian*, the erstwhile Secularist leader presented his experience as an earnest and thirsty searcher after knowledge and truth as confirming Francis Bacon's dictum: 'A little philosophy inclineth men's minds to atheism, but depth in philosophy bringeth men's minds about to religion.'[73] Other life stories—equally valid—would, of course, call into question such a principle. Bebbington's intellectual journey is only one kind among a variety of possibilities—albeit a real and legitimate and too often overlooked kind.

[71] J. B. Bebbington, *A Letter (Short and Sharp) to William Evans* (Hanley: J[ames] Bebbington, 1866).

[72] Information kindly provided some years ago by Chris Latimer, City Archivist, Stoke-on-Trent. I have since checked it and added to it from the information provided at www.familysearch.org.

[73] Bebbington, *Why*, 27.

8

George Sexton

In 1876 George Sexton (1825–98) declared that 'he intended devoting the rest of his life to the preaching of the Gospel and the promulgation of Christian truth'.[1] He made good on this pledge, spending twenty-two years preaching and writing on Christian apologetics. Before that, what a varied life he had led! His position in this study anticipates that he had been a Secularist lecturer. He was for some years an eminent Spiritualist. He was also a Communist, working side by side with Marx and Engels. He was a prominent advocate of medical reform, phrenology, and anti-vaccination. He was a fellow of numerous learned societies and possessed a wide range of degrees—some more respectable than others. Throughout his life, 'Dr Sexton', as he was invariably referred to, was rightly treated even by his enemies as a man of science and learning.

Sexton's life-story has never been fully pieced together, and this chapter is only a partial contribution to that process. His early career is murky, probably in part due to misinformation spread by Sexton himself. On the other hand, I have found that sometimes the claims he made that seem the most improbable end up being proven true. It is never clear if a seeming discrepancy is the result of Sexton himself fudging the truth, if further information would clear it up, or if information provided by third parties has been muddled by them. In any event, Sexton's life as a sceptical leader and then as a reconvert Christian apologist is well documented and quite straightforward.

[1] *Spiritual Magazine* (1876), 234.

George Sexton was born in 1825 at Hainford, Norfolk, the son of a farmer, Samuel Sexton.[2] Already at the age of 24 he appeared before the world in the persona that he would maintain for the rest of his life, as 'Dr. Geo. Sexton, honorary member of various scientific, medical, and literary societies, British and continental, etc.'.[3] One wonders if this was more a prophecy than reality at that time. In the following year, 1850, at the age of 25, he signed a letter to the *Reasoner*, 'G. Sexton, M.D., B.A.'.[4] Again, one has to wonder whether these degrees might have been self-conferred. If they were not, then they were sufficiently dubious not to enter into the final record.[5] His entry in a ministerial directory late in life simply stated that he had studied at University College London and 'Wm. and Charing Cross Mcd. C.'—Charing Cross is a well-known teaching hospital to this day, and 'Wm.' might refer to Westminster Hospital or Dispensary. Extant records confirm that he was a student at University College London for the academic year 1853–4, studying anatomy. He never was awarded any degrees from London, however. In 1869 Sexton mentioned incidentally that he

  [2] This information was found on the Norfolk Transcription Archive website at www.genealogy.doun.org. The fact that he was born in Hainford, Norfolk, is confirmed by the information recorded on him in the 1881 Census. Information from this census was accessed at www.familysearch.org. Sexton was visiting Jabez Tearle in Hindley, Lancashire, when the census was taken. Sexton's entry in a ministerial directory also records his birthplace as Hainford: Edgar Sutton Robinson, *The Ministerial Directory of the Ministers of the Presbyterian Church . . .* (Oxford, Ohio: Ministerial Directory Company, 1898), i. 474. The fact that the Norfolk Transcription Archive information is correct is confirmed by the fact that Sexton mentions that his father died in 1875: George Sexton, *Reasons for Renouncing Infidelity. Two Sermons, preached in Augustine Independent Church, Clapham Road, London, on Sunday, September 10th, 1876* (London: G. S. Sexton, 1876), 26. The fact that George Sexton was born in 1825 is also confirmed by his age as known by University College London when he was a student there (information kindly provided in an email dated 28 June 2005 by Wendy Butler, University College London Records Office).

  [3] George Sexton, *A Portraiture of Mormonism* (London: W. Strange, 1849).

  [4] *Reasoner*, 10 Apr. 1850, pp. 9–10.

  [5] *The London and Provincial Medical Directory* for 1851 has Sexton listed as having been awarded a Doctor of Medicine from Göttingen in 1850. The University of Göttingen, however, has no record of this, and we can take its records as accurate. The *Directory* for 1859 makes no mention of Göttingen, but lists the more recent degrees from Giessen. This information from the *Directories* was kindly provided by Alice Ford-Smith, Assistant Librarian, Wellcome Library for the History and Understanding of Medicine, London. Dr Ulrich Hunger of the archives at the University of Göttingen Library kindly checked their records.

had been 'a pupil' of Dr Willshire (who had just written a letter to a newspaper) at 'Charing Cross Hospital Medical College'.[6] Therefore, Sexton did receive some medical training in London. Nevertheless, if he had some sort of MD in 1850, he clearly thought he was in need of a more respectable one. In 1858 he endeavoured to obtain one by special examination from St Andrews University, but was turned down on the grounds that he 'is or has been connected with the discreditable exhibition advertised in "Kahn's Museum" '.[7]

Sexton eventually found genuine academic respectability through the University of Giessen. He claimed to have been awarded an MA and Ph.D (in 1857) and MD (in 1858) from Giessen. Many of the university's records were destroyed during the Second World War; they do, however, have a list of those awarded Ph.D degrees. Sexton was awarded his on 4 September 1858. He wrote his Ph.D thesis on 'Hollingsworth and Modern Poetry'.[8] Giessen matriculation lists are also extant, and Sexton is not recorded there, revealing that all of his Giessen degrees were awarded for theses submitted or examinations taken. With a genuine Giessen Ph.D in hand, Sexton's right to be addressed as 'Doctor' was stronger than that of the vast majority of Christian ministers and men of letters in Britain who used the title at that time.[9] It would seem then, that he finally could also claim with confidence that he had an MD. A German MD earned in such a manner is not without parallel. The eminent physicist John Tyndall (whom Sexton would later criticize for his apparent materialism) was awarded an MD from Tübingen in 1877 for his research on pasteurization.[10] Nevertheless, although Sexton asserted his medical

[6] George Sexton, *Vaccination Useless and Injurious. A Lecture delivered in the Temperance Hall, Sheffield, on February 11th, 1869* (Sheffield: William Fox, 1869), 17.

[7] St Andrews, St Andrews University Archives, Minutes of the Senatus Academicus, Ref. UYUY452/17/440. Information kindly provided by Mrs Rachel Hart, Archivist, St Andrews University Library Special Collections Department.

[8] George Sexton, *Hollingsworth and Modern Poetry: A Critical and Explanatory Essay* (London: William Freeman, 1858). Sexton also edited Hollingsworth's poetry for publication: George Sexton, *The Poetical Works of the late Alfred Johnstone Hollingsworth*, 2nd edn. (London: C. J. Skeet, 1858).

[9] Timothy Larsen, 'Honorary Doctorates and the Nonconformist Ministry in Nineteenth-Century England', in David Bebbington and Timothy Larsen (eds.), *Modern Christianity and Cultural Aspirations* (London: Sheffield Academic Press, 2003), 139–56.

[10] H. C. G. Matthew and Brian Harrison (eds.), *Oxford Dictionary of National Biography* (Oxford: Oxford University Press, 2004), lv. 792.

identity, he seemed happy to defy the emerging mainstream of the profession. He championed phrenology and opposed vaccination. For several years in the early 1870s he edited *The New Era of Eclecticism! (Positive Organic Medicine), and the Journal of the British Medical Reform Association*. The British Medical Reform Association was a way of organizing doctors who were not in conformity with the emerging standards of the British Medical Association, such as those who concentrated on herbal remedies. Sexton become a Fellow of the Ethnological Society of London in 1853—a body which in 1871 became the (later Royal) Anthropological Institute.[11] Moreover, in the same year—on 28 February 1853—he was elected a Fellow of the Royal Geographical Society.[12] He was elected a Fellow of the Zoological Society in 1866.[13] Therefore, Dr Sexton, whatever tendencies he had to exaggerate his own achievements, was nevertheless truly playing at an impressive level. His writings strike the reader as being far more learned than those of leading popular freethinkers such as Bradlaugh, and his acceptance in learned circles has no parallel in the Victorian Secularist movement. His genuine credentials were well beyond those that any of the other Secularist leaders in his day ever secured.

Sexton once claimed in passing that as a young man he had been 'a Christian minister'.[14] The Presbyterians in America gained the impression that he had once been ordained in the 'Episcopal Ch., Eng.'[15] In 1873, he spoke incidentally about his life in London in the late 1840s in which he attended a church and 'occasionally officiated' there. This has verisimilitude to it, indicating that he did not have a congregation of his own but sometimes had ministry opportunities.[16] A 1874 biographical sketch plausibly claimed that

---

[11] Information kindly provided by Sarah Walpole, Archivist, Royal Anthropological Institute, in an email dated 4 July 2005.

[12] Information kindly provided by Sarah Strong, Archives Officer, Royal Geographical Society, in an email dated 28 July 2005.

[13] Information kindly provided by Michael Palmer, Archivist, the Zoological Society of London, in an email dated 6 June 2005.

[14] Sexton, *Reasons*, 44.

[15] Robinson, *Ministerial Directory*, 474.

[16] George Sexton, *How I Became a Spiritualist. An Oration delivered in the Cavendish Rooms, London, on Sunday Evening, June 8th, 1873* (London: J. Burns, 1873), 7.

as a young man he had entered the ministry of the nascent Free Church of England, and this aligns well with his information given by the American Presbyterians.[17] There is not enough information to say with any hope of reasonable accuracy what the extent of Sexton's experience in Christian ministry was prior to his Secularist days. It is possible that Sexton made multiple, distinct attempts at higher education, Christian ministry, and the medical profession over a stretch of quite a few years and therefore, if all the pieces of the puzzle were present, some of them would fit in at seemingly odd places. He simply did a lot. Sexton's more literary side, for example, lies outside the scope of this study. It was substantial enough, however, for him to end up in 1860 editing a paper entitled, *The Players: a weekly dramatic and literary journal.* In 1869, he gave a lecture on 'The Psychology of Macbeth' that even was reprinted in 1977.[18]

Sexton had a resolute, public, orthodox Christian identity as a young man. In 1849 an anti-Mormon lecture of his was published which left the reader in no doubt that he was a very zealous orthodox Christian. He claimed that it was one of a series of lectures of his on 'false and Antichristian Isms'.[19] Other belief systems that he was railing against included Swedenborgianism, Socinianism, Owenism, deism, and atheism. The book is a learned work, marked by careful research. He frequently refers to the Greek of the New Testament and sprinkles the text with Latin quotations. Sexton's scientific discussions include quoting Erasmus Darwin. One of his main attacks on the Mormons is on the grounds that they believe in the eternity of matter. This is not only (in Sexton's presentation) bad science, it is also an 'infidel' or 'atheist' doctrine—associations that he views at this stage of his career with alarm.[20]

Sexton's exposé of Mormonism shows marked devotion to Jesus Christ as Saviour, Lord, Redeemer, and the Son of God. Scripture is

---

[17] 'George Sexton,' *Human Nature* VIII (1874), pp. 24–25.

[18] Sexton edited this journal under the pseudonym Wilfred Wisgast, MA. It is so like Sexton that even his fictitious identity needed to be adorned with an academic degree. George Sexton, *The Psychology of Macbeth* (1869; New York: AMS Press, 1977).

[19] Sexton, *Portraiture*, advertisement [ii].

[20] Ibid. 94.

referred to as 'that infallible standard of truth—the Bible'.[21] His scientific knowledge in no way undercut that conviction: 'I am one of those who believe that science and the Bible go hand in hand together in their teaching, and that in no single instance can one oppose the other.'[22] The following passage might serve as an earnest expression of his Christian faith at that time:

The sacred oracles of truth [just identified as the Old and New Testaments] have stood the test of examination for ages and ages. Objector after objector has arisen to attempt to disprove their truth, and refute the arguments advanced in favour of the inspiration of their contents, but all in vain, the bible and christianity have stood unmoved and unshaken amidst the downfall of error—the wreck of falsehood—the overthrow of scepticism—and the revolution of systems of atheism and infidelity. . . . christianity has remained firmly fixed upon a foundation which all the united opposition of men and demons could not so much as even shake. Atheists and infidels, one after another, have strove to bring about a downfall of true religion, put the bible out of existence, and cause the very name of God to be buried in oblivion, and raise new and false systems upon the ruins of christianity. . . . in every instance Christianity has returned from the field a victor, triumphing over its greatest opponents and enemies.[23]

In addition to the issue of the eternity of matter, Sexton fills much space endeavouring to refute the claims of Mormons to possess supernatural gifts. He went to Mormon worship services and met with Mormon leaders in order to test the credibility of these assertions. One wonders if Sexton had originally investigated the Church of the Latter-Day Saints in the secret hope that its claims might be true, that perhaps it might be able to display the supernatural for him—the realm of the spirit breaking in on the Victorian age.

In April 1850 Sexton wrote a letter to the *Reasoner* in response to an item it had published. His letter argued that the Hebrew word translated as 'day' in English did not necessarily mean a twenty-four-hour period, hence there was not a contradiction between the days of creation as given in Genesis and geological time.[24] It is patently the letter of a defender of Christianity, and was treated as such.[25] Nevertheless, it is interesting that Sexton was already reading the

21 Sexton, *Portraiture*, advertisement [ii]. 92.
22 Ibid. 94.   23 Ibid. 23.   24 *Reasoner*, 10 Apr. 1850, pp. 9–10.
25 Ibid., 24 Apr. 1850, p. 33.

Reasoner in 1850. Maybe he was just collecting data for his anti-atheism lecture, but perhaps he was in a fluid period in his life, quietly flirting with various possible belief systems. In 1852 Sexton published a lecture arguing against a traditional Christian belief in the devil: *The Existence and Influence of the Devil, Viewed in the Light of Reason, Nature, and the Bible.*[26] Unfortunately, Sexton left the biblical discussion for a second lecture that he intended to publish separately, but apparently never did. He promised a 'critical examination (according to the original Hebrew and Greek) of the various passages in the Old and New Testament, generally looked upon as teaching this doctrine'.[27] It is probable, therefore, that he did not attack the Bible so much as claim that it did not support conservative theological views. He would use this approach later in a discussion of the doctrine of hell. An advertisement refers to an otherwise unknown work of Sexton's entitled 'Trinitarianism Viewed in the Light of the Old Testament'. It is likely that this used the same biblical theology approach to support Unitarianism. In *The Existence and Influence of the Devil* Sexton championed 'more liberal views' against 'the Orthodox (so called)'.[28] He was moving away from his past resolute orthodoxy to a liberal Christian identity or perhaps even deism. The advertisements also revealed that his *A Portraiture of Mormonism* had been favourably reviewed by the sturdily evangelical newspaper the *British Banner*, and the *Wesley Banner*: nothing Sexton would write for the next twenty years would come remotely close to being something that might gain approbation from such journals.

In 1853 Sexton was to be found lecturing on phrenology at the freethinking John Street Institution, and by the mid-1850s he had fully emerged as a Secularist leader.[29] In May 1857 Thomas Cooper, who had himself reconverted a year earlier, wrote to Charles Kingsley identifying Sexton as a Secularist teacher he hoped might be open to rethinking the case for Christianity: 'We had a very interesting meeting last Sunday night: no coarseness—not a shade of it. Dr. Sexton owned that I answered him so as to lead him to <u>reflect</u> a little

---

[26] George Sexton, *The Existence and Influence of the Devil, viewed in the light of Reason, Nature, and the Bible* (London: published by the author, [1852]).

[27] Ibid. [1].

[28] Ibid.

[29] *Reasoner*, 6 July 1853, p. 16.

further, & urges me to spend an evening & smoke a pipe with him.
I consented—for I want to know what he is made of—& whether
I cannot detach him from the staff of Sceptical teachers. He often
talks at John St[reet Institution].'[30] A freethinking address that Sexton gave in April 1858 is particularly interesting as an unequivocal
endorsement of the eternity of matter, a position that, as has been
shown, he once strongly opposed and, as will be shown, he would
adamantly denounce later in life. Using *Vestiges of the Natural History
of Creation* as a prompt, it was an account of the evolution of
species.[31] Sexton was the one popular freethinking lecturer at that
time who had the aptitude to tackle serious scientific themes. He
even sometimes gave what appear to have been straightforward
lectures in science, such as 'The Wonders of a Ray of Light', which
he delivered in January 1860 at the South London Secular Institute.[32]
He also gave a series of lectures at that institute on phrenology. Such
teaching was done alongside the more standard fare for such contexts. For example, he gave a lecture on 'Satan: the doctrine taught
concerning him in Nature, Reason, and the Bible': this was undoubtedly a more stridently freethinking version of his 1852 address.[33]

Sexton wrote for the *National Reformer* under the nom de plume
'Melampus'. As 'Melampus of the *National Reformer*' he penned *The
Doctrine of Eternal Torment Refuted* (1863), a forceful attack on
traditional Christianity. In it, Sexton asserted flatly: 'The God of
orthodoxy is a monster to be feared and dreaded, not loved.'[34] *The
Doctrine of Eternal Torment Refuted*, although polemical in purpose,
is grounded in significant learning. Sexton carefully traces the various words for hell in an array of languages. He has a whole section of
biblical theology in which he pursues the idea through the Old and
New Testaments, giving due attention to the various Hebrew and
Greek words involved. Sexton argued that the Bible, especially the

[30] Amsterdam, Internationaal Instituut Voor Sociale Geschiedenis, Coll. Cooper,
Thomas Cooper to Charles Kingsley, 5 May 1857.

[31] *Reasoner*, 5 May 1858, p. 143. For *Vestiges*, see James A. Secord, *Victorian
Sensation: The Extraordinary Publication, Reception and Authorship of 'Vestiges of the
Natural History of Creation'* (Chicago: University of Chicago Press, 2000).

[32] *Reasoner Gazette*, 8 Jan. 1860, p. 8.

[33] Ibid., 26 Feb. 1860, p. 35.

[34] Melampus (of the 'National Reformer') [George Sexton], *The Doctrine of
Eternal Torment Refuted* (London: George Abington, 1863), 3.

Old Testament, is generally referring merely to death rather than a place of torment. 'The mission of Freethought', he averred when moving toward a conclusion, was to not let the next generation grow up believing in this 'monstrous and pernicious fable'. He concluded with a quotation from Cooper's *The Purgatory of Suicides*. Sexton identified its author as someone who was 'once an earnest champion of Freethought', and found Cooper's indictment of eternal torment still true, 'whatever he may say to the contrary' as a recon-vert.[35]

Another of Sexton's freethinking publications was a tribute to Paine. One passage in which he looks forward to a kind of freethink-ing millennium will serve to illustrate the vigour of his anti-Bible sentiments and the strength of his rejection of orthodox Christian doctrine at that time:

And fathers teaching their sons the rudiments of education, shall excite laughter and mirth among those happy boys by relating how in years gone by men believed that God, whom heaven and earth could not contain, lived on the earth in the shape of a man, eating and drinking and sleeping, and at last dying like other men; that a doctrine called the Trinity was recognised, which set all the laws of mathematics at defiance by teaching that three times one is one and not three; that a donkey talked, and politely enquired why it was beaten, and a man took furnished apartments in the stomach of a whale ... that knowledge grew on a tree like apples, and manna, if not beefsteaks and onions, rained down from heaven in showers ... [36]

Not only the Bible, but also the doctrines of the incarnation and the Trinity, are here dismissed as risible.

A particularly suggestive work of Sexton's from this period is his *The Concessions of Theology to Science: A Lecture* (1868). 'Theology and science have always been antagonistic to each other', he expounded, and theology was the loser in each confrontation.[37] Sexton argues that pleas that the Bible did not really teach ideas opposed to science, but had only been misunderstood in the past as

[35] Ibid. 32.

[36] George Sexton, *Thomas Paine. An Address. Delivered at a Meeting held in Commemoration of the Birthday of the Great Apostle of Freethought* (London: Austin & Co., n.d. [stamped 20 Sept. 1869]).

[37] George Sexton, *The Concessions of Theology to Science: A Lecture* (London: Austin, 1868), 3.

doing so, did not rescue it as an authority: 'Of what use is a book whose plainest teachings are thus liable to misinterpretation?'[38] He even uses as an example the question of the length of the days of creation—the very argument that he had once propounded. He concedes the universality of religion—a point very important to Sexton as a reconvert—but views it as a kind of pervasive oppression. He is aware that many people have an intuitive sense that prompts them to be religious. He has no quarrel with them, but only with 'dogmatic theology'. A religious intuition is not dismissed, but only quarantined: 'any emotional feeling must be felt, not preached, and hence the inutility of advocating it to those not susceptible of it by experience.'[39]

For a final example of Sexton's thought as a freethinker, it will be useful to look at his *The Antiquity of the Human Race*. In the third edition (1871), strikingly, Sexton cites Darwin's *The Descent of Man*, even though he would have had to absorb it within months of its publication. Dr Sexton's *Antiquity of the Human Race* is a careful, learned study in which he presents the findings of numerous contemporary scientists. Sexton also quotes a passage from Huxley's *Evidence as to Man's Place in Nature* (1863) which refers to unresolved issues in the origin of the human race, and then triumphantly announces that elucidation has been provided: 'These questions are now to a large extent answered by the theory of "Natural Selection," propounded by Mr. Darwin.'[40] Sexton's *The Antiquity of the Human Race* is really more a scientific tract than a freethinking one. True, he contends that a belief that the human race came into existence 'as recently as six or seven thousand years ago' is scientifically untenable, but there were not many orthodox Christian thinkers insisting that such a view needed to be retained. The application for purposes of freethinking polemics is confided to a quotation from Baron Bunsen, in which he speaks of the advance of knowledge being held back by 'theological prejudices'. From the mid-1850s to the early 1870s Dr Sexton was a leading Secularist lecturer, widely prized in the

---

[38] George Sexton, *The Concessions of Theology to Science: A Lecture* (London: Austin, 1868), 14.

[39] Ibid. 2.

[40] George Sexton, *The Antiquity of the Human Race*, 3rd edn. (London: Austin & Co., 1871), 23.

movement for his notable speaking gifts and, even more so, as a man of science to an extent unrivalled in their ranks.

In the early 1870s Sexton entered a time of transition. He became a Communist. He was the delegate to the general council of the International for the powerful Manchester branch, and was one of four English delegates to the fifth Congress of the International which met at The Hague in September 1872. The English delegation was divided, but Sexton himself was a strong supporter of Marx and Engels.[41] These were the same years that he was also most active in the cause of medical reform. Defending Marxists and herbalists, however, were not Sexton's only preoccupations in the early 1870s.

Sexton's other new enthusiasm was Spiritualism. As far back as the mid-1850s Robert Owen had enthusiastically reported to Sexton intelligence from the spirit world that the doctor would someday make a significant contribution to the Spiritualist movement.[42] Sexton had laughed this off, and occasionally lectured against Spiritualism thereafter. In 1864 he had been intrigued by the phenomena he had witnessed at a meeting of the famous Davenport Brothers, and had rebuked the *National Reformer* for accusing them of trickery without having bothered to find evidence against them. Sexton did investigate himself and could not discover any way in which the brothers could have been rigging their performance. That experience had not led to his becoming a Spiritualist, however. A more decisive influence was when a member of his own immediate family discovered that she or he was a medium. As Sexton knew this person intimately, he was able to judge their claims fully, and since the manifestations happened in his own home, he had full freedom to look for any secret mechanical arrangement. Once convinced, Sexton quickly became an eminent spokesperson for Spiritualism. The movement was thrilled with his June 1873 lecture, later printed as *Spirit-Mediums and Conjurers*.[43] Sexton argued that he was an intelligent man and he could see straight through the tricks of the

[41] Henry Collins and Chimen Abramsky, *Karl Marx and the British Labour Movement: Years of the First International* (London: Macmillan & Co., 1965), 241–64.

[42] Sexton, *How I Became a Spiritualist*, 11.

[43] George Sexton, *Spirit-Mediums and Conjurers. An Oration delivered in the Cavendish Rooms, London, on Sunday Evening, June 15th, 1873* (London: J. Burns, 1873).

conjurers (which he deliciously detailed, to the consternation of the professionals whose trade secrets he was revealing), but he could not see how some mediums had done through trickery what he had personally witnessed. This response was sufficiently impressive to have been reprinted in 1976.[44]

Indeed, Sexton has been lauded by Spiritualists ever since. Dr Sexton went on to become in 1875 the editor of the *Spiritual Magazine*, the most important organ for the movement in Britain. In 1892 he was featured as a notable investigator of Spiritualism in the entry on the subject in *Chambers's Encyclopaedia*.[45] Arthur Conan Doyle listed Sexton as one of eight examples of eminent materialists who had become Spiritualists in his *The History of Spiritualism* (1926).[46] In 1978 Sexton received his own separate entry in the *Encyclopedia of Occultism and Parapsychology*,[47] and currently a biographical sketch of Sexton can be found on the website of the International Survivalist Society, an organization founded in 2002 to promote psychical research.[48] It is important not to dismiss Sexton anachronistically as far removed from genuine scientific enterprise. In fact, his life parallels in striking ways that of one of the most eminent men of science of his generation, Alfred Russel Wallace (1823–1913), the co-discoverer of what came to be called Darwinism. Wallace too did not have a traditional university education; he too mingled in Secularist circles and then became a champion of Spiritualism; he too was an opponent of vaccination.[49]

Scepticism and Spiritualism did overlap. Indeed, Sexton was apt to receive spectral greetings from John Watts, the deceased editor of the atheistic *National Reformer*.[50] Nevertheless, hard on the heels of Sexton's acceptance of Spiritualism came renewed sympathy for

---

[44] James Webb (ed.), *The Mediums and the Conjurors* [by George Sexton] (New York: Arno Press, 1976).

[45] *Chambers's Encyclopaedia* (London: William and Robert Chambers, 1892). ix. 645–9.

[46] Arthur Conan Doyle, *The History of Spiritualism* (New York: George H. Doran, 1926), ii. 262.

[47] *Encyclopedia of Occultism and Parapsychology* (New York: Avon Books, 1978), 829.

[48] Their website is www.survivalafterdeath.org (accessed on 5 July 2005).

[49] For Wallace, see his entry in the Appendix.

[50] Sexton, *How I Became a Spiritualist*, 15.

Christianity. F. R. Young testifies that Sexton reconverted in 1873. By August he was ready to preach at Young's Unitarian church and receive Holy Communion there.[51] Already in June, Sexton was declaring in *Spirit-Mediums and Conjurers* that one of the truths highlighted by Spiritualism was 'that there is a conscious and personal God who is the Father of all spirits, and that to love and worship Him is man's highest duty on earth'.[52] An overlapping transition from the one cause dominating his life to the other coming to do so can be witnessed in the pages of the *Spiritual Magazine* for 1876. In April he claimed, not without some justification: 'For the past three or four years I have devoted myself almost exclusively to the spiritual movement and have worked harder in the cause than almost any other living man.'[53] In addition to editing this leading organ of the movement, he was busy in the cause in many other ways. He was on the council of the British National Association of Spiritualists, and was commissioned by them to tour the country giving lectures. In 1876 Sexton was a very prominent and energetic Spiritualist.

Still, his rediscovery of Christianity was looming larger and larger. The common ground was his attempts to refute materialism, efforts that have been counted as in the service of both Spiritualism and Christian apologetics. Spiritualists, for example, still cite Sexton's rebuttal of John Tyndall's Belfast Address (discussed below) as labour on their behalf. His explicitly Christian efforts crept more and more into the pages of the *Spiritual Magazine*. There were regular reports on sermons he had preached. There was news of his lecture to Young's congregation on 'Twenty Years' Experience of Scepticism, Sceptics, and Sceptical Teaching'.[54] Even more explicitly, Sexton's discourse on 'the Divine Origin and Authority of the Christian Religion' was noticed.[55] Bringing the chapter-length studies in this volume full circle, Sexton also inserted Hone's reconversion poem.[56] This perpetual Christian sideshow proved to be bad for the financial

---

[51] Frederic Rowland Young, *Indirect Evidences in the New Testament for the Personal Divinity of Christ* (London: W. Stewart & Co., 1884), 106.
[52] Sexton, *Spirit-Mediums*, 6.
[53] *Spiritual Magazine* (1876), 233.
[54] Ibid. 89.
[55] Ibid. 131.
[56] Ibid. 560.

health of the *Spiritual Magazine*. Spiritualists were glad to have such a man of science as Dr Sexton on their side, but many Spiritualists were actively anti-Christian and had no desire for the old faith continually to be rubbed in their faces. Sexton gave this explanation for the drying-up of donations to the journal: 'Dr. Sexton is a believer in the Divine authority of Christianity—the large mass of the Spiritualists are dogmatically anti-Christian. This is the secret of the whole thing.'[57] He prophesied that a division was imminent between the Christian Spiritualists and the anti-Christian ones. Closer to the truth was probably that his Christian identity was starting to squeeze out other issues more and more, and therefore he was becoming increasingly unwilling to work with anti-Christian Spiritualists and was moving more decisively toward exclusively Christian endeavours.

By 1875 Sexton's Christian identity was well established. In the first half of that year he gathered his own non-denominational congregation. Meeting in the Cavendish Rooms, London, it eventually took the name 'The Church of the Lord'. In September 1876 he made a public statement, published as *Reasons for Renouncing Infidelity*. The form of this statement was two sermons preached at the invitation of the eminent Congregational minister David Thomas (1813–94). Thomas, who had an international reputation as the editor of *The Homilist*, became a long-term supporter of Sexton's ministry. That he could gain such a respectable ministerial advocate shows what a sound and impressive figure Dr Sexton was deemed to be. His *Reasons for Renouncing Infidelity* began:

For more than twenty years, as is tolerably well known, I occupied a somewhat conspicuous position in the ranks of the so-called Freethinkers. About five years ago, I was led, by a course of Providential circumstances, to re-consider the whole question of Christian Evidences, which I had so long been accustomed to look upon as closed as far as I was concerned, and the result was the discovery of the utter fallacy of my sceptical views. Gradually I returned—as far as the broad principles of Christian truth were concerned—to the faith of my early life, and finally to the position with which I commenced my public career—that of a preacher of the glad tidings of salvation through Christ. A church arose out of my labours, and for the past

---

[57] *Spiritual Magazine* (1876), 419–21.

eighteen months I have been engaged, more or less, in ministering to a regular congregation in sacred things.[58]

Before moving into the main arguments that Sexton offered, it should also be noted in a general way that this is a learned discourse which is explicitly in dialogue with much of the sceptical thought of its day. A partial list of the thinkers named includes Herbert Spencer, John Tyndall, Aeschylus, Spinoza, Hegel, F. W. J. Schelling, Emerson, T. H. Huxley, Auguste Comte, W. J. Fox, Gibbon, Kant, D. F. Strauss, H. E. G. Paulus, Voltaire, John Stuart Mill, W. E. H. Lecky, Ernest Renan, and Theodore Parker. Many of these are the focus of apposite discussions regarding the degree to which their ideas successfully address the human condition.

Sexton does make an effort at the classic arguments for the existence of God. The ontological argument he considers 'unanswerable', but not serviceable in polemical contexts, as it is 'too abstruse for the popular mind'.[59] The argument from design seemed patently obvious to him at this time, especially given his wealth of knowledge of science, medicine, and natural history, and Sexton could only express bafflement that he had ever doubted it.

Such traditional paths are not walked for long. Sexton spends the bulk of these sermons advancing three lines of argument: (1) that humanity has always worshipped and known instinctively that there is a realm of the divine; (2) that Secularism offers no basis for morality and; (3) that Jesus, as portrayed in the New Testament, is a compelling figure who ought to be acknowledged to be God. On the first point, Sexton declared: 'Atheism is both irrational and opposed to the highest instincts of humanity. It is neither conformable to reason nor to that feeling which lies far deeper down in man's nature which the Germans call God-consciousness.'[60] In this way, Sexton connects the standard argument that reconverts used regarding 'instincts' with a line of thought stemming from Friedrich Schleiermacher, whose thought was indeed a learned and sophisticated theological articulation in a liberal, Romantic vein.[61] Sexton

---

[58] Sexton, *Reasons*, p. iii.
[59] Ibid. 5.
[60] Ibid. 3.
[61] Sexton refers to Schleiermacher by name in another publication: George Sexton, *The Fallacies of Secularism* (London: G. S. Sexton, 1877), 98.

observes that it was sometimes claimed that remote groups of people had been discovered who had no conception of God, but, he argues, even if true this would only prove that 'intelligent and civilised man had always believed in God' and it was only the most 'utterly degraded' tribes that might be deprived of this basic knowledge. The human desire to connect with God was too strong for any intellectual to put a stop to it, whatever they might pronounce. Even some freethinkers recognized this: 'Comte was a sufficiently shrewd observer of human nature to discover that some kind of worship was essential to the success of his system.'[62]

Secondly, religion was essential to morality. Sexton is careful to acknowledge that many atheists are personally moral, but his point is that they do not have a philosophy from which a basis for morality can be derived. Thirdly, more space is taken up on the theme of who Jesus is than on any of the other points. Like Cooper, Sexton had once been convinced by Strauss's mythical theory. Nevertheless, he found that the person of Jesus was a subject that he could not thus dismiss: 'This one subject haunted me night and day.'[63] As had Barker, Sexton came to the conviction that the Jesus of the gospels was too good not to be true:

Even if the miracles were proved to be false, and the supernatural halo that continually surrounded Him were shown to be mythological accumulation of after ages, or a pure invention of the time, still that would in no sense explain away the life of the Being depicted. The character of Christ is perfect, and that perfection has to be accounted for. To say that it was fictitious in no way gets out of the difficulty; for that is only to shift the ground from the real to the ideal, leaving us still in the dark as to how the invention came. For, if Christ be simply an ideal picture, the man who sketched it will be as difficult to account for as the Being Himself... [64]

Moreover, as humanity, in Sexton's reckoning, knew more about God than some philosophers thought they could, so also freethinkers knew more about Jesus than their own principles allowed. Dr Sexton averred that it was inconsistent for freethinkers to eulogize Jesus as a great man who taught admirable principles. Given what Jesus claimed about himself, he must have been either less or more: he

62 Sexton, *Reasons*, 22–3.   63 Ibid. 45.   64 Ibid. 33.

could only have been an impostor or a fanatic or divine. If he was an impostor, it would have been because of some worldly motive, but Jesus lived his life in defiance of all earthly rewards. Nor does it ring true that he was a fanatic: 'The calmness of manner which He invariably displays is quite incompatible with fanaticism. Read that magnificent prayer still called the Lord's Prayer, and tell me whether you think it could have been composed by a madman.'[65] If he was neither of those possibilities, then one is left with door number three, and it leads back to faith.

Reasons for Renouncing Infidelity was followed by *The Fallacies of Secularism* (1877). The titles of the three sections make clear the basic lines of attack: 'Secularism as taught by its leading exponents a bundle of contradictions', 'Secularism distinctively considered, a creed of negations', and 'Secularism destitute of an ethical code, and deficient as a moral guide'. Sexton relentlessly attempts to expose Secularism as bankrupt. What do Secularists have that is constructive to offer? he repeatedly enquires. In fact, Sexton asserted, 'Secularism must necessarily fail, since the whole thing consists of a series of negations, which cannot be made the basis of positive work'.[66] He avers that the Secularist argument that seeking to live in a way that would serve life after death took one away from one's duties here on earth was a false dichotomy. Here he exploits his reputation as a man of science. Secularists claim to champion science against the claims of religion, but this was a hollow boast. Science, he asserts, is often taught under the auspices of churches, by the YMCA, at mechanics' institutes and working-men's clubs—seemingly everywhere but among the Secularists: 'There is a Hall of Science, so-called, at Sheffield, and there is another at Bradford, both of which are devoted mainly to dancing, and could not be kept open for a month in any other way. Occasionally Sunday evening lectures are given always upon the usual threadbare topics—abuse of the Bible, and denunciation of Christianity; but Science is never heard of within their walls.'[67] The main Secularist venue in London, 'as though in satire', was also called the Hall of Science. The only time science had ever been taught there, Dr Sexton claimed, was when he had made the attempt himself. Freethinkers would not come. Sexton also mocks

[65] Ibid. 40.   [66] Sexton, *Fallacies*, 20.   [67] Ibid. 45.

some statements that Bradlaugh had made which betrayed his lack of knowledge of basic science. He then goes on to argue that Secularism does not offer Sunday- or day-schools or do anything else for the general education of people: once again, that is left to the churches. In short, according to Sexton, Secularists have nothing positive to offer and do no constructive work. Secularism exists solely in order to attack Christianity.

The third section applied this critique to the domain of morality. Sexton quotes from a public debate in which (making for rather painful reading) Bradlaugh was unable to answer the straightforward question of what method one could use to discover the difference between right and wrong. Pressed on this point, Secularist leaders had learned to say that they adopted the ethical code of Utilitarianism. Bradlaugh had therefore asserted that he took care of his wife because when she was happy it added to his own happiness: 'I admit it is selfish.' Sexton found such a perspective to provide no backbone for doing what was unpleasant and not to one's own advantage, but nevertheless right. Sexton then attacked the Owenite determinism that so many Secularists had imbibed, arguing that by denying human freedom it undercut the whole notion of morality. Bradlaugh had conceded in a debate that an adulterer might just be a product of his circumstances (in which case he could not be blamed). *The Fallacies of Secularism* concludes with comments on how atheism does not meet the needs of the human heart. Sexton somewhat patronizingly—albeit perhaps effectively with some members of his target audience—argued that Secularism is usually a phase that reckless young men go through before they grow up, recognize that it is hollow, and move on.

Sexton also engaged in debates with leaders of popular freethought. A transcript of his debate with G. W. Foote, held in Batley, Yorkshire, in June 1877 was published after having been approved by the disputants. Foote was already a leading Secularist, and his role as editor of the *Secular Review* made him well known. Nevertheless, he was also a quarter-of-a-century younger than Sexton, and the doctor liked to remind Foote of his own more extended experience in the Secularist world. The transcript reads as a polite and thoughtful debate, in which both speakers made some apt and forceful observations.

The Fallacies of Secularism had just been published, and Sexton not surprisingly reprised many of its arguments. He also aimed, however, to add some new ones, in order to take his opponent off guard. Foote said unequivocally that 'the Secular rule of morality' is Utilitarianism.[68] Sexton would again expound a critique of Utilitarianism as a moral system, but his new approach was to argue that Utilitarianism had no inherent connection to Secularism. Many Utilitarians were not Secularists and some Secularists were not Utilitarians, hence it did not really belong in the discussion, and was only dragged in because Secularism was so impoverished that, when asked for its moral scheme, it had to borrow one. Once again, Sexton contrasted with ruthless precision the reality on the ground as he knew it with the boasts and slogans of Secularists. 'Secularists, as a rule, are more ignorant of science than most other people in the same position in life', he asserted.[69] They had not a single man of science in their ranks, and not one library worth the name. They talk of reason, but 'reason does not, any more than science, belong exclusively to the Secularist. We all have a share in it, and are guided by it as far as it can lead us.'[70] Secularism is 'neither a science, nor a philosophy, nor an ethical system, nor a religion? Then, in the name of all that is rational, what is it? (Applause.)'[71] Sexton went point by point through the list of the stated principles of the National Secular Society, identifying every one save the last as either in no way unique to Secularism (thus providing the movement with no *raison d'être*) or as a mere negation. The one positive principle was somewhat less than a complete philosophy of life: 'the circulation of the *National Reformer* comprises the whole duty of Secular man.'[72] Dr Sexton was enjoying himself. He was a fount of apt quotations from within the movement. Foote himself had given an in-house speech in which he had candidly lamented that the Secularist movement had done nothing to promote the education of the people. Many Secularists were moral, Sexton acknowledged, but that was only because they had gained their moral bearings in a Christian context. Foote had a splendid reply: 'If we simply conformed our conduct to the

---

[68] G. W. Foote and George Sexton, *Is Secularism the True Gospel for Mankind? A Debate Held in the Town Hall, Batley,... June 18th and 19th, 1877*, Revised By Both Disputants (London: Smart & Allen, 1877), 5.
[69] Ibid. 25.   [70] Ibid. 37.   [71] Ibid. 14.   [72] Ibid. 34.

Christian practice around us our moral progress would, I fear, be slight indeed.'[73] The editor of the *Secular Review* nevertheless was obliged to admit that Bradlaugh's conception of morality was 'quite wrong'.

It will be useful to look at the contents of Sexton's other major books as a Christian apologist, before turning to reactions to him as a reconvert by Secularists and others, and his own evolving ecclesiastical identity. At the start of 1879 Sexton's *The Baseless Fabric of Scientific Scepticism* was published. The first essay, the only item that had already been published separately, is a reply to John Tyndall's controversial Belfast Address. Not only does it show enormous intellectual confidence that Sexton would think that he could answer so eminent a man of science as Tyndall, but extraordinarily, Sexton wrote and delivered his reply within a week of Tyndall's speech ('Scientific Materialism. A Reply to Professor Tyndall's Belfast Address' was first delivered on 23 August 1874 at the Marylebone Music Hall, London). Sexton skilfully took Tyndall to task for the way that he had attempted to appropriate classical thought. Interestingly, Sexton praised Ludwig Büchner's *Kraft und Stoff* as 'a work ably written'.[74] Moreover, he then proceeded to offer a careful, accurate, and generous exposition of various theories of the evolution of species, discussing the views of Lamarck, of the anonymous *Vestiges of the Natural History of Creation*, and of Charles Darwin. Sexton's point is not that these theories are wrong, but rather that they are not atheistic. On *Vestiges*, he judged: 'Very little support for atheism and materialism can be gathered from this book, or from the theory which it enunciates.'[75] Sexton praises Darwin highly, and argues that his theory in no way necessitates materialism. Tyndall has overstepped the disciplinary boundaries of science:

The evolution theory might be correct enough as far as it goes, but when it is attempted to push it into regions with which it has no sort of connection, even those who believe in it may reasonably object.... Let science confine

---

[73] G. W. Foote and George Sexton, *Is Secularism the True Gospel for Mankind? A Debate Held in the Town Hall, Batley,... June 18th and 19th, 1877*, Revised By Both Disputants (London: Smart & Allen, 1877), 55.

[74] George Sexton, *The Baseless Fabric of Scientific Scepticism* (London: Smart & Allen, 1879), 28.

[75] Ibid. 47.

herself to the region in which she is all-powerful, and we are content; but the moment she begins to dogmatise on subjects of which she is professedly incompetent to judge, we decline to be guided by her counsel.... When scientific men like Professor Tyndall step out of their domain to tell us that matter is the only existence, because their science and their experience have comprehended nothing else, we reply that there are modes of obtaining information upon these questions apart from test-tubes, galvanic batteries, and other instruments of a like kind.... The science of evolution breaks down at the very point where information is felt to be required by every man who looks in the face the tremendous problem of being.[76]

This line of thought is continued in the next essay, 'Science and Religion'. Sexton is reversing the argument used by freethinking men of science such as Huxley. If they wanted to keep theologians from thinking they had the right to adjudicate on matters of science, Sexton counter-attacks that someone such as Tyndall ought to be respected in the field of physics, but he has no expertise out of which to pronounce authoritatively even on zoology, let alone philosophy or religion. Completing the reversal, Sexton noted that scientists, and not just religious leaders, might also be animated by bigotry and intolerance. Sexton is on good form, picking apart a statement by Huxley on the nature of morality.[77] Sexton's main argument, however, is his familiar one that religion is essential to the human condition. Science must do its work without attempting to rule out categorically the realm of the spirit. Sexton is very candid that theology has dogmatized in a wrongheaded way on scientific matters in the past. He was not defending theology (or even Christianity) in this piece, but rather simply religion—the human instinct that there is a divine reality.

Two essays on immortality followed. Sexton again emphasized that human beings cannot be satisfied simply with negations: 'The wants of the human soul demand more than this, and none know it better than those who have, at some period of their lives, been sceptical.'[78] He evokes scientific thought to present the immorality of the soul as a rational and fitting conclusion: 'If we cannot conceive of the annihilation of an atom of matter—and philosophers tell us that this is so—how much less is it likely that we should be able to

---

[76] Ibid. 55–60.   [77] Ibid. 100.   [78] Ibid. 126.

conceive of the annihilation of mind!'[79] He quotes *The Purgatory of Suicides*, referring to Cooper as a much-esteemed personal friend of his—smoking a pipe together back in 1857 paid dividends in the long run. The next essay is a more technical scientific discussion on 'the New-fangled Theory of Protoplasm'. Sexton cites the *British Medical Journal* and a range of professional literature. On a single page of this essay there are references to Brucke, Cienkowsky, Baer, Stricker, Kühne, Leydig, Schultze, and Huxley.[80] Once again, his target is a reductionistic materialism: 'There is a side of [a human being's] nature that opens up towards God and a spiritual world, and which no theories of protoplasm can account for, and no materialistic hypothesis can explain.'[81] The final essay, 'Man as a Spiritual Being', continues the discussion. The truth of Darwinism is not being challenged, but evolution through natural selection is merely 'the *modus operandi*'—however human beings came to their present state, it now includes a spiritual essence. Mind is more fundamental than matter. Sexton can even sound like a critic of the Enlightenment on this point: 'All knowledge is subjective, and objective things can only be known when an idea of them—which is subjective—has made its way to the mind.'[82] His real philosophical debt would seem to be to Platonism: 'Now, we have said before that the spiritual is the real, and the material the shadow. All material things, therefore, must have a spiritual counterpart, to which, in truth, they owe their very existence. Spiritual things are not only real, but they are the only substantial things in existence. The spiritual world is consequently a real world . . .'[83]

In October 1879 Sexton gave an address in Plymouth under the auspices of the Christian Evidence Society to an audience of well over a thousand people. It was published as *The Folly of Atheism* (1880). This discourse is weighted much more toward classic proofs for the existence of God. Sexton's learning is on display. He quotes Plato, Sophocles, and Anaxagoras in Greek, Cicero in Latin, cites a German source, and begins with an explanation of the meaning of a Hebrew word. His conversation partners include Herbert Spencer, Kant, J. S. Mill, and an array of contemporary men of science including

---

[79] George Sexton, *The Baseless Fabric of Scientific Scepticism* (London: Smart & Allen, 1879), 128.

[80] Ibid. 186.   [81] Ibid. 193.   [82] Ibid. 207.   [83] Ibid. 221.

Huxley, Darwin, and Wallace. Sexton declares that atheism cannot satisfy humanity:

It is cold, negative, cheerless, and gloomy, lacking enthusiasm, feeling, emotion, and sympathy.... [the atheist's] intellect is defective on its higher side—the side that opens up Godward....Atheism must furnish us with some sort of a theory of the universe, or it can never satisfy a rational mind. When therefore, the Atheist shelters himself—as he usually does—behind the statement that he affirms nothing, and cannot be logically expected to prove a negative, he takes a position which we cannot for a moment allow. ...Besides, the human mind cannot rest in a mere negation....Any system, therefore, to be worth a straw, must...hazard some sort of a theory as to the why and the wherefore of things. Herein it is that Atheism has always broken down.[84]

Sexton does not leave it there, however, but endeavours to present a variety of classic apologetic arguments. He deploys a great deal of scientific knowledge to dress up the argument for the necessity of a final cause. He also uses recent scientific thought to bolster the idea of the need for a first mover.[85] Sexton also presents the argument from design; Darwin's theory, in his view, does not dispense with this argument, because design can be seen in the inorganic world as well, from planets to crystals. The universe is wrought through with geometrical design which, he explains optimistically, is 'incontrovertible evidence that a geometer has by this means expressed a geometrical thought'.[86] Sexton rejoices over J. S. Mill's words in favour of the argument from design in his posthumously published essays on theism. He also reasserts the universality of religious convictions: 'If the argument *e consensu gentium* does not prove the existence of God, it certainly does prove that in all ages some sort of evidence has led men to believe in one.'[87] If that were not enough for one address, he throws in the ontological argument, and with it Anselm, Spinoza, Descartes, and Leibniz. As his own critiques required that he should, Sexton had moved from merely attacking

[84] George Sexton, *The Folly of Atheism. A discourse delivered in St. George's Hall, Plymouth, on October 18, 1879, on behalf of the Christian Evidence Society* (London: Smart & Allen, 1880), 5–7.
[85] Ibid. 19.
[86] Ibid. 25–6.
[87] Ibid. 34.

Secularism to the positive work of attempting a reasoned explication of the idea of the existence of God.

A final volume to explore here is Sexton's *Theistic Problems: being Essays on the Existence of God and His Relationship to Man* (1880). Once again his learning is evident, including references to material from German authors that had not been published in English translations. There are also numerous classical references, and others to world religions or the history of religions, from Buddhism to Zoroastrianism. The standard array of contemporary conversation partners are there, such as G. H. Lewes and Huxley. As to Herbert Spencer, Sexton quips that he 'writes so voluminously of the unknowable that one would almost imagine it to be the only thing which he knows all about'.[88] A new target is Matthew Arnold's *Literature and Dogma* (1873). On one of his favourite arguments— the universality of religion—Dr Sexton had this to add: 'The universality of worship no sceptic can account for. I have often been told, in the debates that I have held with unbelievers, that it arose through ignorance. This, however, is no explanation, for the question still arises, Why did ignorance in all lands and in all times take this particular direction?'[89] These comments will suffice to give the heart of Sexton's teaching as a reconvert.

A more rough-and-tumble forum for Sexton's Christian apologetics was the journal the *Shield of Faith*, founded in 1877. Although its first editor was David Blyth of the Christian Evidence Society, Sexton was editor from 1880 until its demise in early 1884. Under Sexton the *Shield* declared flatly that its enemy was Secularism. Atheists were referred to pejoratively as 'God-haters',[90] while atheism is said to have no argument against adultery or suicide. On the other hand, Sexton, as editor of the *Shield*, would steer earnest Christians who were reading the Bible in too wooden a manner back into line with the findings of modern science: 'Certainly death was in the world before it was inhabited by man. The remains of the lower animals are found in the early strata of the earth, deposited, probably, millions of years

[88] George Sexton, *Theistic Problems; being Essays on the Existence of God and His Relationship to Man* (London: Hodder & Stoughton, 1880), 58.

[89] Ibid. 102.

[90] *Shield of Faith* (Jan. 1880), 2.

before man was created. There is nothing in the Bible opposed to this fact.'[91]

The *Shield of Faith* provides a natural transition to consideration of reactions to Sexton as a Christian apologist. His importance as a reconvert may be measured by the vast amount of attention the Secularist community gave to him. The *Secular Review* seemed to have no limit on how many items it wished to publish about him. It offered a surprisingly generous review of his *Fallacies of Secularism*, although it must be borne in mind that this also reflects the general approach of this particular journal and its editors, in contrast to the approaches taken by some others such as Bradlaugh. The *Secular Review* claimed that Sexton's very name would mean that everyone would already know that the work was 'exceedingly well-written'.[92] It did not acknowledge that he had wounded Utilitarianism, but did admit that he had attacked it cleverly and with 'much vigour and ability'. It actually recommended that Secularists should read Sexton's indictment of them for not doing anything positive, and take it to heart: 'They will perceive from it that [Secularism's] weak point is its constructive policy, which has not by some advocates for many years been considered half so important as the destructive.' The Secularist leader Charles Watts worked up a lecture replying to Sexton's book, and gave it repeatedly.[93] Sexton's debate with Watts was covered heavily in the *Secular Review*. One report was by an author who went to the debate because he or she wanted to 'hear "Melampus" defend doctrine' he had once 'eloquently opposed'.[94] Although this report contains more than one polemical jab, the author conceded that Sexton offered 'beautiful sentences strung together so ingeniously'. Even as a reconvert, this Secularist voice recognized Dr Sexton as a man of learning and ability. Another correspondent said that the freethinking community should simply answer Sexton by reprinting his Secularist writings.[95]

A review of Sexton's *Reasons for Renouncing Infidelity* in the *Secular Review* recognized that these two church addresses were 'very well

---

[91] Ibid. (Jan. 1882), 21.
[92] *Secular Review and Secularist*, 9 June 1877, p. 6.
[93] e.g. *Secular Review*, 18 Mar. 1877, p. 53; 8 Apr. 1877, p. 95.
[94] Ibid., 23 June 1877, p. 39.
[95] Ibid., 11 Aug. 1877, pp. 155–6.

written, above the average sermons a long way'.[96] It wittily mocked Dr Sexton as 'a sort of Infidel dove let out of the ark when the whole earth was covered by one vast sea of doubt'. It admitted that he had once dared to 'doubt out-and-out', but had now become 'an out-and-out believer', which might be taken as a sort of acknowledgement that Sexton was a genuine reconvert possessing an honest faith. It ended wistfully, if not bitterly, measuring the loss of such an accomplished man of science: 'Thus the interpreter of Huxley, Tyndall, Darwin, and other great men of our time, has passed over again to the service of one who came to redeem the world, but failed; and who has been expected again "shortly" for the past 2,000 years.' Another article ridiculed him as offering Jesus as 'Dr Sexton's New Patent Mixture' that is good for whatever ails you.[97] Even it conceded, however, that Sexton was making earnest and germane attempts to answer the objections to Christianity raised by Secularists. In an impressive tribute to how seriously this organ of Secularism took George Sexton, his *Reasons for Renouncing Infidelity* was revisited as the lead article in the *Secular Review* eight months after it had already been reviewed once before. The article declared:

When a man has publicly, and conspicuously identified himself with a movement, when he has devoted the best years of his life to the propagation of certain opinions, and has been, perhaps, the means of inducing many others to accept those opinions, if he suddenly disowns his old convictions, and begins to advocate others of an opposite character, it seems to us very proper that he should let the world know what are the reasons which have operated to produce such a change.... imagine our disgust at finding the great bulk of it to consist of the veriest twaddle of the pulpit.... If the Doctor thinks it has the remotest tendency to shake the convictions of any confirmed Sceptic, he must be more sanguine than sensible.[98]

Notice the use of the routine accusation that his change of convictions must have happened 'suddenly'.

The *Secular Review* also kept up a running feud with the *Shield of Faith*, or as Secularists tended to quip, in reference to its tendency to look for immorality in the Secularist camp, the 'Shield of Filth'. When

---

[96] e.g. *Secular Review*, 8 Sept. 1877, p. 215.
[97] Ibid., 22 Sept. 1877, p. 247.
[98] Ibid., 20 Apr. 1878, pp. 241–3.

Sexton made jokes at its expense, the *Secular Review* retorted caustically that he was trying for the role of Court Jester for King Jesus.[99] Still, the *Secular Review* tended to concede that Sexton was defending the untenable with considerable skill.[100] When Sexton critiqued 'Hylo-Idealism', an elusive idea then fashionable among some freethinkers, the Secularist paper owed that Dr Sexton's remarks were true, wise, relevant, and penetrating.[101] Moreover, when the *Shield of Faith* ceased publication in 1884, as the lead item in the *Secular Review* Charles Watts paid a kind tribute to his adversary:

I should like to dance a war-dance over the grave of this divine bantling; but somehow I cannot. I have, for years, noted the work of Dr. Sexton; and my unquenchable hatred for the faith he champions has never blunted the edge of my sympathy with the man who championed it. I have always recognised in him a gallant and chivalrous enemy; and I have, from my boyhood, had too much to do with literary adventures, journalistic and otherwise, not to have a fellow feeling with the man who on principle, against disadvantages, conducts a journal for seven weary and ill-supported years, throwing into it valorously his talents and his purse; but compelled at last to surrender, after having lost everything save honour.

The faith Dr. Sexton supports has no more bitter opponent than I am; but my human sympathies are stronger than even my anti-Christian antipathies.... and now I cannot say that I rejoice that Dr. Sexton, after a gallant fight, is also *hors de combat*. There is one liberally educated, and intellectually capable man the less to defend the sanctity of the litter of that stable in Bethlehem; and, in opposing that sanctity, I am apprehensive that I may have to measure swords with narrower and less gifted men than the Uriah whom the Christian host has just left in the front of the battle to perish utterly but not ignobly.[102]

This is not only a recognition of Sexton as a man of ability and intellectual weight, but also an acknowledgment that, far from declaring himself a Christian in a sordid hunt for pecuniary advantages, Sexton had actually spent what money of his own that he could in order to engage in what was for him the vital work of Christian apologetics.

[99] Ibid., 11 Nov. 1882, p. 311.
[100] Ibid., 7 July 1883, pp. 10–11.
[101] Ibid., 17 Nov. 1883, p. 315.
[102] Ibid., 19 Jan. 1884, p. 33.

The Christian world received Sexton as one of their own with great respect. He could boast that the most eminent Anglican layman, Lord Shaftesbury, and the most eminent Nonconformist layman, Samuel Morley, were supporters of his ministry.[103] He was elected a member of that highbrow Christian apologetics society the Victoria Institute, his name invariably appearing in the alphabetical list of members immediately before that of Lord Shaftesbury.[104] Pulpits across much of the denominational spectrum were open to him. The Church of England was more rigid on such matters, but still sometimes welcoming in its own way. When Sexton spoke in Middlesborough, for example, it was in the town-hall and not the parish church, but he was supported by and the personal guest of the vicar, the Revd J. K. Bealey.[105] David Thomas was so willing to promote Sexton's ministry that he even had him preach the Christmas morning sermon at his chapel.[106] Sexton was a frequent guest in Congregational pulpits in numerous places. Indeed, Dissent as a whole was more or less open to him. To take a random example, an announcement of his forthcoming engagements made in 1882 included Congregational, Countess of Huntingdon, Free Methodist, Primitive Methodist, and United Evangelical (Scotland) pulpits.[107] Dr Sexton became a regular lecturer for the Christian Evidence Society, and he often spoke at local branches of the YMCA.

Another measure of the high regard in which Sexton was held is the praise heaped upon him in reviews of his books. Here is a sample:

Blackpool Times: A great scholar, and a man of large and varied reading.

Essex Telegraph: Tyndall's Belfast Address appears in a sorry plight after its dissection in this book.

Homilist: The author is well known as a man of letters and high scientific attainments.

---

[103] The dedication page of George Sexton, *Biblical Difficulties Dispelled: Being an answer to queries respecting so-called Discrepancies in Scripture, misunderstood and misinterpreted texts, etc., etc.*, 2nd edn. (Toronto: William Briggs, 1887).

[104] The first time he appears as a member is *Journal of the Transactions of the Victoria Institute, or Philosophical Society of Great Britain*, 10 (1877), 409.

[105] *Spiritual Magazine* (1876), 233.

[106] This was published as George Sexton, *The Advent of Christ, and its effects upon the ages* (London: Smart & Allen, 1878).

[107] *Shield of Faith* (Jan. 1882), 44.

Englishman: The writer is a gentleman of very high culture, and of great and varied learning.

Indeed, the *Christian Evidence Journal,* finding Sexton's erudition almost too formidable, said apologetically that an essay of his, 'though sometimes it is rather learned', might still be of use to the ordinary reader.[108]

In conclusion, Sexton's evolving ecclesiastical identity needs to be addressed. His return to Christian worship came through his friendship with Young, and thus was in a Unitarian chapel. Sexton initially thought that he would spend his life in a Unitarian context. Some autobiographical comments he made in April 1876 are revealing:

When it was known that he had abandoned the Secularist platform, and had devoted himself to the promulgation of Christian truth, he had been requested to join the ranks of many denominations. He said this without any vanity, or without wishing to over-rate his own abilities. He had been offered pulpits in different denominations, but up to the present had accepted none. His tendency had been at first towards Unitarianism, and his friends naturally expected that he would settle down in that denomination. He soon came to see, however, that the great central truth of Christianity was the supreme divinity of the Lord Jesus Christ, and that if this were removed the whole fabric would fall.[109]

In describing the religious changes that occurred in him, Sexton later reminisced that, after much reflection, he 'reached what is called the more orthodox form of Unitarianism'.[110] The Unitarian world welcomed him, and he could have found a respected position in it. His own congregation, later called the Church of the Lord, was not at first orthodox. When Sexton became convinced of the divinity of Christ, this again disrupted what he was building and meant another setback: 'Large numbers, consisting of Unitarians, Spiritualists, and other kinds of Rationalists, shook their heads, wondering what next; suggested that I had better join Moody and Sankey, and left.'[111] In Britain, Sexton settled down to being thoroughly

---

[108] All of these quotations are taken from the advertisements printed at the back of his various books.

[109] *Spiritual Magazine* (1876), 233.

[110] Sexton, *Reasons,* 44.

[111] Ibid. 46.

orthodox, continuing to serve his own congregation, and spending much of his time preaching and lecturing in a wide variety of contexts. A measure of how theologically conservative he became is his *Biblical Difficulties Dispelled*, a collection of the answers that he gave to scriptural conundrums sent to the *Shield of Faith* by readers. A total of 127 questions are addressed in this volume, and Dr Sexton deserves full credit for tackling rather than ducking the most forceful objections usually raised by Secularists. He does not articulate a doctrine of Scripture, but the tone tends toward infallibility as he never concedes that a real discrepancy exists. Occasionally he will admit that a passage is perplexing, but a more typical response is for him to breeze in, confidently claiming that the matter can be resolved. Learning is often on display. To take an extreme case, in a single answer we have references to the Syriac Peshito, Origen, Theodoret, Erasmus, Grotius, Luther, Cranmer, Tyndale, Hammond, Adam Clarke, Ellicott, Alford, Chrysostom, Gregory of Nyssa, Wolf, Bengel, Calvin, Owen, De Wette, Olshausen, Oosterzee, Barnes, Conybeare, Wordsworth, Hodge, Dr Arnold, and F. D. Maurice.[112] Scientific knowledge is repeatedly brought to bear. To the question 'Will the Earth Be Destroyed?', Sexton retorted: 'Science, no less than Scripture, declares this consummation to be inevitable. The law of dissipation of energy would of itself bring it about.'[113] Sexton's reading of Scripture was only conservative up to a point. He declared that the Book of Job was entirely an allegory and should in no way be viewed as a record of events that actually happened. He asserted that the biblical flood was local, not universal, as was the apostle Paul's apparent prohibition of women preachers. In the end, Sexton was a defender of a fairly traditional brand of orthodox Christianity.

In August 1884 Sexton travelled to North America. He had originally intended simply to visit, but he found a hearty welcome and a new field of service and, in the end, never returned to Britain. He spent most of these years in Canada. William Briggs of Toronto, a Methodist house, became his main publisher. A preface dated 1 December 1884 has him in Toronto. Two years later he was in Philadelphia.[114] In America he officially took on an orthodox

---

112 Sexton, *Biblical Difficulties*, 135–7.
113 Ibid. 132.
114 Ibid., the prefaces to the first and second editions.

denominational identity and ministry. In 1889 he was received by the Presbytery of Buffalo, New York, as an ordained minister in the Presbyterian Church in the United States of America (Northern).[115] He served in 1889–90 as the minister of First Presbyterian Church, Dunkirk, New York. It is a sure sign of how solid his credentials were deemed to be that he could have made this transition into the ordained ministry of a sound, respectable, orthodox, learned denomination such as the Presbyterians. Sometime during the 1890s Sexton returned to Ontario, where he lived a semi-retired life in which he still gave occasional addresses, including preaching at the flagship evangelical Presbyterian church in the region, Knox Presbyterian Church, Toronto. In fact his death from 'heart disease', at the home where he lived as a guest near St Catharines, Ontario, came on a day when he was writing a new lecture.[116] He died on 11 October 1898 at the age of 73. Dr Sexton's new identity was so complete that the local obituary simply described him as a 'Presbyterian divine', giving no hint of a past life of scepticism, or leadership in Spiritualism or any other movements. The *Toronto Globe*, however, identified him as 'A Well Known Lecturer on the Error of Infidelity and a Distinguished Author'. At the time of his death George Sexton had been a reconvert for twenty-five years, and had devoted the last twenty-two years of his life to offering an intelligent defence and articulation of Christian thought.

[115] Robinson, *Ministerial Directory*, i. 474.
[116] *Toronto Globe*, 13 Oct. 1898, 'Death of Rev. Dr. Sexton. A Well Known Lecturer on the Error of Infidelity and a Distinguished Author Expires Suddenly'; *Daily Standard* (St Catharines, Ontario), 12 Oct. 1898, p. 1.

9

How Many Reconverts Were There?

As I have discussed this research project with scholars in overlapping areas of expertise, I have met the same reactions again and again. When I would say that I was working on nineteenth-century free-thinkers who reconverted, the first reaction was often an assumption that I was speaking of deathbed conversions. I would have to cut off in mid-flow the speech that would then ensue about how this was Christian propaganda and often demonstrably untrue, in order to state that I was studying people who went on to write books on Christian apologetics, participate in debates, or otherwise defend their new-found beliefs, generally for a decade or more before any deathbed scene could be enacted.[1]

This point having been established, the standard follow-up question has been: 'How many reconverts were there?' This question struck me as strange the first few times I encountered it. I doubt very much that people routinely asked Basil Willey, A. O. J. Cockshut, Susan Budd, or A. N. Wilson: 'How many Victorians lost their faith?' To ask 'How many reconverts were there?' seems to assume that this must be such an extreme phenomenon that its limits can easily be delineated with precision, as if one were asking 'How many people have landed on the moon?' Quantifying nineteenth-century

---

[1] For deathbeds, see David S. Nash, ' "Look in Her Face and Lose Thy Dread of Dying": The Ideological Importance of Death to the Secularist Community in Nineteenth-Century Britain', *Journal of Religion*, 19: 2 (Dec. 1995), 158–80. For the urban legend that Darwin reconverted on his deathbed, see James Moore, *The Darwin Legend* (Grand Rapids, Mich.: Baker, 1994). Victorian Secularists often addressed this issue as well. See e.g. Robert Cooper, *Death-bed Repentance: its fallacy and absurdity when applied as a test of the truth of opinion; with authentic particulars of the last moments of distinguished free-thinkers*, 6th edn. (London: E. Truelove, 1875).

reconversions is not a project that naturally interests me (indeed, crisis-of-faith scholars have never bothered to quantify the pattern they were studying), but as I have been persistently asked to address this question I will endeavour to do so. Nevertheless, I would not wish the musings offered in the rest of this chapter to be leaned on too heavily: I recognize that they are contestable, and do not consider them central to the thesis of this book.

How many reconverts were there? How could one possibly know? This project has been interested in a maximalist rather than minimalist principle of selection. It has focused on figures who were well known as popular Secularist leaders or heroes of freethought, who left writings in their own voice from their sceptical days, and who then returned to organized Christianity and left germane writings from those days as well. In other words, to be prime figures for research, not only would it be indisputable that they had once been widely received as prominent religious sceptics but also that they were then well known as active Christians. Moreover, they would also have considered their own change of views intellectually defensible and made an effort to explain how. As every person's story is different, so each figure fits these various stipulations to a greater or lesser extent. Left out are figures who were merely sceptics as opposed to sceptical leaders. Also left out altogether are people who were not prominent enough in either stage of advocacy to have their views noticed or published.

The standard for this project is therefore a much higher one than that adhered to in the loss-of-faith literature. A comparable loss-of-faith volume would be a collection of figures who had been bishops, well-known ministers, or prominent preachers. George Eliot, an archetypal loss-of-faith figure, was a sincere evangelical, but she never even came close to being an influential evangelical voice. Even the figures in the loss-of-faith literature who were ordained were rarely, if ever, Christian leaders in any way comparable to the degree to which figures such as Cooper and Barker were leaders of organized, popular freethought. Moreover, some of the figures commonly discussed in the loss-of-faith literature barely had a faith to lose; one thinks, for example, of John Stuart Mill. To reiterate, if a reconvert is any person who was convinced for a time by sceptical thoughts and who later became a sincere Christian, it is probable that there were hundreds of them in nineteenth-century England. Even if one narrows the field to those who were active in the much smaller world of organized unbelief, given the significant attrition rate from the top Secularist leadership, one can reasonably postulate that numerous rank-and-file members of organized freethought later made a conscientious move into denominational Christianity. Sexton, a well-placed if also biased source, claimed in 1877 that 'a great majority' of Secularists eventually reconverted:

> the so-called Secular societies are largely made up of young men, for whom sceptical views have an attraction, as being calculated to allow a sort of reckless independence, freedom from control, and a kind of intellectual audacity which fascinate for a time; whilst the majority of those who professed infidel principles a few years ago have discovered how sterile and barren the whole thing is, and have left it for something which is better adapted to the deep-felt wants of human nature.... In my own case... I endeavoured to feed my spiritual being on some miserable substitute for religion, but in the end the truth made its way to my heart, as it does, sooner or later, to a great majority of Secularists, that there is nothing that can supply the needs of the soul but the religion of Christ.[2]

That was presumably an exaggeration, but, crucially, an exaggeration of a genuine pattern among the rank and file. I have not even attempted to discover such reconverts. I have, however, stumbled upon enough Christian obituaries, biographical sketches, and testimonies asserting that the subject had once been a sceptic, to have no doubt that a systematic trawl through the sources would produce a numerically significant list of such figures. The methodological problem that this would then raise would be the difficulty of discerning when a previous commitment to scepticism had been exaggerated in order to provide a more dramatic conversion narrative. The chapter-length case studies presented here have avoided this methodological problem by concentrating on figures whose reputations and opinions as sceptics can be assessed from extant sources written before their reconversion. It should also be noted that this study is primarily interested in a cohort of plebeian political radicals, rather than just anyone who had a crisis of doubt across the social spectrum.

---

[2] George Sexton, *The Fallacies of Secularism* (London: G. S. Sexton, 1877), 105.

A more manageable project might be to attempt to quantify what percentage of leaders of popular freethought reconverted. It must be said that it is a slippery task, however, as 'a leader of popular freethought' is a much more contestable category than, for example, a Church of England clergyman. The waters are also muddied by the fact that a freethinking leader who was faithful to the movement to the end of their days would often have their reputation solidified and perpetuated posthumously. On the other hand, it is quite clear that concerted attempts were routinely made to downplay, discredit, or simply ignore the prominent Secularist leadership that had once been given by reconverts. For example, Bradlaugh's reputation is secure and his memory is still honoured by self-identified Secularists today,[3] while Barker was deliberately edited out of the record, but there was a time when Barker got top billing over Bradlaugh on the masthead of the *National Reformer*.

The crisis-of-doubt haemorrhage at the national-leadership level of popular, organized freethought was a significant one. Reading through the *Reasoner*, it is startling to see how often two or more figures who would later reconvert are mentioned on a single page.[4] When Cooper reconverted, the movement put up Barker to answer him, only to have Barker himself reconvert some years later. Repeatedly, the *Reasoner* would attempt to replenish the leadership-supply by promoting an impressive, rising leader such as Young or Gordon, only to see that person reconvert. The lead article in the 1 August 1863 issue of the *Secular World* discussed four popular freethinking leaders who had either just announced their reconversion or had made some statement or movement that made it likely that they soon would under the headline, 'Further Conversions'. It rather wistfully expressed the hope that such people would learn how to

---

[3] See e.g. the page extolling his achievements on the website of the National Secular Society: www.secularism.org.uk/charlesbradlaugh.html (accessed on 6 Jan. 2006).

[4] To take a random example, in the 'Secularist and Progressionist Societies' reports section, *Reasoner Gazette*, 25 Nov. 1860, p. 190, the first report is of Sexton speaking in South London and the second one is of Gordon speaking in Sheffield. In the same section in the next week's issue (2 Dec. 1860, p. 194), the first report is an announcement that Barker will lecture at the Hall of Science, London, then, after an announcement regarding an appeal to raise money for a Secularist hall, the next announcement is a report of Gordon's debate in Birmingham. The next page (*Reasoner Gazette*, 2 Dec. 1860, p. 195) included news of lectures by all three: Gordon, Sexton, and Barker.

convert to Christianity earlier in their careers. The article went on to wish that all the Secularist leaders who ever would might all reconvert at once—even if this meant precipitating an additional purge of their top leadership, when they had not even recovered from the last one—that way, at least they could get the matter decisively behind them.[5] Reminiscent of Jonathan Edwards's *The Distinguishing Marks of a Work of the Spirit of God*, the *Secular World* ran another article a few months later entitled 'Rules for Testing Converts', reckoning: 'In these days, when alleged "conversions" are so frequent, it may be useful if we strive to find some characteristic distinguishing marks between the sincere convert and the worthless turncoat.'[6] There were, however, more reconversions to come beyond that cluster. Even if scholars have not always discerned it, the *Secular World*, at least, knew that it had a crisis of doubt on its hands.

More concretely, a major, unique Secularist camp meeting was organized in 1860. Royle observes: 'This meeting was the greatest single demonstration of Secularist strength.'[7] Although not all of them were able to attend, the organizers recognized eight national leaders of the Secularist movement through their invitations to speakers: G. J. Holyoake, Joseph Barker, Charles Bradlaugh, Austin Holyoake, John Watts, J. H. Gordon, Robert Cooper, and J. B. Bebbington. Three of these eight—Barker, Gordon, and Bebbington—went on to reconvert. Not only is this a startling result in its own terms but, once again, there is nothing like it in the annals of the Victorian loss of faith. A comparable event would be three out of eight members of the executive committee of the Evangelical Alliance, three out of eight Wesleyan superintendents, or three out of eight Anglican bishops losing their faith. It would capture the attention of historians if three out of eight key leaders of a national political party switched sides.

The 12 July 1862 issue of the *Literary Budget* ran an article on 'Infidel and Atheistical Literature'.[8] It identified four journals

[5] *Secular World*, 1 Aug. 1863, 'Further Conversions'.

[6] Ibid., 1 Nov. 1863, 'Rules for Testing Converts'.

[7] Edward Royle, *Victorian Infidels: The Origins of the British Secularist Movement, 1791–1866* (Manchester: Manchester University Press, 1974), 190.

[8] *Literary Budget*, 12 July 1862, 'Infidel and Atheistical Literature', as reprinted in the *Propagandist*, 2 Aug. 1862, pp. 56–7.

currently serving that community: Bradlaugh's *National Reformer*, Holyoake's *Secular World*, *Barker's Review*, and Bebbington's *Propagandist*. Two of those four editors went on to reconvert. It might be said that this was simply a particularly opportune time for the thesis of this study for a snapshot to have been taken. Granted—but has there ever been such an opportune moment from the start of the eighteenth century into the twenty-first century for a corresponding crisis-of-faith snapshot to have been taken? When did half of the leading editors of evangelical, Anglican, or generically Christian journals ever go on to lose their faith? Moreover, to remove the fortuitous-snapshot effect, it is possible to look at Victorian Secularist journals and their editors more systematically. In the 'newspapers and periodicals' section of the bibliography in Royle's *Victorian Infidels*, twenty-seven people are named as editors. Of these, six are so obscure or tangential to the movement that they do not receive a 'biographical summary' in Royle's Appendix V, leaving twenty-one editors. Many of those twenty-one, such as Thornton Hunt, W. J. Linton, and G. J. Harney, were arguably political radicals rather than leaders of religious scepticism, and politics rather than freethought was the domain of their journals. Nevertheless, as that is a more debatable line to draw, we shall leave them in the sample. It should also be noted that contained in these twenty-one (let alone the original twenty-seven) are in all likelihood figures whose later lives are not known well enough to determine whether or not they reconverted. Nevertheless, of these twenty-one, for no fewer than eight of them some sort of cloud would develop over their commitment to the freethinking cause. Bebbington, Barker, and Cooper are clear reconverts. Thomas Paterson was seemingly one as well. Charles Southwell and W. H. Johnson were apparently not, but they behaved in ways that made other freethinking leaders denounce them as reconverts or as engaging in a dishonest pretence that they were Christian. Robert Owen became a champion of Spiritualism, and Richard Carlile re-emerged as a self-identified Christian, albeit of his own quirky and unorthodox variety.[9] Once again, how would such a finding look if it could be demonstrated for the loss-of-faith narrative? A comparable result would be if, of twenty-one editors of Methodist

---

[9] The reader can find entries on each of these figures in the Appendix.

periodicals in nineteenth-century England, three lost their faith altogether for good and wrote about this process, another wrote about how he had become an atheist (for whatever reason or duration), two flirted with scepticism in ways that got them denounced as presumed atheists, one still considered himself a Methodist although he was now also a materialist, and a final one called himself an atheist, although he was still deeply spiritual in various ways. The Victorian loss of faith, of course, did not even remotely make such inroads. For readers who come to this study primarily from an interest in church history, I might also note that the reconverts were a larger and more prominent section of the Secularist leadership than the converts to Rome were of the Church of England. Once again, these comparisons are made to stimulate fresh thinking, and should not be taken too woodenly as ways of accurately measuring the extent of the Victorian crisis of faith. My point is simply that there is sufficient evidence to discern a significant crisis-of-doubt pattern.

Finally, fellow scholars have often gone on to comment, in the words of one professor of modern British history at an English university in a letter to me: 'More people went the other way, of course.' Once again, I have heard this repeatedly from leading scholars of nineteenth-century Britain. What can this possibly mean, however? On one level, it is self-evident to the point of absurdity. As reconverts are, by definition, a subset from the loss-of-faith pool, it would be literally impossible for there to be more reconverts than loss-of-faith figures. Indeed, the reconverts themselves are often primarily known in the existing scholarly literature in the context of the loss of faith. It is, of course, not the majority of people's fate to go through three contradictory phases of thought on any issue—politics, for example, no less than religion. 'More people on the other side', however, is a self-defeating argument for anyone who wishes to maintain the loss-of-faith narrative. It is obvious that many more Victorians retained their faith than lost it. Yet whoever thought to comment to Willey and company, 'More Victorians were sincere Christians than agnostics, of course'? The strength of the loss-of-faith narrative is that, although it is dealing with case studies that reflect a minority, the life stories of these figures are nevertheless offered as a telling sign of the times. This study argues that the reconverts, although also a distinct minority, are no less a telling sign of their times. Indeed, arguably they are a more telling one, for if one wants to understand the Victorians one must primarily attend to faith—with doubt looming large primarily as its bugbear. It is undoubtedly true that more people who once had been ordained ministers became Secularists or agnostics than people who had once been Secularist leaders reconverted, but that is a reflection of how many, many more Christian ministers there were than Secularist leaders. As a percentage, however, it is very apparent that a very much higher percentage of Secularist leaders reconverted than ordained Christian ministers lost their faith.[10]

Several scholars have dismissed the figures discussed in this project with the aid of psychological theories. As one of them put it, in a knowing tone, one suspects that the reconverts were 'addicted to the drama of conversion'. Even with a great deal of poetic licence, it is hard to see how one could call a behaviour engaged in only three times in one's life, with each incident separated by years, an addiction. Those who converted and then dramatically de-converted have not been accused of this—it is that one, last move that reveals that a person is not an honest searcher after truth, but rather a pathetic victim of some exhibitionist compulsion. More to the point, this attempt at an explanation is one sub-category in the wider category of non-intellectual factors. My working assumption has been that non-intellectual factors apply no more and no less to people such as Cooper, Barker, and Bebbington than they do to loss-of-faith figures such as George Eliot, Leslie Stephen, and F. W. Newman. Some people have speculated, for example, that Victorian atheists were motivated by anger at their fathers (I am not particularly sympathetic to such an explanation, however). In the polemical warfare between Victorian Secularists and Christians, each side gave non-intellectual reasons for the other's motivations. For example, Christians often

---

[10] This is a judgement regarding the evidence that is there for historians to weigh. One can always speculate that ministers lost their faith without admitting it (or, on the other hand, as Christian propagandists sometimes asserted, that atheists secretly believed in God but claimed not to out of spite or some other motive). There does not seem to be any warrant for assuming that a greater percentage of Christian ministers discreetly left the ministry because of a crisis of faith than Secularist leaders quietly abandoned freethinking advocacy because of a crisis of doubt.

claimed that sceptics wanted to be freed from Christianity so that they could engage in immoral behaviour; sceptics often returned the compliment by claiming that reconverts were seeking to make money from the Christian community. As a historian, I am all for scholars investigating non-intellectual factors, but any tendency to discuss the loss of faith primarily in the context of intellectual history while discussing the reconverts primarily in terms of psychological, cultural, or social factors should arouse suspicion. Another working assumption of this study has been that, however much a person might be predisposed, due to non-intellectual factors, to either faith or doubt, it is not as easy as people often seem to imagine for reflective and intellectually curious individuals either to rebuild a coherent worldview from an opposing point of view that answers old objections to one's own satisfaction, or to go on in a new context without having done so. Non-intellectual factors might be a prompt, but they lead on to intellectual work that is genuine in its own terms. A person's ideas cannot be dismissed by a theory about how they first became attracted to them. It might be possible to explain how a person became a feminist, a Marxist, or a democrat through non-intellectual factors, but their intellectual efforts within those schools of thought cannot thereby be marginalized.

Having made the decision that this study would focus on the clearest and most thoroughly documented cases, I then found that my interlocutors would sometimes switch tack. If I was not co-opting people into my sample on the strength of dubious deathbed narratives, then perhaps I was excluding people wrongly as a result of too narrow a definition of what a figure's subsequent faith was. 'Does Annie Besant not deserve to count as a reconvert, just because she went into Theosophy rather than organized Christianity?' I was asked. In order to go some way toward satisfying these various requests, questions, and concerns, I have included an Appendix containing short biographical sketches. As each case has its own special features, I have not wished to group them by affinities. Some of these figures listed in the Appendix have clear reconversion narratives that are quite similar to those of the chapter-length case studies. For others, the evidence base is unsatisfactory or unclear in important ways. Still others were Secularists who moved into Spiritualism or Theosophy, or who only appeared to be reconverts. Many of these figures are 'persons of interest' in various ways rather than reconverts: listing them in the Appendix should not be viewed as an effort to co-opt them or to make a definitive judgement on the nature of their stories. The list is in strict alphabetical order.

The Appendix list has been compiled in a thoroughly haphazard way. The only kind of systematic hunt that I have ever engaged in is to pursue keyword searches in library catalogues for probable separately published nineteenth-century reconversion narratives. I have spent more time in the Secularist press than any other primary sources, but I have not even made a systematic trawl through it: it is highly likely that such an effort would reveal more reconverts. Far from allegations that a figure reconverted often being the result of dubious stories circulating in the Christian community, repeatedly people are identified or denounced as reconverts in freethinking sources even though this claim cannot be verified elsewhere. Combing the religious press, which I have not used, would certainly also reveal more hitherto unidentified, genuine reconverts (as well as more urban legends). Many of the figures listed caught my eye because of something intriguing said about them in some scholar's monograph. As scholars have not been generally interested in reconversion stories, and have often even neglected to mention an erstwhile sceptic's subsequent faith, this is not a very reliable way to generate a list. Also, in the very last draft of this book I had to cut seven figures out of the Appendix due to a lack of space. It should also be noted that the sources I am using for these figures are often also a haphazard and incomplete collection. With many of these sketches, it is my hope to arouse curiosity for possible further research, rather than to make a definitive claim about where a particular figure fits into larger patterns. Some of the figures listed are quite famous Victorians who arguably cannot be connected to a crisis-of-doubt narrative in any way: once again, listing them should not be seen as an effort to co-opt them. I have no doubt that a systematic effort to find people in a particular category would yield many more names. For example, I have made no effort to discover figures who moved from Secularism to Spiritualism, but it is clear that that was a noticeable pattern. I have also paid less attention to the Christian Socialist world, but it was one terminus for former popular freethinkers (see, for example, the entry on Lloyd Jones in the Appendix). If nothing else, the list given in the Appendix should draw attention to the fact that there are many promising lines of enquiry yet to be pursued in order to map the contours of nineteenth-century crises of doubt. It should also serve to underline that 'How many reconverts were there?' is not a question that can be answered by reeling off a list of names such as those of the seven figures whose stories have been highlighted in the main chapters of this book.

10

Crisis of Doubt

> We shall not cease from exploration
> And the end of all our exploring
> Will be to arrive where we started
> And know the place for the first time.
>
> (T. S. Eliot, 'Little Gidding')

There was a crisis of faith in nineteenth-century Britain, but there was also a crisis of doubt. Perhaps there were crises of doubt. Future scholars may uncover similar patterns among different social groups or more precisely located in other ways. The one explored in this study has been the crisis of doubt among plebeian radicals. The main focus here has been on Secularist leaders. The loss of faith of figures who later reconverted corresponds fully to the loss-of-faith narratives of Secularist leaders who were supporters of the cause unto death. Secularist leaders who did not reconvert were also generally raised in devout Christian homes and were once earnest believers. Susan Budd, in her extensive research (mainly based on Secularist obituaries, and thus excluding reconverts and obscuring the crisis of doubt), observes: 'It was mainly those who had been actively and sincerely religious who were converted to secularism.'[1] Even more sharply, Budd identifies a very specific mid-Victorian model: 'In the 1850s and 60s, one pattern of conversion to unbelief appears with remarkable frequency. It is that of the nonconformist, often a Wesleyan, who becomes a class teacher or even a lay preacher, and in studying the Bible closely to prepare for lessons from it discovers inconsistencies

---

[1] Susan Budd, *Varieties of Unbelief: Atheists and Agnostics in English Society, 1850–1960* (London: Heinemann, 1977), 120.

and absurdities, and finds that he can no longer regard the Bible as divinely inspired or literally true.'[2] This study has shown how closely that template parallels the life stories of many reconverts such as Barker, Cooper, and Bebbington. Thus, the first of the 'causes of unbelief' that Budd identifies is 'books'. The most prominent book in the loss-of-faith narratives of nineteenth-century Secularists was the Bible itself, followed by Paine's *The Age of Reason*. The second cause that Budd identifies is a political consciousness that came to see the church or religion as part of the problem rather than the solution. Once again, the reconverts studied here were also political radicals with an anticlerical streak. According to Budd, the final causes that the Secularists themselves recognized were reactions against the Christian use of the deathbed-conversion idea and the threat of hell. Once again, this is all typical. Barker often spoke against the deathbed argument, Sexton wrote a tract against the doctrine of hell, and Cooper strikingly railed against it in his *The Purgatory of Suicides*. Budd also explores 'unrecognized causes', such as the possibility that Secularists were motivated by a desire to defy their fathers. Moreover, the loss-of-faith narratives of the reconverts presented in this study also have parallels with those of the members of the social elite whose lives are usually chronicled in the honest-doubt literature. George Eliot's encounter with Hennell's *An Inquiry Concerning the Origin of Christianity* may be paralleled with the impact on Cooper of her translation of Strauss's *Leben Jesu*. In short, it does not seem that there is any way, even retrospectively, to isolate a distinguishing mark of someone who would later reconvert from someone who would not.

As has been shown in Chapter 9, a significant crisis of doubt confronted the leadership of the Victorian Secularist movement. The figures studied in this volume were often top leaders in the movement, some of them once standing among the leading half-dozen or so national leaders of popular, organized freethought. Hone was the most famous 'blasphemer' of his day. Cooper became the most popular freethinking lecturer in London. Gordon had the only full-time Secularist lecturing position in the nation. Barker was arguably at one point the most popular sceptic in the whole

---

[2] Susan Budd, *Varieties of Unbelief: Atheists and Agnostics in English Society, 1850–1960* (London: Heinemann, 1977), 107–8.

movement, certainly in the north of England. Sexton and Bebbington were also prominent leaders, and even Young—the least distinguished of the group—was a recognized freethinking lecturer and author, and held a rare full-time position in Holyoake's operation. Both as a percentage of the entire leadership and in terms of the place of respect they held within that leadership pool, the reconverts represent a significant reality in the story of the nineteenth-century Secularist movement. Despite the way that the narrative of the Victorian loss of faith has loomed so large in the existing literature, the Secularist movement lost a far greater percentage of its top leadership to reconversion than the Christian ministry lost due to a crisis of faith. Moreover, much of the angst in church circles that is chronicled in the loss-of-faith literature has its mirror-image in the Secularist movement. There also can be found anxious commentary on the current state of affairs. George Millar, for example, wrote to the *Secular Review* in 1878: 'I confess that I write in sorrow; for, having devoted a lifetime in working, to the best of my humble abilities, for the promotion of Secular principles, I am bound in truth to record that, as an organisation, Secular principles are in a worse condition throughout the country now than they have ever been during my forty years associated with the Party.'[3]

If articles can be found in the Victorian Christian press which betray a kind of desperation to answer the objections of sceptics, so also the Secularist press was filled with articles that were frantically attempting to answer the critiques of reconverts. In a single issue of the *Secular World* (1 January 1864), for example, there were articles entitled 'Mere Negations' and 'A Sketch of Positive Morality'—both serving as an effort at Secularist apologetics in the face of reconvert arguments. There were also numerous articles that ran in some sections of the freethinking press insisting that Secularism was a religion or the true religion. One of numerous such articles, this one from the *Secular Review,* argued in 1877: 'And just as the Rev. Rowland Hill did not see why the Devil should have all the good tunes, neither do we see why the theologians should keep all the best words, especially when, as in the present case, the word expresses what the thing is, or at least ought to be, better than any other.'[4]

[3] *Secular Review,* 6 Apr. 1878, p. 221.
[4] Ibid., 8 Apr. 1877, 'Secularism As A Religion'.

Despite the picture one often receives from reading the loss-of-faith literature that religion was being vanquished, it is a tribute to the extraordinary strength and vitality of religion in late Victorian Britain that even some Secularists wanted to wrap themselves in its positive glow.

Recurring themes may be observed in the contours of a crisis of doubt. This list is in no particular order, however: factors are not being ranked. First, there was a growing frustration with scepticism as merely negative and destructive. Reconverts came to believe that it was easier to tear down than build up, yet Secularism could only accomplish the former: not being able to build, it left humanity with no place to live. Secularism did not offer an alternative worldview. It did not equip one with a philosophy with which to face life.[5]

Second, reconverts came to believe that Secularism offered no basis for morality or for making ethical choices. Sometimes this was triggered by a specific event, such as a Secularist leader leaving his wife or seemingly advocating promiscuous behaviour in a publication. Often, however, it was thought that even though many Secularist leaders adhered to the same moral vision as Christians, this was only because they had been raised as Christians. Their morality ran on borrowed fuel. Reconverts thought that exclusively Secularist resources offered no rationale for why some acts were deemed moral and others immoral; therefore freethinkers (or perhaps second-generation freethinkers) would not have sufficient internal restraints to prevent them from engaging in any behaviour that appeared likely to enhance their personal pleasure or benefit them in some other way.

Third, reconverts began to wonder whether scepticism was the result of a procrustean system of logic, an oppressively narrow definition of reason. They came to believe that human beings knew more than could be proven by such a method. Humanity had other sources of knowledge, identified with terms such as the heart, instincts, intuition, feeling, and entire or inner consciousness.

---

[5] These assertions by reconverts, as well as those listed below, should not be taken as 'the truth' about the whole of Victorian Secularism. Holyoake in particular was working very hard to make his version of Secularism a positive movement: the judgement of reconverts that he and others had failed in the ways listed here should not be taken for granted.

Fourth, reconverts often cited their reappraisal of the Bible. Gordon spoke as if he did not really know its contents, and there is a shade of this in Hone. It would be more accurate, however, to say that they came to approach the Scriptures with a different disposition. Barker recalls trying for a change to identify what he found to be good rather than bad in the Bible.

Fifth, the reconverts were often figures who were haunted by Jesus of Nazareth. As Secularists they thought that the Jesus they had heard of when young had been destroyed forever as a historical figure by the results of modern biblical criticism. That Jesus, however, had a tendency to rise from the dead. Several of the reconverts came to the conclusion that the Jesus revealed by a traditional reading of the gospels was too good not to be true: it was a portrait so compelling that only a historical original could account for it.

Sixth, reconverts were often led away from materialism by re-engaging with the realm of spirit in a form decoupled from Christianity. Hone was aided by his own mysterious experiences, and Spiritualism was a part of the story of a variety of figures, including Barker, Young, and Sexton. While for the reconverts this led on to or paralleled a new openness to the claims of Christianity, for other Secularists the realm of the spirit was accepted, but a return to Christianity was not. Robert Owen became an enthusiastic supporter of Spiritualism. Annie Besant famously moved from being an atheist leader to being the president of the Theosophical Society.[6]

Seventh, reconverts often reassessed their assumption that the cause of radical politics and the working classes naturally led on to opposition to Christianity. An encounter with a figure such as F. D. Maurice, for example, could do much to dissolve such an assumption.

Finally, due weight must be given to intellectual influences generally—to reading, to the impact of sermons and lectures, to relationships with learned Christians (for example, Charles Kingsley for Cooper), to the study of Christian apologetics, and to the careful reworking of the arguments for and against particular claims.

A belief is neither true nor false because a Victorian once believed it. A story about George Eliot coming to believe that the gospel narratives were mythological must be valued for some other reason

[6] See the Appendix for entries on Owen and Besant.

than that it establishes the point at issue. Likewise, the reasons for reconverting offered here are not given because they necessarily have force in the context of today's discussions. Some reasons given on both sides of the Victorian debate have no doubt had more staying-power than others. If Bradlaugh sometimes offered critiques of the Bible that now seem embarrassingly pedantic,[7] there are other objections to the Scriptures that are more decisive for many people today. If postmodernism has little taste for the kind of scientific rationalism that T. H. Huxley thought trumped all other forms of discourse, nonetheless many postmoderns have their own critique of orthodox Christianity to offer.

This study is making the more modest claim that the reconverts were thinking Victorians who were intellectually honest. They had honest faith because they had read the latest critiques of faith. They knew the literature; they knew the arguments. Often they had lectured and taught on the very themes and lines of thought that are considered most decisive in the loss-of-faith narratives. They did not evade this material, but rather diligently wrestled their way through it. This was a process involving considerable intellectual labour. In the end, they were able to give learned explanations in which they articulated why they no longer found their former convictions compelling. Cooper did the hard work of answering Strauss. Sexton did the heavy lifting of responding to the apparent materialism of Tyndall. Barker reformulated a doctrine of Scripture that took into account the discrepancies in the Bible he had catalogued for so long.

Secularists often could not believe that anyone who had really understood their arguments could reject them in favour of Christian doctrine. Therefore, the reconverts were routinely accused of being insincere and of being prompted by some other motive than a quest for truth. When the freethinking lecturer Henry Knight reconverted, the popular freethinking leader Robert Cooper admitted that it was not likely that he was going to concede that it was an act marked by intellectual integrity: 'I have some difficulty in comprehending how a person can progress *backwards*.'[8] Occasionally the loss-of-faith

---

[7] For Bradlaugh's anti-Bible arguments, see Timothy Larsen, *Contested Christianity: The Social and Political Contexts of Victorian Theology* (Waco, Tex.: Baylor University Press, 2004), chap. 7.

[8] *Reasoner*, 11 Aug. 1852, p. 139. For Knight, see his entry in the Appendix.

scholarship has also imbibed this bias. A. N. Wilson denounced as dishonest seemingly every leading Victorian intellectual who maintained a commitment to orthodox Christianity. E. B. Pusey and John Henry Newman are said to have 'committed the sin against the Intellect' for which, Wilson remarks bitterly, 'it is not easy to forgive' them.[9] W. E. Gladstone, we are told, was guilty of begging all the questions.[10] S. T. Coleridge and William Wordsworth, because they sought 'shelter beneath the arms of Orthodoxy', are deemed to have taken 'a dishonourable position'—which is explicitly contrasted with the 'honourable position' taken by 'stark atheists'.[11] Perhaps when some writers say that most thinking Victorians experienced a crisis of faith, what they really mean is that they *ought* to have. Given such emotive terrain and polemical tendencies, the reconverts will no doubt be quickly marginalized in the minds of some readers. I have repeatedly heard fellow scholars, before even hearing one bit of evidence, put the reconverts in provisional categories such as 'they probably never really felt the force of modern sceptical objections'. Such theories, if they are to be pursued by future scholars or commentators, need to be checked against the control group of Secularists leaders who did not reconvert (and the standard loss-of-faith figures from the social elite as well). If the reconverts seem to be those whose sceptical arguments were not the right ones, compare them with the writings of the acknowledged heroes of the movement such as Bradlaugh, Holyoake, and Foote, and see if a difference can be found between their advocacy and what the reconverts were saying in their freethinking days. If non-intellectual motivations are given to the reconverts, test-drive the same methodology on the loss-of-faith figures such as A. H. Clough and J. A. Froude and see if their lives should also be recast in the same light. This study defends the historical claim that there was honest faith in Victorian Britain.

How, then, do these plebeian radicals relate to the standard story of the crisis of faith among figures in the social elite? It might be tempting for some to dismiss them in a patronizing manner as not really up to assessing scientific and philosophical ideas: stick with the Oxbridge-trained social elite—they are the real intellectuals,

---

[9] A. N. Wilson, *God's Funeral* (New York: W. W. Norton, 1999), 111.
[10] Ibid. 139.   [11] Ibid. 224.

such a response might go. But such a move could easily be open to a double standard. What training did Huxley have, for example, that allowed him to pronounce on biblical interpretation? More to the historical point, it would reflect a basic misreading of how knowledge was discussed, disseminated, and accepted in the Victorian period. In fact, plebeian radicals were often a long way ahead of elite culture when it came to grasping and accepting new ideas. Adrian Desmond has demonstrated this in the field of the history of science. The atheistic newspaper from the early 1840s, the *Oracle of Reason*, was staffed by people who were all 'consistent, thoroughgoing transmutations';[12] in other words, they had an unflinching belief in the evolution of the species, not only almost two decades before Darwin's *On the Origins of the Species* (1859), but even before the publication of *Vestiges of the Natural History of Creation* (1844). In his wonderful book *The Politics of Evolution*, Adrian Desmond shows how the official centres of learning such as the Royal Society and Oxford and Cambridge universities were resistant to new ideas, while the medical and scientific radicals who were being kept at bay were diving with enthusiasm into new theories. Often the establishment would eventually be forced to admit a version of these theories as well.[13] Darwin had a better explanation of how evolution worked (through natural selection), but his ideas were no more radical than ones long in circulation among popular radicals. Older theories of evolution also carried the same shock-value of aligning human beings with monkeys, and were just as much a challenge to certain traditional religious views. Darwin was therefore reluctant to publish his theory because he was well aware that popular radicals were already committed to evolution, and knew that they would latch on to his work for their own purposes. Indeed, many plebeian radicals were thoroughgoing materialists. While Huxley and Tyndall tended to evade accepting a flat-out label of 'materialist', their moves in that direction are sometimes presented as a tremendous breakthrough in the advance of human knowledge. Such a perspective can only be maintained if elite

[12] Adrian Desmond, 'Artisan Resistance and Evolution in Britain, 1819–1848', *Osiris*, 2nd ser., 3 (1987), 102.

[13] Adrian Desmond, *The Politics of Evolution: Morphology, Medicine, and Reform in Radical London* (Chicago: University of Chicago, 1989).

society alone is in view. Many popular radicals were committed materialists who had learned their materialism from an eighteenth-century work, Baron d'Holbach's *System of Nature*. Hence, Darwin and Huxley had nothing shocking to say to many plebeian radicals: popular sceptics had absorbed the impact of such scientific and philosophical moves decades earlier.

The same is true in the field of biblical criticism. Almost every popular radical read a home-grown work on this subject from the eighteenth century, Paine's *The Age of Reason*. Paine denounced the contents of the Bible from cover to cover, arguing that it was filled with discrepancies, myths, impossibilities, absurdities, immoral stories, and demeaning representations of the Almighty. German biblical criticism was more sophisticated and learned, but it offered nothing more radical or shocking. Ideas that were slowly introduced into a wider, socially elite readership later in the century, such as the possibility that portions of the Bible were compilations of multiple anonymous authors rather than the commonly named one (Moses, for example), were standard fare in Secularist lectures long before. Moreover, popular radicals were digesting the new learning first. Cooper was probably the most thorough and faithful public interpreter of Strauss's thought in Britain. His meticulous work should be contrasted with the sloth of the social elite. It is painfully clear that many commentators on Strauss, including a much-reprinted piece that originally appeared in the *Edinburgh Review*, did not even bother to read most of his book.[14] Someone really interested in the latest thought in the field of modern biblical criticism would have been better off going to hear Cooper at the London Hall of Science than an Oxbridge lecture.

A. N. Wilson discusses a succession of lives of Christ that made a splash in Victorian Britain: Strauss's *Leben Jesu* (1835–6), Ernest Renan's *Vie de Jésus* (1863), and Sir John Seeley's *Ecce Homo* (1865). What Wilson does not notice is that each of these was less radical than the one before it. *Ecce Homo* was finally palatable for the social elite. By then, the gospel stories had been treated unceremoniously in radical contexts for a long time. Leslie Stephen's crisis of faith in the early 1860s was marked by the discovery that he could no

---

[14] Larsen, *Contested Christianity*, chap. 4.

longer believe the story of Noah's ark.[15] From the perspective of plebeian radicals, what is surprising about this is not the critique, but rather its late date. One could have gone to a freethinking hall decades earlier and heard a careful catalogue of reasons why the account of the flood, on a standard, literalist reading, could not be squared with what was known of geology, and how it was filled with a wide variety of absurdities.

The same advanced chronological encounter holds true for any of the standard triggers of the loss of faith in the existing literature. The popular radicals had well-developed lines of thought on moral critiques of Christian tradition, such as substitutionary atonement, the doctrine of hell, and stories in the Bible. They were a long way ahead of the kind of political commitment that is sometimes said to have replaced religion later in the century. Sexton was even a member of the International, working side by side with Marx and Engels. Popular radicals were significantly ahead of the social elite when it came to the intellectual ideas that precipitated the crisis of faith.

The full force of doubt came to the social elite only in the last part of the century. This may be explained in part as due to educational and professional realities. Affirming the Thirty-Nine Articles was a prerequisite to obtaining even a bachelor's degree from Oxford and Cambridge universities until the mid-1850s. After that, it was only a very slow process that opened up Oxbridge academic positions to non-Anglicans. The only non-confessional university in England was the University of London, founded in 1836. Many traditional professions were formally or informally controlled by social conservatives who wished to bolster the church and uphold religion. The church itself was a major traditional profession for thoughtful gentlemen to pursue. For much of the century, a member of the social elite who was not a person of independent means would have had a hard time imagining how they could both pursue a successful career with some intellectual life in it, and simultaneously be known publicly as a religious sceptic. The career of being a 'scientist' had not yet been invented. It is easy to forget that Huxley, celebrated though he was, did not have an Oxbridge professorship or any other position

[15] Noel Annan, *Leslie Stephen: The Godless Victorian* (New York: Random House, 1984), 45.

that would be expected today. Rather, he was fortunate to find a living lecturing at the Government School of Mines, and even that was an opportunity that would not have been available earlier in the century. Toward the end of the Victorian period society was opening up, religious or irreligious profession was less likely to affect one's career prospects, and new ways of earning a living were emerging. Moreover, this opening-up in terms of the ending of religious tests had far more to do with the Christian thinking and efforts of Nonconformists than to any supposed process of secularization, in the sense of the populace becoming more indifferent to religion.[16] This change, combined with the new professions and ways of making a living that were emerging, meant that it was becoming more and more possible to find a way to live as a member of the social elite even as a known freethinker. This line of reasoning regarding the influence of educational and professional factors is not confined to the issue of opportunity, and is not intended as an assault on the intellectual honesty of members of the social elite. The social elite were educated in religious contexts and taught to think by sound pillars of the establishment. They were assigned books to read by figures such as Bishop Butler and not by continental atheists, and they discussed them with friends who were also formed in a similar religious context. If they had doubts, a wise and learned member of the establishment could endeavour to put the matter in a better light. They worked their way into institutions that saw it as part of their brief to defend church and state. For many of them, the full impact of sceptical ideas was therefore kept partially at bay for a while.

These factors did not apply to plebeian radicals. A self-employed shoemaker such as Cooper had a great deal of independence: he could think what he liked. It was not likely that knowledge of his ideas would destroy his living through a pious boycott, and if it did he felt he had less to lose anyway and could try his hand in another location or at another occupation. Political radicals frequently suspected that all the great institutions of their society were arrayed against them. This meant that they were naturally suspicious of the

---

[16] See Timothy Larsen, *Friends of Religious Equality: Nonconformist Politics in Mid-Victorian England* (Woodbridge, Suffolk: Boydell, 1999); id., *Contested Christianity*, chap. 10.

conventional wisdom: it might actually be part of a conspiracy to keep them down and to keep the real truth from them. They were therefore not afraid to reach the conclusion that the leading men of science might have it all wrong about the true origin of things; that the doctors of divinity were trading in superstition. If books were banned or denounced, then they were not averse to suspecting that it might be because they contained genuine and important truths that shook the establishment. They were autodidacts, with no kind and wise Oxbridge don to smile at a radical notion and gently guide them back into line with an apposite quotation from classical literature. All of this means that sceptical ideas influenced radical plebeian culture earlier than they did the social elite.

Because plebeian radicals imbibed scepticism earlier, this created a context for a portion of them to experience a crisis of doubt. The crisis-of-doubt life stories given in this study indicate that scepticism was at first thrilling for many. There was a kind of joy in the iconoclasm of attacking Christianity. There was intellectual fulfilment in exposing false ideas and doctrines. It was only after persisting for some years that concerns began to grow regarding what was missing in their new worldview. What resources did they have with which to build? What was their positive philosophy of life? What was the Secularist basis for morality? Such a crisis of doubt is by no means inevitable. Other Secularists lived their whole lives as intellectually satisfied sceptics—quite confident that they did possess a code of ethics, a positive take on life's great questions, and much more. The point is not that a crisis of doubt was inevitable after a sufficient period of time, but rather that, if it should come, one typically had to have gone sufficiently far and deep into scepticism to provoke this kind of reaction. Often, members of the social elite showed a tendency to hedge their bets. A classic loss-of-faith figure such as Matthew Arnold continued a life of Anglican worship, thus drawing on what he still found to be good, true, beautiful, and useful in that tradition. Such an approach was a far cry from the kind of thoroughgoing project undertaken by many popular Secularists, who wanted to throw out all the old traditions, habits, and ideas that could not obviously and immediately pass some strict, rationalistic tests. Save for those few Victorians raised as unbelievers, a crisis of doubt could come only after a crisis of faith: perhaps only popular radical culture was far enough ahead in such a cycle for a pattern of a crisis of doubt to appear in the nineteenth century.

The dust-jacket write-up on Wilson's *God's Funeral* begins: 'By the end of the nineteenth century, almost all the great writers, artists, and intellectuals had abandoned Christianity: many had abandoned belief in God altogether.' This is not the place to take this sweeping statement apart assumption by assumption. If one were to do so, perhaps one would begin by problematizing how someone comes to be deemed 'great' for these purposes. Let us assume however, for purposes of argument, that the statement is more or less accurate. Such statements are often read (and perhaps written) as presenting the permanent fruits of the advance of knowledge. The reader is invited to imagine that since the late Victorian period, henceforth and forevermore, informed people now 'know' that Christianity has been discredited. In reality, to the extent that this statement can be given credence, it reflects a historic moment: a crisis-of-faith bubble. The social elite would spend its sojourn in the 'land of doubt', and eventually a portion of it would decide that this was a barren place and return to religious pastures. Thus, in the inter-war period and thereafter numerous 'great' writers, artists, and intellectuals had reappropriated Christian faith. One thinks of T. S. Eliot, W. H. Auden, Graham Greene, Dorothy L. Sayers, C. S. Lewis, Christopher Dawson, Siegfried Sassoon, J. R. R. Tolkien, John Betjeman, E. F. Schumacher, Edith Sitwell, Malcolm Muggeridge, C. E. M. Joad, G. K. Chesterton, and Evelyn Waugh.[17] Budd records the frustration of rationalists in the first half of the twentieth century as they discovered that many of the most eminent British scientists (she names figures such as A. N. Whitehead, Sir Arthur Eddington, and Sir James Jeans) 'were or became if not precisely Christians at least quasi-religious, and claimed, much to the indignation of the [Rational Press] Association, that the new physics supported, or at least did not contradict,

---

[17] This pattern is documented in Joseph Pearce, *Literary Converts: Spiritual Inspiration in an Age of Unbelief* (London: HarperCollins, 1999). Unfortunately, Pearce's book is marred by a willingness, on the one hand, to count famous figures who became Anglicans as converts while, on the other, also including as 'converts' devout Anglo-Catholics who conformed to Rome. Wilson recognizes that twentieth-century intellectual life was more open to Christianity and religion than a story about the late Victorian crisis of faith would have led one to expect: *God's Funeral*, 353–4.

Christianity'.[18] She also refers in passing to the phenomenon of 'prominent agnostic intellectuals of the post-war period who returned to religion'.[19]

It is also interesting to observe how fashionable Spiritualism, eastern religions, and other such trends became among the freethinking social elite during the Great War and thereafter. Once again, this indicates that a cycle that some plebeian radicals had experienced in the nineteenth century had now reached the same point in these circles. Conan Doyle, for example, had experienced a loss of faith as a young man in the 1870s. His character Sherlock Holmes epitomizes the supremacy of rationalism, hard logic, and scientific habits. Nevertheless, in the inter-war period Doyle was a major champion of Spiritualism—a life-course that figures such as Robert Owen, George Sexton, and Annie Besant had trodden long before him. The case of J. S. Mill is also suggestive. Mill reported that he was 'one of the very few examples, in this country, of one who has, not thrown off religious belief, but never had it'.[20] He therefore was a rare member of the social elite whose commitment to religious scepticism started earlier and went deeper, as it also did for the plebeian radicals. This early start of Mill's led on, not to Christian conversion, to be sure, but still to a crisis in which he was led to conclude that a procrustean logic needed to be contained so that room could be made for the realm of feeling. Mill went on to show a surprising amount of respect for the argument from design and arguably to accept some sort of theism. Willey claims that Mill found 'a ghostly image which was sufficiently God-like to alarm one of his agnostic disciples (John Morley)'.[21]

A parallel case is a crisis of doubt that occurred among French intellectuals toward the end of the nineteenth century and into the twentieth. Hugh McLeod describes it as follows:

In reaction against what they regarded as the aridity of positivism and the vindictiveness of the incessant attacks on the church by anti-clerical politicians, an important section of the intelligentsia had rediscovered

---

[18] Budd, *Varieties*, 165–6.   [19] Ibid. 175.

[20] Alan Millar, 'Mill on Religion', in John Skorupski (ed.), *The Cambridge Companion to Mill* (Cambridge: Cambridge University Press, 1998), 176. My comments on Mill largely depend on this essay by Millar.

[21] Basil Willey, *Nineteenth Century Studies: Coleridge to Matthew Arnold* (London: Chatto & Windus, 1950), 176.

Catholicism. The first high-profile conversion was that of the literary critic Ferdinand Brunetière, who wrote a much debated article in 1895 in which he declared that science had in some respects failed and that morality needed a religious basis. A number of other prominent literary figures announced their conversions at about the same time, and there was a bigger wave of conversions from about 1905. The most prominent personality in this Catholic renaissance was the poet Charles Péguy, who had been an ardent Dreyfusard and Socialist. Another less famous writer who converted at about the same time, Ernest Psichari, carried particular symbolic potency in Catholic eyes, because he was the grandson of Ernest Renan. A number of characteristic themes occurred in these conversions. Science was seen as having excluded important areas of the world and of human experience. Catholicism was regarded as providing a better basis for morality than positivism. . . . [22]

If scholars are attentive to the possibility, it seems likely that patterns of crises of doubt will also be found in still other milieus, places, and time-periods.

Accordingly, a focus on the crisis of doubt of plebeian radicals in the nineteenth century provides a fresh perspective on the intellectual resilience and cogency of faith in general and Christianity in particular in the Victorian period. A relentless focus on the loss of faith has obscured this reality. Future studies of nineteenth-century intellectual history should consider building into their framework a realization that faith was compelling to many Victorian thinkers. It is time to reintegrate faith positively into accounts of Victorian thought. Instead of discussions of faith merely serving as the set-up and foil for the imagined real story—one of the loss of faith—scholars would do well to learn to see that doubt has a subservient role in nineteenth-century Britain as the bugbear of a larger story, one of minds profoundly persuaded by the compelling nature of Christian thought. Most Victorian thinkers did not experience a reconversion: they had no need to, because they never lost their faith to begin with. The reconverts serve to reorientate us toward the intellectual strength of the Christian tradition in nineteenth-century Britain.

---

[22] Hugh McLeod, *Secularisation in Western Europe, 1848–1914* (London: Macmillan, 2000), 214–15. For a study of this French crisis of doubt, see Frédéric Gugelot, *La Conversion des intellectuels au catholicisme en France, 1885–1935* (Paris: CNRS, 1998).

Appendix
More Reconverts and Other
Persons of Interest[1]

Jonathan Barber (1800–1859)

Although Barber was unquestionably a reconvert, he has hitherto only appeared in scholarly studies as a radical champion of the working classes. He is sufficiently prominent in these later causes to have warranted an entry in the *Dictionary of Labour Biography*.[2] Barber was a framework knitter whose fiery Chartist oratory led to his arrest in 1839. He went on to be the animating figure of the most radical physical-force wing of Nottingham Chartists. There is much more that could be said about his political and social radicalism;[3] in this context, however, it is necessary to turn to his religious biography.

In early life Barber was a Christian believer, in the congregation of the Revd J. G. Pike of Derby. At the age of 21 he moved to Nottingham and became acquainted with freethinkers. As a reconvert he recalled: 'First I gave up divine revelation; then I was led to disbelieve the immortality of the soul; and at length I denied the existence of a Supreme Being, and became an Atheist.'[4] Barber emerged as the only sceptic in town who was brave enough to take on Christian ministers in debate. When the Revd J. W. Brooks first

---

[1] The reader should consult Chap. 9 for an account of the nature of this list.

[2] Joyce M. Bellamy and John Saville (eds.), *Dictionary of Labour Biography* (London: Macmillan, 1977), iv. 6–7.

[3] James Epstein, 'Some Organisational and Cultural Aspects of the Chartist Movement in Nottingham', in James Epstein and Dorothy Thompson (eds.), *The Chartist Experience: Studies in Working-Class Radicalism and Culture, 1830–60* (London: Macmillan, 1982), 221–68; Peter Wyncoll, *Nottingham Chartist* (Nottingham: Nottingham Trades Council, 1966).

[4] Jonathan Barber, *The apology for renouncing infidel opinions of Jonathan Barber, Frame-Work Knitter; Delivered at St. Mary's School Room, Nottingham, after a Lecture by the Rev. J. W. Brooks, the Vicar, to the St. Mary's Working Men's Association, on 'The Testimony of Infidels to the Fulfilment of Prophecy.' To which is added an Introduction, and Particulars of his state of mind during his last illness, by the Rev. J. W. Brooks* (London: Simpkin & Marshall, and Nottingham: W. Dearden, n.d. [1859]), 7.

came to minister in Nottingham, he was alarmed to discover that there was a freethinking society, and he challenged its members to a debate which took place in 1844. Brooks testified that 'the chief speaker' and 'the one to whom they all deferred' was 'Jonathan Barber, who, after two or three evenings discussion, became my only antagonist'.[5] This led on to other debates, with the Revd W. Collinson and, in 1852, with the Revd G. W. Conder. The *Dictionary of Labour Biography*'s assessment is that in the early 1850s 'Barber was the most articulate and controversial local secularist'.

Barber faced the usual charges when, in 1858, he reconverted. One of these was to deny that he ever was a Secularist leader. Holyoake, in an article entitled 'Who Is Jonathan Barber?', asserted that Barber was an 'unknown' whom the press should not have identified as an erstwhile Secularist leader in Nottingham.[6] Barber's relation to the Nottingham Secular Society does seem to have been a complex one. He claimed that he had refused to join forces with them formally because they were opposed to universal suffrage. The *Reasoner* argued that 'Barber was a calamity to any party; and the Secularists long since repudiated his connection'.[7] Those two perspectives seem to converge in the assessment that the Secularists were too staid for him and he was too hot for them. Nevertheless, the Nottingham Secularists clearly were glad to have Barber as a co-belligerent. Barber reminded them that, in addition to representing them in debate, they had asked him to move a resolution at one of their meetings; they had also asked him to present an honorarium to the freethinking leader Emma Martin when she came to lecture, and had then showered him with 'golden eulogiums'.[8] Barber was also accused of being motivated by a desire to gain financial help from Christians. The *Reasoner* ran an article entitled 'Rice Christians', which asserted without evidence that Barber should be viewed as being like the indigenous people in 'the East' who, so the author had heard, claim to be Christians merely in order to receive food from the missionaries.[9] Also, Barber was ill, and this would prove to be a sickness unto death, albeit there was a full year between his reconversion and his death when he was able and willing to articulate his new-found views for himself. Still, his illness was deemed evidence that this was not an intellectually credible conversion. Holyoake averred: 'it is to be noticed that his views did not change when

[5] Ibid. 3.
[6] *Reasoner*, 11 Aug. 1858, p. 254.   [7] Ibid., 29 Aug. 1858, p. 274.
[8] Ibid., 5 Sept. 1858, 'Letter from Mr. Jonathan Barber'.
[9] Ibid., 29 Aug. 1858, pp. 274–5.

in health, and able to weigh opinion.'[10] After his death the *Reasoner* offered another classic insinuation: his reconversion was part of a pattern of attention-seeking. This argument was at odds with the earlier thesis that he had been repudiated by the Secularists: 'The desire of his heart was always to be in the public eye. His love of notoriety was pampered and ministered to by a section of the Secularist party.'[11] Barber fought back, as he had done his whole life.

Barber gave his 'Apology for Renouncing Infidel Opinions' as a lecture that was later published. He described his crisis of doubt thus:

Some years since however, I began to doubt my creed.... On those occasions I used to have recourse to the reading of infidel books, which for a short time (to use a homely phrase) bolstered me up... This change in my opinions was by no means sudden.... Even during the discussions to which I have referred... I felt that I could not maintain my ground against the arguments for a Supreme being... and I have sometimes also had misgivings, when pressed by arguments, on other points.[12]

He claims to have spent several years in this state. As a well known 'infidel', he was too proud to admit his new-found respect for Christianity, but his sickness prompted him to become more earnest about deciding what he really believed. Barber argued that he discovered that Secularism was not a philosophy of life in its own right: 'I have been opposing religion, but like all other infidels had nothing to offer.'[13] Barber then argues that the ideas of freethinkers are more incredible than those of Christians. He takes swipes at various books, including Palmer's *Principles of Nature* and Mackintosh's *Electrical Theory*, as they related to the origin of the world or humanity. He also attacks G. H. Toulmin, whose *The Antiquity and Duration of the World* and *The Eternity of the Universe* were republished by Carlile in the 1820s and subsequently by other radical publishers.[14] In contrast to such speculations, Barber asserts that the argument from design is intellectually cogent.

For the last year of his life Barber worshipped at St Mary's Church. He died on 17 January 1859. Barber made sure that he had plenty of witnesses at his deathbed and that they could all testify that he was confessing his faith in Christ to the end. The *Nottingham Journal* reported that he told 'one of the town missionaries' on the day of his death: 'Make no mistake about my conversion. I wish the world to know it, it is important that they should know it.'[15]

---

[10] *Reasoner*, 11 Aug. 1858, p. 254.   [11] Ibid., 17 Apr. 1859, p. 123.
[12] Barber, *Apology*, 7.   [13] Ibid. 8.   [14] Ibid. 10.
[15] *Nottingham Journal*, 18 Feb. 1859, p. 2.

Henry N. Barnett

Barnett was the minister of the leading English freethinking congregation, South Place Chapel, Finsbury, from 1858 to 1863. He therefore is a South Place minister largely erased from the historical record who fills in a gap between the much-celebrated ministries of W. J. Fox and Moncure Daniel Conway. Barnett was also a member of the London Secular Society.[16] His *The Youthful Inquirer Counselled and Encouraged* was described in the *Reasoner*: 'This work advocates the right duty and advantages of free inquiry, and the moral safety of rejecting Christianity if sincerely disbelieved. The work contains a defence of reading anti-Christian works, and a tribute to Paine's "Age of Reason." '[17] Barnett's book was later selected for special recommendation.[18] Barnett's other freethinking publications include a tribute to Theodore Parker.[19] He also lectured at the Secularist Hall of Science, London.[20] It would seem, however, that he resigned from South Place because he had returned to orthodox Christianity. Holyoake complained that he had read Barnett's letter of resignation 'with great pain', and that his statement 'really amounts also to a conversion'. Holyoake, therefore, listed Barnett along with Gordon, Barker, and Bebbington when he counted up freethinking leaders who had recently reconverted.[21]

John Bayley (1814–1880)

Bayley grew up in Newcastle under Lyme. His mother 'was a pious member of the Church of England'.[22] He became a sceptic because he read sceptical books and found that they presented plausible objections to Christianity. Authors he read included Paine, Volney, and Gibbon. In his later teenage years he was a subscriber to the publications of the freethinker Robert Taylor, 'the Devil's chaplain'.

Bayley emigrated to America. On Sundays he would attend anti-Christian lectures at Tammany Hall, New York. He moved to Washington, DC, and became more active than ever as a freethinker. He was deeply affected by the

---

[16] *Reasoner*, 4 June 1854, p. 371.   [17] Ibid., 22 Jan. 1854, p. 63.

[18] Ibid., 19 Mar. 1854, p. 208.

[19] Henry N. Barnett, *Theodore Parker: A Discourse delivered in South-Place Chapel, Finsbury, on Sunday Morning, June 3, 1860* (London: George Manwaring, 1860).

[20] *Reasoner*, 26 Feb. 1854, p. 159.

[21] *Secular World*, 1 Aug. 1863, 'Further Conversions'.

[22] John Bayley, *Confessions of a Converted Infidel* (Richmond, Virginia: T. L. D. Walford, 1875), 1.

beautiful piety of a Methodist family, but this was not decisive: 'I had gone too far into the domains of error to be brought back all at once.'[23] He heard a celebrated preacher, and this too fostered further reflection: 'I was led to read, think, and converse upon the subject until one after another the props upon which I leaned were broken.'[24]

At this point he began to read works of Christian apologetics and to find their arguments compelling, especially Butler's *Analogy of Religion.* He had a protracted period of transition as he made his way back toward Christianity. His reconversion took place *c.*1839. He joined the Methodist Episcopal Church and was ordained in 1843. Later he made a trip to England in order to make a public profession of Christ to people who had known him there as a vocal unbeliever. This reunion was not always a happy one: 'It was by no means pleasant to hear the petty cavils and objections against Christianity, with which I had been familiar in my boyish days, urged by the very persons to whom I had furnished them; and when I observed that there was no force in them, to be told "You used to think differently."'[25] As a Christian apologist, he informed himself regarding the current state of English scepticism, paying attention to the arguments of Holyoake, Bradlaugh, Watts, and Barker.

Annie Besant (1847–1933)

The literature about Annie Besant is voluminous.[26] She is arguably the most prominent nineteenth-century Secularist leader to defect. Born Annie Wood, she become a devout adherent of the Oxford Movement. In 1867 she married a clergyman, Frank Besant. In 1871 she began to move into religious scepticism. Her freethinking *On the Deity of Jesus of Nazareth* (1872) was published anonymously. Frank insisted that his wife should be an active Anglican, and as she could not be one, they separated.

Besant joined the National Secular Society in 1874. She quickly became one of the most popular Secularist leaders. She was a regular contributor to the *National Reformer* and eventually co-proprietor with Bradlaugh. This leading duo of organized scepticism also founded and ran together the Freethought Publishing Company. Bradlaugh was the president of the

---

[23] Bayley, *Confessions*, 27.   [24] Ibid. 29.   [25] Ibid. 68.

[26] For the basic facts of Besant's chronology, I have tended to rely on the entry by Anne Taylor in H. C. G. Matthew and Brian Harrison (eds.), *Oxford Dictionary of National Biography* (Oxford: Oxford University Press, 2004), v. 504–7. Taylor has also written a full-length study, *Annie Besant: A Biography* (Oxford: Oxford University Press, 1992). See also Mark Bevir, 'Annie Besant's Quest for Truth: Christianity, Secularism and New Age Thought', *Journal of Ecclesiastical History*, 50: 1 (Jan. 1999), 62–93.

National Secular Society and Besant vice-president. She was very popular among the rank and file and became the most prominent leader of organized atheism in Britain beside 'Iconoclast' himself. Her atheistic writings were manifold. *My Path to Atheism* (1877) may serve as a representative example.[27] The unequivocal embracing of the 'atheist' label is significant. It is also revealing that many of the essays in this collection are anti-Bible or anti-Christian ones. There are also more general attacks on religion, which are significant given later developments, including 'On the Nature and the Existence of God' and 'On Prayer'.

In 1889 Besant joined forces with Madame Blavatsky and converted to Theosophy. A measure of how far Besant was to travel is a version of this conversion that she told much later in life. She claimed she was, of all places, in the offices of Britain's greatest atheistic paper, the *National Reformer*, when she heard a voice say: 'Are you willing to give up everything for the sake of truth?' To which one of Britain's most prominent atheists responded: 'Yes, Lord.'[28] Bradlaugh was deeply disappointed. Trotting out the standard innuendo, he complained that her acceptance of these new beliefs had been 'somewhat of suddeness'.[29] Besant, however, was in earnest. She rose to the presidency of the Theosophical Society and contributed extensively to its literature. She was a serious student of Hindu thought. Her scholarly accomplishments include her own translation from Sanscrit of the *Bhagavad Gita*. Besant became convinced that a young brahmin, Jiddu Krishnamurti, was the reincarnation of the World Teacher. Her *My Path to Atheism*, published by the Freethought Publishing Company, may be contrasted with a volume of hers published exactly twenty years later. In perfect symmetry, the publisher this time was the Theosophical Publishing Society, and the title echoed a key word, *The Three Paths to Union with God* (1897).[30]

Albert T. Bradwell

My knowledge of Bradwell is confined to his published conversion narrative: *Autobiography of a Converted Infidel: being a record of his experience from childhood to his conversion under the ministry of the Rev. J. Caughey at Sheffield, and including A History of his Infidel Opinions* (1844).[31]

[27] Annie Besant, *My Path To Atheism* (London: Freethought Publishing Co., 1877).
[28] David Tribe, *President Charles Bradlaugh, M.P.* (London: Elek Books, 1971), 270.
[29] Taylor, *Annie Besant*, 245.
[30] Annie Besant, *The Three Paths to Union with God* (London: Theosophical Publishing Society, 1897).
[31] Albert T. Bradwell, *Autobiography of a Converted Infidel: being a Record of His Experience from childhood to his conversion under the ministry of the Rev. J. Caughey at Sheffield, and including A History of his Infidel Opinions* (Sheffield: George Chaloner, 1844).

Bradwell's father was a plebeian autodidact and a deist, who died when his son was 8 years old. Bradwell also pursued his father's love of learning. At the age of 12 he worked for twelve-to-fourteen hours a day and still found time to read Rousseau, Shelley, and other authors. He went on to conquer Locke, Voltaire, and Kant. His scepticism led him to abandon Methodism. He read deeply in the English and continental sceptical traditions, as well as classical authors. As a reconvert, he claims that he had been an atheist. Bradwell reconstructs his freethinking reasoning as follows: '*Matter is eternal. . . . The Universe is infinite in magnitude*: That as an infinite universe cannot have a comprehender, consequently no ruler,—therefore, *There is no God*.'[32] He argues that sceptics resist the struggles of their souls to be freed from 'the dark doctrines of Materialism' by 'thinking it unphilosophical to yield to natural emotions'.[33]

Bradwell experienced a dramatic crisis of doubt. In an inversion of sceptical rejections of the Christian idea of eternal life, Bradwell claims that he began to doubt the 'doctrine of Eternal Death'—that is, that there was no afterlife. At the age of 20 he was briefly infatuated with 'the visionary schemes of Paine, of Owen, and other theorists'.[34] The catalyst for his conversion was the ministry of the Methodist revivalist James Caughey.[35] Bradwell was not impressed with Caughey at first: 'I heard a series of anecdotes of the lives and last hours of infidels; and I was very much inclined to believe that all I heard was false, and went away with the conviction on my mind that the preacher was either a knave or a fool, or both.'[36] Still, this led him to read the New Testament, and he was struck by what he found there. Thereafter, a desire to go to hear Caughey was a perpetual temptation to the poor conflicted sceptic. Once he was spared from going by having 'got into a long metaphysical dispute with [a friend] as to the difference between sorrow and grief'.[37] Nevertheless, he would find himself hearing Caughey proclaim the gospel. Once he so forgot himself as to shout out 'Glory!' when the revivalist was on particularly good form. Nevertheless, Bradwell was well aware of the difference between emotionalism and reason, between sentiment and truth, and he could not just ignore the intellectual obstacles in his path:

I could not make out why a man should be blessed for believing what his reason and the evidence of his senses contradicted. Some years before I had endeavoured to prove that Christ was either an impostor or an enthusiast,

[32] Bradwell, *Autobiography*, 8–9.   [33] Ibid. 9–10.   [34] Ibid.
[35] For Caughey, see his entry in Donald M. Lewis (ed.), *Dictionary of Evangelical Biography, 1730–1860* (Oxford: Blackwell, 1995), i. 207–8.
[36] Bradwell, *Autobiography*, 14.   [37] Ibid. 15.

but after reading the gospels through for evidence against him, I was forced to admit that this character was *almost* too perfect to warrant such an inference.... Suppose I begin now with the Bible—Is the Bible true, and can I comprehend it?[38]

He told his friends that 'if they should ever hear of my conversion, they must give me credit for more sense than to think me sincere'. He knew that, if he converted, they 'will not believe me, and to be taunted with hypocrisy on every hand will be unbearable'.[39]

A business acquaintance began to help him with the intellectual obstacles that still lay in his path to faith:

His lucid views of Christian principles, and the acute reasoning he brought to bear on them, were of invaluable service to me. In a few days I had brought my mind to assent to the truth of the Bible, but was still in doubt what were the doctrinal truths it maintained. On the subject of the Trinity my mind was undecided; the Divinity of Christ appeared not only above human comprehension, but also opposed both to reason and scripture.[40]

Bradwell went to hear the revivalist yet again. He came away with assurance of salvation.

Bradwell's account was written just ten weeks after this conversion. As he had feared, he had endured the charge of hypocrisy. Bradwell was astute enough to wonder if he would subsequently return to scepticism. He says that even if he did, it would be impossible to deny that he had once had this spiritual breakthrough. The account ends with Christian apologetics, in which he explains why he had come to see that it is more rational to believe that matter is not eternal. He concludes with the argument from design. This is advanced partially through a quotation (probably) from Balguy's *Divine Benevolence asserted and vindicated from the objections of ancient and modern sceptics* (1781).[41] Bradwell had found a way to think philosophically about his revivalist faith.

Richard Carlile (1790–1843)

Carlile has been rightly canonized as a hero of freethought. He was the pre-eminent leader of plebeian atheism in the early 1820s. The first of a series of indictments came when he republished Hone's parodies, an act that cost him eighteen weeks imprisonment. He was incarcerated, in total, for the best part

[38] Ibid. 16.   [39] Ibid. 18–19.   [40] Ibid. 23.
[41] Thomas Balguy, *Divine Benevolence asserted and vindicated from the objections of ancient and modern sceptics* (London: L. Davis, 1781).

of a decade, going on with his radical work undaunted whenever he could. Later in life, however, he revelled in a Christian identity and biblical language. He used allegorical methods to appropriate this material in non-supernatural ways. He never became an orthodox Christian in the sense that such a label would standardly be defined. Still, he was no longer anti-Christian or anti-Bible in the defiant manner that was usually a distinguishing mark of plebeian sceptics. He became a licensed preacher by swearing:

I, Richard Carlile, profess faith in God the Father, and in Jesus Christ, his eternal Son, the true God, and in the Holy Spirit, one God, blessed for evermore, and do acknowledge the Holy Scriptures of the Old and New Testament to be given by divine inspiration. I, Richard Carlile, do solemnly declare, in the presence of Almighty God, that I am a Christian and a Protestant; and as such that I believe that the scriptures of the Old and New Testament as commonly received among Protestant churches, do contain the revealed will of God, and that I do receive the same as the rule of any doctrine and practice.[42]

Carlile offered his own interpretation of this statement, which was certainly not what its framers intended, but the fact that he wanted to make this effort is itself curious.

Carlile styled himself a 'Reverend' and spoke glowingly of the second birth, the Trinity, and Jesus, asserting that he was 'wholly, and in every respect a Christian'. He would defend his views by citing biblical passages. He was increasingly interested in Swedenborg's writings. He edited the *Phoenix: or, the Christian Advocate of Equal Knowledge*, the *Church*, and, just before his death, the *Christian Warrior, or New Catholic Church Militant*. Joel Wiener notes: 'Carlile was denounced by working-class atheists.... he stood branded by working-class freethinkers as an apostate to the cause of infidelity'.[43] Freethinkers have subsequently rehabilitated Carlile by simply ignoring all this religiosity. His entry in *A Biographical Dictionary of Free-thinkers of All Ages and Nations* not only does not touch on any of this, but, when listing his journals, it simply leaves out all religious titles.[44] Ludovic Kennedy, in a study exploring the history of religion and secular thought, has taken this tack as well. In two-and-a-half pages on Carlile, not a hint of his religious turn is given. Instead, Kennedy reports deceptively: 'During the

[42] Anon., *Extraordinary Conversion and Public Declaration of Richard Carlile of London, to Christianity* (Glasgow: H. Robinson, 1837), 7.

[43] Joel H. Wiener, *Radicalism and Freethought in Nineteenth-Century Britain: The Life of Richard Carlile* (Westport, Conn.: Greenwood Press, 1983), 250.

[44] J. M. Wheeler, *A Biographical Dictionary of Freethinkers of All Ages and Nations* (London: Progressive Publishing Co., 1889), 68–9.

last years of life Carlile undertook a series of speaking engagements... His subjects were all aspects of working-class reform.'[45] The entry on Carlile in the *Oxford DNB* apologizes for Carlile's appropriation of Christianity by saying 'it is clear he never retreated to orthodoxy'.[46] It is not clear why, if he had returned to orthodox Christianity, such a move would need to be viewed pejoratively as a retreat.

Walter Cooper (b. 1814)

Cooper grew up in poverty in Aberdeenshire. 'In his early life he became deeply imbued with the tenets of and principles of Wesleyan Methodism', and was initially shocked by Carlile's attacks on the church.[47] He became a political radical. Convinced that religion was on the side of the rich, he lost his faith. Cooper became a prominent radical lecturer and an organizer of working-class movements. John Ludlow described meeting him in 1848:

there was a remarkable man, a tailor named Walter Cooper, a professed chartist and infidel, and Lecturer on Strauss... He was then, I am bound to say, a perfectly genuine man, whatever he may have become eventually. A Scotchman, he had been brought up a strict Calvinist, and had lain awake whole nights praying to be delivered from hell-fires. Then his faith had by degrees dropped away, and he had become a Chartist, Socialist, and un-believer. He knew Thomas Cooper, the poet of the *Purgatory of Suicides*... [48]

It is not entirely clear how a person could be both a Wesleyan and a Calvinist, even in Scotland, and one wonders if the 'Lecturer on Strauss' indicates a jumbling together of the biographies of the two Coopers. Thomas Cooper, however, did indeed know Walter Cooper before the latter had ever met Ludlow—or either of them had reconverted.[49]

Ludlow brought Walter Cooper to hear F. D. Maurice preach. He was intrigued and came to hear him repeatedly, eventually being reconciled to Christianity. Cooper then suggested that other plebeian sceptics might benefit from hearing Maurice. This led to a series of meetings. Figures such as Holyoake and Henry Hetherington were not impressed, but others were. Like Spiritualism, Christian Socialism became a movement that

---

[45] Ludovic Kennedy, *All in the Mind: A Farewell to God* (London: Hodder & Stoughton, 1999), 203–5.

[46] *Oxford DNB*, x. 127.

[47] *Reynold's Political Instructor*, 16 Mar. 1850, 'Mr. Walter Cooper'.

[48] A. D. Murray (ed.), *John Ludlow: The Autobiography of a Christian Socialist* (London: Frank Cass, 1981), 144–5.

[49] Thomas Cooper, *The Life of Thomas Cooper* (London: Hodder & Stoughton, 1882), 313.

allowed some figures to make the transition from avowed unbelief back to organized Christianity. Cooper became a prominent figure in the Christian Socialist movement and its efforts at Cooperation and trade-unionism. After quite a few years of service Cooper abused his position by committing fraud, and moved off the scene in disgrace.[50]

W. S. Ellison

Apparently the only source that exists regarding Ellison's story is his own reconversion narrative. Ellison was 'apprenticed to a mechanical trade' at the age of 13. His parents were devout, and he became a Sunday-school teacher. Ellison tells a classic autodidact tale: 'I was naturally inquisitive and studious having a strong predilection for books. . . . I devoted most of my leisure hours to the pursuit of knowledge.'[51] His work led him to a town where he lodged with 'an avowed infidel'. He read Paine's *The Age of Reason* and this prompted a loss of faith. Ellison moved into a 'labyrinth of metaphysical speculations': 'My faith exhibited many indistinct phases before it was entirely eclipsed by a perverted reason. From doubts as to the authority of the Bible, I proceeded to reject its authority, and to acknowledge only the authority of nature. I need not tell you with what zest I pondered over the seductive pages of Atheistical literature. Hume, Gibbon, Voltaire, and Rousseau were my philosophical oracles and moral mentors . . .'[52] He then joined a group of Secularists: 'I was regarded as a valuable accession to the "free thought movement," and was soon identified as an active promoter of the cause, and learnt to descant and rhapsodize about virtue and liberty—to rail at religion and ridicule its professors. I did not scruple to denounce the Bible as the most tremendous medley of incongruous lies that ever human ingenuity devised, or human credulity accepted.'[53]

His father was troubled by his loss of faith, but he was immune to this: 'I maintained a stolid, self-sufficient indifference to everything that was not directly addressed to my *logical* nature in the acumen of which I had begun to pride myself. . . . The only maxims which I did *not* doubt, were that the volume of Nature supplied the only legitimate basis of morality; that Reason was an absolute and sufficient guide for human conduct.'[54] He convinced other young men to become unbelievers. As his work brought him to a new town, he

[50] Charles E. Raven, *Christian Socialism, 1848–1854* (London: Macmillan, 1920), 142.

[51] W. S. Ellison, *Statement delivered by W. S. Ellison, (Formerly a Secularist,) in Ebenezer Chapel, Leeds, on Wednesday Evening, Oct. 8, 1862, containing his reasons for having abandoned Secularism, and an account of his conversion* (Leeds: Charles Goodall, A. Mann, & B. Summersgill, 1862).

[52] Ibid. 5.   [53] Ibid. 5–6.   [54] Ibid. 7.

always sought out the Secularists. The work ran out, however, with the downturn resulting from the American Civil War. Three weeks of seeking work brought him to Leeds. Ellison was broke, unemployed, tired, hungry, and homeless. He then discovered that Secularist thinking did not provide resources for facing life's trials. He contemplated committing suicide. The next day he stumbled upon some revival services taking place at Ebenezer Chapel. He was impressed, 'but when I got out, reason began to attribute it to a sort of enthusiasm'.[55] He went again, and this encounter resulted in a conversion: 'Reason was humbled and reduced to its legitimate function and sphere.'

Ellison gave a statement regarding 'his reasons for having abandoned Secularism' at Ebenezer Chapel on 8 October 1862. This event attracted a full house of some 1,000 people. Ellison reported that he had faced some of the usual charges: 'it has been insinuated that my conversion is fictitious—that my motives are mercenary.... It has been intimated that presumption, vanity, egoism, and other kindred attributes, have prompted me to obtrude myself into notice.'[56] His critique of Secularism was equally standard. He called Bradlaugh, Holyoake, and company 'the apostles of Negation'. Their sceptical perspective was insufficient: 'Secularism is then only adapted to a part of man's nature. Religion is adapted to the physical, intellectual, moral, and spiritual constitution of man; it appeals to every element in human nature.'[57] Ellison had once considered Holyoake his 'beau ideal of a logician—of a metaphysical thinker'. He saw cracks in Holyoake's armour, however, even when he was still a Secularist, and as a reconvert Ellison asserted that the ontological argument for the existence of God was intellectually compelling.

David Knell Fraser

Fraser was an important organizer of Secularism. In 1864 he can be found as the secretary for the freethinking Cleveland Street Institute, London, and by 1865 he was secretary for Tarlington Hall as well.[58] By the early 1870s he was secretary of the leading organization of the movement, the National Secular Society. Fraser also wrote for the *National Reformer* under the pen-name 'Free Lance'.[59] Some of these 'Free Lance' articles were published in book form by a leading Secularist, Charles Watts.[60] Fraser also served without pay

---

[55] Ibid. 10.
[56] Ibid. 3.   [57] Ibid. 12.
[58] *National Reformer*, 29 Oct. 1864, p. 525; 19 Nov. 1865, p. 743; 3 Dec. 1865, p. 777.
[59] Ibid., 18 Aug. 1872, p. 108.   [60] Ibid., 5 July 1874, p. 15.

as the secretary of the Freethinkers' Benevolent Fund, a charity in which all the key leaders were active, including Holyoake, Bradlaugh, and Watts.[61]

The only source for Fraser's reconversion is the following item in the *National Reformer*:

MR. DAVID KNELL FRASER, one of the persons of whose conduct we complained at the Conference, has, we are glad to say, joined the Christians, and announces his public renunciation of Atheism. We are not aware that Mr. Fraser ever professed Atheism. We can only hope that he will be as uncomfortable to his new colleagues as he has been to ourselves.[62]

Since it was so common for Secularists to strike the pose that they were 'glad' a reconvert had left, it cannot be assumed that this statement reveals that there ever was any significant frustration with Fraser beside any signs that he was about to reconvert. He had hitherto only been presented as a prominent, hard-working, and loyal servant of the freethinking cause. It is clear that he was not motivated by a desire for attention or by spite, as he never gave a reconversion lecture or published an attack on the freethinking camp.

James Keir Hardie (1856–1915)

Hardie, a founder of the Labour Party, was a classic autodidact, given to wide reading. Although he was raised in a family committed to organized freethought, as a young man Hardie became a devout Christian and even a lay preacher for the Evangelical Union denomination. Walter L. Arnstein observes: 'Secularists indeed came to look upon a man like Keir Hardie as an archapostate: that the son of Glasgow secularists should convert to both socialism and Christianity was seen as the ultimate insult.'[63]

Henry Hurdis Hodson (1810–1832)

The only source on Hodson is a pious tale of his deathbed conversion: D.B., *A Short Account of some circumstances connected with the last Illness and Death of Henry Hurdis Hodson, Esq., of Hart Street, Bloomsbury, A Convert from the Principles of Infidelity* (1833). This account at least has the merit of being well grounded in specifics. Hodson was a gentleman from 'a very ancient family'.[64]

---

[61] *National Reformer*, 6 July 1873, p. 12.   [62] Ibid., 25 June 1876, p. 409.

[63] Walter L. Arnstein, *The Bradlaugh Case: Atheism, Sex, and Politics Among the Late Victorians* (Columbia, Miss.: University of Missouri Press, 1983), 359.

[64] D.B., *A Short Account of some circumstances connected with the last Illness and Death of Henry Hurdis Hodson, Esq., of Hart Street, Bloomsbury, A Convert from the Principles of Infidelity, in a letter from one of his friends in London to a Gentleman in the Country* (London: W. J. Sparrow, 1833), [5].

He was the grandson of the Revd John Hodson, rector of Thornham, Kent. Hodson moved to London and experienced a loss of faith:

Like other young men however, he had greedily perused those publications so widely circulated at the present day, the leading principles of which are Deism, or Atheism. In addition to this, he became a constant attendant at the places where the same principles were publicly maintained. The result was that Henry became an unbeliever. The Bible, and every thing derived from it, were now objects of aversion to him. Those parts of it which were above his comprehension, he condemned as irrational: its plain and practical precepts he turned into ridicule.[65]

Paine and Carlile are named as among his influences, but primarily he is identified as an Owenite, and Robert Owen was the lecturer he most liked to hear.

Infected with smallpox, Hodson sensed that his death was imminent and this prompted a crisis of doubt. He found that his freethinking philosophy offered no 'consolation'. Someone asked if he wanted Owen to be sent for. This has a calculated ring to it, as if to show that a priest of rationalism had no last rites to perform or pastoral resources to bring. Eventually, Hodson has a full reconversion and makes an orthodox confession of faith. He also gives a speech ostensibly addressed to Owen:

Tell Mr. Owen that I listened to him with attention, and that as a young man, I was pleased with his philosophy; but tell him at the same time, that I would now give worlds that I had never heard it, it was vanity on my part, and on his, foolishness. Tell him also not to lead other young men astray as he did me: I was wrapped up in him; and was deluded, fatally deluded. Beseech him, in the name of God, to search the Scriptures, with a desire to understand them, and not for the purpose of vain caviling, and unprofitable dispute.[66]

William Harral Johnson (b. 1834)

Johnson was a prominent leader of popular freethought. He was the editor of the atheistic journal the *Investigator*, 1857–8. He sometimes wrote under the pseudonym 'Anthony Collins'. With Bradlaugh and John Watts, he

[65] Ibid. 8.   [66] Ibid. 13–14.

edited *Half-Hours with Freethinkers*, 1857.[67] He was rumoured to be a reconvert, but his is apparently a case of dishonest doubt. Around 1857 James Robertson outed Johnson as someone who 'rents, and regularly occupies a pew in St. Paul's Church, in the town of Blackburn, wherein he may be seen flourishing an elegantly bound prayer-book, and demurely contemplating his own initials graven on the golden clasp thereof. . . . Does not this seem slightly incompatible with the stern solemnity of Atheism?'[68] Royle notes that in the late 1850s Johnson withdrew from freethinking advocacy in deference to his family, but came back to it in 1865. Holyoake reported in December 1861 that Johnson 'happily, has a second time been converted to Christianity, to which his personal eccentricity naturally allies him'.[69]

(Patrick) Lloyd Jones (1811–1886)

Lloyd Jones grew up as a Catholic in County Cork.[70] He moved to England as a teenager. He went on to become a paid Owenite 'social missionary'. Holyoake paid tribute to Jones in the most emphatic terms as '*the* Champion of Socialism'.[71] In this capacity, Jones debated with Christian ministers. These debates reveal that he was what would later be called an agnostic: 'Now, what is an Atheist? Is it not a man who denies the existence of God? Did I do that? Did I not tell you that my knowledge was not sufficient to enable me to say that that being did *not* exist? Did I not tell I could not say he was there, nor positively say he was not there?'[72] Jones was also blatantly anti-Christian, claiming that Christianity had produced 'a great portion' of the evils in the world.[73] He made anti-Bible comments and criticized Christ himself. He defended his belief that all known religions

[67] This information is primarily drawn from Edward Royle, *Victorian Infidels: The Origins of the British Secularist Movement, 1791–1866* (Manchester: Manchester University Press, 1974), esp. 313.

[68] James Robertson, *Secularists and their Slanders: or, the 'Investigator' Investigated* (London: J. B. Bebbington, n.d. [*c.*1857]), 14.

[69] *Counsellor* (Dec. 1861), 31.

[70] *Oxford DNB*, xxx. 581–2.

[71] Royle, *Victorian Infidels*, 149.

[72] *Report of the Discussion betwixt Mr Troup, Editor of the Montrose Review, on the part of the Philalethean Society, and Mr Lloyd Jones, of Glasgow, on the part of the Socialists, in the Watt Institution Hall, Dundee, on the evenings of Tuesday and Wednesday, 17th and 18th September 1839, on the propositions, I. That Socialism is Atheistical; and, II. That Atheism is Incredible and Absurd* (Dundee: James Chalmers, & Alexander Reid, 1839), 46.

[73] *The Influence of Christianity: report of a discussion which took place at Oldham, 19th, 20th February 1839 between the Rev. J. Barker and Mr. Lloyd Jones* (Manchester: Cave & Sever, 1839), 7.

were demonstrably false.[74] At least one of his debates was on 'Christianity v. Socialism'.[75]

Nevertheless, Jones was perhaps the most prominent plebeian radical who went on to join the Christian Socialists. Holyoake was disappointed. In a review of the contents of the *Christian Socialist*, he averred of erstwhile Owenites in that camp (naming Jones and Walter Cooper specifically): 'these publications contain so much which those who at present retail them have often shown to be false, that they must put a restraint upon themselves greater than they were wont, and greater than the writers of these papers put upon themselves, not to do battle for their own truth and confute the articles they sell.'[76] Jones responded: 'All I now ask is, permission to do my work in my own way; I have no desire to meddle with yours.'[77] Jones was still attacked by freethinkers, however. A report of a lecture by the free-thinker Charles Southwell said: 'It abounded in personal reflections upon Mr. Lloyd Jones, Mr. Walter Cooper, and the Christian Socialists, in Mr. Southwell's favourite style of imputation.'[78]

Jones spent the rest of his life—some thirty years—in Christian Socialist circles. For what it is worth, John Ludlow testified that Jones had become a Christian: 'I must add that, though singularly reticent as to spiritual matters, Lloyd Jones once told a friend of mine that since he had come to know Mr. Maurice and his friends he believed that Jesus Christ was the Son of God, and I can vouch from personal experience that his death-bed was that of a Christian.'[79] Jones's earlier work in the service of freethought was of sufficient significance that he was given an entry in *A Biographical Dictionary of Freethinkers of All Ages and Nations* (1889).[80] This entry, although it includes his death date, makes no mention of three decades of work on behalf of Christian Socialism.

Henry Knight

Knight was a lecturer at the freethinking John Street Institute, London, and at other venues. He specifically avowed atheism, and led a discussion in which he defended it at the Hall of Science. His importance to the Secularist movement can be judged by the fact that when he converted to Christianity, Robert Cooper lectured in reply, and the *Reasoner* ran a whole series of articles on Knight's change of views, including a lead story. Knight's conversion took place in 1852. He confessed that he had gone through

[74] *Report of the Discussion*, 42.   [75] *Reasoner*, Nov. 1847, p. 51.
[76] Ibid., 15 Jan. 1851, p. 265.   [77] Ibid., 19 Feb. 1851, p. 332.
[78] Ibid., 15 Oct. 1851, p. 335.   [79] Murray, *John Ludlow*, 149.
[80] Wheeler, *Biographical Dictionary*, 187.

a crisis of doubt in a letter to the Revd Henry Townley, dated 21 May 1852.[81] The *Reasoner* minimized the damage by claiming that Knight had not been a very good Secularist lecturer, but rather went in for 'mere antagonism'.[82] Robert Cooper offered the charge that 'such a *speedy* process' of change was suspicious. Moreover, however slow or fast, for Robert Cooper it was not readily conceivable as an intellectual move: 'I have some difficulty in comprehending how a person can progress *backwards*.'[83] Cooper reports that Knight used Paley's argument from design in order to defend the intellectual credibility of his new-found faith.[84]

Eliza Mills (b. 1796)

All I know of Mills comes from an edifying tale: Christopher Woollacott's *Eliza Mills or the Infidel Reclaimed* (1852). Still, this is a story grounded in specifics. Mills was born in London to Anglican parents. She was a quick learner, a favourite with her Sunday-school teachers, and herself became one at the age of 16. There is a long account of her *first* conversion: 'The change that had been wrought in Eliza was of God.'[85] She became convinced of Baptist principles, was baptized as a believer, and began attending a Baptist chapel. Her brother then started to challenge her with sceptical thinking, and she lost her faith. Then she fell ill. When a minister came to visit her she rebuffed him: 'I fear, sir, that you are labouring under some mistake; you speak as if you believed me to be a Christian, but *I am a disciple of the man commonly called Tom Paine!*'[86] Her scepticism had also been informed by Volney's *Ruins of Empires*. The minister persuaded her to read Watson's *Apology for the Bible* and Simpson's *Plea for Religion*. These books slowly led to a reconversion. The whole process is said to have taken several months. She gave a full testimony of her renewed Christian faith, and died a believer.

Michael Cyprian O'Byrne (1848–1928)

O'Byrne had an Irish father and was raised as a Catholic. He later claimed that his parents had intended him for the priesthood. He taught in the early

[81] Henry Townley (ed.), *Report of a Public Discussion carried on by Henry Townley, . . . and George Jacob Holyoake . . . in the Scientific Institution, John Street, Fitzroy Square* (London: Ward & Co., 1852), 12.

[82] *Reasoner*, 7 July 1852, 'The Conversion of Mr. Henry Knight'.

[83] Ibid., 11 Aug. 1852, 139.

[84] Ibid., 25 Aug. 1852, 172.

[85] [Christopher Woollacott], *Eliza Mills or the Infidel Reclaimed* (London: Baptist Tract Society, n.d. [1852]), 5.

[86] Ibid. 10.

1870s at St Colman's College, which was affiliated to the Catholic University of Ireland. In 1873 he came to London and joined the freethinking cause. He was a regular lecturer on Secularist platforms, especially at the North London Secular Society's Claremont Hall. He was also a regular contributor to the Secularist press, including the *Secular Chronicle* and the *Secular Review*, sometimes using the pen-name 'Thalassoplekos'.

In 1878 O'Byrne put himself forward as a reconvert. With the chair occupied by someone from the Christian Evidence Society, O'Byrne engaged in a 'Christianity versus Secularism' debate with Charles Watts at the Hall of Science. In a report of it in the *Secular Review*, O'Byrne is acknowledged to be a man of real ability. It is said that he was better at attacking Secularism than defending Christianity. He spoke of 'the moral value of Christianity' and made a distinction between 'the original Christian system as defined in the New Testament' and what some people had done in the name of Christianity.[87]

In 1882 O'Byrne emigrated to Boston, going on to farm in North Carolina. His private correspondence from 1884–5 makes it clear that he had either been insincere in his reconversion or had since experienced a re-deconversion (I suppose, in any event, this study inevitably prompts one to wonder about the existence of such a category). At that time O'Byrne was annoyed that a freethinking orator, George Chainey, had recently announced his conversion to Spiritualism. In typical fashion, he denounced Chainey as someone the movement should be glad to be rid of: 'Freethought never loses anything by the desertion of unscientific and unintellectual men.'[88] O'Byrne wanted to give some lectures in Boston on 'Materialism versus Spiritualism', and throughout the letters his identity is as a resolute materialist. O'Byrne said of one article he had written with the hope that the *Atlantic Monthly* might publish it: 'We shall do a great thing for Freethought if we can succeed in opening the high-toned monthlies to avowed Materialists.'[89] There is a poignant letter to a grieving friend in which he unflinchingly asserted that materialism was a philosophy that brought more consolation than the spurious notion of the immortality of the soul.[90] O'Byrne also hoped to become a freethinking lecturer in America.[91]

In 1886 O'Byrne moved to Illinois, where he would rise to be a pillar of the community in LaSalle County. He was admitted to the bar and elected a justice of the peace and a police magistrate. He wrote a *History of LaSalle County Illinois*. The story becomes still more intriguing in 1897, when

[87] *Secular Review*, 9 Mar. 1878, 'The Debate in the Hall of Science'.

[88] Ann Arbor, Mich., University of Michigan Library Special Collections. M. C. O'Byrne Collection. O'Byrne to K. F. Heinzen, 22 Sept. 1884.

[89] Ibid., O'Byrne to Louis Prang, 12 Aug. 1884.

[90] Ibid., O'Byrne to Louis Prang, 11 May 1884.

[91] Ibid., O'Byrne to Louis Prang, 4 Nov. 1884.

O'Byrne self-published his long poem *Song of the Ages: A Theodicy*. It is, of course, the business of a religious apologist to write a theodicy—to defend the ways of God. On the one hand, O'Byrne's poem is not an orthodox work. God's 'Son', for example, is defined in a footnote as 'man', less anyone be misled into Christology.[92] On the other hand, the very first footnote in the whole poem reads: 'Apparently oblivious of the purpose of this poem, a "clever" publisher's reader objected that this and the succeeding lines were atheistic. It was scarcely worth while to controvert so learned a Theban.'[93] If that is not a denial that he is an atheist, then it is an attempt to lull pious readers into assuming he is not one. Moreover, O'Byrne's poem is written in the form of a prayer to 'the great All-Father': 'O Fount Divine', 'O Father', 'Lord of Judgments', 'O righteous God', and so on. Reminiscent of Carlile, O'Byrne might have still been a materialist, only one who now wished to appropriate religious language. Still, if one were to read this poem without knowledge of O'Byrne's past materialism, one would assume that the author was a pantheist, at the very least. It is possible that O'Byrne experienced some sort of re-reconversion and ended up as a pantheistic freethinker. In sketches of his life published in 1911 and 1924 (and probably written by himself), religious connections are made explicit (he had been a student of Anglican clergymen and had taught at a Catholic college), while his free-thinking advocacy is completely hidden in the claim that he had been a 'journalist and litterateur' in London.[94] On the other hand, the second sketch celebrates his poem *Nyssia* by quoting a positive review of it that appeared in 1905 in a Toronto journal, *Secular Thought*. This journal would have never thought to review it if the author was not, at the very least, still keeping up with his Secularist friends.

Moreover, the family church was St Paul's Episcopal. O'Byrne's son, Vincent, was married there, its priest, the Revd Fleming, officiating. His wife, Elizabeth, widowed for several years, was living with another son, Michael, away from LaSalle when she died. Nevertheless, the funeral service was held in St Paul's Episcopal Church, LaSalle, with 'the Rev. Father Quinter Kephart', who was then the priest there, officiating.[95] It is impossible to say for certain what O'Byrne's final position on matters of faith was. If

[92] M. C. O'Byrne, *Song of the Ages, A Theodicy* (La Salle, Ill.: H. E. Wickham, 1897), 28.
[93] Ibid. 9.
[94] *La Salle Tribune*, Twentieth Anniversary Edition (July 1911), 122; Michael Cyprian O'Byrne, *History of LaSalle County Illinois* (Chicago: Lewis Publishing Company, 1924), iii. 652.
[95] I am grateful for the help I received from Laura Frizol, Director of the LaSalle Public Library, and from Jenan Jobst, corresponding secretary of the LaSalle County Genealogy Guild. Jobst found O'Byrne's death date in the records of Oakwood Cemetery, LaSalle, Ill. Unfortunately, unlike his wife, no obituary appears to have been printed. He died on 22 December 1929, and it is possible that an obituary in the local paper was thwarted by the Christmas holiday.

I were to guess, I would speculate that, despite efforts at Christian Evidence Society-style Christianity and at materialistic atheism, in the end O'Byrne was reconciled to the fact that he was both incurably unorthodox and incurably religious.

Robert Owen (1771–1858)

Owen was a patriarch of popular anti-Christian thought. He was widely venerated across the freethinking movement, including by Holyoake and Bradlaugh. His critique of Christianity was done in the name of rationality. He wished to remove Christianity's 'superstition', especially its belief in miracles. Owen pointed the way with an alternative, 'the Rational Society'. Here is a sample of his anti-Christian rhetoric:

christianity is *not* of divine origin; and . . . its doctrines are now anything but beneficial to mankind. . . . its miracles and mysteries are of man's contrivance, to impose on the great mass of mankind, who have never yet been taught reason . . . its doctrines are now, by turning aside the mind from investigating its own powers, the only obstacle in Christendom to the most important improvements; and that the whole system, in its principles and practice . . . is the greatest bar to the progress of knowledge, that now exists . . . [96]

Owen explained his opposition to Christianity by declaring that he was opposed 'to all mysteries beyond our comprehension—and to all miracles opposed to the laws of nature'.[97]

In 1853 Owen announced his conversion to Spiritualism. It is ironic that he accepted communications with departed spirits as 'an apparent miracle'.[98] A *Biographical Dictionary of Freethinkers* apologizes for this with the words: 'As his mind began to fail he accepted the teachings of Spiritism.'[99] This, however, was no deathbed conversion. Owen had years of advocacy of Spiritualism ahead of him.[100] Moreover, his famous freethinking son,

[96] *The Evidence of Christianity; A Debate between Robert Owen . . . and Alexander Campbell* (Cincinnati: Bosworth, Chase, & Hall, 1874), 405.

[97] *Weekly Tribune*, 1 June 1850, 5.

[98] Frank Podmore, *Robert Owen: A Biography* (London: George Allen & Unwin, 1906), 603.

[99] Wheeler, *Biographical Dictionary*, 244.

[100] Robert Owen, *The Future of the Human Race; or a great, glorious, and peaceful revolution, near at hand, to be effected through the agency of departed spirits of good and superior men and women* (London: Effingham Wilson, 1853); id., *Address on Spiritual Manifestations, delivered by Robert Owen, at the Literary Institution, John Street, Fitzroy Square, On Friday, July the 27ᵗʰ, 1855* (London: J. Clayton & Son, 1855).

Robert Dale Owen, who was in no sense on the decline, took up the cause with enthusiasm.

Thomas Paterson

Paterson, a Scotsman, became a prominent advocate of the freethinking cause in the 1840s. He worked at the Hall of Science, Sheffield, and was known at that time as Holyoake's 'curate'. Later, he began to work with Charles Southwell. For a period during 1842–3 he edited a leading free-thinking journal, the *Oracle of Reason*. Royle notes that Paterson was 'accepted as the leader of the atheists during the time of Southwell's and Holyoake's imprisonment'.[101] Convicted for his anti-Christian placards, Paterson was sentenced to a three-month prison term. He took God to be his accuser, and he endeavoured to discredit such a plaintiff by bringing his character (as revealed in the Bible) into question. This stunt, which delighted the movement, was published as *God v. Paterson*. When distributors of anti-Christian literature were shut down in Edinburgh, Paterson bravely continued the work. He opened a branch of the 'Blasphemy Depot' there, and sold works by Volney, Paine, Carlile, and others. One could also procure from him a copy of: 'The Bible, an improper book for youth, and dangerous to the easily excited brain—with immoral and contradictory passages.'[102] Convicted for blasphemy, he spent over a year in Perth prison. He was released on 10 February 1845.

His trial and prison time made him a hero of the movement. He was presented with a testimonial at a meeting where Henry Hetherington presided. Holyoake praised him in the highest terms:

It is not flattery to say, that two men like Thomas Paterson are not given to one cause in a century. In disinterestedness, bravery, and endurance, he has no known equal. No man has appeared capable of bearding religious tyrants after his fashion. . . . On the occasion of his trial in Bow Street, he delivered such a defence as was never before attempted under like circumstances, and probably never will. He has rendered a service to infidelity which lookers-on neither understand nor reward. Future time will reveal its value.[103]

There was a spectacular falling out between Paterson and Southwell. Paterson put this down to Southwell's jealousy. They both started accusing one another of disreputable behaviour, including whoring and pimping. In 1848 Paterson announced his reconversion in a tract entitled *The Devil's*

101 Royle, *Victorian Infidels*, 82.
102 *The Trial of Thomas Paterson for Blasphemy* (London: H. Hetherington, 1844), 10.
103 Ibid. 9.

Looking-Glass or Mirror of Infidelity! It argued that the leaders of popular atheism in Britain were sexually immoral. It includes a coy admission that, as an atheist, he also engaged in the behaviour he is now denouncing.[104] It must be said, it does not read so much like the work of a man weighed down by guilt regarding his past sinfulness, as of a man relishing the role of exposé journalist. His rationale for this work included his declaration of his new-found Christian identity:

From being an expounder of that worst type of Infidelity—'*Atheism,*' and an associate of its advocates, I here publicly proclaim my entire renunciation of any future connection with them; and, consequently, as a Christian Member of Society, I am bound to assist in staying the further progress of a pestilence which is spreading a moral death amongst the ignorant and inexperienced of all classes. Secondly, because being no longer captivated by the sophistry and outward appearances put on by Infidel leaders for every nefarious purpose, and having witnessed the hideous enormities that characterize their private lives, it would little accord with the sincerity of my new convictions, and be the height of criminality not to lay bare the sunken rock upon which many a Christian soul has been wrecked.[105]

Not surprisingly, Paterson denounces Southwell—whose personal life does seem to have been irregular—at length. He goes on, however, to name or allude to a string of other freethinking advocates who had left their wives, taken mistresses, and like behaviour, including Hetherington. His comments on Hetherington's private life (which are known from other sources to be accurate) were unlikely to be motivated by personal dislike. Paterson claimed that by putting all this dirty laundry out in public he had 'made some amends to the Christian World for my former efforts of stigmatizing religion', and had warned those who might be tempted of 'the vital danger of embracing Atheistic principles'.[106]

Joss Marsh has presented Paterson's reconversion as jailbird religion: 'Courage dwindled as prison treatment worsened; fifteen months' solitary confinement in harsh Perth Penitentiary turned loud-mouthed Paterson into a hysterical Christian convert.'[107] This is simply wrong.[108] Actually, Paterson

[104] Thomas Paterson, *The Devil's Looking-Glass, or Mirror of Infidelity!* (London: T. Paterson, 1848), 3.

[105] Ibid. 2.

[106] Ibid.

[107] Joss Marsh, *Word Crimes: Blasphemy, Culture, and Literature in Nineteenth-Century England* (Chicago: University of Chicago Press, 1998), 123.

[108] I must admit that I would have never been tipped off to Paterson as a reconvert if it were not for Marsh's book, which is, overall, a brilliant piece of scholarship.

emerged from prison as a triumphant infidel. Once released, he continued to participate in the movement, including writing his *Letters to Infidels*, in which he argued that Southwell was disgracing the good cause of atheism.[109] Paterson's reconversion happened almost three years after he had been freed from prison. Moreover, his *Devil's Looking-Glass* is no more 'hysterical' in tone than Southwell's own attacks on him. All sources agree that Paterson eventually emigrated to America. Southwell had this to say of Paterson's reconversion: 'Before leaving England he subsisted upon the charity of credulous Christians, whose notions of religion he pretended to have suddenly, through God's help, discovered the divinity of. They are heartily welcome to such a convert, and if God, in consequence of hypocrisy so detestible, should have mercy on his soul, I beg it may be well understood that in no case would I have mercy on his body.'[110] This is a masterpiece of concision. In a mere two sentences can be found almost all of the standard charges made against reconverts: (1) he was insincere; (2) he was after pecuniary advantages; (3) it happened 'suddenly'; (4) the movement is glad to see such a person go. Holyoake, writing after Paterson's death, testified—again, in flat contrast to Marsh's claim—that he had not been broken by his prison experience: 'No danger and no imprisonment intimidated Paterson.'[111] Holyoake also claimed to have remained lifelong friends with Paterson. Minus any mention of his attacks on Southwell and his reconversion, Paterson has an entry in *A Biographical Dictionary of Freethinkers.*[112]

William Peplow (1814–1856)

The freethinking *London Investigator* (January 1857) reported: 'In October last, a Mr. Wm. Peplow of that town [Stafford], an old Chartist and sceptic, and an intimate friend of Mr. Thomas Cooper, died after a lingering illness. It is said he "recanted," and considerable exultation has been evinced by the

Dr Marsh was kind enough to take time when she was on leave to email me information regarding how to track down Paterson's elusive reconversion tract (a copy is held at the Bishopsgate Library, London).

[109] Thomas Paterson, *Letters to Infidels* (London: T. Paterson, n.d.). This was written after his time in prison (which is referred to) and before his reconversion tract (which refers to this earlier publication).

[110] Charles Southwell, *The Confessions of a Free-Thinker* (London: printed for the author, n.d.) This work is usually identified as having been published in 1845, but the chronology does not fit. An anonymous reader of this manuscript for OUP has helpfully written 'actually 1849–50'.

[111] G. J. Holyoake, *Sixty Years of an Agitator's Life* (London: T. Fisher Unwin, 1906), i. 111.

[112] Wheeler, *Biographical Dictionary*, 252.

local clergy on the subject.'[113] Peplow's road back to faith was said to have begun with a letter from Cooper in August 1856. A death notice in the *Staffordshire Advertiser* stated that he had been ill for fourteen months and had died on 18 October 1856. He had been a shoe manufacturer. A 'friend of the deceased' observed:

He possessed a mind of high order, and by diligent self-culture he had amassed ample stores of information. We regret, however, to say that for twenty years he threw his talents and influence into the cause of scepticism; but we have reason to believe that when bound with the cords of affliction he was led utterly to renounce his long-cherished principles, and from his heart to embrace the Gospel scheme, and to plead for acceptance with God through the merits of a dying Saviour.[114]

At Peplow's request, the funeral service was conducted by the Revd G. Swann of Zion (Congregationalist) Chapel, Stafford.

George William MacArthur Reynolds (1814–1879)

Reynolds is well known as a journalist, popular radical, and author of sensational fiction. As a young man, Reynolds was an avowed sceptic. He wrote an anti-Bible tract that was published by Carlile: *The Errors of the Christian Religion Exposed, by a comparison of the Gospels of Matthew and Luke* (1832).[115] Here is his account, as an unbeliever, of his loss of faith:

I am now eighteen years old, and till within this year have been a firm believer in Christianity. My father and my mother, both of whom are now dead, were also of the same creed, and the whole of my surviving relatives also are what they call Christians. About a year ago I began to be sceptical. People may wonder how I came to muse on this matter so young, and with so little experience; but truth may be descried from fallacy even by a youth, and an infant child can distinguish the luminous mid-day from the deep shades of night.... About six months ago I perused the "Age of Reason;" and this entirely opened my eyes to the errors in which I had so lately trodden. Had I known of the inconsistencies and false interpretations of many passages in the Bible before this period, I should have also embraced the creed of Deism before; but it is only when we read, reason, and compare, that we find the Old and New Testament to be false. And the reason of this

[113] *London Investigator* (Jan. 1857), 342.
[114] *Staffordshire Advertiser*, 25 Oct. 1856, p. 5.
[115] G. W. M. Reynolds, *The Errors of the Christian Religion Exposed, by a comparison of the Gospels of Matthew and Luke* (London: Richard Carlile, 1832).

long blindness is thus. We are brought up in the Christian creed, and we are taught to believe it as true with our earliest impressions.[116]

The Errors of the Christian Religion Exposed itself contains an unflinching attack on the clergy and church of Reynolds's day, before moving on to the work of cataloguing gospel discrepancies. This robust anticlericalism is significant, as Reynolds will later make his peace with the church. In this early work Christians are always the opposing camp. The divinity of Jesus is denied. In summary, the gospels are 'books of deceptions and lies', marked by 'impiety, impossibility, mystery, and nonsense'.

Later in life, however, Reynolds was an active member of his parish church, St Andrew's, Wells Street, London. He attended services regularly, gave money generously (including to the clergy fund), and from 1864 to 1878 served as a steward at the church's annual festival. At the time of his death Reynolds was a churchwarden.[117] Indeed, Michael Shirley has argued that Christianity was central to his mature thought: 'God, and religion—specifically Christianity—were at the center of much of his rhetoric... The Christianity established by Christ—as Reynolds interpreted it—was the subtext of Reynolds's political writing.'[118]

George John Romanes (1848–1894)

Romanes was a prominent evolutionary biologist. I have no wish to co-opt him as a reconvert. Nevertheless, further reflection on his life and thought by other scholars might benefit from an awareness of the patterns presented in this study. Romanes's faith was undermined by his exposure to scientific thinking. His most sceptical work, *A Candid Examination of Theism* (1878), apparently affirmed materialism. Later in life, however, he become more open to spiritual realities, as reflected in his posthumously published *Thoughts on Religion*. He became willing to take Spiritualism seriously. The *Oxford DNB* speaks of his later views in tones that are resonant with arguments that have often been presented in this study: 'he had begun to

---

[116] Reynolds, *Errors*, pp. xii–xiii.
[117] Rohan McWilliam, 'The mysteries of G. W. M. Reynolds: Radicalism and Melodrama in Victorian Britain', in Malcolm Chase and Ian Dyck (eds.), *Living and Learning: Essays in Honour of J. F. C. Harrison* (Aldershot: Scholar Press, 1996), 190. I am grateful to Dr McWilliam for giving me a copy.
[118] Michael H. Shirley, 'On Wings of Everlasting Power: G. W. M. Reynolds and Reynolds's Newspaper, 1848–1876', Ph.D thesis, University of Illinois at Urbana-Champaign, 1997). The text of this thesis that I have restarts the pagination with each chapter. The quotations are from page 1 of chapter. 7. I am grateful to Dr Shirley for giving me a copy.

consider that feeling, as well as reason, might be a legitimate source of truth.... His notes ... enabled his wife and clerical friends to believe he had nearly returned, as indeed he wished to return, to the full Christian faith. He certainly came to believe that his rational rejection of religion in the 1870s was faulted by an undue reliance on reason to the exclusion of emotional sources of truth.'[119]

John Roughly (1817–1873)

Roughly grew up in poverty in Leigh, Lancashire. His parents were hand-loom weavers. Around the age of 18 he moved to the village of Lowton Common. According to his edifying denominational memoir:

When a young man there was a clique in the village who were followers of the late Robert Owen, and to these persons John attached himself. He listened to their arguments and drank in their animadversions on religion, for their doctrines were quite congenial to his state of mind. Having imbibed the spirit of infidelity, he cast off the last vestige of moral restraint and abandoned himself to a career of recklessness and viciousness seldom equalled.[120]

Becoming a husband moderated his wild living, 'but still there was the same enmity to God and religion in his heart. He indulged in the same cynical sneers at religious people.' His wife worshipped at the Independent Methodist Church. In June 1857 William Prestcott, 'one of Roughly's old companions in infidelity' who had converted, persuaded him to come to a revival meeting at his wife's chapel. This led to Roughly's own conversion: 'The news soon spread in the village that Roughly had got converted; Roughly, the blasphemer, the infidel.' He could not be tempted back to his old identity by his erstwhile companions, and lived the rest of his life as a well-respected believer.

Thomas Shorter (1823–1875)

Shorter grew up in poverty in London. His story is one of an autodidact reading voraciously. He was a watch-case joint-finisher. Shorter took an active part in working-class self-improving culture, and while still a teenager

---

[119] *Oxford DNB*, xlvii. 649–52.

[120] *Independent Methodist Magazine* (1874), 300–3. I am grateful for the assistance of John Dolan, Connexional Archivist, Independent Methodist Churches. Roughly came to my attention because his conversion is mentioned in Michael R. Watts, *The Dissenters*: Volume II: *The Expansion of Evangelical Nonconformity* (Oxford: Claren-don Press, 1995), 561.

was being called upon to lecture. He was appointed the honorary secretary of an Owenite society in Finsbury.[121] A birthday tribute to Owen by Shorter was published in *Cooper's Journal*.[122] He also became a Chartist.

Shorter was one of those plebeian radicals who were drawn into the Christian Socialist movement. He was loyal to Christian Socialism to the end of his life, serving as the secretary of its Working Men's College from 1854 till his retirement. Shorter was also attracted to Spiritualism, writing a letter to the *Spiritual Magazine* defending it against its attackers. Sexton listed Shorter as one of the prominent Spiritualists who was also a Christian.[123]

Charles Southwell (1814–1860)

Southwell is one of the better-known figures in the history of popular, organized freethought in Victorian Britain. His services to the cause have merited him entries in *A Biographical Dictionary of Freethinkers of All Ages and Nations*, the *Biographical Dictionary of Modern Radicals*, and the *Oxford DNB*. He became a martyr to the cause by serving jail time for blasphemy. His fiery advocacy was particularly prominent when he edited the *Oracle of Reason* in the early 1840s.

In 1856 Southwell emigrated to New Zealand. It was then reported in the sceptical press that he had converted. The freethinking *London Investigator* was edited by Robert Cooper, who had worked closely with Southwell. In January 1857 it ran an article denouncing a pair of turncoats: 'Mr C. Southwell and Mr T. Cooper': 'Mr Thomas Cooper has not been long alone in his apostacy [*sic*]. A companion has been found in no less a personage than Charles Southwell. Doubtless the incident will afford an agreeable variety in the renegade camp.... We would advise Messrs Spurgeon and Brewin Grant to prepare for rivals. The "converts" are quite in their wake.'[124] It reprinted an article from the *Southern Cross*. When Southwell spoke in favour of the Bible at a meeting and was challenged by the Revd Hamer, who knew of his past activities, Southwell claimed: 'he had now changed his sentiments; he had renounced the opinions held by Mr. Owen and his followers; was a believer in the Bible, and was the subject of other important mental changes.' At his deathbed, it was made apparent that Southwell was still an unbeliever. He had apparently been feigning to be a Christian in order to improve his prospects for making a living.

121 *Bee-Hive*, 20 Nov. 1875, pp. 1–2.
122 *Cooper's Journal* (1850), 370–1.
123 *Spiritual Magazine* (1876), 192, 420.
124 *London Investigator* (Jan. 1857), 341–3.

An interesting feature of Southwell's story is how delighted Secularists have always been to learn of his hypocrisy. When Holyoake first learned the truth, he did say a few words of censure for such behaviour. Before he reached the end of the paragraph, however, Holyoake was ready to extol Southwell: 'He considered that bigotry asked for a lie, and he spat it out, but he told only one. He lied with his lips, but not in his heart—nor in his life. His conduct was true, bold, defiant, as ever. . . . he died true to his convictions.'[125] From that point on, Southwell has been honoured. Just a year later the *Propagandist* was promoting a scheme to have a monument erected to his memory. He is lauded in its pages, without a hint being breathed of his pretended conversion.[126] In 1876 the *Secular Review*, in an article praising Southwell, laughed it off: 'Nothing fell to him available except the editorship of a Wesleyan newspaper. It must have been a livelier publication in his hands than his readers had known it before. Its orthodox articles must have been written by proxy. . . . He, however, preferred to die in the principle in which he had lived. He was an Atheist.'[127] In 1877 and 1878 the *Secular Review* ran a long series of tribute articles on 'The Life & Times of Charles Southwell', by J. P. Adams.

An even longer series of articles on 'Charles Southwell in Australia and N.Z.' appeared in 1957 and 1958 in the *New Zealand Rationalist*. The author, Harry Hastings Pearce, set it as his goal to defend Southwell in the light of the reconversion charge. Addressing his subject, Pearce proclaims: 'Charles Southwell, though man and years have let you lay neglected, and under a cloud, I am indeed proud to have been able to rescue your name and reputation, and rehabilitate you into your proper place among the true heroes of historic Freethought.'[128] Southwell's place as a hero of the movement seemed quite secure even before Pearce's work, however. Moreover, Pearce's method of rehabilitating Southwell is to reassure readers that his recantation could not have been 'genuine' in the sense of reflecting what he actually believed. Pearce avers: 'Whatever the immediate motives were, I am satisfied myself that Southwell played the actor in that "recantation".'[129] Following Pearce's lead, Bill Cook suggested that the story of Southwell's reconversion should be put down to Holyoake's malice: 'Holyoake, recently estranged from his erstwhile friend, had insinuated that, on arrival in New Zealand, Southwell had edited a Wesleyan newspaper there, and had in fact died a Wesleyan. The story was repeated by Joseph McCabe in his two volume

---

[125] *Counsellor* (Sept. 1861), 'Mr. Southwell's Recantation'.
[126] *Propagandist*, 31 May 1862, p. 30; 2 Aug. 1862, p. 55.
[127] *Secular Review*, 20 Aug. 1876, p. 21.
[128] *New Zealand Rationalist* (Sept. 1958), 8.
[129] Ibid. (Apr. 1958), 8.

biography of Holyoake. But it was never true.'[130] This is very odd. First, McCabe does not quote Holyoake or claim to be expressing his opinion; McCabe (himself a freethinker) was simply speaking as a chronicler. Second, this is what he actually says: 'for want of better employment, he edited a Wesleyan journal, and horrified his employers by a death-bed avowal of atheism after having controlled their paper for several years.'[131] Far from claiming that Southwell died a Wesleyan, McCabe explicitly states that he died an atheist. Moreover, Cook's theory—even if it had been what McCabe said—would still not fit the facts. First, the original report appeared not in a Holyoake paper, but rather in the *London Investigator*. Second, no one has ever questioned the fact that Southwell said what he said. Third, it does not appear that any scholar has ever found the article in the *Counsellor* where Holyoake announces the good news that he had 'read with unmixed satisfaction' that Southwell had died an atheist.

That piece was based on an article printed in full from Archibald Campbell of Auckland, New Zealand, dated 30 March 1861 (less than a year after Southwell's death). Campbell's article was entirely admiring of Southwell in tone. It also stated correctly that he had been editing the *Auckland Examiner* (which, Pearce points out, was not a Wesleyan paper). In another effort to handle the issue with humour, Campbell explained that Auckland freethinkers 'were disposed to take a mythical view of his avowal of change'.[132] He also reported that Southwell read Holyoake's *Reasoner* regularly and 'spoke of a letter from Mr. Holyoake which lay unanswered, as a duty unfulfilled'. This means that Southwell knew that he was thought of as a reconvert in Britain and had done nothing to disabuse his former co-labourers of that notion. Moreover, Campbell revealed that Southwell's funeral was conducted by the Revd Hamer—the very minister associated with his recantation. Nevertheless, it must be kept in mind that Campbell was writing to honour Southwell. Campbell reassured readers that the really frightening spectre of Southwell having found his way to a genuine intellectual commitment to Christianity need not be feared any longer: 'no one who could form anything like an estimate of the strength and logical clearness of Mr. Southwell's intellect, could imagine or believe the possibility of that intellect ever returning in faith to the vulgar theology of our time.' Currently, the New

[130] Bill Cooke, 'Charles Southwell: New Zealand's First Freethinker', *New Zealand Rationalist and Humanist* (Spring 1998), 10–12.

[131] Joseph McCabe, *Life and Letters of George Jacob Holyoake* (London: Watts & Co., 1908), i. 211.

[132] *Counsellor* (Sept. 1861), 'Mr. Charles Southwell in Auchland', by Archibald Campbell.

Zealand Association of Rationalists and Humanists awards one prize annually: the Charles Southwell Award.[133]

James Spilling (1825–1897)

Spilling grew up in Ipswich. His Swedenborgian obituary says of his commitment to organized freethought as a young man:

Together with a number of young men also capable of thinking deeply and feeling strongly, he developed views of the most fervid radicalism in politics, and of skepticism in religion. He became a student of the writings of Voltaire, of Thomas Paine, and others; he was instrumental in founding a freethinking association called the Ipswich Utilitarian Society, afterwards introduced into one of his stories as the 'Society of the Daring Doubters.' Of this he was for a long time a leading spirit.[134]

He had read Emerson's lecture on Swedenborg and consented to join a Swedenborgian reading group, but 'it would seem that the aggressive and disputative spirit which he had acquired whilst he was connected with the Utilitarian Club was for a long time a barrier to his acceptance of the truths of the New Church'. Eventually, however, he read Swedenborg's *Arcana Coelestia*: 'This was the turning point in his mental career. The arguments of the skeptics were brushed aside like cobwebs.' Spilling went on to become a Swedenborgian leader.

The 'Daring Doubters' appear in Spilling's heavily autobiographical novel *Charles Robinson: A Phase in the History of a Soul* (1890).[135] It is set in the 1840s and 1850s, in a radical context where 'the theological guides in popular favour were such men as Charles Southwell and George Jacob Holyoake'. Robinson had been raised a Methodist, but had become an unbeliever. His model of a philosopher was Volney, of a theologian, Paine. His science came from *Vestiges of the Natural History of Creation*. His newspaper was the *Reasoner*. He became the president of the 'Daring Doubters'. He informed his Methodist sweetheart of his new views: 'No reasonable man can believe in the Bible. The light of science and philosophy

---

[133] I am grateful to David Ross, the secretary of the New Zealand Association of Rationalists and Humanists, for his kind attentiveness to my requests for information.

[134] *Morning Light*, 2 Oct. 1897, 'The Late Mr. James Spilling'. I am grateful for the assistance of Michael Yockey, Library Director, Swedenborgian House of Studies, Berkeley, California.

[135] James Spilling, *Charles Robinson: A Phase in the History of a Soul* (London: James Speirs, 1890).

has stricken it dead—dead—never to live again.'[136] He believed that recon-version was an impossibility.[137] He lectured on four reasons to reject the Bible: it is unscientific, unphilosophical, immoral, and inhumane. He underlined his revulsion at the doctrine of hell by quoting Cooper's *The Purgatory of Suicides.*

Robinson's reconversion comes about under the influence of the local doctor, Mr. Locker, and his folksy gardener, Ben Brame, who are both Swe-denborgians. In conversations with them Robinson is shown how a Sweden-borgian approach is one that accepts the Bible and is rich in faith, but which evades the problems he had latched on to. Robinson begins to read his way back to faith, finding intellectual stepping-stones in Pope's *Essay on Man* and Carlyle's *Sartor Resartus.* The decisive moment of his reconversion comes while reading Swedenborg.

Robinson then felt it was his duty to address the Daring Doubters for a final time, explaining his change of views. He gives them a version of the ontological argument. They attribute his motives to non-intellectual factors: 'You have been in the light; how can you return into the darkness? The poet says the love of woman is a fearful thing. I never knew it to be more fully exemplified than in your case. The most charitable conclusion I can come to is that it has unhinged your brain. (Uproarious laughter.)'[138] If the fictional loss-of-faith character Robert Elsmere reflects a real Victorian pattern, so does Spilling's Charles Robinson.

Henry Townley (1784–1861)

Townley was born at Great Ealing, Middlesex, and raised in the Church of England. His father was a proctor in Doctors' Commons, and he was educated to follow him in this profession.[139] His studies led him to adopt sceptical views. A serious illness in 1810 prompted him to reconsider the evidences for Christianity, leading to his reconversion. He studied at Horton Academy in preparation for the Congregational ministry. Townley spent some time as a missionary in India, but most of his ministry was fulfilled in English pastorates. In 1852 he debated with Holyoake. He spoke of his own crisis of doubt:

I have travelled the road of unbelief, and know its dismal scenery, and the gloomy goal to which it leads. When a young man, I read Hume's Essays; I associated with infidels, I imbibed their sentiments, and neglected all religious observances of every kind. My worldly calling was respectable

---

[136] Spilling, *Charles Robinson*, 9.   [137] Ibid. 21.   [138] Ibid. 135.
[139] There is an obituary in the *Congregational Year Book* for 1862, pp. 265–7.

and lucrative, and I bore a fair character among my kindred, my clients, and my neighbours. All things outwardly were prosperous and smiling, when suddenly the symptoms of a wasting disorder, which I thought in about three months would end my life, appeared. Death did then indeed appear to me as an unwelcome visitor clothed in crape. My conscience told me that I had not acted ingenuously with a book professing to be the Word of God; that I had not given it that thorough and candid investigation which it deserved. I resolved to spend the remnant of my days in the earnest pursuit of truth. I determined that if that book, upon due examination, should answer to its appellation, I would act in harmony with its dictates; if otherwise, I would lay it aside and meet death without it in the best way I could. I read, and pondered what I read. I searched, and made inquiry. My health soon returned; but I continued my investigation of the Scriptures, I think I may say, without a day's intermission, for a year. The result was, that all my doubts and objections were cleared away, and I became a believer.[140]

Henry Vincent (1813–1878)

Vincent is well known as a political radical. He is a model plebeian auto-didact. Later in life he was an active Christian. The *Oxford DNB* records: 'Vincent frequently conducted services on Sundays in free church chapels as a lay preacher.'[141] In his youth, however, he was elected 'vice-president of a local Paineite discussion group'.[142] Holyoake reported unequivocally that Vincent was a reconvert, pairing him with Thomas Cooper as figures who had similar life-stories. Holyoake testified to a time when Vincent was anti-Christian and when in his fiery speeches he 'said as much against Christianity as against political oppression'.[143] After his return to faith, Holyoake credited him with being the kind of Christian who 'dwelt on the hills of orthodoxy, where some light of reason falls'.

Alfred Russel Wallace (1823–1913)

Wallace was an eminent naturalist, who is most famous for independently discovering the principle of evolution by natural selection and presenting it alongside the first public airing of Darwin's thoughts. Wallace was not a reconvert. Nevertheless, it is possible that his story might relate in some ways to wide patterns and concerns discussed in this study. As a young man he became an Owenite and (as he would later tell it) 'as thorough an Agnostic

---

[140] Townley, *Report*, 74–5.   [141] *Oxford DNB*, lvi. 535–6.
[142] Ibid.   [143] Holyoake, *Sixty Years*, i. 104.

as Mr. Blatchford himself, and I am afraid almost as dogmatic and one-sided in my opinions'.[144] In his autobiography, he observes that the term at that time for agnosticism was 'secularism', and he also refers to his views then as 'religious scepticism'.[145] He recalls reading sceptical literature, including *The Age of Reason*. In 1866 Wallace converted to Spiritualism. He later reflected: 'For thirty years before I became convinced of the truth of spiritualism I was an agnostic. My only religion is that which I get out of spiritualism'.[146] He accepted Jesus as a medium who really did perform wonders and healings. The *Oxford DNB* observed that one of the things that attracted Wallace to Spiritualism was its moral teachings—a concern that has often reappeared in this study. It also speculates that he might have been dissatisfied with the limitations of Darwinian materialism.[147]

'A Working Man' (b. 1811)

Scenes from My Life (1858), by 'A Working Man', is an anonymous autobiography that tells a reconversion story. There are enough specific details given for it to be possible that someone might be able to uncover the name of the author. The work has a preface by the Revd Robert Maguire, who vouches for the authenticity of the narrative. 'Working Man' grew up as a Methodist in Coventry. He experienced Christian conversion at the age of 6. This 'spark of Divine light . . . was never extinguished, but was overlaid for many years with a worse than Egyptian night'.[148]

He was sent to work as a ribbon-weaver. He joined a local Political Union that was animated by freethinkers who admired Paine and Henry Hethering-ton. He moved to a village where he and a companion gained a local reputation for not believing in God. His companion, Thomas Simmons Mackintosh, later became an 'itinerating Lecturer to the Socialist Institution in Theobald's Road, Holborn'.[149]

[144] Letter to the Editor from Alfred Russel Wallace, *Christian Commonwealth*, 11 Sept. 1912, p. 815 (as reprinted at www.wku.edu/~smithch/wallace/S699.htm).

[145] Alfred Russel Wallace, *My Life: A Record of Events and Opinions* (New York: Dodd, Mead, & Co., 1905), i. 87–8.

[146] Interview with Alfred Russel Wallace, *Bookman*, January 1898 (as reprinted at www.wku.edu/~smithch/wallace/S738.htm).

[147] *Oxford DNB*, lvi. 920–6.

[148] *Scenes from My Life, By A Working Man*, with a preface by the Rev. Robert Maguire, M.A. (London: Seeleys, 1858), 19.

[149] James A. Secord's magnificent book on the *Vestiges* is where I learned of the existence of *Scenes from My Life*: see *Victorian Sensation: The Extraordinary Publication, Reception, and Secret Authorship of 'Vestiges of the Natural History of Creation'* (Chicago: Chicago University Press, 2000), 325.

Our working-man later fell into debt and became weary of life. He was befriended by a Wesleyan. This relationship led him on the road to Christian faith: 'There was plenty of food for reflection that week, and the next, and the next. Slowly, very slowly, light broke in upon his mind'. At last, he reconverted.[150] This happened in his twenties. He wrote his narrative after twenty-two years of Christian faith. James Secord describes him as a 'reclaimed Owenite socialist'.[151]

---

[150] *Scenes*, 83.　　[151] Secord, *Victorian Sensation*, 325.

Works Cited

Primary Sources

Manuscripts

Joseph Barker Collection, Douglas County Historical Society, Omaha, Nebraska

Joseph Barker Papers, John Rylands University Library of Manchester

Thomas Cooper Collection, Internationaal Instituut Voor Sociale Geschiedenis, Amsterdam

Thomas Cooper Collection, Local Studies, Lincoln Central Library, Lincoln

Thomas Cooper Collection, Lincolnshire Archives, Lincoln

Thomas Cooper to James Andrew, 24 Feb. 1860, Timothy Larsen, personal collection

George Jacob Holyoake Correspondence Collection, The Co-operative College Archives, Manchester

William Hone Collection, Special Collections, Adelphi Universities Libraries, Garden City, New York

William Hone Papers, Washington State University, Pullman, Washington, DC

M. C. O'Byrne Collection, University of Michigan Library Special Collections, Ann Arbor, Michigan

Minutes of the Senatus Academicus, St Andrews University Archives, St Andrews

Newspapers, Magazines, and Journals

Baptist Handbook
Baptist Magazine
Barker's Review
Bee-Hive
Bookman
Bradford Review
British Banner
British Quarterly Review
Carlisle Patriot
Christian Commonwealth
Congregational Year Book

Cooper's Journal
Counsellor
Daily Standard
Eclectic Review
Edinburgh Review
Evangelical Christendom
Independent Methodist Magazine
Inquirer
International Herald
Investigator
Journal of the Transactions of the Victoria Institute, or Philosophical Society of
    Great Britain
LaSalle Tribune
Literary Budget
London Investigator
Methodist New Connexion Magazine
Morning Light
National Reformer
Newcastle Weekly Chronicle
Nonconformist
Norfolk News
North Wilts Herald
Nottingham Journal
Nottingham and Midland Counties Express
The People
Potteries Telegraph
Propagandist
Quarterly Review
Reasoner
Reasoner Gazette
Reynold's Political Instructor
Secular Chronicle
Secular Review
Secular Review and Secularist
Secular World
Shield of Faith
Spiritual Magazine
Staffordshire Advertiser
Toronto Globe
Unitarian Herald
Weekly Tribute

Contemporary Printed Material

ASPLAND, R. BROOK, *Memoir of the Life, Works and Correspondence, of the Rev. Robert Aspland, of Hackney* (London: Edward T. Whitfield, 1850).

BALGUY, THOMAS, *Divine Benevolence asserted and vindicated from the objections of ancient and modern sceptics* (London: L. Davis, 1781).

BARBER, JONATHAN, *The apology for renouncing infidel opinions of Jonathan Barber, Frame-Work Knitter; Delivered at St. Mary's School Room, Nottingham, after a Lecture by the Rev. J. W. Brooks, the Vicar, to the St. Mary's Working Men's Association, on 'The Testimony of Infidels to the Fulfilment of Prophecy.' To which is added an Introduction, and Particulars of his state of mind during his last illness, by the Rev. J. W. Brooks* (London: Simpkin & Marshall, and Nottingham: W. Dearden, n.d. [1859]).

BARKER, JOSEPH, *Mercy triumphant, or, Teaching the children of the poor to write on the Sabbath Day, proved to be in perfect agreement with the oracles of God* (Manchester: Cave & Sever, 1840).

—— *Water Baptism: A letter to Thomas Allin, corresponding member of the Annual Committee of the Methodist New Connexion* (Newcastle: J. Blackwell, 1841).

—— *The Inspiration of the Sacred Scriptures* (Newcastle upon Tyne: J. Barker, n.d. [c.1845]).

—— *The History and Confessions of a Man, as put forth by Himself* (Wortley: J. Barker, 1846).

[——], *A Review of the Bible* (London: J. Watson, 1848).

—— *The Popular Imperfections of the Bible. A Speech delivered by Mr. Joseph Barker, President of the Bible Convention in Salem, U.S.* (London: Holyoake & Co., 1854).

—— *Seven Lectures on the Supernatural Origin & Divine Authority of the Bible* (Stoke-on-Trent: George Turner, 1854).

—— 'What harm have the Scriptures ever done you?', *Reasoner*, 17 Sept. 1854.

—— *Confessions of Joseph Barker, a Convert from Christianity* (London: Holyoake & Co., 1858).

—— 'Mr. Thomas Cooper—Remarks on his reputed conversion', *Reasoner*, 15 Aug. 1858.

—— *'I am not ashamed of the Gospel of Christ.' A Sermon preached by Mr. Joseph Barker, in the Athenaeum, Sunderland, on Sunday Evening, November 8th, 1863* (Newcastle upon Tyne: J. G. Forster, 1863).

—— *Noah's Ark* (London: Barker & Co., 1863).

—— *Unitarianism: What claims has it to respect and favour? A Lecture* (n.p., n.d. [probably 1866]).

—— *The Bible, Its Great Worth and Divine Origin* (Philadelphia: Methodist Episcopal Book Room, 1873).

—— *Jesus: A Portrait* (Philadelphia: Methodist Episcopal Book Room, 1873).

—— *Modern Skepticism: A journey through the land of doubt and back again. A Life Story* (Philadelphia: Smith, English, & Co., 1874).

—— *Teachings of Experience, or, lessons I have learned on my way through life* (London: E. W. Allen, 1885).

—— *The Duty of Christians to Provide for their Poor Members, and the impropriety of professing Christians connecting themselves with benefit societies, rechabite societies, life insurances, loan funds, or with any societies founded on worldly principles* (Newcastle: J. Blackwell, n.d.).

BARKER, J. T. (ed.), *The Life of Joseph Barker, Written by Himself* (London: Hodder & Stoughton, 1880).

BARNETT, HENRY N., *Theodore Parker: A Discourse delivered in South-Place Chapel, Finsbury, on Sunday Morning, June 3, 1860* (London: George Manwaring, 1860).

BATCHELOR, HENRY, *The Logic of Atheism* (London: Judd & Glas, 1858).

BAYLEY, JOHN, *Confessions of a Converted Infidel* (Richmond, Va.: T. L. D. Walford, 1875).

BEBBINGTON, J. B., *Freethought Biographies, a series of sketches of the Lives and Writings of the most remarkable British Freethinkers,* 'Reprinted from the "Reasoner" ' (London: Holyoake & Co., 1858).

—— *Why I Was An Atheist, and Why I Am Now A Christian*, 2nd edn. (London: H. J. Tresidder, n.d. [1865]).

—— *A Letter (Short and Sharp) to William Evans* (Hanley: J[ames] Bebbington, 1866).

The Belief in a Personal God and a Future Life. Six Nights' Discussion between Thomas Cooper and Joseph Barker, held in St. George's Hall, Bradford, September, 1860 (London: Ward & Co., n.d.).

BESANT, ANNIE, *My Path to Atheism* (London: Freethought Publishing Co., 1877).

—— *The Three Paths to Union with God* (London: Theosophical Publishing Society, 1897).

BONNER, HYPATIA BRADLAUGH, *Charles Bradlaugh: His Life and Work*, 2 vols. (London: T. Fisher Unwin, 1895).

BOWES, JOHN, *A Hired Ministry Unscriptural* (Manchester: W. Irwin, 1845).

BRADLAUGH, CHARLES, *The Bible: What It Is* (London: Austin, 1870).

BRADWELL, ALBERT T., *Autobiography of a Converted Infidel: being a Record of His Experience from childhood to his conversion under the ministry of the*

Rev. J. Caughey at Sheffield, and including A History of his Infidel Opinions (Sheffield: George Chaloner, 1844).

BRIDGES, CHARLES, *Life and Works of Miss Mary Jane Graham* (New York: Robert Carter & Bros., 1849).

BUCHANAN, JAMES, *Modern Atheism* (Boston: Gould & Lincoln, 1857).

BUTLER, SAMUEL, *The Genuine and Apocryphal Gospels compared. A Charge, delivered to the clergy of the Archdeaconry of Derby, at the Visitations at Derby and Chesterfield, June 6 & 7, 1822, and published at their request* (Shrewsbury: Wm. Eddowes, 1822).

—— *The Life and Letters of Dr. Samuel Butler*, 2 vols. (London: John Murray, 1896).

CARLILE, RICHARD, *Extraordinary Conversion and Public Declaration of Richard Carlile of London, to Christianity* (Glasgow: H. Robinson, 1837).

Chambers's Encyclopaedia (London: William & Robert Chambers, 1892).

The Child and the Traveller. A True Story (London: Paternoster Road, n.d.).

Christianity v. Secularism: report of a public discussion between David King and Charles Bradlaugh, held in the Co-operative Hall, Bury, Lancashire, September, 27, 28, 29, and 30, October 25 and 26, 1870 (Birmingham: D. King, 1870).

'Church and State.' Controversy between the Rev. S. G. Potter, D.D., and 'Pastor Gordon,' in fourteen letters (London: W. Macintosh, 1874).

CONDER, EUSTACE E., *Josiah Conder: A Memoir* (London: John Snow, 1857).

COOPER, ROBERT, *Death-bed Repentance: its fallacy and absurdity when applied as a test of the truth of opinion; with authentic particulars of the last moments of distinguished free-thinkers*, 6th edn. (London: E. Truelove, 1875).

COOPER, THOMAS, *The Purgatory of Suicides. A Prison-Rhyme* (London: Jeremiah How, 1845).

—— *Eight Letters to the Young Men of the Working-Classes* (London: J. Watson, 1851).

—— *The Bridge of History Over the Gulf of Time* (London: Hodder & Stoughton, 1871).

—— *The Life of Thomas Cooper*, with an introduction by John Saville (1872; Leicester: Leicester University Press, 1971).

—— *God, the Soul, and a Future State* (London: Hodder & Stoughton, 1875).

—— *The Verity of Christ's Resurrection from the Dead* (London: Hodder & Stoughton, 1875).

—— *The Verity and Value of the Miracles of Christ* (London: Hodder & Stoughton, 1876).

—— *Evolution, the Stone Book, and the Mosaic Record of Creation* (London: Hodder & Stoughton, 1878).

—— *The Life of Thomas Cooper. Written by Himself* (1872; London: Hodder & Stoughton, 1882).

—— *Thoughts at Fourscore and Earlier* (London: Hodder, 1885).

—— and ROBERT TAYLOR, *A Calm Inquiry into the Nature of Deity* (London: Farrah, 1864).

D.B., *A Short Account of some circumstances connected with the last Illness and Death of Henry Hurdis Hodson, Esq., of Hart Street, Bloomsbury, A Convert from the Principles of Infidelity, in a letter from one of his friends in London to a Gentleman in the Country* (London: W. J. Sparrow, 1833).

[D'HOLBACH, PAUL H. T.], *The System of Nature; or, The Laws of the Moral and Physical World*, 3 vols. (London: G. Kearsley, 1797).

Discussion between Mr. Thomas Cooper and Mr. C. Bradlaugh (London: Freethought Publishing Co., 1883 [1864 debate]).

ELIOT, T. S., 'Four Quartets: Little Gidding', in *Collected Poems: 1909–1962* (San Diego: Harcourt Brace Jovanovich, 1970).

ELLISON, W. S., *Statement delivered by W. S. Ellison, (Formerly a Secularist,) in Ebenezer Chapel, Leeds, on Wednesday Evening, Oct. 8, 1862, containing his reasons for having abandoned Secularism, and an account of his conversion* (Leeds: Charles Goodall, A. Mann, & B. Summersgill, 1862).

EVANS, GEORGE EYRE, *Vestiges of Protestant Dissent* (Liverpool: F. & E. Gibbons, 1897).

The Evidence of Christianity; A Debate between Robert Owen . . . and Alexander Campbell (Cincinnati, Ohio: Bosworth, Chase, & Hall, 1874).

FOOTE, G. W. and GEORGE SEXTON, *Is Secularism the True Gospel for Mankind? A Debate Held in the Town Hall, Batley, . . . June 18th and 19th, 1877*, 'Revised By Both Disputants' (London: Smart & Allen, 1877).

GORDON, J. H., *The Exodus of the Priests: A Secularist's Dream of Better Times*, Essays by the Way—No. 1, Series 1861 (London: Holyoake & Co., 1861).

—— *The Public Statement of Mr. J. H. Gordon, (Late Lecturer to the Leeds Secular Society,) with reference to his repudiation of secular principles, and his adoption of the Christian faith [Delivered in the Music Hall, Leeds, on Tuesday, August 5th, 1862. The Rev. G. W. Conder in the Chair]* (Leeds: J. Hamer, 1862).

—— *Helps to Belief; or, Essays by the Way, No. 2—Earnest Appeal to Secularists. No. 3.—Corroborations of Christianity* (Leeds: J. Hamer, 1863).

—— *Helps to Belief; or Essays by the Way, No. 4. Just-What-You-Like-Ism. A brief explanation of Mr. G. J. Holyoake's 'Principles of Secularism Briefly Explained'* (Leeds: J. Hamer, 1863).

GORDON, J. H., *Thoughts for the Million; or, Buds, Blossoms, and Berries* (London: Haughton & Co., 1874).

GRAHAM, MARY JANE, *The Test of Truth* (Philadelphia: J. Whetham, 1834).

Great Discussion on the Origin, Authority, & Tendency of the Bible, between Rev. J. F. Berg, D.D., of Philadelphia, and Joseph Barker, of Ohio (Stoke-on-Trent: George Turner, 1854).

HACKWOOD, FREDERICK W., *William Hone: His Life and Times* (1912; New York: Burt Franklin, n.d. [1967]).

[HOGBEN, JOHN], *Richard Holt Hutton of 'The Spectator': A Monograph* (Edinburgh: Oliver & Boyd, 1899).

HOLYOAKE, G. J., *Trial of Theism* (London: Holyoake & Co., 1858).

—— *Thomas Cooper Delineated as Convert and Controversialist: A Companion to his Missionary Wanderings* (London: Austin Holyoake, 1861).

—— *Sixty Years of an Agitator's Life* (London: T. Fisher Unwin, 1906).

[HONE, WILLIAM], *The Apocryphal New Testament, Being all the Gospels, Epistles, and other pieces now extant attributed in the first four centuries to Jesus Christ, His Apostles, and their companions, and not included in the New Testament by its compilers*, 2nd edn. (London: William Hone, n.d. [c.1821; 1st edn., 1820]).

—— *Aspersions Answered. An explanatory statement to the public at large, and to every reader of The Quarterly Review in particular* (London: William Hone, 1824).

—— (ed.), *The Early Life and Conversion of William Hone [Sr.] . . . A Narrative Written By Himself* (London: T. Ward & Co., 1841).

HOWARD, J. E., *Recollections of William Hone. Thirty Years an Atheist, Afterwards a Happy Christian* (London: Religious Tract Society, n.d.).

HUME, DAVID, *Dialogues Concerning Natural Religion*, ed. Norman Kemp Smith (Indianapolis: Bobbs-Merrill Co., 1947).

—— *An Essay on Miracles* (London: J. B. Bebbington, [n.d.]).

'Iconoclast' [Charles Bradlaugh], *Who Was Jesus Christ?* (n.p., n.d.).

The Influence of Christianity. Report of the Public Discussion which took place at Oldham, . . . February 19th and 20th, 1839, between the Rev. J. Barker . . . and Mr. Lloyd Jones, Of Manchester, Social Missionary (Manchester: Cave & Sever, 1839).

JEFFERSON, THOMAS, *The Jefferson Bible: The Life and Morals of Jesus of Nazareth* (Boston: Beacon Press, 1989).

KING, DAVID and CHARLES BRADLAUGH, *Christianity v. Secularism: report of a public discussion between David King and Charles Bradlaugh, held in the Co-operative Hall, Bury, Lancashire, September, 27, 28, 29, and 30, October 25 and 26, 1870* (Birmingham: D. King, 1870).

KINGSLEY, F. E., *Charles Kingsley: His Letters and Memories of His Life*, 2 vols. (London: Macmillan & Co., 1901).

Leeds Secular Society, *The Converted Lecturer, or, Mr. Gordon's Repudiation of Secular Principles Examined* (Leeds: B. Summersgill, 1862).

MCCABE, JOSEPH, *Life and Letters of George Jacob Holyoake* (London: Watts & Co., 1908).

MARTINEAU, HARRIET, *History of the Peace: Pictorial History of England during the Thirty Years' Peace 1816–1846*, new edn. (London: W. & R. Chambers, 1858).

'Melampus' (of the 'National Reformer') [George Sexton], *The Doctrine of Eternal Torment Refuted* (London: George Abington, 1863).

Minutes of the General Assembly of the Presbyterian Church in the United States of America, 1899 (Philadelphia: MacCalla & Co., 1899).

O'BYRNE, M. C., *Song of the Ages, A Theodicy* (LaSalle, Ill.: H. E. Wickham, 1897).

—— *History of LaSalle County Illinois*, 3 (Chicago: Lewis Publishing Co., 1924).

Origin and Authority of the Bible. Report of the Public Discussion between Joseph Barker, Esq., and the Rev. Brewin Grant, B.A., Held at Halifax on Ten Nights... 1855 (Glasgow: Robert Stark, n.d. [1855]).

OWEN, ROBERT, *The Future of the Human Race; or a great, glorious, and peaceful revolution, near at hand, to be effected through the agency of departed spirits of good and superior men and women* (London: Effingham Wilson, 1853).

—— *Address on Spiritual Manifestations, delivered by Robert Owen, at the Literary Institution, John Street, Fitzroy Square, On Friday, July the 27th, 1855* (London: J. Clayton & Son, 1855).

PAINE, THOMAS, *The Age of Reason* (1795–6; The Thinker's Library; London: Watts & Co, 1938).

PATERSON, THOMAS, *The Devil's Looking-Glass, or Mirror of Infidelity!* (London: T. Paterson, 1848).

—— *Letters to Infidels* (London: T. Paterson, n.d.).

PEAKE, ARTHUR S., *The Bible, Its Origin, Its Significance, and Its Abiding Worth* (London; New York: Hodder & Stoughton, 1913).

PODMORE, FRANK, *Robert Owen: A Biography* (London: George Allen & Unwin, 1906).

POTTER, S. G. and J. H. GORDON, *'Church and State.' Controversy between the Rev. S. G. Potter, D.D., and 'Pastor Gordon,' in fourteen letters* (London: W. Macintosh, 1874).

PRATT, JOSIAH, *Remains of the Rev. Richard Cecil* (Boston: Samuel T. Armstrong, 1817).

PUTNAM, SAMUEL P., *400 Years of Freethought* (New York: Truth Seeker Co., 1894).

REID, WILLIAM HAMILTON, *The Rise and Dissolution of the Infidel Societies in the Metropolis* (London, J. Hatchard, 1800): facsimile in Victor E. Neuburg (ed.), *Literacy and Society* (London: Woburn, 1971).

RENNELL, THOMAS, *Proofs of Inspiration, or the Ground of Distinction between the New Testament and the Apocryphal Volume: occasioned by the recent publication of the Apocryphal New Testament by Hone* (London: F. C. & J. Rivington, 1822).

Report of the Discussion betwixt Mr Troup, Editor of the Montrose Review, on the part of the Philalethean Society, and Mr Lloyd Jones, of Glasgow, on the part of the Socialists, in the Watt Institution Hall, Dundee, on the evenings of Tuesday and Wednesday, 17th and 18th September 1839, on the propositions, I. That Socialism is Atheistical; and, II. That Atheism is Incredible and Absurd (Dundee: James Chalmers, and Alexander Reid, 1839).

The Report of the Public Discussion, at Stockport, between Mr. John Bowes... and Mr. Joseph Barker, ... 'Are the Scriptures of the Old & New Testaments of Supernatural Origin and Divine Authority; Are the Doctrines contained therein Conducive to Morality and Virtue?' (London: R. Bulman, 1855).

REYNOLDS, G. W. M., *The Errors of the Christian Religion Exposed, by a comparison of the Gospels of Matthew and Luke* (London: Richard Carlile, 1832).

ROBERTSON, JAMES, *Secularists and their Slanders: or, the 'Investigator' Investigated. Mr. Holyoake and his assailants, their defeat, and the votes of confidence in Fleet Street House, from Manchester and Elsewhere* (London: J. B. Bebbington, n.d. [c.1857]).

ROBINSON, EDGAR SUTTON, *The Ministerial Directory of the Ministers of the Presbyterian Church...* (Oxford, Ohio: Ministerial Directory Co., 1898).

[ROLLESTON, FRANCES], *Some Account of the Conversion from Atheism to Christianity of the late William Hone*, 2nd edn. (London: Francis & John Rivington, 1853).

Scenes from My Life, By A Working Man, with a preface by the Rev. Robert Maguire, M.A. (London: Seeleys, 1858).

SEXTON, GEORGE, *A Portraiture of Mormonism* (London: W. Strange, 1849).

—— *The Existence and Influence of the Devil, viewed in the light of Reason, Nature, and the Bible* (London: Published by the Author, n.d. [1852]).

—— *Hollingsworth and Modern Poetry: A Critical and Explanatory Essay* (London: William Freeman, 1858).

—— *The Poetical Works of the late Alfred Johnstone Hollingsworth*, 2nd edn. (London: C. J. Skeet, 1858).

—— *The Doctrine of Eternal Torment Refuted* (London: George Abington, 1863).

—— *The Concessions of Theology to Science: A Lecture* (London: Austin, 1868).

—— *The Psychology of Macbeth* (1869; New York: AMS Press, 1977).

—— *Thomas Paine. An Address. Delivered at a Meeting held in Commemoration of the Birthday of the Great Apostle of Freethought* (London: Austin & Co., n.d. [stamped 20 Sept. 1869]).

—— *Vaccination Useless and Injurious. A Lecture delivered in the Temperance Hall, Sheffield, on February 11th, 1869* (Sheffield: William Fox, 1869).

—— *The Antiquity of the Human Race*, 3rd edn. (London: Austin & Co., 1871).

—— *How I Became A Spiritualist. An Oration delivered in the Cavendish Rooms, London, on Sunday Evening, June 8th, 1873* (London: J. Burns, 1873).

—— *Spirit-Mediums and Conjurers. An Oration delivered in the Cavendish Rooms, London, on Sunday Evening, June 15th, 1873* (London: J. Burns, 1873).

—— *Reasons for Renouncing Infidelity. Two Sermons, preached in Augustine Independent Church, Clapham Road, London, on Sunday, September 10th, 1876* (London: G. S. Sexton, 1876).

—— *The Fallacies of Secularism* (London: G. S. Sexton, 1877).

—— *The Advent of Christ, and its effects upon the ages* (London: Smart & Allen, 1878).

—— *The Baseless Fabric of Scientific Scepticism* (London: Smart & Allen, 1879).

—— *The Folly of Atheism. A discourse delivered in St. George's Hall, Plymouth, on October 18, 1879, on behalf of the Christian Evidence Society* (London: Smart & Allen, 1880).

—— *Theistic Problems; being Essays on the Existence of God and His Relationship to Man* (London: Hodder & Stoughton, 1880).

—— *Biblical Difficulties Dispelled: Being an answer to queries respecting so-called Discrepancies in Scripture, misunderstood and misinterpreted texts, etc., etc.*, 2nd edn. (Toronto: William Briggs, 1887).

SOUTHWELL, CHARLES, *The Confessions of a Free-Thinker* (London: Printed for the Author, n.d.).

SPILLING, JAMES, *Charles Robinson: A Phase in the History of a Soul* (London: James Speirs, 1890).

SPINOZA, BENEDICTUS DE, *A Treatise on Politics*, ed. William Maccall (London: Holyoake, 1854).

STRAUSS, DAVID FRIEDRICH, *The Life of Jesus Critically Examined*, trans. George Eliot [1846], ed. Peter C. Hodgson (Ramsey, NJ: Sigler, 1994).

—— *The Old Faith and the New* (London: Asher & Co., 1874).

SUGDEN, EDWARD H. (ed.), *John Wesley's Fifty-Three Sermons* (Nashville, Tenn.: Abingdon Press, 1983).

The Three Trials of William Hone, for publishing Three Parodies; viz.—the late John Wilkes's Catechism, the Political Litany, and the Sinecurist's Creed (facsimile of London: William Hone, 1818; London: Freethought Publishing Co., 1880).

TOWNLEY, HENRY (ed.), *Report of a Public Discussion Carried on by Henry Townley and George Jacob Holyoake . . . in the Scientific Institution, John Street, Fitzroy Square* (London: Ward, 1852).

Trial By Jury and the Liberty of the Press. The Proceedings at the Public Meeting, December 29, 1817, at the City of London Tavern, for the purpose of enabling William Hone to surmount the difficulties in which he has been placed by being selected by the ministers of the crown as the object of their persecution (London: William Hone, 1818).

The Trial of Thomas Paterson for Blasphemy (London: H. Hetherington, 1844).

WALLACE, ALFRED RUSSEL, *My Life: A Record of Events and Opinions* (New York: Dodd, Mead, & Co., 1905).

WATTS, J., 'Iconoclast' [CHARLES BRADLAUGH], and A. COLLINS [WILLIAM HARRAL JOHNSON] (eds.), *Half-Hours with the Freethinkers* (London: Holyoake & Co., 1857).

WHEELER, J. M., *A Biographical Dictionary of Freethinkers of All Ages and Nations* (London: Progressive Publishing Co., 1889).

[WOOLLACOTT, CHRISTOPHER], *Eliza Mills or the Infidel Reclaimed* (London: Baptist Tract Society, n.d. [1852]).

YOUNG, FREDERIC ROWLAND, *Hints How To Make Home Happy* (London: Edward Truelove, 1854).

—— *Our Lord Jesus Christ the Personal Revelation of God* (Belfast: Depository of the Unitarian Society for the Diffusion of Christian Knowledge, 1865).

—— *Five Hundred Hymns for the Use of Free Christian Churches,* (London: E. T. Whitfield, 1870).

—— *Indirect Evidences in the New Testament for the Personal Divinity of Christ* (London: W. Stewart & Co., 1884).

Secondary Sources

ALTICK, RICHARD D., *Victorian People and Ideas: A Companion for the Modern Reader of Victorian Literature* (New York: W. W. Norton, 1973).

ANNAN, NOEL, *Leslie Stephen: The Godless Victorian* (New York: Random House, 1984).

ARNSTEIN, WALTER L., *The Bradlaugh Case: Atheism, Sex, and Politics among the Late Victorians* (Columbia, Miss.: University of Missouri Press, 1983).

BAYLEN, JOSEPH O. and NORBERT J. GOSSMAN (eds.), *Biographical Dictionary of Modern British Radicals: Volume 2: 1830–1870* (Brighton: Harvester Press, 1984).

BEBBINGTON, D. W., *Evangelicalism and Modern Britain: A History from the 1730s to the 1980s* (1989; London: Routledge, 1993).

—— and TIMOTHY LARSEN (eds.), *Modern Christianity and Cultural Aspirations*, Essays in Honour of Clyde Binfield, OBE (London: Sheffield Academic Press, 2003).

BELLAMY JOYCE E. and JOHN SAVILLE (eds.), *The Dictionary of Labour Biography* (Basingstoke: Macmillan, 1993).

BEVIR, MARK, 'Annie Besant's Quest for Truth: Christianity, Secularism and New Age Thought', *Journal of Ecclesiastical History*, 50: 1 (Jan. 1999), 62–93.

BONNER, HYPATIA BRADLAUGH, *Penalties Upon Opinion* (London: Watts & Co., 1913).

BRETT, R. L., *Faith and Doubt: Religion and Secularization in Literature from Wordsworth to Larkin* (Macon, Ga.: Mercer University Press, 1997).

BROWN, KENNETH D., *A Social History of the Nonconformist Ministry in England and Wales, 1800–1930* (Oxford: Clarendon Press, 1988).

BUDD, SUSAN, 'The Loss of Faith: Reasons for Unbelief Among Members of the Secular Movement in England, 1850–1950', *Past & Present*, 36 (Apr. 1967), 106–25.

—— *Varieties of Unbelief: Atheists and Agnostics in English Society, 1850–1960* (London: Heinemann, 1977).

BURN, W. L., *The Age of Equipoise* (London: Unwin University Books, 1964).

CHADWICK, OWEN, *The Secularization of the European Mind in the Nineteenth Century* (Cambridge: Cambridge University Press, 1998).

CLAEYS, GREGORY (ed.), *Encyclopedia of Nineteenth-Century Thought* (London: Routledge, 2005).

COCKSHUT, A. O. J., *The Unbelievers: English Agnostic Thought, 1840–1890* (London: Collins, 1964).

COLE, G. D. H., *Chartist Portraits* (1941; New York: Macmillan, 1965).

COLLINS, HENRY and CHIMEN ABRAMSKY, *Karl Marx and the British Labour Movement: Years of the First International* (London: Macmillan & Co., 1965).

CONKLIN, ROBERT J., *Thomas Cooper, the Chartist (1805–1892)* (Manila: University of the Philippines Press, 1935).

COOKE, BILL, 'Charles Southwell: New Zealand's First Freethinker', *New Zealand Rationalist and Humanist* (Spring 1998), 10–12.

COREY, MELINDA and GEORGE OCHOA, *The Encyclopedia of the Victorian World: A Reader's Companion to the People, Places, Events, and Everyday Life of the Victorian Era* (New York: Henry Holt & Co., 1996).

CULE, JOHN, *Wreath on the Crown: The Story of Sarah Jacob, the Welsh Fasting Girl* (Llandysul: Gomerian Press, 1967).

DAVIS, PHILIP, *The Victorians*, The Oxford English Literary History: Vol. 8: *1830–1880* (Oxford: Oxford University Press, 2002).

DESMOND, ADRIAN, 'Artisan Resistance and Evolution in Britain, 1819–1848', *Osiris*, 2nd ser., 3 (1987), 77–110.

—— *The Politics of Evolution: Morphology, Medicine, and Reform in Radical London* (Chicago: University of Chicago Press, 1989).

DICKSON, NEIL, *Brethren in Scotland, 1838–2000: A Social Study of an Evangelical Movement* (Carlisle: Paternoster, 2002).

DOWNER, ARTHUR CLEVELAND, *A Century of Evangelical Religion in Oxford* (London: The Church Book Room, 1938).

DOYLE, ARTHUR CONAN, *The History of Spiritualism* (New York: George H. Doran, 1926).

EDWARDS, WIL JON, *From the Valley I Came* (London: Angus & Robertson, 1956).

Encyclopedia of Occultism and Parapsychology (New York: Avon Books, 1978).

EPSTEIN, JAMES and DOROTHY THOMPSON (eds.), *The Chartist Experience: Studies in Working-Class Radicalism and Culture, 1830–60* (London: Macmillan, 1982).

FYFE, AILEEN, *Science and Salvation: Evangelical Popular Science Publishing and Salvation* (Chicago: University of Chicago Press, 2004).

GARNETT, JANE, 'Bishop Butler and the *Zeitgeist*: Butler and the Development of Christian Moral Philosophy in Victorian Britain', in Christopher Cunliffe (ed.), *Joseph Butler's Moral and Religious Thought: Tercentenary Essays* (Oxford: Clarendon Press, 1992), 63–96.

GRODZINS, DEAN, *American Heretic: Theodore Parker and Transcendentalism* (Chapel Hill, NC: University of North Carolina Press, 2002).

GUGELOT, FRÉDÉRIC, *La Conversion des intellectuels au catholicisme en France, 1885–1935* (Paris: CNRS, 1998).

HAMBRICK, MARGARET, *A Chartist's Library* (London: Mansell Publishing, 1986).

HELMSTADTER, RICHARD J. and BERNARD LIGHTMAN (eds.), *Victorian Faith in Crisis: Essays on Continuity and Change in Nineteenth-Century Religious Belief* (London: Macmillan, 1990).

HEYCK, THOMAS WILLIAM, *The People of the British Isles: A New History:* Volume 2: *From 1686 to 1870* (Belmont, Calif.: Wadsworth, 1992).

—— *The People of the British Isles: A New History:* Volume 3: *From 1870 to the Present* (Belmont, Calif.: Wadsworth, 1992).

HILTON, BOYD, *The Age of Atonement: The Influence of Evangelicalism on Social and Economic Thought, 1795–1865* (Oxford: Clarendon Press, 1988).

HOPPEN, K. THEODORE, *The Mid-Victorian Generation, 1846–1886* (Oxford: Clarendon Press, 1998).

JAY, ELISABETH, *Faith and Doubt in Victorian Britain* (London: Macmillan, 1986).

KENNEDY, LUDOVIC, *All in the Mind: A Farewell to God* (London: Hodder & Stoughton, 1999).

KENT, JOHN, *From Darwin to Blatchford: The Role of Darwinism in Christian Apologetic, 1875–1910* (London: Dr Williams's Trust, 1966).

KUDUK, STEPHANIE, 'Sedition, Chartism, and Epic Poetry in Thomas Cooper's *The Purgatory of the Suicides*', *Victorian Poetry*, 39: 2 (Summer 2001), 165–85.

LARSEN, TIMOTHY, *Friends of Religious Equality: Nonconformist Politics in Mid-Victorian England* (Woodbridge, Suffolk: Boydell, 1999).

—— 'Honorary Doctorates and the Nonconformist Ministry in Nineteenth-Century England', in David Bebbington and Timothy Larsen (eds.), *Modern Christianity and Cultural Aspirations*, Essays in Honour of Clyde Binfield, OBE (London: Sheffield Academic Press, 2003), 139–56.

—— ' "Living by Faith": A Short History of Brethren Practice', *Emmaus Journal*, 12: 2 (Winter 2003), 277–315.

—— *Contested Christianity: The Political and Social Contexts of Victorian Theology* (Waco, Tex.: Baylor University Press, 2004).

—— 'A. S. Peake, the Free Churches, and Modern Biblical Criticism', *Bulletin of the John Rylands University Library of Manchester*, 86: 3 (forthcoming).

—— (ed.), *Biographical Dictionary of Evangelicals* (Leicester: Inter-Varsity Press, 2003).

LEWIS, DONALD M. (ed.), *The Blackwell Dictionary of Evangelical Biography, 1730–1860* (Oxford: Blackwell, 1995).

McLEOD, HUGH, *Religion and Society in England, 1850–1914* (New York: St Martin's, 1996).

—— *Secularisation in Western Europe, 1848–1914* (London: Macmillan, 2000).

McWILLIAM, ROHAN, 'The Mysteries of G. W. M. Reynolds: Radicalism and Melodrama in Victorian Britain', in Malcolm Chase and Ian Dyck (eds.),

Living and Learning: Essays in Honour of J. F. C. Harrison (Aldershot: Scholar Press, 1996), 182–98.

MARSH, JOSS, *Word Crimes: Blasphemy, Culture, and Literature in Nineteenth-Century England* (Chicago: University of Chicago Press, 1998).

MATTHEW, H. C. G. and BRIAN HARRISON (eds.), *Oxford Dictionary of National Biography* (Oxford: Oxford University Press, 2004).

MILLAR, ALAN, 'Mill on Religion', in John Skorupski (ed.), *The Cambridge Companion to Mill* (Cambridge: Cambridge University Press, 1998), 176–202.

MITCHELL, SALLY, *Daily Life in Victorian England* (Westport, Conn.: Greenwood Press, 1996).

MOORE, JAMES, *The Darwin Legend* (Grand Rapids, Mich.: Baker, 1994).

MULLEN, SHIRLEY A., *Organized Freethought: The Religion of Unbelief in Victorian England* (New York: Garland Publishing, 1987).

MURRAY, A. D. (ed.), *John Ludlow: The Autobiography of a Christian Socialist* (London: Frank Cass, 1981).

NASH, DAVID, ' "Look in Her Face and Lose Thy Dread of Dying": The Ideological Importance of Death to the Secularist Community in Nineteenth-Century Britain', *Journal of Religion,* 19: 2 (Dec. 1995), 158–80.

—— *Blasphemy in Modern Britain: 1789 to the Present* (Aldershot: Ashgate, 1999).

NETHERCOT, ARTHUR H., *The First Five Lives of Annie Besant* (Chicago: University of Chicago Press, 1960).

OUTLER, ALBERT C. (ed.), *John Wesley* (New York: Oxford University Press, 1964).

PALS, DANIEL L., *The Victorian 'Lives' of Jesus* (San Antonio: Trinity University Press, 1982).

PEARCE, HARRY HASTINGS, 'Charles Southwell in Australia and N.Z.', *New Zealand Rationalist,* (May 1957), 1–4; (June 1957), 5–8; (July 1957), 8–11; (Aug. 1957), 9–12; (Sept. 1957), 7–10; (Oct. 1957), 6–7; (Nov. 1957), 6–8; (Dec. 1957–Jan. 1958), 7–10; (Feb. 1958), 11–13; (Mar. 1958), 9–10; (Apr. 1958), 7–9; (May 1958), 9–11; (June 1958), 6–8; (July 1958), 7–9; (Aug. 1958), 5–6; (Sept. 1958), 5–8.

PEARCE, JOSEPH, *Literary Converts: Spiritual Inspiration in an Age of Unbelief* (London: HarperCollins, 1999).

RAVEN, CHARLES E., *Christian Socialism, 1848–1854* (London: Macmillan, 1920).

READ, DONALD, *England 1868–1914* (London: Longman, 1979).

ROBERTS, ADAM C., *Victorian Culture and Society: The Essential Glossary* (London: Arnold, 2003).

ROBERTS, CLAYTON and DAVID ROBERTS, *A History of England*: Volume II: *1688 to the Present* (Englewood Cliffs, NJ: Prentice-Hall, 1991).

ROBERTS, STEPHEN, 'Joseph Barker and the Radical Cause, 1848–1851', *Publications of the Thoresby Society: The Leeds Historical Society: Miscellany*, 2nd ser., vol. 1 for 1990 (1991), 59–73.

ROBERTSON, J. M., *A History of Freethought in the Nineteenth Century* (London: Watts & Co., 1929).

ROSE, JONATHAN, *The Intellectual Life of the British Working Classes* (New Haven: Yale University Press, 2001).

ROYLE, EDWARD, *Victorian Infidels: The Origins of the British Secularist Movement, 1791–1866* (Manchester: Manchester University Press, 1974).

—— *Radicals, Secularists and Republicans: Popular Freethought in Britain, 1866–1915* (Manchester: Manchester University Press, 1980).

—— *Modern Britain: A Social History, 1750–1997* (London: Arnold, 1997).

SCOTLAND, NIGEL, '*Good and Proper Men*': *Lord Palmerston and the Bench of Bishops* (Cambridge: James Clarke, 2000).

SECORD, JAMES A., *Victorian Sensation: The Extraordinary Publication, Reception, and Secret Authorship of 'Vestiges of the Natural History of Creation*' (Chicago: University of Chicago Press, 2000).

SHIRLEY, MICHAEL H., 'On Wings of Everlasting Power: G. W. M. Reynolds and *Reynolds's Newspaper*, 1848–1876', Ph.D thesis, University of Illinois at Urbana-Champaign (1997).

SYMONDSON, ANTHONY (ed.), *The Victorian Crisis of Faith* (London: SPCK, 1970).

TAYLOR, ANNE, *Annie Besant: A Biography* (Oxford: Oxford University Press, 1992).

THOMPSON, DAVID M., *Let Sects and Parties Fall: A Short History of the Association of Churches of Christ in Great Britain and Ireland* (Birmingham: Berean Press, 1980).

TRIBE, DAVID, *President Charles Bradlaugh, M.P.* (London: Elek Books, 1971).

WARDROPER, JOHN, *The World of William Hone: A New Look at the Romantic Age in Words and Pictures of the Day* (London: Shelfmark Books, 1997).

WATTS, MICHAEL R., *The Dissenters*: Volume II: *The Expansion of Evangelical Nonconformity* (Oxford: Clarendon Press, 1995).

WEBB, JAMES (ed.), *The Mediums and the Conjurors* (New York: Arno Press, 1976).

WHITLEY, W. T., *Baptists of North-West England, 1649–1913* (London: Kingsgate Press, 1913).

WIENER, JOEL H., *Radicalism and Freethought in Nineteenth-Century Britain: The Life of Richard Carlile* (Westport, Conn.: Greenwood Press, 1983).

WILKINSON, JOHN T., *Arthur Samuel Peake: A Biography* (London: Epworth Press, 1971).

WILLEY, BASIL, *Nineteenth Century Studies: Coleridge to Matthew Arnold* (London: Chatto & Windus, 1950).

—— *More Nineteenth Century Studies: A Group of Honest Doubters* (London: Chatto & Windus, 1956).

WILSON, A. N., *God's Funeral* (New York: W. W. Norton, 1999).

WOLFF, ROBERT LEE, *Gains and Losses: Novels of Faith and Doubt in Victorian England* (London: J. Murray, 1977).

WYNCOLL, PETER, *Nottingham Chartist* (Nottingham: Nottingham Trades Council, 1966).

Index

Canning, George, 20
Carlile, Richard, 19, 36, 139, 141, 233, 261–3, 267, 272, 274
Carlisle, 110, 111
Carlyle, Thomas, 6, 9, 73, 164, 284
Cartesian, 166
Castereagh, Lord, 22
Castle Hill, 112, 183
Castle Street, 64
Catholic, 4, 253, 268, 270, 272
    anti-Catholic rhetoric, 10
Catholicism, 253
Catholic University, 271
Caughey, James, 260
Cavendish College (Manchester), 130
Cavendish Rooms (London), 210
Cecil, Richard, 45, 46, 47
Chadwick, Owen, 7, 8
Chainey, George, 271
Chalmers, Thomas, 3, 165
Chandler, Samuel, 105
Channing, William Ellery, 164, 165
Charles Southwell Award, 283
Chartism, 75, 145
Chartist, 72, 75, 76, 77, 160, 254, 263, 276, 280
    Nottingham Chartists, 254
Chartists, 76, 155
Chesterton, G. K., 134, 251
Chicago, 57
Childs, John, 189
Christ – *see* Jesus Christ
Christendom, 273
Christian, vii, 2, 3, 12, 13, 18, 19, 21, 23, 24, 25, 26, 28, 31, 34, 40, 42, 45, 47, 48, 49, 53, 58, 62, 67, 68, 70, 74, 78, 82, 88, 89, 90, 93, 94, 95, 98, 101, 103, 104, 107, 108, 119, 124, 125, 128, 130, 132, 135, 138, 144, 147, 148, 154, 155, 163, 164, 165, 168, 175, 176, 183, 188, 191, 193, 194, 195, 197, 199, 200, 201, 202, 203, 205, 206, 209, 215, 216, 220, 221, 223, 224, 225, 227, 228, 229, 230, 233, 234, 237, 239, 240, 241, 244, 248, 249, 252, 253, 257, 260, 262, 264, 266, 268, 270, 271, 275, 278, 279, 280, 285, 286, 287

Christian Brethren, 142
Christian Defense Association, 63, 70
Christian Evidence Society, 218, 220, 224, 271, 272
Christian faith, vii, 251
Christianism, 185
Christianity, vii, 1, 4, 5, 7, 13, 14, 16, 17, 24, 25, 36, 37, 40, 42, 44, 45, 46, 51, 57, 61, 70, 73, 74, 75, 81, 85, 86, 89, 94, 97, 107, 113, 114, 116, 119, 125, 126, 127, 128, 129, 134, 135, 136, 139, 140, 141, 145, 155, 156, 161, 162, 163, 164, 166, 167, 169, 171, 172, 178, 182, 184, 185, 188, 189, 193, 194, 202, 203, 204, 209, 210, 213, 214, 217, 222, 226, 228, 230, 232, 236, 243, 244, 245, 250, 251, 252, 253, 256, 257, 258, 263, 264, 266, 268, 269, 271, 272, 277, 278, 282, 284, 285
Christianity, evangelical, 47, 48
Christianity, orthodox, 16, 21, 30, 43, 84, 86, 87, 91, 104, 119, 160
Christians, vii, 6, 13, 25, 45, 53, 59, 61, 65, 81, 125, 141, 149, 150, 151, 161, 163, 168, 177, 178, 193, 195, 228, 234, 235, 242, 243, 255, 256, 266, 276, 277, 278
    orthodox, 21, 22, 35, 36, 165
Christian Socialism, 263, 269, 280
Christian Socialist, 237, 264, 280
Christological, 168
Christology, 47, 57, 58, 60, 65, 67, 116, 272
Chrysostom, John, 226
Churchill, Winston, 171
Church of England, 20, 132, 200, 224, 231, 258, 284
Church of England Catechism, 18
Church of England Litany, 18
Church of the Latter-Day Saints, 202
Church of the Lord, 210
Cicero, 138, 164, 218
Cienkowsky, Leon de, 218
City Road, 80
City Temple (London), 130
Clapham Sect, 13
Claremont Hall, 271
Clarke, Adam, 226

Unitarian Society for the Diffusion of
Christian Knowledge (Belfast),
57–58
United, Evangelical (Scotland), 224
University College London, 198
Utilitarian Club, 283
Utilitarianism, 215, 221
Utilitarianists, 215

Vanderbilt University, 32
Vicarage Street (Unitarian) Chapel, 57
Victoria, Queen, 10, 190
Victoria Institute, 224
Victorian, vii, 1, 2, 3, 4, 5, 7, 8, 10, 11, 13,
14, 15, 17, 39, 73, 72, 88, 95, 96,
100, 129, 132, 161, 164, 172, 182,
202, 232, 234, 235, 239, 241, 242,
243, 244, 245, 246, 247, 249, 251,
253, 284
evangelicals, 44
pre-Victorian, 12
Victorians, vii, 1, 2, 3, 5, 7, 8, 9, 10, 11,
13, 16, 131, 143, 228, 234, 235, 237,
244, 245, 250
Villiers, Henry Montagu, 110
Vincent, Henry, 285
Virchow, Rudolf, 101
Virgil, 138
Vogt, Carl, 101
Volney, C. F., 30, 74, 96, 174, 175, 177,
258, 270, 274, 283
Voltaire, 30, 56, 74, 83, 153, 211, 260,
264, 283

Wallace, Alfred Russel, 208, 219, 285–6
Ward, Mary Augusta, 11
Wardlaw, Ralph, 106
Washington, DC, 257
Washington, George, 84
Watson, Richard, 29, 30, 106
Watson, James, 51, 52, 53, 56
Watts, Charles, 63, 221, 223, 265, 266,
271
Watts, Isaac, 24
Watts, John, 112, 153, 180, 183, 190, 208,
232, 258, 267
Waugh, Evelyn, 251
Weigh House, 32, 47, 48
Wellington, duke of, 84

Welsh Fasting Girl, 59
Wesley, John, 12, 13, 28, 32, 137, 164
Wesleyan(s), 75, 138, 176, 232, 239, 263,
280, 281, 282, 287
West, Gilbert, 105
Westminster Hospital or Dispensary,
198
Wheeler, J. M., 33
Weiner, Joel, 262
Whewell, William, 101, 165
Whigs, 47, 48
Whit Sunday, 93
Whitehead, A. N., 251
Whitwell, Mr., 100, 103
Wilberforce, William, 13
Willey, Basil, 6, 7, 8, 15, 17, 228, 252
Williams, Benjamin, 74
Willshire, Dr, 199
Wilks, Washington, 110, 111, 120
Wilson, A. N., 8, 9, 15, 228, 245, 247,
251
Wiltshire, 57
Wolff, Robert, 9, 226
Wolverhampton, 57
Wood, Annie, *see* Besant, Annie
Woollacott, Christopher, 270
Woolston, Thomas, 83, 105
Wordsworth, William, 245, 226
Working Men's College, 280
Wortley, 144
Wright, Henry C., 144, 145, 149
W. Stewart & Co., 69

Xenophon, 12

Yeovil, 57
YMCA, 68, 94, 110, 213, 224
Yorkshire, 214
Young, Betsy, 50
Young, Frederick Rowland, 50–71, 209,
225, 243
Young, Joseph, 50

Zion Congregationalist Chapel
(Stafford), 277
Zionism, 5
Zoological Society, 200
Zoroastrianism, 220
Zurich, 88